TULSIAN'S

Fundamentals of Operations Research

(Theory and Practice)

For B.Com., M.Com., BBA, MBA, ICWA and Other Degree and Professional Courses

CA (Dr.) P.C. TULSIAN

M.Com., Ph.D., FCA, PGDFM

Additional Director (Former)
Board of Studies
The Institute of Chartered Accountants of India, New Delhi
Head
Department of Commerce
Ramjas College
University of Delhi
DELHI

CA BHARAT TULSIAN

Chartered Accountant
Senior Executive, KPMG
Alumnus of Sri Ram College of Commerce (SRCC) University of Delhi, DELHI
Recepient of An Award for the Best Article in All India
by The Institute of Chartered Accountants of India, New Delhi

S. CHAND
PUBLISHING

S Chand And Company Limited

(ISO 9001 Certified Company)

S Chand And Company Limited

(ISO 9001 Certified Company)

Head Office: Block B-1, House No. D-1, Ground Floor, Mohan Co-operative Industrial Estate, New Delhi – 110 044 | Phone: 011-66672000

Registered Office: A-27, 2nd Floor, Mohan Co-operative Industrial Estate, New Delhi – 110 044 Phone: 011-49731800

www.**schandpublishing.com**; e-mail: **info@schandpublishing.com**

Branches

Chennai	:	Ph: 23632120; chennai@schandpublishing.com
Guwahati	:	Ph: 2738811, 2735640; guwahati@schandpublishing.com
Hyderabad	:	Ph: 40186018; hyderabad@schandpublishing.com
Jalandhar	:	Ph: 4645630; jalandhar@schandpublishing.com
Kolkata	:	Ph: 23357458, 23353914; kolkata@schandpublishing.com
Lucknow	:	Ph: 4003633; lucknow@schandpublishing.com
Mumbai	:	Ph: 25000297; mumbai@schandpublishing.com
Patna	:	Ph: 2260011; patna@schandpublishing.com

First Edition 2012

ISBN: 978-81-219-4087-0

PRINTED IN INDIA

By Vikas Publishing House Private Limited, Plot 20/4, Site-IV, Industrial Area Sahibabad, Ghaziabad – 201 010 and Published by S Chand And Company Limited, A-27, 2nd Floor, Mohan Co-operative Industrial Estate, New Delhi – 110 044.

PREFACE

This book adopts a fresh and novel approach to the study of **Fundamentals of Operations Research**. It has been written in a "Teach Yourself Style", strictly following a student friendly approach and is essentially meant to serve as a tutor at home.

The distinct features of the book are as follows :

PEDAGOGICAL FEATURES	
• **Simple Language**	: The Text is presented in the simplest language, meant to serve beginners.
• **Heading for each Paragraph**	: Each paragraph has been arranged under a suitable heading for easy retention of concepts.
• **Tabular Form**	: Wherever possible the text matter relating to a particular topic/subtopic has been presented in a Tabular Form.
• **Eye-catching Screens**	: All important equations, formulae, figures and practical steps have been presented in screen format to catch the eye.
• **Uniform Format of Chapter**	: Each chapter has been uniformly organised under suitable headings, Text supported by suitable Illustrations, Solved Problems.
DISTINCTIVE FEATURES	
• **50 Exhibits**	: To acquaint students with various Practical steps.
• **Over 175 Solved Practical Problems**	: To aid better understanding of the text. Along with necessary working notes and alternative solutions (if any)
• **Over 40 Theoretical Questions**	: To enable students to revise Important Theoretical Questions.

We are confident that all these features would make this book an invaluable asset to students learning Corporate Accounting.

We wish to express our sincere thanks to several individuals who have been a source of inspiration and support both personally and professionally including Dr. R.P. Tulsian, Dr. Renu Gupta, Dr. Amit Singhal, Dr. Sonal Gupta, Dr. S.C. Gupta, Dr. Naresh Gupta, Dr. S.C. Garg, Dr. N.K. Aggarwal, Dr. K.B. Gupta, Dr. M.M. Goyal, Dr. Sandeep Aggarwal, Dr. Sushma Aggarwal, Dr. Himanshu Garg, Dr. Poonam, Dr. Indu Jain, Dr. P.V. Khatri, Dr. Madhu Gupta, Dr. Kusum Gupta, Dr. V.K. Jain, Dr. Harpal Singh, Dr. Pradeep Aggarwal, Dr. J.M. Gupta, Dr. N.K. Puri, Dr. Y.P. Tyagi, Dr. R.D. Arora, Dr. S.K. Gupta, Dr. Rajeev Goel.

Special word of thanks are also due to our favourite students **Vishal, Prarthana, Piyush, Pranav and Arushi** who provided incisive comment and useful feedback.

We must conclude that this book would never have been written without the support, encouragement and prodding of our family members. Many thanks to all of them.

Any suggestion for improvement will be gratefully acknowledged and appreciated

CA (Dr.) PC Tulsian
pctulsian@gmail.com

CA Bharat Tulsian
bharattulsian88@gmail.com

CONTENTS

APPENDIX

1 LINEAR PROGRAMMING — FORMULATION

PRACTICAL STEPS INVOLVED IN THE FORMULATION OF LP PROBLEM

The practical steps involved in the formation of linear programming problem are as follows:

Step 1→ *Identify the **Decision Variables** of interest to the decision maker and express them as x_1, x_2, x_3 ....*

Step 2→ *Ascertain the **Objective** of the decision maker whether he wants to minimize or to maximize.*

Step 3→ *Ascertain the **cost** (in case of minimization problem) or the **profit** (in case of maximization problem) per unit of each of the decision variables.*

Step 4→ *Ascertain the **constraints** representing the maximum availability or minimum commitment or equality and represent them as less than or equal to (≤) type inequality or greater than or equal to (≥) type inequality or 'equal to' (=) type equality respectively.*

Step 5→ *Put **non-negativity restriction** as under:*

$x_j \geq 0;\ j = 1, 2 \ldots.n$ *(non-negativity restriction)*

Step 6→ *Now **formulate the LP problem as under**:*

Maximize (or Minimize) $Z = c_1x_1 + c_2x_2 \ldots..c_nx_n$

Subject to constraints:

$a_{11}x_1 + a_{12}x_2 ,\ldots.a_{1n}x_n \leq b_1$ *(Maximum availability)*

$a_{21}x_1 + a_{22}x_2 ,\ldots.a_{2n}x_n \geq b_2$ *(Minimum commitment)*

$a_{31}x_1 + a_{32}x_2 ,\ldots.a_{3n}x_n = b_3$ *(Equality)*

$a_{m1}x_1 + a_{m2}x_2 ,\ldots.a_{mn}x_n \lesseqgtr b_m$

$x_1;\ x_2 \ldots.\ x_n \geq 0$ *(Non-negativity restriction)*

where,

x_j = *Decision Variables i.e. quantity of jth variable of interest to the decision maker.*

c_j = *Constant representing per unit contribution (in case of Maximization Problem) or Cost (in case of Minimization Problem) of the jth decision variable.*

a_{ij} = *Constant representing exchange coefficients of the jth decision variable in the ith constant.*

b_i = *Constant representing i^{th} constraint requirement or availability.*

PROBLEM 1.1

A firm produces three products A, B and C. It uses two types of raw materials I and II of which 5,000 and 7,500 units respectively are available. The raw material requirements per unit of the products are given below:

Raw Material	*Requirement per unit of Product*		
	A	B	C
I	3	4	5
II	5	3	5

The labour time for each unit of product A is twice that of Product B and three times that of Product C. The entire labour force of the firm can produce the equivalent of 3,000 units. The minimum demand of the three products is 600, 650 and 500 units respectively. Also the ratios of the number of units produced must be equal to 2 : 3 : 4. Assuming the profits per unit of A, B and C as Rs. 50, 50 and 80 respectively.

Required: Formulate the problem as a linear programming model in order to determine the number of units of each product, which will maximize the profit.

Solution

Let X_1, X_2 and X_3 be the units produced & sold of Product A, B and C respectively.

The labour time for each unit of Product A is twice that of Product B and three times that Product C. Also the entire labour force can produce the equivalent of 3000 units.

$$x_1 + \frac{x_2}{2} + \frac{x_3}{3} \leq 3000$$

or
$$6x_1 + 3x_2 + 2x_3 \leq 18000$$

Since the ratios of the number of units produced must be equal to 2 :3 :4, therefore,

$$\frac{1}{2}x_1 = \frac{1}{3}x_2, \text{ and } \frac{1}{3}x_2 = \frac{1}{4}x_3$$

or
$$3x_1 = 2x_2 \text{ and } 4x_2 = 3x_3 \qquad \text{...(v)}$$

Since the objective of the firm is to maximize the profit, therefore, the objective function is given by–

Maximise $Z = 50x_1 + 50x_2 + 80x_3$

Subject to the constraints

$3x_1 + 4x_2 + 5x_3 \leq 5000$ [Maximum Raw-Material I]

$5x_1 + 3x_2 + 5x_3 \leq 7500$ [Maximum Raw-Material II]

$6x_1 + 3x_2 + 2x_3 \leq 18000$ [Maximum Labour Time]

$3x_1 = 2x_2$ and $4x_2 = 3x_3$ [Ratio of No. of units Produced]

$x_1 \geq 600$, $x_2 \geq 650$ and $x_3 \geq 500$ [Minimum Demand for Products]

PROBLEM 1.2

In a chemical industry two products A and B are made involving two operations The production of B also results in a by-product C. The product A can be sold at a profit of Rs. 3 per unit and B at a profit of Rs. 8 per unit. The by-product C has a profit of Rs, 2 per unit. Forecasts show that upto 5 units of C can be sold. **The company gets 3 units of C for each unit of B produced.** The manufacturing times are 3 hours per unit for A on each the operation one and two and 4 hours and 5 hours per unit for B on operation one and two respectively. Because the product C results from producing B, no time is used in producing C. The available times are 18 hours and 21 hours of operation one and two respectively. The company desires to know that how much A and B should be produced keeping C in mind to make the highest profit. Formulate LPP model for this problem.

Solution

Let x_1 x_2, x_3 be the number of units produced & sold of products A, B, and C respectively.

In first operation, A takes 3 hours of manufacturer's time and B takes 4 hours of manufacturer's time Therefore, total number of hours required in first operation becomes,

$$3x_1 + 4x_2$$

Further, the company gets three units of by product C for every unit of product B produced, therefore

$$x_3 = 3x_2$$

Now, the allocation problem of the industry can be finally put in the following linear programming problem:

Maximise $Z = 3x_1 + 8x_2 + 2x_3$

Subject to the constraints

$3x_1 + 4x_2 \leq 18$ [Maximum Hours in First Operation]

$3x_1 + 5x_2 \leq 21$ [Maximum Hours in Second Operation]

$x_3 \leq 5,$ [Maximum Sales units of Product C]

$x_3 = 3x_2$ [Ratio of Product C to Product B]

$x_1, x_2, x_3 \leq 0$ [Non-Negativity]

PROBLEM 1.3

A firm buys castings of P and Q type of parts and sells them as finished product after machining, boring and polishing. The purchasing cost for castings are Rs. 3 and Rs. 4 each for parts P and Q and selling prices are Rs. 8 and Rs. 10 respectively. The per hour capacity of machines used for machining, boring and polishing for two products is given below:

Capacity (per hour)	*P*	*Q*
Machining	30	50
Boring	30	45
Polishing	45	30

The running costs for machining, boring and polishing are Rs. 30, Rs, 22.5 and Rs. 22.5 per hour respectively.

Formulate the linear programming problem to find out the product mix to maximize the profit.

Solution

Let the firm buy x units of castings of P and y units of castings of Q which are sold as finished product after machining , boring and polishing. According to the given data, the capacity constraints of machining, boring and polishing machines on per hour basis have been formulated as below:

$\frac{x}{30} + \frac{y}{50} \leq 1$ *or* $50x + 30y \leq 1500$ (*Machining Constraint*) ...(i)

$\frac{x}{30} + \frac{y}{45} \leq 1$ *or* $45x + 30y \leq 1350$ (*Boring Constraint*) ...(ii)

$\frac{x}{45} + \frac{y}{30} \leq 1$ *or* $30x + 45y \leq 1350$ (*Polishing Constraint*) ...(iii)

Calculation of Total Cost and Profit per unit

	Cost/per unit	
	Castings of P type	*Castings of Q type*
Machining	Rs.30/30 = Rs. 1.00	Rs.30/50 = Rs 0.60
Boring	Rs. 22.5/30 = Rs. 0.75	Rs .22.5/45 = Rs. 0.50
Polishing	Rs. 22.5/45 = Rs. 0.50	Rs. 22.5/30 = Rs. 0.75
Purchasing Cost	Rs. 3.00	Rs. 4.00
Total Cost	Rs. 5.25	Rs. 5.85
Sale Price	Rs. 8.00	Rs. 10.00
Profit	Rs. 2.75	Rs. 4.15

The required product mix to maximise the profit of the firm will be given by the following relation:

Maximise $Z = 2.75x + 4.15\,y$

Subject to the Constraints

$$50\,x + 30\,y \leq 1500$$
$$45x + 30y \leq 1350$$
$$30\,x + 45\,y \leq 1350$$

where $x, y, \geq 0$

PROBLEM 1.4

A manufacturer produces three products Y_1, Y_2, Y_3 from three raw materials X_1, X_2, X_3. The cost of raw materials X_1, X_2 and X_3 is Rs. 30, Rs. 50 and Rs. 120 per kg respectively and they are available in a limited quantity viz 20 kg of X_1, 15 kg of X_2 and 10 kg of X_3. The selling price of Y_1, Y_2 and Y_3 is Rs. 90, Rs. 100 and Rs. 120 per kg respectively. In order to produce 1 kg of Y_1, ½ kg of X_1, ¼ kg of X_2 and ¼ kg of X_3 are required. Similarly to produce 1 kg of Y_2, 3/7 kg of X_1, 2/7 kg of X_2 and 2/7 kg of X_3 and to produce 1 kg of Y_3, 2/3 kg of X_2 and 1/3 kg of X_3 will be required.

Formulate the linear programming problem to maximize the profit.

Solution

The information given in the question can be presented of the following tabular form.

	Raw material (in kg) required to produce one kg of product			*Selling*
Products	X_1	X_2	X_3	*Price (per kg)*
Y_1	1/2	1/4	1/4	Rs. 90
Y_2	3/7	2/7	2/7	Rs. 100
Y_3	—	2/3	1/3	Rs. 120
Cost of raw material (per kg)	Rs. 30	Rs. 50	Rs. 120	
Availability of raw material	20 kg	15 kg	10 kg	

From the above table, the cost of producing 1 kg of Y_1, Y_2 and Y_3 can be calculated as given below:

Cost to produce 1 kg of $Y_1 = ½$ Rs. 30 + ¼ Rs. 50 + ¼ Rs. 120
= Rs. 15 + Rs. 12.50 + Rs. 30 = Rs. 57.50

∴ Profit per kg of Y_1 = Rs. 90 – Rs. 57.50 = Rs. 32.50

Similarly, Cost to produce 1 kg of Y_2 = 3/7 Rs. 30 + 2/7 Rs. 50 + 2/7 Rs. 120
= 1/7(Rs. 90 + Rs. 100 + Rs. 240)
= Rs. 430/7 = Rs. 61.43

Profit per kg of Y_2 = Rs.100 – Rs.61.43 = Rs.38.57

and cost to produce 1 kg of Y_3 = 2/3 Rs.50 + 1/3 Rs.120 = Rs.220/3 = Rs.73.33

Profit per kg of Y_3 = Rs.120 – Rs.73.33 = Rs.46.67

Let the manufacturer produce y_1, y_2 and y_3 units of the products Y_1, Y_2 and Y_3 respectively.

Since the manufacturer wants to maximise the profit, the objective function is given by

Maximise $Z = 32.50\ Y_1 + 38.57\ Y_2 + 46.67\ Y_3$

Subject to the constraints

$$½\ Y_1 + 3/7\ Y_2 \le 20 \text{ or } 7\ Y_1 + 6\ Y_2 \le 280$$

$$¼\ Y_1 + 2/7\ Y_2 + 2/3\ Y_3 \le 15 \text{ or } 21\ Y_1 + 24\ Y_2 + 56\ Y_3 \le 1260$$

$$¼\ Y_1 + 2/7\ Y_2 + 1/3\ Y_3 \le 10 \text{ or } 21\ Y_1 + 24\ Y_2 + 28\ Y_3 \le 840$$

where Y_1, Y_2 and $Y_3 \ge 0$

PROBLEM 1.5

An agriculturist has a farm with 125 acres. He produces Radish, Muttar and Potato. Whatever he raises is fully sold in the market. He gets Rs. 5 for Radish per kg. Rs.4 for Muttar per kg. and Rs. 5. For Potato per kg. The average yield is 1,500 kg. of Radish per acre, 1,800 kg. of Muttar per acre and 1,200 kg. of Potato per acre. To produce each 100 kg. of Radish and Muttar and to produce each 80 kg. of Potato, a sum of Rs. 12.50 has to be used for manure. Labour required for each acre to raise the crop is 6 man days for Radish and Potato each and 5 man days for Muttar. A total of 500 man days of labour at a rate of Rs. 40 per man day are available.

Formulate this as a Linear Programming model to maximize the Agriculturist's total profit.

Solution

Let x_1, x_2 and x_3 be the number of acres allotted for cultivating radish, mutter and potato respectively.

Sales Revenue/acre (Radish) = Rs. 5 × 1500 = Rs. 7,500

Sales Revenue/acre (Matter) = Rs. 4 × 1800 = Rs. = 7,200

Sales Revenue/acre (Patato) = Rs. 5 × 1200 = Rs. 6,000

Now, the selling price, manure cost, labour cost and profit per acre of land for will be as fallows:

Per acre	Radish	Muttar	Potato
A. Selling Price	Rs. 7,500	Rs. 7,200	Rs. 6,000
B. Manure Cost	$\frac{\text{Rs. } 12.50 \times 1500}{100}$ = Rs. 187.50	$\frac{\text{Rs. } 12.50 \times 1800}{100}$ = Rs. 225	$\frac{\text{Rs. } 12.50 \times 1200}{80}$ = Rs. 187.50
C. Labour Cost	Rs.40 × 6 = Rs.240	Rs.40 × 5 = Rs.200	Rs.40 × 6 = Rs. 240
D. Profit [A – B – C]	= Rs.7,072.50	= Rs.6,775	= Rs. 5,572.50

Since, the agriculturist wants to maximise the total profit, hence the objective function of the problem is given by:

Maximise $Z = 7072.5x_1 + 6775x_2 + 5572.5x_3$

Subject to following constraints:

$x_1 + x_2 + x_3 \leq 125$ [Maximum Land Area]

$6x_1 + 5x_2 + 6x_3 \leq 500$ [Maximum Man Days]

where x_1, x_2 and $x_3 \geq 0$

PROBLEM 1.6

Three grades of coal A, B and C contains phosphorus and ash as impurities. In a particular industrial process, **fuel up to 100 ton (maximum) is required which could contain ash not more than 3% and phosphorus not more than .03%.** It is desired to maximize the profit while satisfying these conditions. There is an unlimited supply of each grade. The percentage of impurities and the profits of each grade are as follows:

Coal	*Phosphorus (%)*	*Ash (%)*	*Profit in Rs. (per ton)*
A	.02	3.0	12.00
B	.04	2.0	15.00
C	.03	5.0	14.00

You are required to formulate the Linear-programming (LP) model.

Solution

Let X_1, X_2 and X_3 respectively be the amounts in tons of grades A, B, and C used. The constraints are

(i) Phosphorus content must not exceed 0.03%

$$.02\ X_1 + .04\ X_2 + 0.03\ X_3 \leq .03\ (X_1 + X_2 + X_3)$$

$$2\ X_1 + 4\ X_2 + 3\ X_3 \leq 3\ (X_1 + X_2 + X_3) \text{ or} - X_1 + X_2 \leq 0$$

(ii) Ash content must not exceed 3%

$$3\ X_1 + 2\ X_2 + 5\ X_3 \leq 3(X_1 + X_2 + X_3) \text{ or} - X_2 + 2\ X_3 \leq 0$$

(iii) Total quantity of fuel required is not more than 100 tons. $X_1 + X_2 + X_3 \leq 100$

The Mathematical formulation of the problem is

Maximize $Z = 12\ X_1 + 15\ X_2 + 14X_3$

Subject to the constraints:

$$-X_1 + X_2 \leq 0$$

$$-X_2 + X_3 \leq 0$$

$$X_1 + X_2 + X_3 \leq 100$$

$$X_1, X_2, X_3 > 0$$

PROBLEM 1.7

An oil refinery can blend three grades of crude oil to produce quality A and quality B petrol. Two possible blending processes are available. For each production run, the older process uses 5 units of crude Q, 7 units of crude P and 2 units of crude R and produces 9 units of A and 7 units of B. The newer process uses 3 units of crude Q, 9 unit of crude P and 4 units of crude R to produce 5 units of A and 9 units of B.

Because of prior contract commitments, the refinery must produce at least 500 units of A and at least 300 units of B for the next month. It has 1,500 units of crude Q, 1,900 units of crude P and 1,000 of crude R. For each unit of A, refinery receives Rs. 60 while for each unit of B, it receives Rs. 90.

Formulate the problem as linear programming model so as to maximize the revenue.

Solution

Maximize $Z = 60(9x_1 + 5x_2) + 90(7x_1 + 9x_2) = 1170x_1 + 1110x_2$

Subject to $9x_1 + 5x_2 \geq 500$ commitment for A

$7x_1 + 9x_2 \leq 300$ commitment for B

$5x_1 + 3x_2 \leq 1500$ availability of Q

$7x_1 + 9x_2 \leq 1900$ availability of P

$2x_1 + 4x_2 \leq 1000$ availability of R

and $x_1 \geq 0,\ x_2 \geq 0.$

PROBLEM 1.8

A refinery makes 3 grades of petrol (A, B, C) from 3 crude oils (d, e, f,). Crude can be used in any grade but the others must satisfy the following specifications

Grade	*Specification*	*Selling price per litre*
A	Not less than 50% crude d Not more than 25% crude e.	16
B	Not less than 25% crude d Not more than 50% crude e	13
C	No specifications	11

There are capacity limitations on the amounts of the three crude elements that can be used.

Crude	*Capacity*	*Price/litre*
d	2,50,000	19
e	2,50,000	11
f	1,50,000	13

Build a LPP to produce the maximum profit.

Solution

Let there be x_1 litres of d in A

x_2 litres of e in A

x_3 litres of f in A

y_1 litres of d in B

y_2 litres of e in B

y_3 litres of f in B

z_1 litres of d in C

z_2 litres of e in C

z_3 litres of f in C

Calculation of Profit per Litre in each Grade

	x_1	x_2	x_3	y_1	y_2	y_3	z_1	z_2	z_3
Selling Price	16	16	16	13	13	13	11	11	11
Cost	19	11	13	19	11	13	19	11	13
Profit	-3	5	3	-6	2	0	-8	0	-2

Since the objective is to maximize profit, the objective function is given by —

Maximize $Z = -3x_1 + 5x_2 + 3x_3 - 6y_1 + 2y_2 - 8z_1 - 2z_3$

Subject to constraints:

$$\frac{x_1}{x_1 + x_2 + x_3} \geq \frac{1}{2} \quad \text{i.e.} \; - x_1 + x_2 + x_3 \leq 0$$

$$\frac{x_1}{x_1 + x_2 + x_3} \geq \frac{1}{4} \quad \text{i.e.} \; - x_1 + 3x_2 - x_3 \leq 0$$

$$\frac{y_1}{y_1 + y_2 + y_3} \geq \frac{1}{4} \quad \text{i.e.} \; - 3y_1 + y_2 + y_3 \leq 0$$

$$\frac{y_1}{y_1 + y_2 + y_3} \geq \frac{1}{4} \quad \text{i.e.} \; - y_1 + y_2 - y_3 \leq 0$$

$$x_1 + y_1 + z_1 \leq 2{,}50{,}000$$

$$x_2 + y_2 + z_2 \leq 2{,}50{,}000$$

$$x_3 + y_3 + z_3 \leq 1{,}50{,}000$$

PROBLEM 1.9

A Mutual Fund Company has Rs. 20 lakhs available for investment in Government Bonds, Blue Chip Stocks, Speculative Stocks and Short-term Bank Deposits. The annual expected return and risk factor are given below:

Type of Investment	*Annual Expected Return %*	*Risk Factor (0 to 100)*
Government Bonds	14	12
Blue Chip Stocks	19	24
Speculative Stocks	23	48
Short-term Deposits	12	6

Mutual fund is required to keep at least 10% of funds in short-term deposits and not to exceed an average risk factor of 42, Speculative stocks must be at most 20 percent of the total amount invested.

Govt. Bonds must be at least 10% of Total Investment. Mutual Fund will not accept on Average Rate of Return below 15%.

How should mutual fund invest the funds so as to maximize its total expected annual return ? Formulate this as a Linear Programming Problem. Do not solve it.

Solution

Let x_1 x_2, x_3 and x_4 denote the amount of funds to be invested in Government Bonds, Blue chip Stocks, Speculative Stocks and Short term Deposits respectively. Let Z denote the Total Expected Return.

The average risk factor is given by—

$$\frac{12x_1 + 24x_2 + 48x_3 + 6x_4}{x_1 + x_2 + x_3 + x_4}$$

$$x_1 \geq 0.10\,(x_1 + x_2 + x_3 + x_4)$$

Since the average risk factor for Mutual Fund should not exceed 42, we get the following . constraint

$$\frac{12x_1 + 24x_2 + 48x_3 + 6x_4}{x_1 + x_2 + x_3 + x_4} \leq 42$$

or $12\, x_1 + 24\, x_2 + 48\, x_3 + 6\, x_4 \leq 42 \quad (x_1 + x_2 + x_3 + x_4)$

or $30x_1 - 18x_2 + 6x_3 - 36x_4 \leq 0$

Further, speculative stock must be at most 20 per cent of the total amount invested, hence

$$x_3 \leq 0.20\,(x_1 + x_2 + x_3 + x_4)$$

or $-0.2\, x_1 - 0.2\, x_2 + 0.8\, x_3 - 0.2\, x_4 \leq 0$

For Minimum Average Rate of Return

$$0.14x_1 + 0.19x_2 + 0.23x_3 + 0.12x_4 \geq 0.15\,(x_1 + x_2 + x_3 + x_4)$$

$$-0.01x_1 + 0.04x_2 + 0.08x_3 + 0.03x_4 \geq 0 \text{ (Minimum Average Rate of Return)}$$

For Minimum Govt. Bonds

$$x_1 \geq 0.10\,(x_1 + x_2 + x_3 + x_4)$$

$$0.9x_1 - 0.1x_2 - 0.1x_3 - 0.1x_4 \geq 0$$

Since, the objective is to maximise the total expected annual return, the objective function for Mutual Fund is given by:

Maximise $Z = 0.14\, x_1 + 0.19\, x_2 + 0.23\, x_3 + 0.12\, x_4$

Subject to the constraints:

$$x_1 + x_2 + x_3 + x_4 \leq 20{,}00{,}000 \text{ [Maximum Total Investment]}$$

$$x_4 \geq 2{,}00{,}000 \text{ [Minimum Short-term Deposit]}$$

$$-30x_1 - 18x_2 + 6\, x_3 - 36\, x_4 \leq 0 \text{ [Maximum Average Risk Factor]}$$

$$-0.2\, x_1 - 0.2\, x_2 + 0.8\, x_3 - 0.2\, x_4 \leq 0 \text{ [Maximum Speculative Stocks]}$$

$$0.9x_1 - 0.1x_2 - 0.3x_3 - 0.1x_4 \geq 0 \text{ [Maximum Govt. Bonds Investments]}$$

$$-0.01x_1 + 0.04x_2 + 0.08x_3 + 0.03x_4 \geq 0 \text{ (Minimum Average Rate of Return)}$$

where $x_1 \geq 0,\ x_2 \geq 0,\ x_3 \geq 0$ *and* $x_4 \geq 0$

PROBLEM 1.10

An investor has money making activities A_1, A_2, A_3 and A_4. He has only Rs. 1 lakh to invest. In order to avoid excessive investment, no more than 50% of the total investment can be placed in Activity A_2 and for Activity A_3. Activity A_1 is very conservative, while Activity A_4 is speculative. To avoid excessive speculation at least Re. 1 must be invested in Activity A_1 for every Rs. 3 invested in Activity A_4. The data on the return on investment are as follows:

Activity	***Anticipated return On investment (%)***
A_1	10
A_2	12
A_3	14
A_4	16

Investor wishes to know how much to invest in each activity to maximize the total return on the investment.

Solution

Let x_1, x_2, x_3 and x_4 represent the percentages of the total fund invested in securities A_1, A_2, A_3 and A_4 respectively. Since the objective of the investor is to maximize total return on the investment,

Let x_1, x_2 and x_3 be the number of acres allotted for cultivating radish, mutter and potato respectively.

Sales Revenue/acre (Radish) = Rs. 5 × 1500 = Rs. 7500

Sales Revenue/acre (Matter) = Rs. 4 × 1800 = Rs. = 7,200

Sales Revenue/acre (Patato) = Rs. 5 × 1200 = Rs. 6,000

Now, the selling price, manure cost, labour cost and profit per acre of land for will be as fallows:

Per acre	*Radish*	*Muttar*	*Potato*
A. Selling Price	Rs. 7,500	Rs. 7,200	Rs. 6,000
B. Manure Cost	$\frac{\text{Rs. } 12.50 \times 1500}{100}$	$\frac{\text{Rs. } 12.50 \times 1800}{100}$	$\frac{\text{Rs. } 12.50 \times 1200}{80}$
	= Rs. 187.50	= Rs. 225	= Rs. 187.50
C. Labour Cost	Rs.40 × 6 = Rs.240	Rs.40 × 5 = Rs.200	Rs.40 × 6 = Rs. 240
D. Profit [A – B – C]	= Rs.7,072.50	= Rs.6,775	= Rs. 5,572.50

Since, the agriculturist wants to maximise the total profit, hence the objective function of the problem is given by:

Maximise $Z = 7072.5x_1 + 6775x_2 + 5572.5x_3$

Subject to following constraints:

$x_1 + x_2 + x_3 \le 125$ [Maximum Land Area]

$6x_1 + 5x_2 + 6x_3 \le 500$ [Maximum Man Days]

where x_1, x_2 *and* $x_3 \ge 0$

Z = 10% (rupees invested in A_1) + 12% (rupees invested in A_2) + 14% (rupees invested in A_3) + 16% (rupees invested in A_4).

$= 0.10\ x_1 + 0.12\ x_2 + 0.14\ x_3 + 0.16\ x_4$

Since total money invested in activities is Rs. 1 lakh,

$$x_1 + x_2 + x_3 + x_4 \le 1{,}00{,}000$$

Also money invested in activity A_2 and activity A_3 is less than or equal to 50% of money invested in four activities, therefore,

$$x_2 + x_3 \leq 0.50\ (x_1 + x_2 + x_3 + x_4)$$

or, $$-0.5x_1 + 0.5x_2 + 0.5x_3 - 0.5x_4 \leq 0$$

or, $$-x_1 + x_2 + x_3 - x_4 \leq 0$$

Further, the money invested in activity A_1 being greater than or equal to one-third of the money invested in activity A_4,

$$x_1 \geq 1/3x_4 \text{ or } \quad 3x_1 - x_4 \geq 0$$

Thus, the appropriate mathematical formulation of the LP problem is:

Maximize $Z = 0.10x_1 + 0.12x_2 + 0.14x_3 + 0.16x_4$

Subject to the constraints:

$x_1 + x_2 + x_3 + x_4 \leq 1{,}00{,}000$ (Funds Constraint)

$-x_1 + x_2 + x_3 - x_4 \leq 0$ (Maximum Constraint)

$3x_1 - x_4 \geq 0$ (Minimum Constraint)

$x_1, x_2, x_3 \geq 0$ (Non-Negativity Constraint)

PROBLEM 1.11

A leading Chartered Accountant is attempting to determine a 'best' investment portfolio and is considering six alternative investment proposals. The following table indicates point estimates for the price per share, the annual growth rate in the price per share, the annual dividend per share and a measure of the risk associated with each investment.

PORTFOLIO DATA

	Shares under consideration					
	A	*B*	*C*	*D*	*E*	*F*
Current price per share (Rs.)	80	100	160	120	150	200
Projected annual growth rate	0.08	0.07	0.10	0.12	0.09	0.15
Projected annual dividend per share (Rs.)	4.00	4.50	7.50	5.50	5.75	0.00
Projected risk in return	0.05	0.03	0.10	0.20	0.06	0.08

1. The total amount available for investment is Rs. 25 lakhs and the following conditions are required to be satisfied.
2. The maximum rupee amount to be invested in alternative F is Rs. 2,50,000.
3. No more than Rs. 5,00,000 should be invested in alternatives A and B combined.
4. Total weighted risk should not be greater than 0.10, where

$$\text{Total weighted risk} = \frac{\text{(Amount invested in alternative) (risk of alternative)}}{\text{Total amount invested in all the alternatives}}$$

5. For the sake of diversity, at least 100 shares of each stock should be purchased.
6. At least 10 percent of the total investment should be in alternatives A and B combined.
7. Dividends for the year should be at least Rs. 10,000.

Rupees return per share of stock is defined as price per share one year hence less current price per share PLUS dividend per share. If the objective is to maximise total rupee return, formulate the linear Programming model for determining the optimal number of shares to be purchased in each of the shares under consideration. You may assume that the time horizon for the investment is one year. The formulated LP problem is not required to be solved.

SOLUTION

Let x_1, x_2, x_3, x_4, x_5 and x_6 denote the number of shares to be purchased in each of the six investment proposals A, B, C, D, E and F.

Rupee return per share = Price per share one year hence
Less Current price per share
Plus dividend per share
= Current price per share × Projected annual growth rate
(i.e. Project growth for each share)
Plus dividend per share.

Thus, we get following table of data.

Investment alternatives	*A*	*B*	*C*	*D*	*E*	*F*
No. of shares purchased	x_1	x_2	x_3	x_4	x_5	x_6
Projected growth for each share (Rs.)	6.40	7.00	16.00	14.40	13.50	30.00
Projected annual dividend per share (Rs.)	4.00	4.50	7.50	5.50	5.75	0.00
Rupee return per share	10.40	11.50	23.50	19.90	19.25	30.00

The objective of the Chartered Accountant is to maximise the total rupee return, the objective function of the linear programming problem is given by:

Maximise $Z = 10.40x_1 + 11.50x_2 + 23.50x_3 + 19.90x_4 + 19.25x_5 + 30x_6$

Various constraints are as follows:

Since the total amount available for investment is Rs. 25 lakhs, hence

(I) $80x_1 + 100x_2 + 160x_3 + 120x_4 + 150x_5 + 200x_6 \leq 25{,}00{,}000$

(II) $200x_6 \leq 2{,}50{,}000$ [from condition (i)]

(III) $80x_1 + 100x_2 \leq 5{,}00{,}000$ [from condition (ii)]

(IV) As per condition (iii) of the problem

≤ 0.10

or $4x_1 + 3x_2 + 16x_3 + 24x_4 + 9x_5 + 16x_6 \leq 8x_1\ 10x_2 + 16x_3 + 12x_4 + 15x_5 + 20x_6$

or $-4x_1 - 7x_2 + 0x_3 + 12x_4 - 6x_5 - 4x_6 \leq 0$

(V) Also $x_i \geq 100$, i = 1, 2, 3, 4, 5, 6 ...[from condition (iv)]

(VI) $80x_1 + 100x_2 \geq 0.10\ (80x_1 + 100x_2 + 160x_3 + 120x_4 + 150x_5 + 200x_6)$

[from condition (v)]

on simplification, we get

$80x_1 + 100x_2 \geq 8x_1 + 10x_2 + 16x_3 + 12x_4 + 15x_5 + 20x_6$

or $72x_1 + 90x_2 - 16x_3 - 12x_4 - 15x_5 - 20x_6 \geq 0$

(VII) $4x_1 + 4.5x_2 + 7.5x_3 + 5.5x_4 + 5.75x_5 \geq 10{,}000$ [from condition (vi)]

Combining all the constraints from I...VII, the linear programming problem becomes

Maximise $Z = 10.40x_1 + 11.50x_2 + 23.50x_3 + 19.90x_4 + 19.25x_5 + 30x_6$

Subject to the constraints:

$80x_1 + 100x_2 + 160x_3 + 120x_4 + 150x_5 + 200x_6 \le 25,00,000$ (Maximum Funds)

$200x_6 \le 2,50,000$ (Max. Investment in Proposal F)

$80x_1 + 100x_1 \le 5,00,000$ (Max. Investment in Proposal A & B)

$-4x_1 - 7x_2 + 0x_3 + 12x_4 - 6x_5 - 4x_6 \le 0$ (Maximum Risk)

$xi, x_2, x_3, x_4, x_5, x_6, \ge 100$ (Minimum No. of Shares)

$72x_1 + 90x_2 - 16x_3 - 12x_4 - 15x_5 - 20x_6 \ge 0$ (Minimum Investment in Proposal A & B)

$4x_1 + 4.5x_2 + 7.5x_3 + 5.50x_4 + 5.75x_5 + 0x_6 \ge 10,000$ (Minimum Dividend)

PROBLEM 1.12

An advertising firm desires to reach two types of audiences - customers with annual income of more than Rs. 40,000 (target audience A) and customers with annual income of less than Rs. 40,000 (target audience B), The total advertising budget is Rs. 2,00,000. One programme of T.V. advertising costs Rs. 50,000 and one programme of Radio advertising costs Rs. 20,000. Contract conditions ordinarily require that there should be at least 3 programmes on T.V. and the number of programmes on Radio must not exceed 5. Survey indicates that a single T.V. programme reaches 7,50,000 customers in target audience A and 1,50,000 in target audience B. One Radio programme reaches 40,000 customers in target audience A and 2,60,000 in target audience B.

Formulate this as a linear programming problem and determine the media mix to maximize the total reach using graphic method.

Solution

Let x_1 be the number of programmes of T.V. advertising and X_2 denote the number of programmes of radio advertising.

Since the advertising firm desires to determine the media mix to maximise the total reach, the objective function is given by

Maximise $Z = (7,50,000+1,50,000)\ x_1 + (40,000+2,60,000)\ x_2$

Subject to the constraints

$5x_1 + 2x_2 < 20$ [Maximum Adv. Budget]

$x_1 \ge 3$, [Minimum T.V. Programmes]

$x_2 \le 5$ [Maximum Radio Programmes]

where $x_2, x_2 > 0$

Point of intersection for lines $x_1 = 3$ and $5x_1 + 2x_2 = 20$ is P(3, 5/2).

Similarly, lines $x_2 = 5$ and $5x_1 + 2x_2 = 20$ intersect at point (2, 5).

Line $x_1 = 0$ meets $5x_1 + 2x_2 = 20$ at point (0, 10)

Line $x_2 = 0$ meets $5x_1 + 2x_2 = 20$ at point Q(4, 0)

The graphical solution for the problem is given below:

The feasible region is given by the shaded area PQR, and the feasible points are *P*(3,5/2), *Q*(3, 0) and *R*(4, 0).

Value of the objective function Z at P(3, 5/2) is

$$9,00,000 \times 3 + 3,00,000 \times 5/2 = 27,00,000 + 7,50,000 = 34,50,000$$

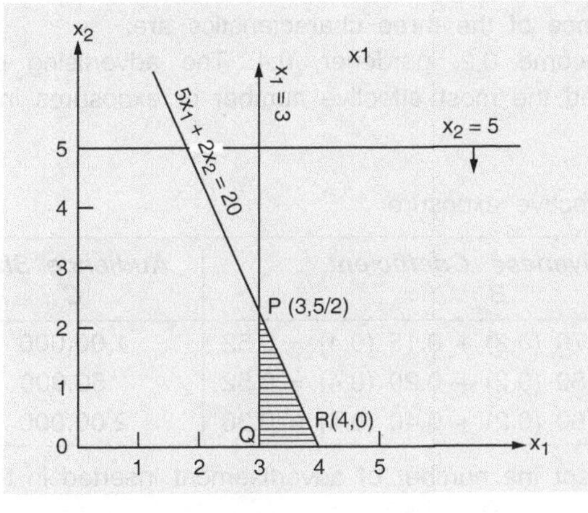

Fig. 1.1

Value of Z at Q(3, 0) is

$$9{,}00{,}000 \times 3 = 27{,}00{,}000$$

and value of Z at R(4, 0) is given by

$$9{,}00{,}000 \times 4 = 36{,}00{,}000$$

It can be seen that the value of Z is maximum at point R (4, 0). Thus, the solution to the given problem is:

$x_1 = 4$, $x_2 = 0$ and Maximum Z = 36,00,000.

In other words, the advertising firm should give 4 programmes on TV and no programme on Radio in order to achieve a maximum reach of 36,00,000 customers.

PROBLEM 1.13

Bharat Advertisers Ltd. is preparing a proposal for an advertising campaign for a client who are manufacturers of law products. An optimal allocation of advertising funds to maximise the total number of exposures has to be made for the client. The characteristics of the three alternative publications are shown in the following table.

	Home Beautiful	*Home and Garden*	*Law Care*
	Rs.	*Rs.*	*Rs.*
Cost Per Advertisement	12,000	16,000	900 0
Maximum no. of advertisements	12	24	12
Minimum no. of advertisements	3	6	2
Characteristics			
Homeowner	80%	70%	20%
Income : Rs. 10,000 or more	70%	80%	60%
Occupation : Gardener	15%	20%	40%
Audience size	1,00,000	50,000	2,00,000

The relative importance of the three characteristics are:

Homeowner, 0.4; income 0.2; gardener, 0.4. The advertising budget is Rs. 4,00,000. Formulate the LPP to find the most effective number of exposures in each magazine.

Solution

Let us first calculate, effective exposure

Media ***A***	***Effectiveness Coefficient*** ***B***	***Audience Size*** ***C***	***Effective Exposure*** ***D = B 5 C***
1	0.80 (0.4) + 0.70 (0.2) + 0.15 (0.4) = 0.52	1,00,000	52,000
2	0.70 (0.4) + 0.80 (0.2) + 0.20 (0.4) = 0.52	50,000	26,000
3	0.20 (0.4) + 0.60 (0.2) + 0.40 (0.4) = 0.36	2,00,000	72,000

Let x_1, x_2 and x_3 represent the number of advertisement inserted in the three media 1, 2 and 3 respectively.

Since the objective is to maximize the effective exposure, the objective function is given by:

Maximize $Z = 52{,}000x_1 + 26{,}000x_2 + 72{,}000x_3$

Subject to:

$12{,}000x_1 + 16{,}000x_2 + 9{,}000x_3 \leq 4{,}00{,}000$ (Budget Amount constraint)

$x_1 \geq 3$ (Minimum No. of Advertisement in Home Beautiful constraint)

$x_2 \geq 6$ (Minimum No. of Advertisement in Home and Garden constraint)

$x_3 \geq 2$ (Minimum No. of Advertisement in Law Care constraint)

$x_1 \leq 12$ (Maximum Number of Advertisement in Home Beautiful constraint)

$x_2 \leq 24$ (Maximum Number of Advertisement in Home and Garden constraint)

$x_3 \leq 12$ (Maximum Number of Advertisement in Law Care constraint)

PROBLEM 1.14

The ABC Company, manufacturers of 'ZOLO', a leading brand of hair dye, are planning the media-mix for the next year within their and budget of Rs. 1,00,000. The characteristics of target audience for 'ZOLO' and weightages for each are as follows:

	Characteristics	***Weightage (%)***
Age	Over 35 years	50
Monthly income	Over Rs. 1,200	40
Education	Graduate and above	10

The audience characteristics for the three magazines under consideration are given below:

	Characteristic	***Magazine X(%)***	***Magazine Y(%)***	***Magazine Z(%)***
Age	Over 35 years	50	30	45
Monthly Income	Over Rs. 1,200	70	60	55
Education	Graduate and above	60	50	50

The cost per insertion and the readership for the three magazines are as follows:

Magazine	*Cost per insertion (Rs.)*	*Readership (in 000's)*
X (Monthly)	4,000	170
Y (Fortnightly)	3,500	220
Z (Monthly)	5,000	160

Also at least 2 insertions are necessary in X and Y to create an impact, whilst minimum 3 insertions will be required in case of Z.

Formulate a Linear Programming Model for the given problem to maximize the expected effective exposure.

Solution

Let x_1, x_2 and x_3 represent the number of advertisement inserted in the three magazines X, Y and Z respectively. In order to formulate the objective function, we shall first calculate the effectiveness coefficients as follows:

Media	*Effectiveness Coefficient*
Magazine X	0.50 5 0.50 + 0.70 5 0.40 + 0.60 5 0.10 = 0.59
Magazine Y	0.30 5 0.50 + 0.60 5 0.40 + 0.50 5 0.10 = 0.44
Magazine Z	0.45 5 0.50 + 0.55 5 0.40 + 0.50 5 0.10 = 0.495

The effective exposures for all the three media employed can be computed as follows:

Effective exposure = Effectiveness coefficient × Audience size, where effectiveness coefficient is a weighted average of audience characteristics. Thus effective exposure for

$$\text{Magazine (X)} = 0.59 \times 170{,}000 = 1{,}00{,}300$$

$$\text{Magazine (Y)} = 0.44 \times 220{,}000 = 96{,}800$$

$$\text{Magazine (Z)} = 0.495 \times 160{,}000 = 79{,}200$$

Now the objective function and constraints of the linear programming model can be written as:

$$\text{Maximize } Z = 1{,}00{,}300x_1 + 96{,}800x_2 + 79{,}200x_3$$

Subject to the constraints:

$4{,}000x_1 + 3{,}500x_2 + 5{,}000x_3 \leq 1{,}00{,}000$ (Budget constraint)

$x_1 \geq 2,\ x_2 \geq 2,\ x_3 \geq 3$ (Minimum number of advertisements allowed constraints)

$x_1 \geq 0,\ x_2 \geq 0,\ x_3 \geq 0$ (Non-Negetivity constraints)

PROBLEM 1.15

Computer Company produces three types of models, which are first required to be machined and then assembled. The time (in hours) for these operations for each model is given below:

Model	*Machine Time*	*Assembly Time*
PIII	20	5
P II	15	4
Celeron	12	3

The total available machine time and assembly time are 1,000 hours and 1,500 hours respectively. The selling price and other variable costs for three models are:

	PIII	*PII*	*Celeron*
Selling Price (Rs.)	3,000	5,000	15,000
Labour, Material and other Variable Costs (Rs.)	2,000	4,000	8,000

The company has taken a loan of Rs. 50,000 from a Nationalised Bank, which is required to be repaid on 1.4.2011. In addition, the company has borrowed Rs. 1,00,000 from XYZ Cooperative Bank. However, this bank has given its consent to renew the loan.

The Balance Sheet of the company as on 31.3.2011 is as follows:

Liabilities	*Rs.*	*Assets*	*Rs*
Equity Share Capital	1,00,000	Land	80,000
Capital reserve	20,000	Buildings	50,000
Profit & Loss Account	30,000	Plant & Machinery	1,00,000
Long-term Loan	2,00,000	Furniture etc.	20,000
Loan from XYZ		Vehicles	40,000
Cooperative Bank	1,00,000	Cash	2,10,000
Loan from National Bank	50,000		
	5,00,000		5,00,000

The company is required to pay a sum of Rs. 15,000 towards the salary. Interest on long-term loan is to be paid every month @ 18% per annum. Interest on loan from XYZ Cooperative and Nationalised Banks may be taken as Rs. 1,500 per month. The company has already promised to deliver three P III, Two P II and five Celeron Type of Computer to M/s ABC Ltd. next month. The level of operation in the company is subject to the availability of cash next month.

The Company Manager is willing to know that how many units of each model must be manufactured next month, so as to maximize the profit.

Required: Formulate a linear programming problem for the above.

Solution

Let X_1, X_2 and X_3 denote the number of P Hi, P II and Celeron computers respectively to be manufactured in the company. The following data is given:

	PIII	*PII*	*Celeron*
Selling Price per unit (Rs.)	3,000	5,000	15,000
Labour, Material & Other variable cost per unit (Rs.)	2,000	4,000	8,000
Profit per unit (Rs.)	1,000	1,000	7,000

Calculation of cash availability for the next month from the balance sheet:

Cash balance (Rs. 2,10,000)

Loan to repay to Nationalized bank (Rs. 50,000)

Interest on loan from XYZ cooperative bank and Nationalized bank (Rs. 1500)

Interest on long term loans $\left[\dfrac{0.18 \times 2{,}00{,}000}{12}\right] = \text{Rs. } 3{,}000$

Salary to staff (Rs. 15,000)

Or, Cash availability = Rs. 2,10,000 – (Rs. 50,000 + Rs. 1,500 + Rs. 3,000 + Rs. 15,000)

= Rs. 1,40,500

Since the company wants to maximize the profit, hence the objective function is given by:

Maximize $Z = 1000X_1 + 1000X_2 + 7000X_3 -$ (Rs. 15,000 + Rs. 3,000, + Rs. 1,500) Subject to the constraints:

$20X_1 + 15X_2 + 12X_3 < 1000$ (Machine Time Restriction)

$5X_1 + 4X_2 + 3X_3 < 1500$ (Assembly Time Restriction)

$2000X_1 + 4000X_2 + 8000X_3 <$ Rs. 1,40,500 (Cash Requirements & Availability)

$X_1 \geq 3, X_2 > 2, X_3 > 5$ (Minimum Deliveries)

X_1, X_2 and $X_3 \geq 0$

PROBLEM 1.16 [Capital Mix Problem]

The most recent audited summarised Balance Sheet of Stop and Shop Financial Services is given below:

Balance Sheet as on March 31, 20X1

Liabilities	*(Rs. in lakhs)*	*Assets*	*(Rs. in lakhs)*
Equity Share Capital	65	**Fixed Assets:**	
Reserves & Surplus	110	— Assets on Leave	
Term Loan from IFCI	80	(original cost: Rs. 550 lakhs)	375
Public Deposits	150	— Other Fixed Assets	50
Bank Borrowings	147	Investments (on wholly owned	
Other Current Liabilities	50	subsidiaries)	20
		Current Assets:	
		— Stock on Hire	80
		— Receivables	30
		— Other Current Assets	35
		Miscellaneous expenditure	
		(not written off)	12
	602		**602**

The company intends to enhance its investment in the lease portfolio by another Rs. 1,000 lakhs. For this purpose it would like to raise a mix of debt and equity in such a way that the overall cost of raising additional funds is minimised. The following constraints apply to the way the funds can be mobilised:

1. Total debt divided by net owned funds, cannot exceed 10.
2. Amount borrowed from financial institutions cannot exceed 25% of the net worth.
3. Maximum amount of bank borrowings cannot exceed three times the net owned funds.
4. The company would like to keep the total public deposit limited to 40% of the total debt.

The post-tax costs of the different sources of finance are as follows :

Equity	:	25%
Term Loans	:	8.5%
Public Deposits	:	7%
Bank Borrowings	:	10%

Formulate the funding problem as a LPP.

Note: (a) Total Debt = Term Loans from Financial Institutions + Public Deposits + Bank Borrowings
(b) Net Worth = Equity Share Capital + Reserve & Surplus
(c) Net Owned Funds= Net Worth – Miscellaneous Expenditures

Solution

Let x_1, x_2, x_3 and x_4 be the quantum of additional funds (all figures here are in lakhs) raised by way of additional equity, additional term loans, additional public deposits and additional bank borrowings respectively. The objective function to minimise the cost of additional funds raised by the company is as follows:

Minimize $Z = 0.25x_1 + 0.085x_2 + 0.07x_3 + 0.1x_4$

subject to the following constraints:

(1) $\dfrac{\text{Total debt}}{\text{Net owned funds}} \le 10$

or $\dfrac{(\text{Existing debt} + \text{Additional debt})}{(\text{Equity share capital} + \text{Reserves \& Surplus})} \le 10$

or $\dfrac{(80 + 150 + 147 + x_2 + x_3 + x_4)}{(65 + 110 + x_1) - 12} \le 10$

or $\dfrac{x_2 + x_3 + x_4 + 377}{(x_1 + 163)} \le 10$

or $x_2 + x_3 + x_4 + 377 \le 10x_1 + 1630$

or $-10\,x_1 + x_2 + x_3 + x_4 \le 1253$

(2) Amount borrowed (financial institutions) $\le$ 25% of net worth

or (Existing long term loan from financial institutions + Additional loan) $\le$ 25% (Existing Equity Capital + Reserves & Surplus + Addl. Equity Capital)

or $(80 + x_2) \le 0.25\,(175 + x_1)$

$(80 + x_2) \le 1/4\,(175 + x_1)$

PROBLEM 1.17

The costs and selling prices per unit of two products manufacturing by a company are as under:

Product	*A (Rs.)*	*B (Rs.)*
Selling Price	500	450
Variable costs:		
Direct Materials @ Rs. 25 per kg.	100	100
Direct Labour @ Rs. 20 per hour	80	40
Painting @ Rs. 30 per hour	30	60
Variable overheads	190	175
Fixed Costs @Rs. 17.50/D.LHr.	70	35
Total Costs	470	410
Profit	30	40

In any month the maximum availability of inputs is limited to the following:

Direct Materials	480 kg.
Direct Labour hours	400 hours
Painting hours	200 hours

Required:

(I) Formulate a linear programme to determine the production plan which maximizes the profits by using graphical approach.

(ii) State the optimal product mix and the monthly profit derived from your solution in (i) above.

If the company can sell the painting time at Rs. 40 per hour as a separate service, show what modification will be required in the formulation of the linear programming problem. You are requi'ed to re-formulate the problem but not to solve.

Solution

Contribution Analysis

Products	*A (Rs.)*	*B (Rs.)*
A. Selling Price	500	450
B. Variable Costs:		
Direct Materials	100	100
Direct Labour	80	40
Painting	30	60
Variable Overheads	190	115
Total Variable Costs	400	375
C. Contribution (A – B)	100	175
Direct Material per unit	100/25 = 4 kg.	100/25 = 4 kg.
Direct Labour hour per unit	80/20 = 4 hours	40/20 = 2 hours
Painting hour per unit	30/30 = 1 hour	60/30 = 2 hours

Let A be the units to be produced of Product A and B be the units to be produced of Product B.

LP Problem formulation:

Max Z	$= 100A + 75B$	Maximisation of contribution
Subject to:		
	$4A + 4B \le 480$	Raw material constraint
	$4A + 2B \le 400$	Direct Labour hour constraint
	$A + 2B \le 200$	Painting hour constraint
	$A, B \ge 0$	Non negativity constraint

Raw Material Constraint:	Put B = 0, A = 120
	Put A = 0, B = 120
Direct Labour Constraint:	Put B = 0, A = 100
	Put A = 0, B = 200
Painting Constraint:	Put B = 0, A = 200
	Put A = 0, B = 100

The graphical representation will be as under:

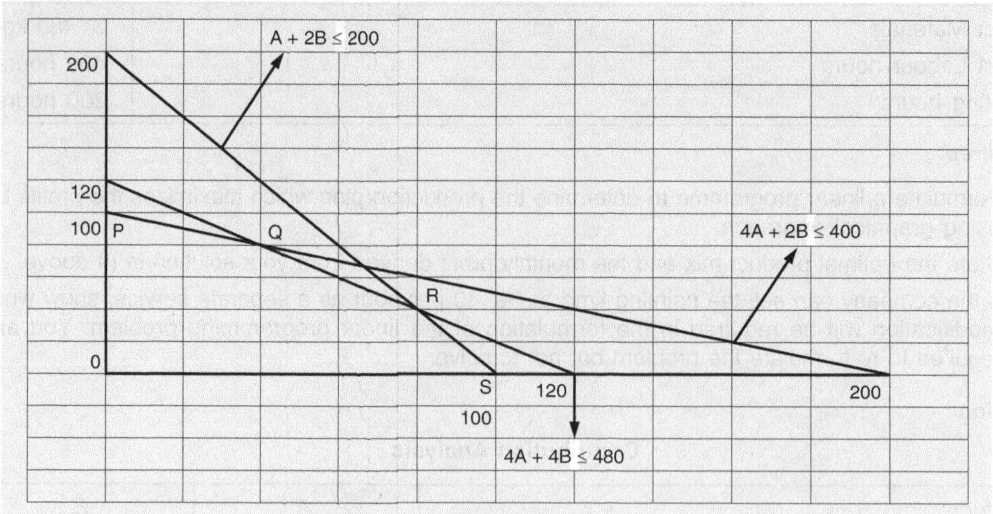

Fig.1.2

Q Intersects $4A + 2B = 400$ ...(1)

and $4A + 4B = 480$ ...(2)

Subtracting (2) from (1), we get $-2B = -80$

$\Rightarrow B = 80/2 = 40$

Putting value of B in (1). we get $4A + 2 \times 40 = 400$

$$\Rightarrow A = \frac{400 - 80}{4} = 80$$

R Intersects $4A + 4B = 480$ ...(3)

and $A + 26 = 200$ ...(4)

Multiplying (4) by (2) and then subtracting from (3), we get

$2A = 80$

$\Rightarrow A = 40$

Putting the value of A in (4), we get $2B = 200 - 40$

$\Rightarrow B = 80.$

Evaluation of Corner Points:

Point	*Products*		*Contribution*		*Total Contribution*
	A	B	A (Rs.) 100 perunit	B (Rs.) 75 per unit	Rs.
P	0	100	0	7,500	7,500
Q	80	40	8,000	3,000	11,000
R	40	80	4,000	6,000	10,000
S	100	0	10,000	0	10,000

Optimal Product Mix is Q

Product	*Units*	*Contribution Rs.*
A	80	8,000
B	40	3,000
Total Contribution		11,000
Less: Fixed costs 400 D.L. Mrs. × Rs. 17.50		7,000
Optimal Profit		4,000

(iii) If the painting time can be sold at Rs. 40 per hour the opportunity cost is calculated as under:

	A (Rs.)	*B (Rs.)*
Income from Sale per hour	40	40
Painting variable Cost per hour	30	30
Opportunity Cost	10	10
Painting hours per unit	1	2
Opportunity Cost	10	20
Revised Contribution	100 – 10 = 90	75 – 20 = 55

Hence, modification is required in the objective function.

Re-formulated problem will be:

Z Max.	$90A + 55B$	Maximisation of contribution Subject to:
	$4A + 4B \leq 480$	Raw Material constraint
	$4A + 2B \leq 400$	Direct Labour hour constraint
	$A + 2B \leq 200$	Painting hour constraint
	$A, B \geq 0$	Non-negativity constraint

PROBLEM 1.18

Transport Ltd. provides tourist vehicles of 3 types - 20-seater vans, 8-seater big cars and 5-seater small cars. These seating capacities are excluding the drivers. The company has 4 vehicles of the 20-seater van type, 10 vehicles of the 8-seatcr big car types and 20 vehicles of the 5-seater small car types. These vehicles have to be used to transport employees of their client company from their residences to their offices and back. All the residences are in the same housing colony. The offices are at two different places, one is the Head Office and the other is the Branch. Each vehicle plies only one round trip per day, if residence to office in the morning and office to residence in the evening. Each day, 180 officials need to be transported in Route I (from residence to Head Office and back) and 40 officials need to be transported in Route II (from Residence to Branch office and back). The cost per round trip for each type of vehicle along each route is given below.

You are required to formulate the information as a linear programming problem, with the objective of minimising the total cost of [hiring vehicles] for the client company, subject to the constraints mentioned above, (only formulation is required. Solution is not needed).

	20-Seater Vans	*8-Seater Big Cars*	*Figs. – Rs. /round trip* *5-seater Small Cars*
Route I— Residence —Head Office and Back	600	400	300
Route II— Residence—Branch Office and Back	500	300	200

Solution

(a) Type	I 20 – Seater vans	II 8 – Sealer Big cars	III 5 – Seater Small cars	Total no. of Passengers
Route I Residence H.O. Residence	600	400	300	180
Route II Residence Br. Residence	500	300	200	40
No. of Vehicles	4	10	20	
Max. Capacity	80	80	100	220
			260	
No. of Passengers				

Let i be the ith route,

and j be the type of vehicle, so that

S_{11} = no. of vans (vehicles on Route I, Type I)

S_{12} = no. of 8 seater cars on Route I

S_{13} = no. of 5 seater cars on Route I

S_{21} = no. of vans — on Route II

S_{22} = no. of 8 seater cars on Route II

S_{23} = no. of 5 seater cars on Route II

LPP

Minimise Cost $Z = 600\ S_{11} + 400\ S_{12} + 300\ S_{13} + 500\ S_{21} + 300\ S_{22} + 200\ S_{23}$

Subject to

$20\ S_{11} + 8\ S_{12} + 5\ S_{13} = 180$

$20\ S_{21} + 8\ S_{22} + 5\ S_{23} = 40$

$S_{11} + S_{21} \leq 4$

$S_{21} + S_{22} \leq 10$

$S_{31} + S_{32} \leq 20$

All $S_{ij} \geq 0$

PROBLEM 1.19

The following matrix gives the unit cost of transporting a product from production plants P_1, P_2 and P_3 to destinations. D_1, D_2 and D_3. Plants P_1, P_2 and P_3 have a maximum production of 65, 24 and 111 units respectively and destinations D_1, D_2 and D_3 must receive at least 60, 65 and 75 units respectively:

To / *From*	D_1	D_2	D_3	*Supply*
P_1	400	600	800	65
P_2	1,000	1,200	1,400	24
P_3	500	900	700	111
Demand	60	65	75	200

You are required to formulate the above as a linear programming problem. (Only formulation is needed. Please do not solve).

Solution

(b) Let p_i, d_j, be the variable to denote the number of units of product from the ith plant to this jth destination, so that

$$P_1\, d_1 = \text{transport from plant } P_1 \text{ to } D_1$$

$$P_2\, d_2 = \text{transport from plant } P_2 \text{ to } D_2 \text{ etc.}$$

Objective function

$$\text{Minimize } Z = 400\, p_1d_1 + 600\, p_1d_2 + 800\, p_1d_3 + 1000\, p_2d_1 + 1200\, p_2d_2 + 1400\, p_2d_3$$
$$+ 500\, p_3d_1 + 900\, p_3d_2 + 700\, p_3d_3.$$

Subject to:

$$\left.\begin{aligned} p_1d_1 + p_1d_2 + p_1d_3 &\le 65 \\ p_2d_1 + p_2d_2 + p_2d_3 &\le 24 \\ p_3d_1 + p_3d_2 + p_3d_3 &\le 111 \end{aligned}\right\} \text{(Plant constraints)}$$

and

$$\left.\begin{aligned} p_1d_1 + p_2d_1 + p_3d_1 &\le 60 \\ p_1d_2 + p_2d_2 + p_3d_2 &\le 65 \\ p_1d_3 + p_2d_3 + p_3d_3 &\le 75 \end{aligned}\right\} \text{(destination constraints)}$$

all $p_1d_1 \ge 0$

PROBLEM 1.20 [Transportation Problem]

A company is to subcontract work on four assemblies. The five subcontractors have agreed to submit a bid price on each assembly type and a limit on the total number of assemblies (if any combination) for which they are willing to contract. These bids, the contract times, and time requirements for assemblies are given in the following matrix.

	Subcontractor					
	A	**B**	**C**	**D**	**E**	***Assemblies Required***
Assembly 1	10	11	12	13	14	500
Assembly 2	11	12	11	10	9	300
Assembly 3	12	13	8	9	10	300
Assembly 4	13	8	9	10	11	400
Contract Limits	250	280	330	360	380	

Formulate the LP model.

Solution

Let x_{11} be Assembly 1 to Subcontractor A, x_{12} be assembly to Subcontractor B and so on.

	Subcontractor					
	A	**B**	**C**	**D**	**E**	***Assemblies Required***
Assembly 1	10 x_{11}	11 x_{12}	12 x_{13}	13 x_{14}	14 x_{15}	500
Assembly 2	11 x_{21}	12 x_{22}	11 x_{23}	10 x_{24}	9 x_{25}	300
Assembly 3	12 x_{31}	13 x_{32}	8 x_{33}	9 x_{34}	10 x_{35}	300
Assembly 4	13 x_{41}	8 x_{42}	9 x_{43}	10 x_{44}	11 x_{45}	400
Contract Limits	250	280	330	360	380	

It is a minimization problem since the objective is to minimize the cost of sub-contract price of the assembly. Hence, objective function is given by—

$$\begin{aligned}\text{Minimum} \quad Z = {} & 10x_{11} + 11x_{12} + 12x_{13} + 13x_{14} + 14x_{15} \\ & + 11x_{21} + 12x_{22} + 11x_{23} + 10x_{24} + 9x_{25} \\ & + 12x_{31} + 13x_{32} + 8x_{33} + 9x_{34} + 10x_{35} \\ & + 13x_{41} + 8x_{42} + 9x_{43} + 10x_{44} + 11x_{45}\end{aligned}$$

Subject to the following constraints:

$x_{11} + x_{21} + x_{31} + x_{41} \le 250$ (No. of Contract limits)

$x_{12} + x_{22} + x_{32} + x_{42} \le 280$ (No. of Contract limits)

$x_{13} + x_{23} + x_{33} + x_{43} \le 330$ (No. of Contract limits)

$x_{14} + x_{24} + x_{34} + x_{44} \le 360$ (No. of Contract limits)

$x_{15} + x_{25} + x_{35} + x_{45} \le 380$ (No. of Contract limits)

$x_{11} + x_{12} + x_{13} + x_{14} + x_{15} \leq 500$ (No. of Assemblies required)

$x_{21} + x_{22} + x_{23} + x_{24} + x_{25} \leq 300$ (No. of Assemblies required)

$x_{31} + x_{32} + x_{33} + x_{34} + x_{35} \leq 300$ (No. of Assemblies required)

$x_{41} + x_{42} + x_{43} + x_{44} + x_{45} \leq 400$ (No. of Assemblies required)

$x_{ij} \geq 0$ for all i and j (Non-Negativity constraint)

PROBLEM 1.21

North-East Aircraft Company, which operates out of a central terminal, has 8 aircraft of Type I, 15 aircraft of Type II, and 12 aircraft of Type III available for today's flights. The tonnage capacities (in thousands of tons) are 4.5 for Type I, 7 for Type II and 4 for Type III.

The company dispatches its planes to cities A and B. Tonnage requirements (in thousands of tons) are 20 at city A and 30 at city B; excess tonnage capacity supplied to a city has no value. A plane can fly once only during the day.

The cost of sending a plane from the terminal to each city is given by the following table:

	Type I	*Type II*	*Type III*
City A	23	5	1.4
City B	58	10	3.8

Formulate the LP model to minimise the air-transportation cost.

Solution

Let x_{11} be the I planes coming to A, x_{12} the II plane coming to A; and so on.

		Aircraft Type			
		I	*II*	*III*	
		8	15	12	(Nos.)
		4.5	7	4	(Capacity in tons)
	Tons A(20)	x_{11}	x_{12}	x_{13}	Cost matrix
		23	5	1.4	
Requirements	B(30)	x_{21}	x_{22}	x_{23}	(Cost of sending a plane)
		58	10	3.8	

$$\text{Min. } Z = 23x_{11} + 5x_{12} + 1.4x_{13} + 58x_{21} + 10x_{22} + 3.8x_{23}$$

$$4.5x_{11} + 7x_{12} + 4x_{13} \geq 20$$

$$4.5x_{21} + 7x_{22} + 4x_{23} \geq 30$$

$$x_{21} + x_{11} \leq 8$$

$$x_{22} + x_{12} \leq 15$$

$$x_{23} + x_{72} \leq 12$$

$$xij \geq 0$$

PROBLEM 1.22 [Assignment Problem]

A company has two grades of inspectors, 1 and 2 to undertake quality control inspection. At least 3,500 pieces must be inspected in an 8 hour day. Grade 1 inspector can check 50 pieces in an hour with an accuracy of 95%. Grade 2 inspector checks 25 pieces an hour with an accuracy of 90%.

The daily wages of grade 1 inspectors are Rs. 6 per hour while those of grade 2 inspectors are Rs. 5 per hour. Any error made by an inspector costs Rs. 4 per piece to the company. If there are, in all, 20 grade 1 inspectors and 25 grade 2 inspectors in the company, find the optimal assignment of inspectors that minimizes the daily inspection cost. Formulate the LP problem.

Solution

Let x_1 and x_2 be the number of grade 1 and 2 inspectors

Calculation of Inspection Cost of Inspectors

	Grade 1 (x_1)	Grade 2 (x_2)
A. Wage rate per hour	Rs. 6	Rs. 5
B. Inspection error cost per piece	Rs. 4	Rs. 4
C. Probability of Inspection Error	5%	10%
D. No. of pieces checked per hour	50	25
E. Cost of Inspection Error per hour [B 5 C 5 D]	Rs. 10	Rs. 10
F. Total Inspection cost per hour [A + E]	Rs. 16	Rs. 15
G. Total Inspection cost per day [F 5 8]	Rs. 128	Rs. 120

The above inspection problem can now be formulated in an appropriate mathematical from as follows:

Minimize (Daily inspection cost) $Z = 128x_1 + 120x_2$

Subject to the constraints:

$400x_1 + 200x_2 \geq 3500$ (Inspection pieces constraint)

$x_1 \leq 20$ (Grade 1 inspectors constraint)

$x_2 \leq 25$ (Grade 2 inspectors constraint)

$x_1, x_2 \geq 0$ (Non-Negetivity constraint)

PROBLEM 1.23 [Trim Problem]

The Fine Paper Company produces rolls of paper used in cash registers. Each roll of paper is 500 ft. in length and can be produced in widths of 1, 2, 3 and 5 inch. The company's production process results in 500' rolls that are 12 inches in width. Thus, the company must cut its 12 inch roll to the desired widths. It has six basic cutting alternatives as follows:

Cutting Alternative	*No . of Rolls*				*Waste (inches)*
	1"	*2"*	*3"*	*5"*	
1	6	3	0	0	0
2	0	3	2	0	0
3	1	1	1	1	1
4	0	0	2	1	1
5	5	2	1	0	1
6	4	2	1	0	1

The minimum demand requirements for the four rolls are as follows:

Roll Width (inches)	*Demand Requirements (Rolls)*
1	6000
2	4000
3	3000
5	2000

The company wishes to minimise the wastes generated by its production process, while meeting its demand requirements. Formulate the LP model.

Solution

Let x_j be the number of times cutting alternative (j = 1, 2, ... 6) is employed.

Since the objective is to minimize the waste generated, the objective function is given by—

Minimise (waste produced) $Z = 1x_3 + 1x_4 + 1x_5 + 1x_6$

Subject to constraints:

$6x_1 + 1x_3 + 5x_5 + 4x_6 \geq 6000$ (Minimum Demand Requirement of 1" Roll)

$3x_1 + 3x_2 + 1x_3 + 4x_5 + 2x_6 \geq 4000$ (Minimum Demand Requirement of 2" Roll)

$2x_2 + 1x_3 + 2x_4 + 1x_5 + 1x_6 \geq 3000$ (Minimum Demand Requirement of 3" Roll)

$1x_3 + 1x_4 \geq 2000$ (Minimum Demand Requirement of 5" Roll)

$x_j \geq 0$, for all j (Non-Negativity constraint)

PROBLEM 1.24 [Job Schedulings]

A big hospital has the following minimal daily requirements of doctors:

Period	*Clocktime (24 hours.)*	*No. of doctors required*
1	6 a.m. - 10 a.m.	72
2	10 a.m. - 2 p.m.	77
3	2 p.m. - 6 p.m.	85
4	6 p.m. - 10 p.m.	68
5	10 p.m. - 2 a.m.	25
6	2 a.m. - 6 a.m.	23

Doctors report to the hospital at the beginning of each period and work for 8 consecutive hours. Formulate this problem as a linear programming problem to minimise the total number of doctors to meet the needs of the hospital throughout the day.

Solution

Let x_1 represent the number of doctors required at starting period k (k = 1, 2, ..., 6). Then the objective function and constraints can be written as:

Minimise (total number of doctors)

$$Z = x_1 + x_2 + x_3 + x_4 + x_5 + x_6$$

Subject to the constraints:

(i) $\begin{pmatrix}\text{Number of doctors}\\ \text{starting period 1}\end{pmatrix} + \begin{pmatrix}\text{Number of doctors that started}\\ \text{at period 6 and still on duty}\end{pmatrix} \geq 72$

or, $x_1 + x_6 \geq 72$

(ii) $\begin{pmatrix}\text{Number of doctors}\\ \text{starting period 2}\end{pmatrix} + \begin{pmatrix}\text{Number of doctors that started}\\ \text{at period 1 and still on duty}\end{pmatrix} \geq 77$

or, $x_2 + x_1 \geq 77$

(iii) $\begin{pmatrix}\text{Number of doctors}\\ \text{starting period 3}\end{pmatrix} + \begin{pmatrix}\text{Number of doctors that started}\\ \text{at period 2 and still on duty}\end{pmatrix} \geq 85$

or, $x_3 + x_2 \geq 85$

(iv) $\begin{pmatrix}\text{Number of doctors}\\ \text{starting period 4}\end{pmatrix} + \begin{pmatrix}\text{Number of doctors that started}\\ \text{at period 3 and still on duty}\end{pmatrix} \geq 68$

or, $x_4 + x_3 \geq 68$

(v) $\begin{pmatrix}\text{Number of doctors}\\ \text{starting period 5}\end{pmatrix} + \begin{pmatrix}\text{Number of doctors that started}\\ \text{at period 4 and still on duty}\end{pmatrix} \geq 25$

or, $x_5 + x_4 \geq 25$

(vi) $\begin{pmatrix}\text{Number of doctors}\\ \text{starting period 6}\end{pmatrix} + \begin{pmatrix}\text{Number of doctors that started}\\ \text{at period 5 and still on duty}\end{pmatrix} \geq 23$

or, $x_6 + x_5 \geq 23$

Alternative Solution:

Minimize $Z = x_1 + x_2 + x_3 + x_4 + x_5 + x_6$

Subject to constraints:

$x_1 + x_2 \geq 72$

$x_2 + x_3 \geq 77$

$x_3 + x_4 \geq 85$

$x_4 + x_5 \geq 68$

$x_5 + x_6 \geq 25$

$x_6 + x_1 \geq 23$

$x_1 \geq 0,\ x_2 \geq 0,\ x_3 \geq 0,\ x_4 \geq 0,\ x_5 \geq 0,\ x_6 \geq 0,$

Note: There also exist other alternative solutions.

MISCELLENEOUS SOLVED PROBLEMS

PROBLEM 1.25

Piyush is an aspiring freshman at Delhi University. He realizes that "all work and no play make Piyush a dull boy." As a result, Piyush wants to apportion his available time of about 10 hours a day between work and play. He estimates that play is twice as much fun as work. He also wants to study at least as much as he plays. However, he realizes that if he is going to get all his homework assignments done, he cannot play more than 4 hours a day. How should Piyush allocate his time to miximize his pleasure from both work and play?

Solution

Let x_1 = play hours per day, x_2 = work hours per day

Maximize $Z = 2x_1 + x_2$

Subject to,

$x_1 + x_2 \leq 10$ [Maximum Total Time constraint]

$x_1 + x_2 \leq 0$ [Minimum Work Hours constraint]

$x_1 \leq 4$ [Maximum Play Hours constraint]

$x_1, x_2 \geq 0$ [Non negativity constraint]

PROBLEM 1.26

An assembly line consisting of three consecutive stations produces two radio models: HiFi-1 and HiFi-2. The following table porvides the assembly times for the three workstations.

Workstation	*Minutes per unit*	
	HiFi-1	*HiFi-2*
1	6	4
2	5	5
3	4	6

The daily maintenance for stations 1, 2, and 3 consumes 10%, 14%, and 12%, respectively, of the maximum 480 minutes available for each station each day. Determine the optimal product mix that will minimize the idle (or unused) time in the three workstations.

Solution

Let x_1 = Number of HiFi 1 units, x_2 = Number of HiFi 2 units

Minimize $Z = 1267.2 - (15x_1 + 15x_2)$

As, Total Minutes per unit of HiFi 1 = 6 + 5 + 4 = 15 minutes &

Total Minutes per unit of HiFi 2 = 4 + 5 + 6 = 15 minutes

Total Available Time = 432 + 412.8 + 422.4 = 1267.2 minutes

Subject to,

$6x_1 + 4x_2 \leq 432$ I[st] constraint [480 – 10% of 480] [Time constraint]

$5x_1 + 5x_2 \leq 412.8$ IInd constraint [480 – 14% of 480] [Time constraint]

$4x_1 + 6x_2 \leq 422.4$ IIIrd constraint [480 – 12% of 480] [Time constraint]

$x_1, x_2 \geq 0$ [Non negativity constraint]

PROBLEM 1.27

A city will undetake five urban renewal housing projects over the next five years. Each project has a different starting year and a different duration. The following table provides the basic data of the situation:

	Year 1	*Year 2*	*Year 3*	*Year 4*	*Year 5*	*Cost (million \$)*	*Annual income (million \$)*
Project 1	Start		End			5.0	.05
Project 2		Start			End	8.0	.07
Project 3	Start				End	15.0	.15
Project 4			Start	End		1.2	.02
Budget (million \$)	3.0	6.0	7.0	7.0	7.0		

Projects 1 and 4 must be finished completely within their durations. The remaining two projects can be finished partially within budget limitations, if necessary. However, each project must be at least 25% completed within its duration. At the end of each year, the completed section of a project is immediately occupied by tenants and a proportional amount of income is realized.

Solution

Let x_{11} = Portion of project 1 completed in year 1
x_{12} = Portion of project 1 competed in year 2
x_{13} = Portion of project 1 completed in year 3 [Project End]
x_{22} = Portion of project 2 completed in year 2 [As Project 2 starts in year 2]
x_{23} = Portion of project 2 completed in year 3
x_{24} = Portion of project 2 completed in year 4
x_{25} = Portion of project 2 completed in year 5
x_{31} = Portion of project 3 completed in year 1
x_{32} = Portion of project 3 completed in year 2
x_{33} = Portion of project 3 completed in year 3
x_{34} = Portion of project 3 completed in year 4
x_{35} = Portion of project 3 completed in year 5
x_{43} = Portion of project 4 completed in year 3 [As project 4 starts in year 3]
x_{44} = Portion of project 4 completed in year 4 [Project End]

Note: Year 5 will not be considered, for revenue for revenue come in next year and we are considering 5 year horizon. Now optimum function of project 1 is

Year 2 Year 3 Year 4 Year 5

$$[x_{11} \times 0.05] + [(x_{11} + x_{12})\, 0.05] + [(x_{11} + x_{12} + x_{13})\, 0.05] + [(x_{11} + x_{12} + x_{13})\, 0.05]$$

i.e. $$0.05\, [x_{11} + (x_{11} + x_{12}) + (x_{11} + x_{12} + x_{13}) + (x_{11} + x_{12} + x_{13})]$$

$$= 0.05(4x_{11} + 3x_{12} + 2x_{13})$$

Similarly for project 2, 3 and 4

$$0.07\,(3x_{22} + 2x_{23} + x_{24})$$

$$0.15\,(4x_{31} + 3x_{32} + 2x_{33} + x_{34})$$

$0.02\,(2x_{43} + x_{44})$ respectively

$$\text{Maximize } Z = 0.05\,(4x_{11} + 3x_{12} + 2x_{13}) + 0.07\,(3x_{22} + 2x_{23} + x_{24}) + 0.15\,(4x_{31} + 3x_{32} + 2x_{33} + x_{34}) + 0.02\,(2x_{43} + x_{44})$$

Subject to

$x_{11} + x_{12} + x_{13} = 1$ I[st] constraint [Project 1 to be completed at given time]

$x_{43} + x_{44} = 1$ IInd constraint [Project 4 to be completed at given time]

$x_{22} + x_{23} + x_{24} + x_{25} \geq 0.25$ IIIrd constraint [Minimum completion constraint]

$x_{22} + x_{23} + x_{24} + x_{25} \leq 1$ IVth constraint

$x_{31} + x_{32} + x_{33} + x_{34} + x_{35} \geq 0.25$ V[th] constraint [Minimum completion constraint]

$x_{31} + x_{32} + x_{33} + x_{34} + x_{35} \leq 1$ VIth constraint

$5x_1 + 15x_{31} \leq 3$ VIIth constraint [Budget constraint]

$5x_{12} + 8x_{22} + 15x_{32} \leq 6$ VIIIth constraint [Budget constraint]

$5x_{13} + 8x_{23} + 15x_{33} + 1.2x_{43} \leq 7$ IXth constraint [Budget constraint]

$8x_{24} + 15x_{34} + 1.2x_{44} \leq 7$ X[th] constraint [Budget constraint]

$8x_{25} + 15x_{35} \leq 7$ XIth constraint [Budget constraints]

$x_{11}, x_{12}, x_{13}; x_{22}, x_{23}, x_{24}; x_{31}, x_{32}, x_{33}, x_{34}; x_{43}, x_{44} \geq 0$ [Non negativity constraint]

PROBLEM 1.28

Prarthna Mittal owns 800 acres of undeveloped land on a scenic lake in the heart of the Ozark Mountains. In the past, little or no regulation was imposed upon new developments around the lake. The lake shores are now dotted with vacation homes, and septic tanks, most of them improperly installed, are in extensive use. Over the years, seepage from the septic tanks led to severe water pollution. To curb further degradation of the lake, county officials have approved stringent ordinances applicable to all future developments: (1) Only single, double, and triple-family homes can be constructed, with single-family homes accounting for at least 50% of the total. (2) To limit the number of septic tanks, minimum lot sizes of 2, 3, and 4 acres are required for single, double, and triple-family homes, respectively. (3) Recreation areas of 1 acre each must be established at the rate of one area per 200 families. (4) To preserve the ecology of the lake, underground water may not be pumped out for house or garden use. The president of Realco is studying the possiblity of developing the 800-acre property. The new development will include single, double, and triple-family homes. It is estimated that 15% of the acreage will be allocated to streets and utility easements. Realco estimates the returns from the different housing units as follows:

Housing unit	*Single*	*Double*	*Triple*
Net return per unit (Rs.)	10,000	12,000	15,000

The cost of connecting water service to the area is proportionate to the number of units constructed. However, the county charges a minimum of Rs. 100,000 for the project. Additionally, the expansion of the water system beyond its present capacity is limited to 200,000 gallons per day during peak periods. The following data summarize the water service connection cost as well as the water consumption, assuming an average size family:

Housing unit	*Single*	*Double*	*Triple*	*Recreation*
Water service connection cost per unit (Rs.)	1000	1200	1400	800
Water consumption per unit (gal/day)	400	600	840	450

Develop an optimal plan for Prarthna Mittal.

Solution

Let x_1 = Single Family Home
x_2 = Double Family Home
x_3 = Triple Family Home
x_4 = Recreation Area

Now,

$$(10{,}000 - 1000)x_1 + (12{,}000 - 1200)x_2 + (15000 - 1400)x_3 - 800\,x_4$$

i.e. Maximize $Z = 9000x_1 + 10{,}800x_2 + 13{,}600x_3 - 800x_4$

Subject to

$2x_1 + 3x_2 + 4x_3 + x_4 \le 680$ Ist constraint as [800 – 15% of 800] [size constraint]

$x_1 \ge \frac{1}{2}(x_1 + x_2 + x_3)$... [at least 50% of total constraint]

$\Rightarrow$ $0.5x_1 - 0.5x_2 - 0.5x_3 \ge 0$ IInd constraint

$x_4 \ge \dfrac{x_1 + 2x_2 + 3x_3}{200}$ [Recreation area per family constraint]

$\Rightarrow$ $200x_4 - x_1 - 2x_2 - 3x_2 \ge 0$ IIIrd constraint

$400x_1 + 600x_2 + 840x_3 + 450x_4 \le 2{,}00{,}000$ IVth constraint [water capacity constraint]

$x_1, x_2, x_3, x_4 \ge 0$ [Non negativity constraint]

PROBLEM 1.29

Investor Piyush Jindal has Rs. 10,000 to invest in four projects. The following table gives the cash flow for the four investments.

Project	*Cash flow (Rs. 1000) at the start of* Year 1	Year 2	Year 3	Year 4	Year 5
1	–1.00	0.50	0.30	1.80	1.20
2	–1.00	0.60	0.20	1.50	1.30
3	0.00	–1.00	0.80	1.90	0.80
4	–1.00	0.40	0.60	1.80	0.95

The information in the table can be interpreted as follows: For project 1, Rs. 1.00 invested at the start of year 1 will yield Rs. 50 at the start of year 2, Rs. .30 at the start of year 3, Rs. 1.80 at the start of year 4, and Rs. 1.20 at the start of year 5. The remaining entries can be interpreted similarly. The entry 0.00 indicates that no transaction is taking place. Doe has the additional option of investing in a bank account that earns 6.5% annually. All funds accumulated at the end of one year can be reinvested in the following year. Formulate the problem as a linear program to determine the optimal allocation of funds to investment opportunities.

Solution

Let x_1 = Amount invested in project 1 in beginning of year 1
x_2 = Amount invested in project 2 in beginning of year 1
x_3 = Amount invested in project 3 in beginning of year 2
x_4 = Amount invested in project 4 in beginning of year 1

y_1 = Amount invested in Bank in beginning of year 1
y_2 = Amount invested in Bank in beginning of year 2
y_3 = Amount invested in Bank in beginning of year 3
y_4 = Amount invested in Bank in beginning of year 4
y_5 = Amount invested in Bank at the end of year 4

Maximize $Z = Y_5$

Subject to

$x_1 + x_2 + x_4 + y_1 \leq 10{,}000$ I[st] constraint [Budget constraint]
$0.5x_1 + 0.6x_2 - x_3 + 0.4x_4 + 1.065y_1 - y_2 = 0$ IInd constraint [Budget constraint]
$0.3x_1 + 0.2x_2 + 0.8x_3 + 0.6x_4 + 1.065y_2 - y_3 = 0$ IIIrd constraint [Budget constraint]
$1.8x_1 + 1.5x_2 + 1.9x_3 + 1.8x_4 + 1.065y_3 - y_4 = 0$ IVth constraint [Budget constraint]
$1.2x_1 + 1.3x_2 + 0.8x_3 + 0.95x_4 + 1.065y_4 - y_5 = 0$ V[th] constraint [Budget constraint]
$x_1, x_2, x_3, x_4; y_1, y_2, y_3, y_4 \geq 0$ [Non negativity constraint]

PROBLEM 1.30

TULSIAN Construction can bid on two 1-year projects. The following table provides the quarterly cash flow (in millions of dollars) for the two projects.

Project	Cash flow (in millions of Rs.) at				
	1/1/11	*4/1/11*	*7/1/11*	*10/1/11*	*12/31/011*
I	–1.0	–3.1	–1.5	1.8	5.0
2	–3.0	–2.5	1.5	1.8	2.8

TULSIAN has cash funds of Rs. 1 million at the beginning of each quarter and may borrow at most Rs. 1 million at a 10% nominal annual interest rate. Any borrowed money must be returned at the end of the quarter. Surplus cash can earn quarterly interest at an 8% nominal annual rate. Net accumulation at the end of one quarter is invested in the next quarter.

Assume that TULSIAN is allowed partial or full participation in the two projects. Determine the level of participation that will maximize the net cash accumulated on 31.12.2011.

Solution

Let x_1 = Degree of participation in project 1
x_2 = Degree of participation in project 2
b_1 = Borrowings in beginning of quarter 1
b_2 = Borrowings in beginning of quarter 2
b_3 = Borrowings in beginning of quarter 3
b_4 = Borrowings in beginning of quarter 4
S_1 = Surplus in beginning of quarter 1
S_2 = Surplus in beginning of quarter 2
S_3 = Surplus in beginning of quarter 3
S_4 = Surplus in beginning of quarter 4
S_5 = Surplus in beginning of quarter 4

Maximize S_5

Subject to

$x_1 + 3x_2 + S_1 - b_1 = 1$ I[st] constraint [Budget constraint]
as $[x_1 + 3x_2 + S_1 = 1 - b_1]$
$3.1x_1 + 2.5x_2 + 1.025b_1 - b_2 - 1.02\ S_1 + S_2 = 1$ IInd constraint [Budget constraint]
[as $3.1x_1 + 2.5x_2 + 1.025b_1 - 1.02\ S_1 + S_2 = 1 + b_1$]

$1.5x_1 - 1.5x_2 + 1.025b_3 - 1.02\ S_2 - b_3 + S_3 = 1$ IIIrd constraint [Budget constraint]
$-1.8x_1 - 1.8x_2 + 1.025b_3 - 1.02S_3 - b_4 + S_4 = 1$ IVth constrain [Budget constraint]
$5x_1 - 2.8x_2 + 1.025b_4 - 1.02S_4 + S_5 = 0$ V[th] constraint [Budget constraint]
$b_1 \leq 1,\ b_2 \leq 1,\ b_3 \leq 1,\ b_4 \leq 1$ VIth constraint [As borrowings can not be more than 1]
$x_1, x_2, b_1, b_2, b_3, b_4, S_1, S_2, S_3, S_4, S_5 \geq 0$ [Non negativity constraint]

PROBLEM 1.31

A business executive has the option to invest money in two plans: Plan A guarantees that each dollar invested will earn Rs. .70 a year later, and plan B guarantees that each rupee invested will earn Rs. 2 after 2 years. In plan A, investments can be made annually, and in plan B, investments are allowed for periods that are multiples of two years only. How should the executive invest Rs. 100,000 to maximize the earnings at the end of 3 years?

Solution

Let A_1 = Amount Invested in plan A in beginning of year 1
A_2 = Amount Invested in plan A in beginning of year 2
A_3 = Amount Invested in plan A in beginning of year 3
A_4 = Amount Invested in plan A in beginning of year 3
B_1 = Amount Invested in plan B in beginning of year 1
B_2 = Amount Invested in plan B in beginning of year 2

Maximize A_4

$A_1 + B_1 = 1,00,000$ I[st] constraint [Budget constraint]
$-1.70A_1 + A_2 + B_2 = 0$ IInd constraint [Budget constraint]
$-1.70A_2 + A_3 - 3B_1 = 0$ IIIrd constraint [Budget constraint]
$1.70A_3 - A_4 + 3B_2 = 0$ IVth constraint [Budget constraint]
$A_1, A_2, A_3, A_4, B_1, B_2 \geq 0$ [Non negativity constraint]

PROBLEM 1.32

TUSHAR Manufacturing Company has contracted to deliver home windows over the next 6 months. The demands for each month are 100, 250, 190, 140, 220 and 110 units, respectively. Production cost per window varies from month to month depending on the cost of labor, material, and utilities. Acme estimates the production cost per window over the next 6 months to be \$50, \$45, \$55, \$48, \$52, and \$50, respectively. To take advantage of the fluctuations in manufacturing cost, Acme may elect to produce more than is needed in a given month and hold the excess units for delivery in later months. This, however, will incur storage costs at the rate of \$8 per window per month assessed on end-of-month inventory. Develop a linear program to determine the optimum production schedule.

Solution

Let x_1 = No. of units produced in 1st month
x_2 = No. of units produced in 2nd month
x_3 = No. of units produced in 3rd month
x_4 = No. of units produced in 4th month
x_5 = No. of units produced in 5th month
x_6 = No. of units produced in 6th month
S_1 = Inventory at the end of 1st month
S_2 = Inventory at the end of 2nd month
S_3 = Inventory at the end of 3rd month
S_4 = Inventory at the end of 4th month
S_5 = Inventory at the end of 5th month

Minimize $Z = 50x_1 + 45x_2 + 55x_3 + 48x_4 + 52x_5 + 50x_6 + 8S_1 + 8S_2 + 8S_3 + 8S_4 + 8S_5$

Subject to,

$x_1 - S_1 = 100$ Ist constraint [Demand constraint]

$x_2 + S_1 - S_2 = 250$ IInd constraint [Demand constraint]

$x_3 + S_2 - S_3 = 190$ IIIrd constraint [Demand constraint]

$x_4 + S_3 - S_4 = 140$ IVth constraint [Demand constraint]

$x_5 + S_4 - S_5 = 220$ Vth constraint [Demand constraint]

$x_6 + S_5 = 110$ VIth constraint [Demand constraint]

$x_1, x_2, x_3, x_4, x_5, x_6, S_1, S_2, S_3, S_4, S_5 \geq 0$ [Non negativity constraint]

PROBLEM 1.33

A company will manufacture a product for the next four months: March, April, May and June. The demands for each month are 520, 720, 520 and 620 units, respectively. The company has a steady workforce of 10 employees but can meet fluctuating production needs by hiring and firing temporary workers, if necessary. The extra costs of hiring and firing in any month are Rs. 200 and Rs. 400 per worker, respectively. A permanent worker can produce 12 units per month, and a temporary worker, lacking comparable experience, only produce 10 units per month. The company can produce more than needed in any month and carry the surplus over to a succeeding month at a holding cost of Rs. 50 per unit per month. Develop an optimal hiring/firing policy for the company over the four-month planning horizon.

Solution

Let H_1 = Hired labour in month of March

H_2 = Hired labour in month of April

H_3 = Hired labour in month of May

H_4 = Hired labour in month of June

F_2 = Fired labour in month of April

F_3 = Fired labour in month of May

F_4 = Fired labour in month of June

S_1 = Inventory in month of March

S_2 = Inventory in month of April

S_3 = Inventory in month of May

Minimize $Z = 200(H_1 + H_2 + H_3 + H_4) + 400 (F_2 + F_3 + F_4) + 50(S_1 + S_2 + S_3)$

Subject to

$10H_1 - S_1 = 400$ Ist constraint [Demand for month of March constraint]

as $10H_1 + (12 \times 10) - S_1 = 520$

$\Rightarrow$ $10H_1 - S_1 = 520 - 120 = 400$

Similary

$10H_2 + 10(H_1 - F_2) + S_1 - S_2 = 600$ IInd constraint [Demand for month of April constraint]

$10H_3 + 10(H_2 + H_1 - F_2 - F_3) + S_2 - S_3 = 400$ IIIrd constraint

[Demand for the month of May constraint]

$10H_4 + 10(H_3 + H_2 + H_1 - F_2 - F_3 - F_4) + S_3 = 500$

[Demand for the month of June constraint]

$H_1, H_2, H_3, H_4, F_2, F_3, F_4, S_1, S_2, S_3 \geq 0$ [Non negativity constraint]

PROBLEM 1.34

A firm wants to reach two types of customers: House holds having Rs 5 lakhs or more of annual family income and those having income of less than Rs 5 lakhs. The first category purchases twice as much as the second group. One unit of TV advertisement reaches 2,000 families of first group and 8000 families of second group and costs Rs 20,000 while advertisements in a magazine costs Rs 12,000 and reaches 6,000 and 3,000 families respectively. Not more than 12 advertisements can be given in the magazine and at least 6 TV advertisements have to be given. The advertisement budget is Rs. 1,80,000. Assume that every contracted family purchases the company product. The firm wants to maximize its sales. Formulate the above problem as a linear programming model.

Solution

Determination of Revenue Function

Let,

No. of T.V advertisement to be given x_1

No. of magazine advertisement to be given x_2

As T.V advertisement reaches 2000 families of first group and 8000 families of second group.

Therefore effective reach $[(2000 \times 2) + 8000] = 12000$.

In case of magazine advertisement

$= 6000 \times 2 + 3000 = 15000.$

Therefore Maximise $Z = 12000x_1 + 15000x_2$

Subject to

$x_2 \leq 12$ Ist constraint [Maximum no. of Magazine Advertisement constaint]

$x_1 \geq 6$ IInd constraint [Minimum no. of T.V Advertisement constraint]

$20,000\ x_1 + 12,000x_2 \leq 1,80,000$ IIIrd constraint [Budget constraint]

$x_1, x_2 \geq 0$ Non negativity constraint.

PROBLEM 1.35

Industrial design company has been awarded a contract to design a label for a new medicine produced by a pharmaceutical company. The company estimates that 150 hours will be required to complete the project. The firm's three graphic designers available with the company for this project are Leena a senior designer and team leader; Rahul, a senior designer and Sarah, a junior designer. Because Leena has worked on several projects for the company, and that she must be assigned 40% of the total number of hours assigned to the two senior designers. To provide label designing experience for Sarah, she must be assigned at least 15% of the total project time. However, the number of hours assigned to Sarah must not exceed 25% of the total number of hours assigned to the two senior designers. Due to other projects commitments, leena has a maximum of 50 hours available to work on the project.

Hourly wage rate are Rs 1,500 for Leena, Rs 1,250 for Rahul and Rs 900 for Sarah.

Formulate a linear programme problem to determine number of hours each graphic designer should be assigned for the project to minimize the total cost.

Solution

Let x_1 = Work hours of Leena

x_2 = Work hours of Rahul

x_3 = Work hours of Sarah

Minimize $Z = 1500x_1 + 1250x_2 + 900x_3$

Subject to,

$x_1 + x_2 + x_3 = 150$ Ist constraint [Total hours constraint]

also $x_1 \geq \frac{2}{5}[x_1 + x_2]$ [Leena should work 40% i.e. (2/5) of works of senior managers]

i.e. $5x_1 - 2x_1 - 2x_2 \geq 0$

$\Rightarrow$ $3x_1 - 2x_2 \geq 0$ IInd constraint

also, $x_3 \geq \frac{15}{100}(x_1 + x_2 + x_3)$ [Sarah should work at least 15%]

i.e. $100x_3 - 15x_1 - 15x_2 - 15x_3 \geq 0$

$\Rightarrow$ $-15x_1 - 15x_2 + 85x_3 \geq 0$ IIIrd constraint

$x_3 \leq \frac{1}{4}(x_1 + x_2)$ [Sarah can work maximum 25%. i.e. 1/4 of work of senior managers]

i.e. $4x_3 - x_1 - x_2 \leq 0$

$\Rightarrow$ $-x_1 - x_2 + 4x_3 \leq 0$ IVth constraint

$x_1 \leq 50$ Vth constraint [Leena can work maximum 50 hours]

$x_1, x_2, x_3 \geq 0$ [Non negativity constraint]

PROBLEM 1.36

A complete unit of certain product consists of 4 units of component A, 3 units of component B and 2 units of component C. The three components (A, B and C) are manufactured from two different raw materials of which 500 units and 800 units, respectively are available. Four departments are engaged in the production process. The following table give the raw material requirement per production run and the resulting units of each component. The objective is to determine the number of production runs for each department which will maximise the total number of complete units of the final product. Formulate the problem as a linear programming problem:

	Input per run (units)		*Output per run (units)*		
Deptd.	*Raw material 1*	*Raw material 2*	*Component A*	*Component B*	*Component C*
1	6	4	5	3	3
2	3	7	4	7	6
3	1	6	6	2	5
4	2	5	7	3	2

Solution

Let y be the number of find units

x_1 = No. of production run in deptt. 1

x_2 = No. of production run in deptt. 2

x_3 = No. of production run in deptt. 3

x_4 = No. of production run in deptt. 4

Maximise Z = y

Subject to constraint

$6x_1 + 3x_2 + x_3 + 2x_4 \leq 500$ [Raw material 1 constraint]

$4x_1 + 7x_2 + 6x_3 + 5x_4 \leq 800$ [Raw material 2 constraint]

$$\frac{5x_1 + 4x_2 + 6x_3 + 7x_4}{4} \geq y$$

$5x_1 + 4x_2 + 6x_3 + 7xy - 4y \geq 0$ (Component units of A constraint)

$$\frac{3x_1 + 7x_2 + 2x_3 + 3x_4}{3} \geq y$$

$3x_1 + 7x_2 + 2x_3 + 3x_4 - 3y \geq 0$ (Component units of B constraint)

$$\frac{3x_1 + 6x_2 + 5x_3 + 2x_4}{2} \geq y$$

$3x_1 + 6x_2 + 5x_3 + 2xy_4 - 2y \geq 0$ (Component units of C constraint)

$x_1, x_2, x_3, x_4, y \geq 0$ (Non negativity constraint).

PROBLEM 1.37

The PQR stone company sells stone secure feam any of three adjacent quaries. The stone sold by the company must conform to the following specifications:

Material X equal to 30%
Material Y equal to less than 40%
Material Z between 30% and 40%

Stone from quarry A costs Rs 100 per tonne and has the following properties:

Material X – 20%

Material Y – 60%

Material Z – 20%

Stone from quarry B costs Rs 120 per tonne and has the following properties:

Material X – 20%
Material Y – 30%
Material Z – 30%

Stone from quarry C costs Rs 150 per tonne and has the following properties:

Material X – 10%
Material Y – 40%
Material Z – 50%

From what quarries should PQR stone company secure rock in order to minimise the cost per tonne of rock.

Solution

Let,

x_1 = Proportion of tonne of rock to be secured from quarry A
x_2 = Proportion of tonne of rock to be secured from quarry B
x_3 = Proportion of tonne of rock to be secured from quarry C

Minimise $Z = 100x_1 + 120x_2 + 150x_3$

Subject to constraints

$0.20x_1 + 0.40x_2 + 0.10x_3 = 0.30$ [Material X constraint]
$0.60x_1 + 0.30x_2 + 0.40x_3 \leq 0.40$ [Material Y constraint]
$0.20x_1 + 0.30x_2 + 0.50x_3 \geq 0.30$ [Minimum material 2 constraint]
$0.20x_1 + 0.30x_2 + 0.50x_3 \leq 0.40$ [Maximum material 2 contraint]
$x_1 + x_2 + x_3 = 1$
$x_1, x_2, x_3 \geq 0$ [Non negativity constraint]

PROBLEM 1.38

A certain forming organisation operates 3 forms of comparable productivity. The output of each farm is limited both by the usable acreage and by the amount of water available for irrigation. The data for upcoming season is as shown below:

Farm	*Usable Acreage*	*Water available (is cubic feet)*
1	400	1,500
2	600	2,000
3	300	900

The organisation is considering planting crops which differ primarily in their expected profit per acre and in their consumption of water. Furthermore, the total acreage that can be devoted to each of te crops is limited by the amount of appropriate harvesting equipment available.

Crop	*Maximum Acreage*	*Water Consumption (in cubic feet)*	*Expected profit per Acre (Rs)*
A	700	5	4,000
B	800	4	3,000
C	300	3	1,000

In order to maintain a uniform work load among the 3 farms, it is the policy of the organisation that the percentage of the usable acreage planted by the same for each form. However any combination of the crops may be grown at any of the farms. The organisation wishes to know how much of each crop should be planted at the respective farms in order to maximise expected profit. Formulate this problem as an LP model in order to maximise the total expected profit.

Solution

Let

x_{11} = Crop A to be planted in farm 1
x_{12} = Crop A to be planted in farm 2
x_{13} = Crop A to be planted in farm 3
x_{21} = Crop B to be planted in farm 1
x_{22} = Crop B to be planted in farm 2
x_{23} = Crop B to be planted in farm 3
x_{31} = Crop C to be planted in farm 1
x_{32} = Crop C to be planted in farm 2
x_{33} = Crop C to be planted in farm 3

Maximise $Z = 4{,}000(x_{11} + x_{12} + x_{13}) + 3{,}000(x_{21} + x_{22} + x_{23}) + 1{,}000(x_{31} + x_{32} + x_{33})$

Subject to constraints

$x_{11} + x_{12} + x_{13} \leq 700$ [Crop A Requirements]
$x_{21} + x_{22} + x_{23} \leq 800$ [Crop B Requirements]
$x_{31} + x_{32} + x_{33} \leq 300$ [Crop C Requirements]
$x_{11} + x_{21} + x_{31} \leq 400$ [Available average for farm 1]
$x_{12} + x_{22} + x_{32} \leq 600$ [Available average for farm 2]
$x_{13} + x_{23} + x_{33} \leq 300$ [Available average for farm 3]
$5x_{11} + 4x_{21} + 3x_{31} \leq 1{,}500$ [Water availability is farm 1]
$5x_{12} + 4x_{22} + 3x_{32} \leq 1{,}500$ [Water availability is farm 2]
$5x_{13} + 4x_{23} + 3x_{33} \leq 900$ [Water availability is farm 3]

$$\frac{x_{11} + x_{21} + x_{31}}{400} = \frac{x_{12} + x_{22} + x_{32}}{600} \quad \text{[Uniform workload constraint]}$$

$$\frac{x_{12} + x_{22} + x_{32}}{600} = \frac{x_{13} + x_{23} + x_{33}}{300} \quad \text{[Uniform workload constraint]}$$

$$\frac{x_{13} + x_{23} + x_{33}}{300} = \frac{x_{11} + x_{21} + x_{31}}{400} \quad \text{[Uniform workload constraint]}$$

$$x_{11}, x_{12}, x_{13}, x_{21}, x_{22}, x_{23}, x_{31}, x_{32}, x_{33} \geq 0 \quad \text{[Non negativity constraint.]}$$

2 LINEAR PROGRAMMING — GRAPHICAL METHOD

PRACTICAL STEPS INVOLVED IN SOLVING LPP BY GRAPHICAL METHOD

The practical steps involved in solving linear programming problems by Graphical Method are given below:

Step 1 → *Consider each inequality constraint as equation.*

Step 2 → *Take one variable (say x) in a given equation equal to zero and find the value of other variable (say y) by solving that equation to get one co-ordinate [say (0, y)] for that equation.*

Step 3 → *Take the second variable (say y) as zero in the said equation and find the value of first variable (say x) to get another co-ordinate [say (x, 0)] for that equation.*

Step 4 → *Plot both the co-ordinates so obtained [i.e., (0, y) and (x, 0)] on the graph and join them by a straight line. This straight line shows that any point on that line satisfies the equality and any point below or above that line shows inequality. Shade the feasible region which may be either convex to the origin in case of less than type of inequality (<) or opposite to the origin in case of more than type of inequality (>).*

Step 5 → *Repeat Steps 2 to 4 for other constraints.*

Step 6 → *Find the common shaded feasible region and mark the co-ordinates of its corner points.*

Step 7 → *Put the co-ordinates of each of such vertex in the Objective Function. Choose that vertex which achieves the most optimal solution (i.e., in the case of Maximisation, the vertex that gives the maximum value of 'Z' & in case of Minimisation the vertex that gives the minimum value of 'Z). Solution can be obtained in the following manner:*

Vertex No.	*Co-ordinates of vertices of Common shaded feasible region*	*Value of Z*
1	(x_1, y_1)	Z_1 = ...
2	(x_2, y_2)	Z_2 = ...
3	(x_3, y_3)	Z_3 = ...
4 & so on	(x_4, y_4)	Z_4 = ...

Step 8 → Optimal Solution:

Type of Problem	*Optimal Solution*
(a) In case of Maximisation Problem	The vertex which gives the maximum value of Z is the optimal solution.
(b) In case of Minimisation Problem	The vertex which gives the minimum value of Z is the optimal solution.

PROBLEM 2.1

Sky Ltd. has two products Cloud and Wind. To produce one unit of Cloud, 2 units of material X and 4 units of material Y are required. To produce one unit of Wind, 3 units of material X and 2 units of material Y are required. As the raw material X is in short supply so not more than 16 units of material X can be used. Atleast 16 units of material Y must be used in order to meet the committed sales of Cloud and Wind. Cost per unit of material X and material Y are Rs. 2.50 and Rs. 0.25 respectively. The selling price per unit of cloud and wind are Rs. 12 and Rs. 16 respectively.

You are required:

(i) To formulate mathematical model.

(ii) To solve it for maximum contribution (Graphically).

Solution

Calculation of Contribution per Unit of each Product

	Particulars		*Cloud (Rs.)*		*Wind (Rs.)*
A	Selling price per unit		12.00		16.00
B	*Less :* cost per unit				
	(i) Material X	(Rs. 2.50 × 2)	5.00	(Rs. 2.50 × 3)	7.50
	(ii) Material Y	(Rs. 0.25 × 4)	1.00	(Rs. 0.25 × 2)	0.50
	Total (i) + (ii)		6.00		8.00
C	Contribution (A – B)		6.00		8.00

Part (i)

Since the objective is to maximise the profit, the objective function is given by:

Maximise $Z = 6x + 8y$

Subject to constraints:

$2x + 3y \leq 16$ (Maximum material X constraint) ...(i)

$4x + 2y \geq 16$ (Minimum material Y constraint) ...(ii)

$x, y \geq 0$ (Non-Negativity constraint)

Part (ii)

Step 1: Finding the vertex for each constraint by treating the constraint of inequality nature as equality.

Constraint (i) in limiting form $2x + 3y = 16$

When $x = 0$, $y = \frac{16}{3}$

When $y = 0,\ x = \frac{16}{2} = 6$

Thus, the vertices are $(0, \frac{16}{3})$ & $(8, 0)$

Constraint (ii) in limiting form $4x + 2y = 16$

When $x = 0,\ y = \frac{16}{2}$

When $y = 0,\ x = \frac{16}{4} = 4$

Thus, the vertices are (0, 8) & (4, 0)

Step 2: Plotting both the co-ordinates of the 1st constraint on the graph and joining them by straight line and shading the feasible region which is convex to origin in case of less than type of inequality. Similarly drawing straight line and shading feasible region for other constraint.

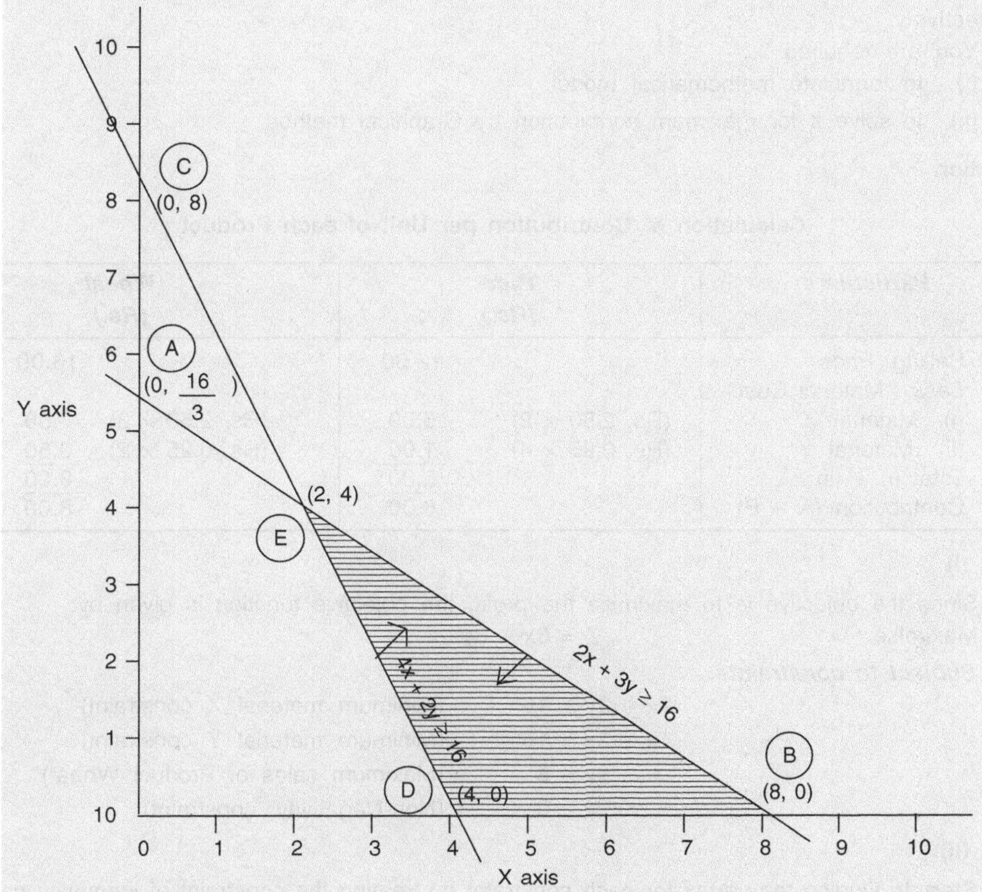

Step 3: Reading the co-ordinates of the vertices of common shaded feasible region and putting the co-ordinates of each of such vertex in the objective function. Selecting those vertices which achieve the most optimal solution (i.e. in case of maximisation vertices which give the maximum value of Z).

Set No.	Co-ordinates of vertices of Common shaded feasible region	Value of Z
1	E (2, 4)	$Z_1 = 6 \times 2 + 8 \times 4 = 44$
2	B (8, 0)	$Z_2 = 6 \times 8 + 8 \times 0 = 48$
3	D (4, 0)	$Z_3 = 6 \times 4 + 8 \times 0 = 24$

Optimal Solution: Thus, set no. 2 gives the max. value of 2 with $x = 8$ and $y = 0$.

PROBLEM 2.2

Seed Ltd has two products Rice and Wheat. To produce one unit of Rice 2 units of material X and 4 units of material Y are required. To produce one unit of Wheat 3 units of material X and 2 units of material Y are required. Atleast 16 units of each material must be used in order to meet committed sales of Rice and Wheat. Due to moderate marketing facilities not more than 8 units of product wheat can be sold. Cost per unit of material X and material Y are Rs. 2.50 and Rs. 0.25 respectively. The selling price per unit of Rice and Wheat are Rs. 12 and Rs. 16 respectively.

You are required:

(i) to formulate mathematical model.

(ii) to solve it for maximum contribution by Graphical method.

Solution

Calculation of Contribution per Unit of each Product

	Particulars	Rice (Rs.)		Wheat (Rs.)	
A	Selling Price		12.00		16.00
B	*Less :* Material Cost				
	(i) Material X	(Rs. 2.50 × 2)	5.00	(Rs. 2.50 × 3)	7.50
	(ii) Material Y	(Rs. 0.25 × 4)	1.00	(Rs. 0.25 × 2)	0.50
	Total (i) + (ii)		6.00		8.00
C	Contribution (A – B)		6.00		8.00

Part (i)

Since the objective is to maximise the profit, the objective function is given by:

Maximise $Z = 6x + 8y$

Subject to constraints:

$2x + 3y \geq 16$ (Minimum material X constraint) ...(i)

$4x + 2y \geq 16$ (Minimum material Y constraint) ...(ii)

$y \leq 8$ (Maximum sales of Product Wheat) ...(iii)

$x, y \geq 0$ (Non-Negativity constraint)

Part (ii)

Step 1: Finding the vertex for each constraint by treating the constraint of inequality nature as equality.

Constraint (i) in limiting form $2x + 3y = 16$

When $x = 0$, $y = \frac{16}{3}$

When $y = 0,\ x = 8$

Thus, the vertices are $(0, \frac{16}{3})$ & $(8, 0)$

Constraint (ii) in limiting form $4x + 2y = 16$

When $x = 0,\ y = 8$

When $y = 0,\ y = 4$

Thus, the vertices are (0, 8) & (4, 0)

Step 2: Plotting both the co-ordinates of the 1st constraint on the graph and joining them by straight line and shading the feasible region which is opposite to origin in case of more than type of inequality. Similarly drawing straight line and shading feasible region for other constraints.

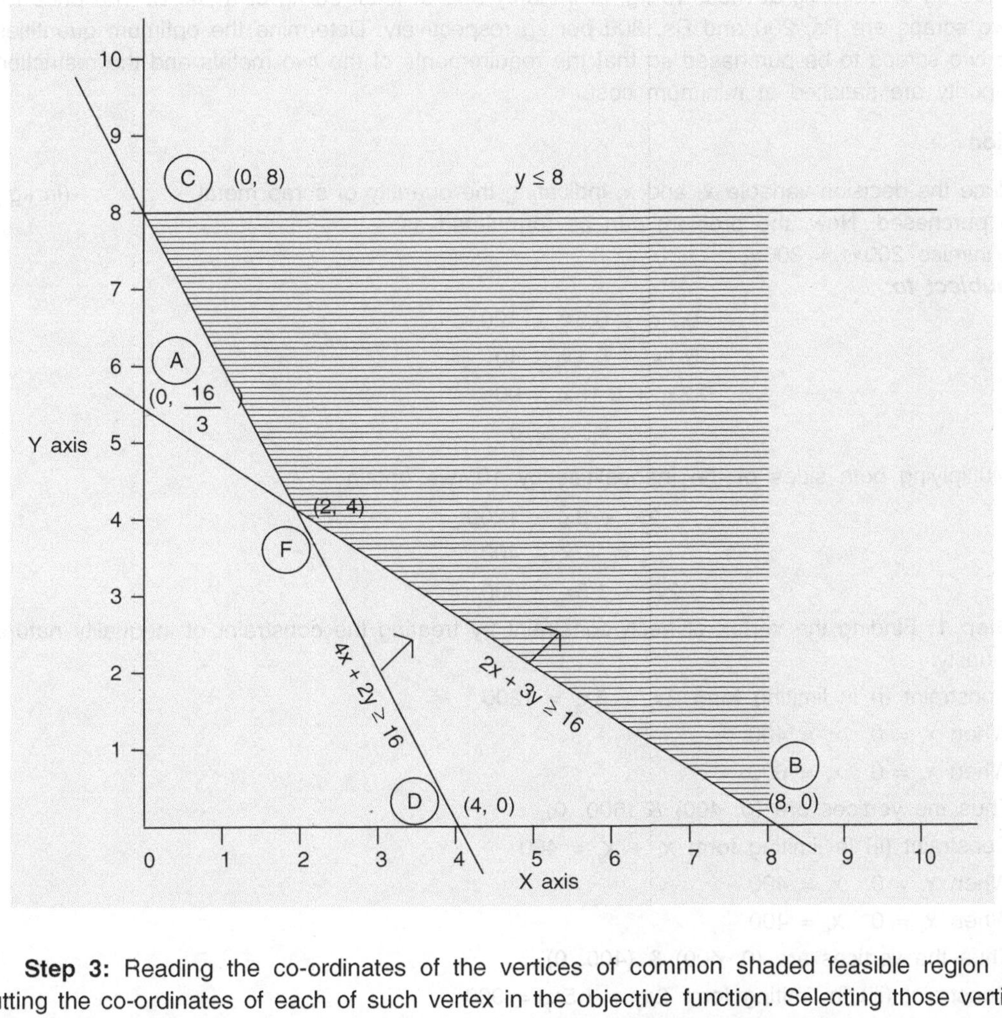

Step 3: Reading the co-ordinates of the vertices of common shaded feasible region and putting the co-ordinates of each of such vertex in the objective function. Selecting those vertices which achieve the most optimal solution (i.e. in case of maximisation vertices which give the maximum value of Z).

Set No.	Co-ordinates of vertices of Common shaded feasible region	Value of Z
1	C (0, 8)	$Z_1 = 6 \times 0 + 8 \times 8 = 64$
2	F (2, 4)	$Z_2 = 6 \times 2 + 8 \times 4 = 44$
3	B (8, 0)	$Z_2 = 6 \times 8 + 8 \times 0 = 48$

The solution of this problem is **unbounded**.

PROBLEM 2.3

A company buying scrap metal has two types of scrap available to them. The first type of scrap has 20% of metal A, 10% of impurity and 20% of metal B by weight. The second type of scrap has 30% of metal A, 10% of impurity and 15% of metal B by weight. The company requires at least 120 kg of metal A, at most 40 kg. of impurity and at least 90 kg of metal B. The price for the two scraps are Rs. 200 and Rs. 300 per kg respectively. Determine the optimum quantities of the two scraps to be purchased so that the requirements of the two metals and the restriction on impurity are satisfied at minimum cost.

Solution

Introduce the decision variable x_1 and x_2 indicating the quantity of scrap metal (in kg.) to be purchased. Now, the problem can be formulated as –

Minimise $200x_1 + 300x_2$

subject to:

$$0.2x_1 + 0.3x_2 \geq 120$$
$$0.1x_1 + 0.1x_2 \leq 40$$
$$0.2x_1 + 0.15x_2 \geq 90$$
$$x_1, x_2 \geq 0$$

Multiplying both sides of the inequalities by 10, we obtain

$$2x_1 + 3x_2 \geq 1200$$
$$x_1 + x_2 \leq 400$$
$$2x_1 + 1.5x_2 \geq 900$$

Step 1: Finding the vertex of each constraint by treating the constraint of inequality nature as equality.

Constraint (i) in limiting form $2x_1 + 3x_2 = 1200$

When $x_1 = 0 \quad x_2 = 400$

When $x_2 = 0 \quad x_1 = 600$

Thus the vertices are (0, 400) & (600, 0).

Constraint (ii) in limiting form $x_1 + x_2 = 400$

When $x_1 = 0 \quad x_2 = 400$

When $x_2 = 0 \quad x_1 = 400$

Thus the vertices are (0, 400) & (400, 0).

Constraint (iii) in limiting form $2x_1 + 1.5x_2 = 900$

When $x_1 = 0 \quad x_2 = 600$

When $x_2 = 0 \quad x_1 = 450$

Thus the vertices are (0, 600) & (450, 0)

Step 2: Plotting the co-ordinates of 1st constraint on the graph and joining them by a straight line, and shading the feasible region. Similarly drawing a straight line and shading feasible region for other constraints.

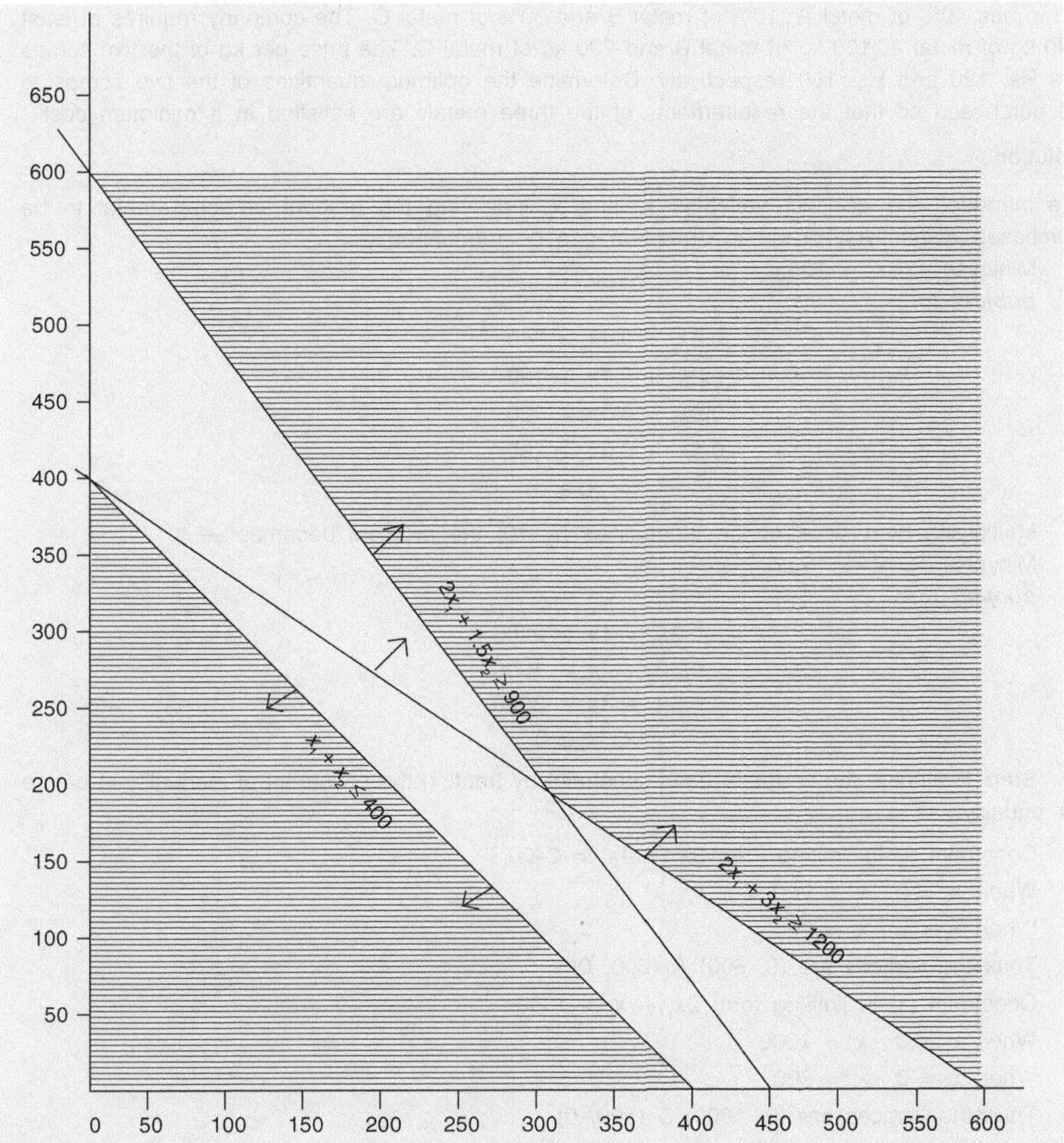

Step 3: There exists **no feasible solution** for this problem since there is no common shaded feasible region.

PROBLEM 2.4

A company buying scrap metal has two types of scrap metals available to him. The first type of scrap metal has 30% of metal A, 20% of metal B and 50% of metal C by weight. The second scrap has 40% of metal A, 10% of metal B and 30% of metal C. The company requires at least 240 kg of metal A, 100 kg of metal B and 290 kg of metal C. The price per kg of the two scraps are Rs. 120 and Rs. 160 respectively. Determine the optimum quantities of the two scraps to be purchased so that the requirements of the three metals are satisfied at a minimum cost.

Solution

We introduce the decision variables x_1 and x_2 indicating the amount of scrap metal to be purchased respectively. Then the problem can be formulated as

Minimise $120x_1 + 160x_2$

subject to:

$$0.3x_1 + 0.4x_2 \geq 240$$
$$0.2x_1 + 0.1x_2 \geq 100$$
$$0.2x_1 + 0.3x_2 \geq 120$$
$$0.5x_1 + 0.3x_2 \geq 290$$
$$x_1, x_2 \geq 0$$

Multiplying both sides of the inequalities by 10, the problem becomes —

Minimise $120x_1 + 160x_2$

subject to:

$$3x_1 + 4x_2 \geq 2400$$
$$2x_1 + x_2 \geq 1000$$
$$5x_1 + 3x_2 \geq 2900$$
$$x_1, x_2 \geq 0$$

Step 1: Finding the vertex of each constraint by treating the constraint of inequality in nature as equality.

Constraint (i) in limiting form $3x_1 + 4x_2 = 2400$

When $x_1 = 0$ $x_2 = 600$

When $x_2 = 0$ $x_1 = 800$

Thus the vertices are (0, 600) & (800, 0)

Constraint (ii) in limiting form $2x_1 + x_2 = 1000$

When $x_1 = 0$ $x_2 = 1000$

When $x_2 = 0$ $x_1 = 500$

Thus the vertices are (0, 1000) & (500, 0)

Constraint (iii) in limiting form $5x_1 + 3x_2 = 2900$

When $x_1 = 0$ $x_2 = 966.67$

When $x_2 = 0$ $x_1 = 580$

Thus the vertices are (0, 966.67) & (580, 0)

Step 2: Plotting the co-ordinates of 1st constraint on the graph and joining them by a straight line, and shading the feasible region. Similarly drawing a straight line and shading feasible region for other constraints.

Step 3: Reading the co-ordinates of the vertices of the common shaded feasible region & putting the co-ordinates of each of such vertex in the objective function. Selecting those vertices which achieve the most optimal solution (i.e. in case of minimisation vertices which give the minimum value of Z).

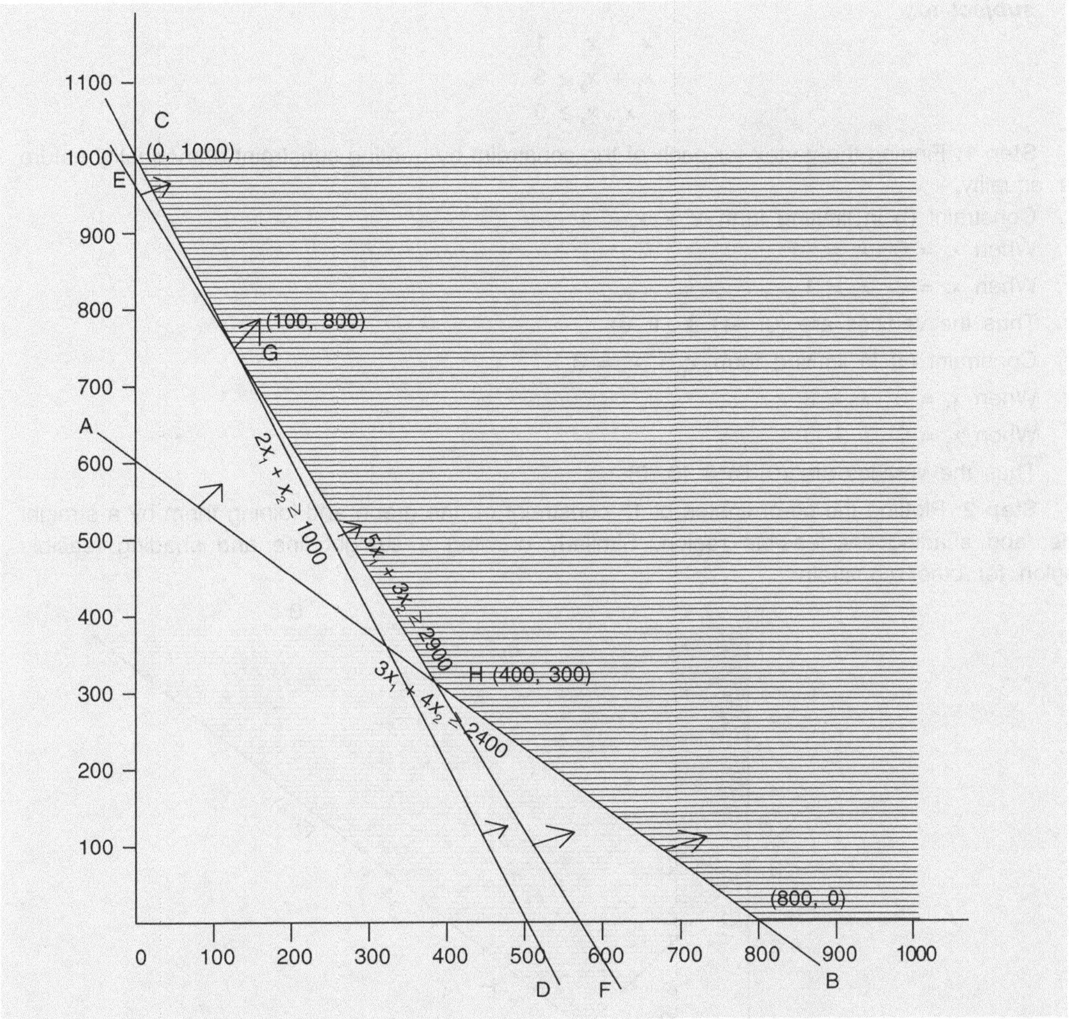

Set No.	Co-ordinates of vertices of Common shaded feasible region	Value of Z
1	C (0, 1000)	$Z_1 + 120 \times 0 + 160 \times 1000 = 1{,}60{,}000$
2	G (100, 800)	$Z_2 = 120 \times 100 + 160 \times 800 = 1{,}40{,}000$
3	H (400, 300)	$Z_3 = 120 \times 400 + 160 \times 300 = 96{,}000$
4	B (800, 0)	$Z_4 = 120 \times 800 + 160 \times 0 = 96{,}000$

Optimal Solution: Thus at both sets i.e. set No. 3 and 4, value of Z is minimum, at $x_1 = 400$ and $x_2 = 300$ or $x_1 = 800$ and $x_2 = 0$.

PROBLEM 2.5

Solve graphically the following linear programming problems:

Maximise $3x_1 + 2x_2$

subject to:

$$x_1 - x_2 \le 1$$
$$x_1 + x_2 \ge 3$$
$$x_1, x_2 \ge 0$$

Step 1: Finding the vertex for each of the constraint by treating constraint of inequality nature as equality.

Constraint (I) in limiting form $x_1 - x_2 = 1$

When $x_1 = 0 \quad x_2 = -1$

When $x_2 = 0 \quad x_1 = 1$

Thus the vertices are (0, –1) & (1, 0)

Constraint (ii) in limiting form $x_1 + x_2 = 3$

When $x_1 = 0 \quad x_2 = 3$

When $x_2 = 0 \quad x_1 = 3$

Thus the vertices are (0, 3) & (3, 0).

Step 2: Plotting the co-ordinates of 1st constraint on the graph and joining them by a straight line, and shading the feasible region. Similarly drawing a straight line and shading feasible region for other constraint.

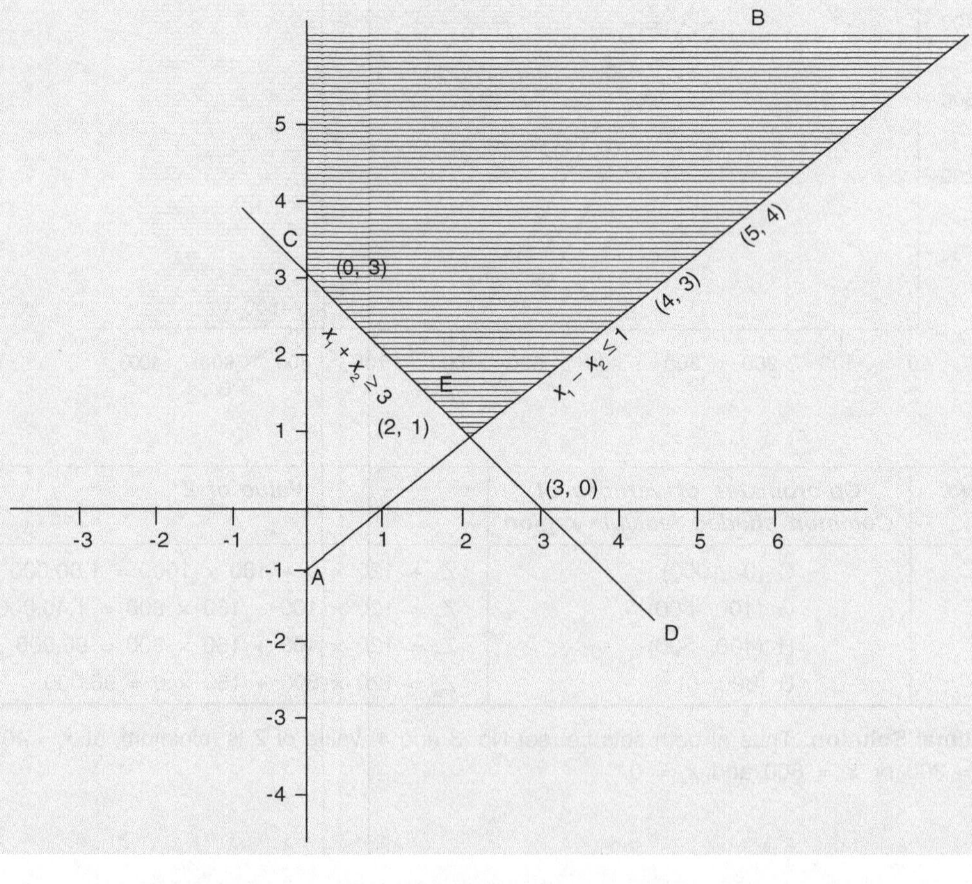

Step 3: Reading the co-ordinates of the vertices of the common shading feasible region & putting the co-ordinates of each of such vertex in the objective function. Selecting those vertices which achieve the most optimal solution (i.e. in case of maxmisation vertices which give the maximum value of Z).

Set No.	*Co-ordinates of vertices of Common shaded feasible region*	*Value of Z*
1	(0, 3)	$Z_2 = 3 \times 0 + 2 \times 3 = 6$
2	(2, 1)	$Z_1 = 3 \times 2 + 2 \times 1 = 8$
3	(4, 3)	$Z_3 = 3 \times 4 + 2 \times 3 = 18$
4	(5, 4)	$Z_4 = 3 \times 5 + 2 \times 4 = 23$

It seems from solution that solution is **unbounded**. As we take, higher values, Z proportionately increases. But this type of problem does not exist in actual practice.

PROBLEM 2.6

A local travel agent is planning a charter trip to a major island resort. The eight day seven-night package includes the fare for round-trip travel, surface transportation, board and lodging and selected tour options. The charter trip is restricted to 200 persons and past experience indicates that there will not be any problem for getting 200 persons. The problem for the travel agent is to determine the number of Deluxe, Standard, and Economy tour packages to offer for this charter. These three plans each differ according to seating and service for the flight, quality of accommodations, meal plans and tour options. The following table summarises the estimated prices for the three packages and the corresponding expenses for the travel agent. The travel agent has hired an aircraft for the flat fee of Rs. 2,00,000 for the entire trip.

Price and Costs for Tour Packages per Person

Tour Plan (Rs.)	*Price (Rs.)*	*Resort Costs (Rs.)*	*Meals & other Expenses*
Deluxe	10,000	3,000	4,750
Standard	7,000	2,200	2,500
Economy	6,500	1,900	2,200

In planning the trip, the following considerations must be taken into account:

(i) At least 10 per cent of the packages must be of the deluxe type.

(ii) At least 35 percent but not more than 70 percent must be of the standard type.

(iii) At least 30 percent must be of the economy type.

(iv) The maximum number of deluxe packages available in any aircraft is restricted to 60.

(v) The resort desires that at least 120 of the tourists should be on the deluxe and standard packages together.

The travel agent wishes to determine the number of packages to offer in each type so as to maximise the total profit.

(a) Formulate the above as a linear programming problem.

(b) Restate the above linear programming problem in terms of two decision variables, taking advantage of the fact that 200 packages will be sold.

(c) Find the optimum solution using graphical methods for the restated linear programming problem and interpret your results.

Solution

Let x_1, x_2, x_3 denote the number of Deluxe, Standard and Economy tour packages to be offered to 200 persons that will maximise the profit. It other words, the total number of tours of three types offered by the concern is restricted to 200 only to maximise its profits.

The contribution (per person) arising out of each type of tour package offered is as follows:

Packages Offered	*Price (Rs.) (1)*	*Resort costs (Rs.) (2)*	*Meals & Other Expenses (Rs.) (3)*	*Net profit (Rs.) (4)=(1) – [(2)+(3)]*
Deluxe	10,000	3,000	4,750	2,250
Standard	7,000	2,200	2,500	2,300
Economy	6,500	1,900	2,200	2,400

The travel agent has to pay the flat fee of Rs. 2,00,000 for the chartered aircraft for the entire trip. Consequently the objective function (profit function) will be:

Maximise Z = Rs. $2{,}250x_1$ + Rs. $2{,}300x_2$ + Rs. $2{,}400x_3$ – Rs. 2,00,000

Part (a)

Condition (1): $x_1 + x_2 + x_3 \le 200$

Condition (2): $x_1 \ge \frac{10}{100}(x_1 + x_2 + x_1)$

or, $x_1 \ge \frac{1}{10}(x_1 + x_1 + x_1)$

or, $9x_1 - x_2 - x_3 \ge 0$

Condition (3): $x_2 \ge \frac{35}{100}(x_1 + x_2 + x_3)$

or, $-35x_1 + 65x_2 - 35x_3 \ge 0$

Condition (4): $x_2 \le \frac{70}{100}(x_1 + x_2 + x_3)$

or, $-70x_1 + 30x_2 - 70x_3 \le 0$

Condition (5): $x_3 \ge \frac{30}{100}(x_1 + x_2 + x_3)$

or, $-30x_1 - 30x_2 + 70x_3 \ge 0$

Condition (6): $x_1 \le 60$

Condition (7): $x_1 + x_2 \ge 120$

Now, the linear problem is:

Maximize Z = $2{,}250x_1 + 2{,}300x_2 + 2{,}400x_3 - 2{,}00{,}000$

Subject to contraints:

$x_1 + x_2 + x_3 \le 200$ (Seat availability constraint)

$9x_1 - x_2 - x_3 \ge 0$ (Minimum number of Delux type)

$-35x_1 + 65x_2 - 35x_3 \ge 0$ (Minimum number of Standard type)

$-70x_1 + 30x_2 - 70x_3 \le 0$ (Maximum number of Standard type)

$-30x_1 - 30x_2 + 70x_3 \ge 0$ (Minimum number of Economy type)

$x_1 \le 60$ (Maximum seat available for Delux type)

$x_1 + x_2 \ge 120$ (Toursit constraint)

$x_1, x_2, x_3 \ge 0$ (Non-Negativity constraint)

Part (b)

Since the value of $x_1 + x_2 + x_3 = 200$, the value of x_3 will be equal to $200 - x_1 - x_2$ and substituting the value of x_3, the LP model will be formulated as under

Maximise $Z = 2{,}250x_1 + 2{,}300x_2 + 2{,}400\ (200 - x_1 - x_2) - 2{,}00{,}000$

or $Z = 2{,}250x_1 + 2{,}300x_2 + 4{,}80{,}000 - 2{,}400x_1 + 2400x_2 - 2{,}00{,}000$

$Z = -150x_1 - 100x_2 + 2{,}80{,}000$

Subject to constraints:

$x_1 \geq 20$ (i.e. 10% of 200) (Minimum number of Delux type)

$x_2 \geq 70$ (i.e. 35% of 200) (Minimum number of Standard type)

$x_2 \leq 140$ (i.e. 70% of 200) (Maximum number of Standard type)

$x_1 \leq 60$ (i.e. 70% of 200) (Maximum seat available for Delux type)

$x_1 + x_2 \geq 120$ (Tourist constraint)

$x_3 \geq 60$ (Minimum no. of Economy type)

$-x - x_2 + 200 \geq 60$

or, $-x - x_2 \geq -140$

or, $x_1 + x_2 \leq 140$

$x_1 + x_2 \geq 0$ (Non-Negativity constraint)

Part (c)

Step 1: Finding the vertex of each constraint by treating the constraint of inequality nature as equality.

Constraint (v) in limiting form $x_1 + x_2 = 120$

when $x_1 = 0 \quad x_2 = 120$

when $x_2 = 0 \quad x_1 = 120$

Thus the vertices are (0, 120) & (120, 0)

Constraint (vii) in limiting form $x_1 + x_2 = 140$

when $x_1 = 0 \quad x_2 = 140$

when $x_2 = 0 \quad x_1 = 140$

Thus the vertices are (0, 140) & (140, 0)

Step 2: Plotting the co-ordinates of 1st constraint on the graph and joining them by a straight line, and shading the feasible region. Similarly drawing a straight line and shading feasible region for other constraints. (Graph on next page)

Step 3: Reading the co-ordinates of the vertices of the common shaded feasible region & putting the co-ordinates of each of such vertex in the objective function. Selecting those vertices which achieve the most optimal solution (i.e. in case of maxmisation vertices which give the maximum value of Z).

Point	***Co-ordinates of the corner points of the feasible region (values of x_1 and x_2)***	***Values of the objective function $Z = -150x_1 - 100x_2 + 2{,}80{,}000$***
A	(50, 70)	Rs. 2,65,500
B	(60,70)	Rs. 2,64,000
C	(60, 80)	Rs. 2,63,000
D	(20,120)	Rs. 2,65,000
E	(20,100)	Rs. 2,67,000

The maximum profit is attained at the point E, whose coordinates are (20, 100)

Interpretation: The profit of the objective function stated under (a) becomes maximum i.e. Rs. 2,67,000 when

$x_1 = 20$; $x_2 = 100$ and $x_3 = 80$ {∴ $x_3 = 200 - (x_1 + x_2) = 200 - (20 + 100)$}

i.e. the travel agent should offer 20 Deluxe, 100 Standard and 80 Economy tour packages so as to get the maximum profit of Rs. 2,67,000.

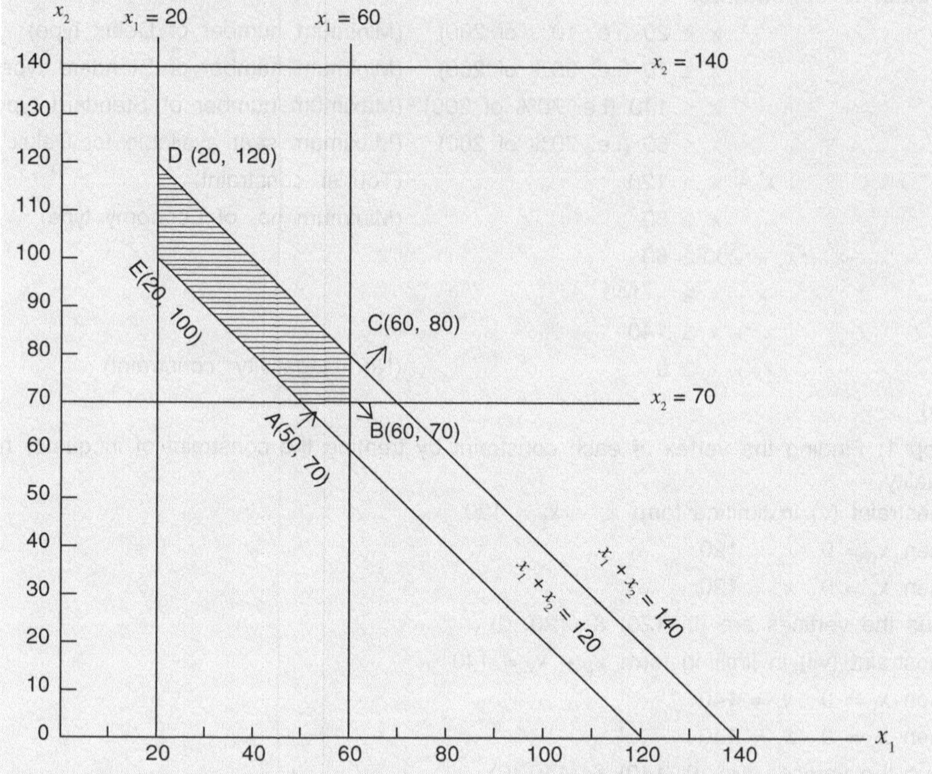

PROBLEM 2.7

Semicond is an electronics company manufacturing tape recorders and radios. Its per unit labour costs, raw material costs and selling prices are given in Table 1. An extract form from its balance sheet on 31.3.20X1 is shown in Table 2. Its current asset/current liability ratio (called the current ratio) is 2.

Table 1 : Cost Information

Items	*Products*	
	Tape Recorder Rs.	***Radio Rs.***
Selling Price	1,000	900
Labour Cost	500	350
Raw Material Cost	300	400

Table 2 : Extract from Balance Sheet as on 31.3.20X1

	Current Liabilities Rs.	*Current Assets* Rs.
Cash		1,00,000
*Accounts Receivable		30,000
**Inventory		70,000
Short-Term Bank Borrowing	1,00,000	

* Accounts receivable is amount due from customers.

** 100 units of raw material used for tape recorder and 100 units of raw material used for radio.

Semicond must determine how many tape recorders and radios should be produced during April 20X1. Demand is large enough to ensure that all goods produced will be sold. All sales are on credit and payment for goods sold in April 20X1 will not be received until 31.5.20X1. During April 20X1, it will collect Rs. 20,000 in accounts receivable and it must pay off Rs. 10,000. On 30.4.20X1 it will receive a shipment of raw material worth Rs. 20,000, which will be paid for on May 31, 20X1. The management has decided that the cash balance on April 30, 20X1 must be at least Rs. 40,000. Also its banker requires that the ratio of current assets to current liabilities as on April 30, 20X1 be at least 2. In order to maximise the contribution to profit for April 20X1 production it has to find the product mix for April 20X1. Assume that labour costs (wages) monthly rent (Rs. 10,000) are paid in the month in which they are incurred.

Formulate this as a Linear Programming Problem and graphically solve it.

Solution

Let x_1 = Number of tape recorders to be produced

x_2 = Number of tape radios to be produced

Since the objective is to maximise, the objective function is given by —

Maximise Z = $200x_1 + 150x_2$

Condition (1) Regarding funds available for production

$500x_1 + 350x_2 \leq 60{,}000$

Calculation of Funds Available for Production

A	Balance of cash		1,00,000
B	*Add :* Collection from Debtors		20,000
C	*Less :* Payment of Bank Loan	10,000	
	Payment of monthly rent	10,000	20,000
D	Balance (A + B – C)		1,00,000
E	Minimum Balance required		40,000
F	Funds available (D – E)		60,000

Condition (2) Regarding Maximum Raw Material

$$x_1 \leq 100 \text{ (i.e. } \frac{30,000}{300})$$

$$x_2 \leq 100 \text{ (i.e. } \frac{30,000}{300})$$

Condition (3) Ragarding Ratio of Current Assets to Current Liabilities

Calculation of Current Assets

A Cash available	100,000
B *Less :* Utilised for Production	$(800x_1 + 750x_2)$
C *Add :* (i) Sales Revenue	$1000x_1 + 900x_2$
(ii) Stock	70,000
(iii) Debtors	10,000
(iv) New Stock	20,000
D Current Assets (A – B + C)	$2,00,000 + 200x_1 + 150x_2$

Calculation of Current Liabilities

A Bank loan (1,00,000 – 10,000)	90,000
B Liabilities due to supplies	20,000
C Current Liability (A + B)	1,10,000

$$\text{Current Ratio} = \frac{\text{Current Assets}}{\text{Current Liabilities}}$$

$$\frac{2,00,000 + 200x_1 + 150x_2}{1,10,000} \geq 2$$

$$2,000,000 + 200x_1 + 150x_2 \geq 2,20,000$$

or $$200x_1 + 150x_2 \geq 20,000$$

Now, LP problem can be shown below:

Maximise $Z = 200x_1 + 150x_2$

Subject to constraints:

$500x_1 + 350x_2 \leq 60,000$ (Funds availability constraints)

$x_1 \leq 100$ (Maximum Raw material available for Tape recorder)

$x_2 \leq 100$ (Maximum Raw material available for Radio)

$200x_1 + 150x_2 \geq 20,000$ (Current Ratio constraint)

$x_1, x_2 \geq 0$ (Non-Negativity constraint)

Step 1: Finding the vertex of each constraint by treating the constraint of inequility value as equality

Constraint (i) in limiting form $500x_1 + 350x_2 = 60,000$

when $x_1 = 0$ $x_2 = 171.43$

when $x_2 = 0$ $x_1 = 120$

Thus the vertices are (0, 171.43) & (120, 0)

Constraint (iv) in limiting form $200x_1 + 150x_2 = 20,000$

when $x_1 = 0$ $x_2 = 133.33$

when $x_2 = 0$ $x_1 = 100$

Thus the vertices are (0, 133.33) & (100, 0)

Step 2: Plotting the co-ordinates of 1st constraint on the graph and joining them by a straight line, and shading the feasible region. Similarly drawing a straight line and shading feasible region for other constraints.

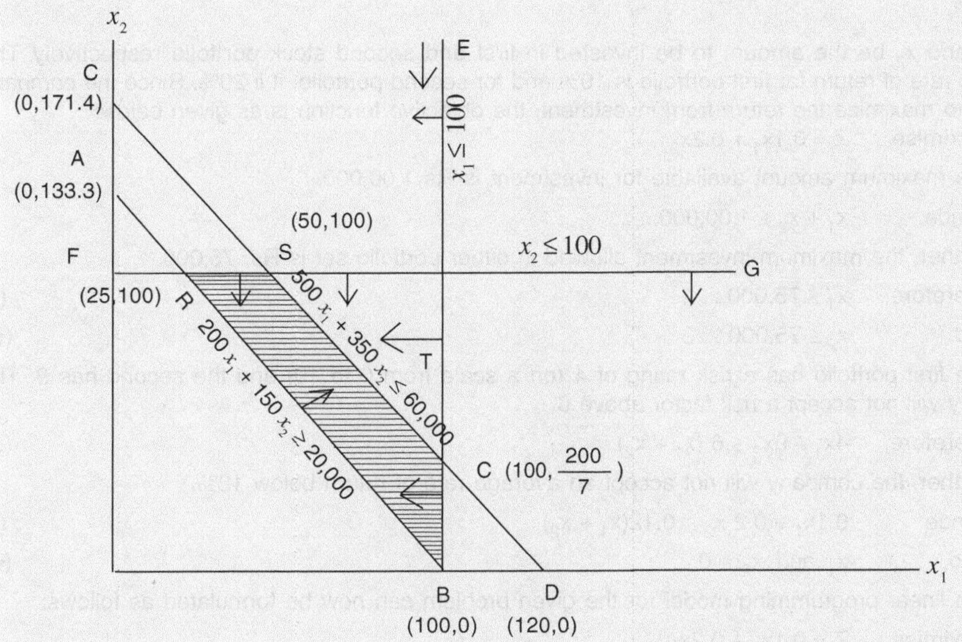

Step 3: Reading the co-ordinates of the vertices of the common shaded feasible region & putting the co-ordinates of each of such vertex in the objective function. Selecting those vertices which achieve the most optimal solution (i.e. in case of maxmisation vertices which give the maximum value of Z).

Set No.	*Co-ordinates of vertex of Common shaded region*	*Value of Z*
1	R (25, 100)	$Z_1 = 200 \times 25 + 150 \times 100 = 20{,}000$
2	S (50, 100)	$Z_2 = 200 \times 50 + 150 \times 100 = 25{,}000$
3	T (100, 200/7)	$Z_3 = 200 \times 100 + 150 \times 200/7 = 24{,}285.70$
4	D (100, 0)	$Z_4 = 200 \times 100 + 150 \times 0 = 20{,}000$

Optimal Solution: Thus, Set No. 2 gives the maximum value of Z (i.e. Rs. 25,000) at $x_1 = 50$ & $x_2 = 100$.

PROBLEM 2.8

Let us assume that you have inherited Rs. 1,00,000 from your father-in-law that can be invested in a combination of only two stock portfolios, with the maximum investment allowed in either portfolio set at Rs. 75,000. The first portfolio has an average rate of return of 10%, whereas the second has 20%. In terms of risk factors associated with these portfolios, the first has a risk rating of 4 (on a scale from 0 to 10), and the second has 9. Since you wish to maximize your return, you will not accept an average rate of return below 12% or a risk factor above 6. Hence, you then face the important question. How much should you invest in each portfolio?

Formulate this as a Linear Programming Problem and solve it by Graphic Method.

Solution

Let x_1 and x_2 be the amount to be invested in first and second stock portfolio respectively. The average rate of return for first portfolio is 10% and for second portfolio, it ii 20%. Since the company wishes to maximize the return from investment, the objective function is as given below:

Maximise $Z = 0.1x_1 + 0.2x_2$

The maximum amount available for investment is Rs 1,00,000.

Hence, $x_1 + x_2 \leq 1{,}00{,}000$... ... (i)

Further, the maximum investment allowed in either portfolio set is Rs. 75,000.

Therefore, $x_1 \leq 75{,}000$ ...... (ii)

and $x_2 \leq 75{,}000$ ...... (iii)

The first portfolio has a risk rating of 4 (on a scale from 0 to 10) and the second has 9. The company will not accept a risk factor above 6.

Therefore, $4x_1 + 9x_2 \leq 6\,(x_1 + x_2)$ (iv)

Further, the company will not accept an average rate of return below 12%.

Hence, $0.1x_1 + 0.2\,x_2 \geq 0.12(x_1 + x_2)$ (v)

Also, x_1 and $x_2 \geq 0$. (vi)

The linear programming model for the given problem can now be formulated as follows:

Maximise $Z = 0.1x_1 + 0.2x_2$

Subject to the constraints

$x_1 + x_2 \leq 1{,}00{,}000$...... (i)

$x_1 \leq 75{,}000$...... (ii)

$x_2 \leq 75{,}000$........ (iii)

$4x_1 + 9x_2 \leq 6(x_1 + x_2)$

or $-2x_1 + 3x_2 \leq 0$ (iv)

$0.1x_1 + 0.2x_2 \geq 0.12\,(x_1 + x_2)$

or $-0.02x_1 + 0.08x_2 \geq 0$.... (v)

where $x_1, x_2 \geq 0$

The problem is solved graphically below:

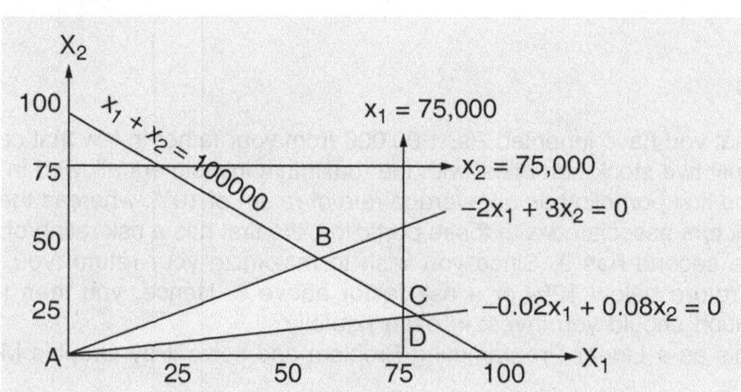

The point of intersection for the lines

$$-2x_1 + 3x_2 = 0$$

and $\quad x_1 + x_2 = 1,00,000$

is given by B(60,000, 40,000)

The point of intersection for the lines

$$x_1 = 75,000$$

and $\quad x_1 + x_2 = 1,00,000$

is given by C(75,000, 25,000)

Similarly, the lines $x_1 = 75,000$

and $\quad -0.02x_1 + 0.08x_2 = 0$

intersect at point D(75,000, 18,750)

Thus, the feasible region is bounded by ABCDA and feasible points are A(0, 0); B(60,000, 40,000); C(75,000, 25,000) and D(75,000, 18,750)

Value of the objective function at the above mentioned feasible points is calculated below:

At A, $\quad Z = 0$

At B, $\quad Z = 0.1 \times 60,000 + 0.2 \times 40,000$

$\quad = 6,000 + 8,000 = $ Rs 14,000

At C, $\quad Z = 0.1 \times 75,000 + 0.2 \times 25,000$

$\quad = 7,500 + 5,000 = $ Rs. 12,500

At D, $\quad Z = 0.1 \times 75,000 + 0.2 \times 18,750$

$\quad = 7,500 + 3,750 = $ Rs. 11,250

We find that the value of the objective function is maximum (= Rs. 14,000) at point B(60,000, 40,000).

Hence, the company should invest Rs. 60,000 in first portfolio and Rs. 40,000 in second portfolio to achieve the maximum average rate of return of Rs. 14,000.

PROBLEM 2.9

A Sports Club is engaged in the development of their players by feeding them certain minimum amount of Vitamins (say A, B and C), in addition to their normal diet. In view of this, two types of products X and Y are purchased from the market. The contents of Vitamin constituents per unit, are shown in the following table:

Vitamin Constituents	*Vitamin contents in products* X	*Y*	*Minimum requirement for each player*
A	36	06	108
B	03	12	36
C	20	10	100

The cost of product X is Rs. 20 and that of Y is Rs. 40.

Formulate the linear programming problem for the above and minimize the total cost, and solve problem by using graphic method.

Solution

Let x & y quantity of X & Y product is purchased respectively.

Minimize $Z = 20x + 40y$

Subject to the conditions.

$$36x + 6y \geq 108$$
$$3x + 12y \geq 36$$
$$20x + 10y \geq 100$$

and $x, y \geq 0$

For finding the solution, we plot above equations on x – y plane as shown below.

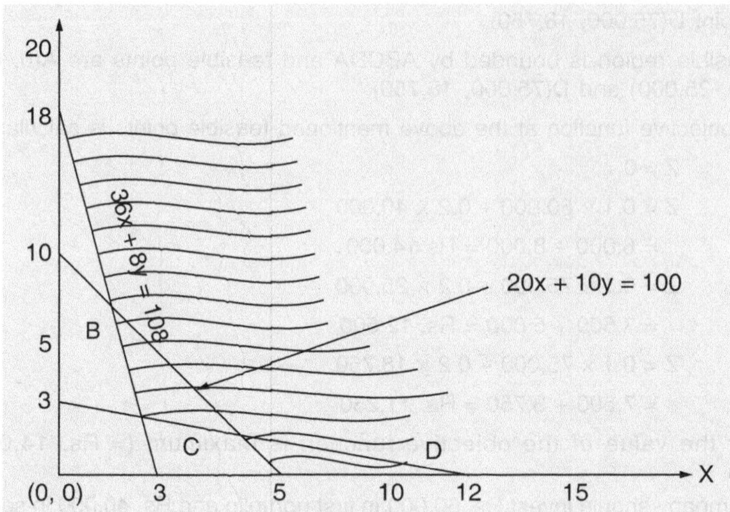

The feasible region is represented by the shaded area.

The extreme points are A, B, C & D which have the coordinates as

A = (0,18), B = (2, 6), C = (4, 2), D = (12, 0)

Extreme point	*(x, y)*	*Value of z = 20x + 40y at extreme point*
A	(0, 18)	720
B	(2,6)	280
C	(4, 2)	160 ⇐ Minimum
D	(12,0)	240

Hence, the optimal solution is to purchase 4 units of product X and 2 units of product Y in order to maintain a minimum cost of Rs. 160.

PROBLEM 2.10

A farm is engaged in breeding pigs. The pigs are fed on various products grown in the farm. In view of the need to ensure certain nutrient constituents (call them X, Y and Z), it becomes necessary to buy two additional products say, A and B. One unit of product A contains 36 units ofX, 3 units of Y and 20 units of Z. One unit of product B contains 6 units of X, 12 units of Y and 10 units of Z. The minimum requirement of X, Y and Z is 108 units, 36 units and 100 units respectively. Product A costs Rs. 20 per unit and product B Rs. 40 per unit.

Formulate the above as a linear programming problem to minimize the total cost and solve this problem by using graphic method.

Solution

The data of the given problem can be summarized as under:

Nutrient constituents	*Nutrient contents in products* A	B	*Minimum requirement of nutrient*
X	36	06	108
Y	03	12	36
Z	20	10	100
Cost of product	Rs. 20	Rs. 40	

Let x_1 units of product A and x_2 units of product B are purchased. Making use of the above table, the required mathematical formulation of L.P. problem is as given below:

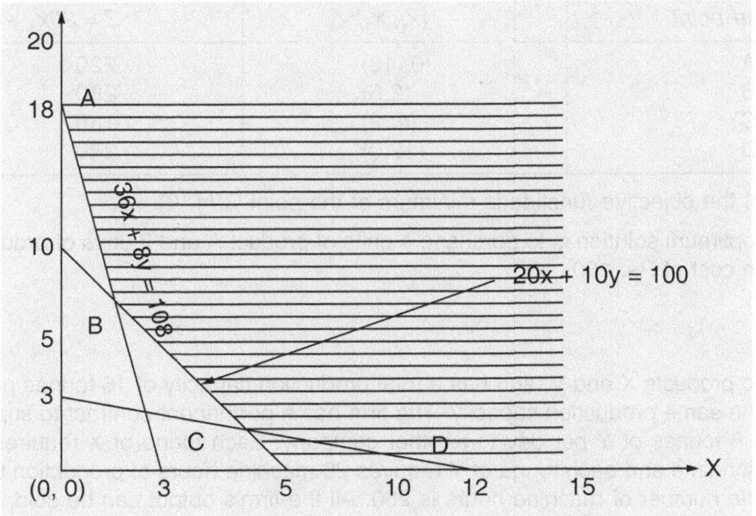

Minimize $Z = 20x_1 + 40x_2$

Subject to the constraints

$$36x_1 + 6x_2 \geq 108$$
$$3x_1 + 12x_2 \geq 36$$
$$20x_1 + 10x_2 \geq 100$$

and $x_1, x_2 \geq 0$

For solving the above problem graphically, consider a set of rectangular axis in the plane. As each point has the coordinates of type (x_1, x_2), any point satisfying the conditions $x_1 \geq 0$ and $x_2 \geq 0$ lies in the first quadrant only.

The constraints of the given problem as described earlier are plotted by treating them as equations:

$$36x_1 + 6x_2 = 108$$
$$3x_1 + 12x_2 = 36$$
$$20x_1 + 10x_2 = 100$$

or

$$\frac{x_1}{3} + \frac{x_2}{18} = 1$$
$$\frac{x_1}{12} + \frac{x_2}{3} = 1$$
$$\frac{x_1}{5} + \frac{x_2}{10} = 1$$

The area beyond these lines represents the feasible region in respect of these constraints, any point on the straight lines or in the region above these lines would satisfy the constraints. The coordinates of the extreme points of the feasible region are given by—

A = (0, 18), B = (2, 6), C = (4, 2) and D = (12, 0)

The value of the objective function at each of these points can be evaluated as follows:

Extreme point	*(x_1, x_2)*	*$Z = 20x_1 + 40x_2$*
A	(0, 18)	720
B	(2,6)	280
C	(4, 2)	160
D	(12,0)	240

The value of the objective function is minimum at the point C (4, 2).

Hence, the optimum solution is to purchase 4 units of product A and 2 units of product B in order to have minimum cost of Rs. 160.

PROBLEM 2.11

A firm makes two products X and V, and has a total production capacity of 16 tonnes per day. X and Y are requiring the same production capacity. The firm has a permanent contract to supply at least 3 tonnes of X and 6 tonnes of Y per day to another company. Each tonne of X requires 14 machine hours of production time and each tonne of Y requires 20 machine hours of production time, the daily maximum possible number of machine hours is 280. All the firm's output can be sold, and the profit made is Rs. 20 per tonne of X and Rs. 25 per tonne of Y.

Required: Formulate a linear programme to determine the production schedule for maximum profit by using graphical approach and calculate the optimal product mix and profit. ***(Nov., 2010)***

Solution

Maximise Z $20x + 25y$

Subject to $x + y \leq 16$

$x \geq 3$

$y \geq 6$

$14x + 20y \leq 280$

$x, y > 0$

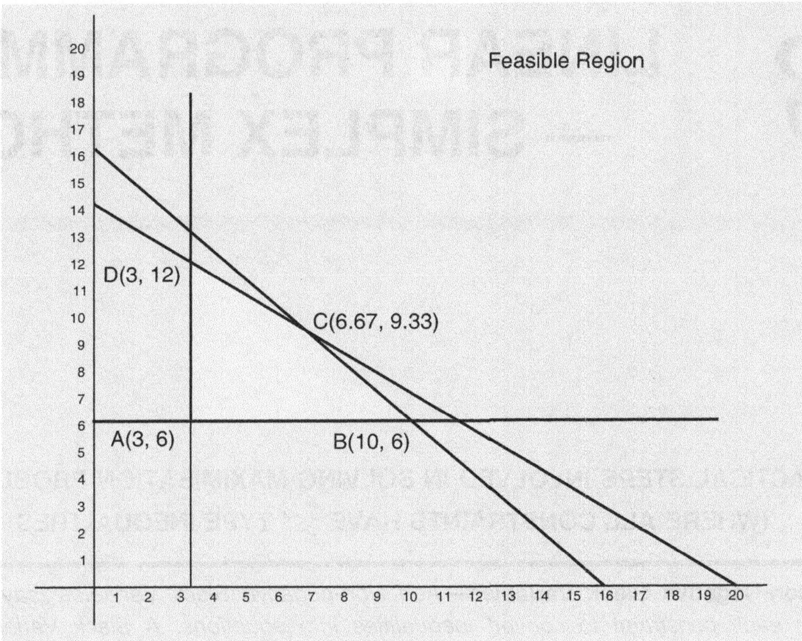

Figure

Z =	20 x +	25y	Total Contribution
Point	X	Y	
A	3	6	210
B	10	6	350
C	6.67	9.33	367 (Optimal)
D	3	12	360

The maximum value of objective function Z= 370 occurs at extreme point C (6.67,9.33).

Hence company should produce x_1 = 6.67 tonnes of product X and x_2 = 9.33 tones of product Y in order to yield a maximum profit of Rs. 367.

3 LINEAR PROGRAMMING — SIMPLEX METHOD

PRACTICAL STEPS INVOLVED IN SOLVING MAXIMISATION PROBLEMS (WHERE ALL CONSTRAINTS HAVE "≤" TYPE INEQUALITIES

Step 1→ Non-Negative Slack Variables—*Add Non-negative Slack Variables (say S_1, S_2 etc.) in each constraint to convert inequalities into equations. A Slack Variable indicates under-utilisation of capacity of the constraint; hence, its contribution to Objective Function is assumed to be zero (or negative, if given). This Slack Variable is also called as Basic Variable. Other variables are called Non-basic Variables.*

Step 2→ Value of Basic Variable—*Assuming the value of each Non-basic Variable equal to 'zero' (i.e. assuming that no performance has taken place), calculate the value of each Basic Variable from the equations.*

Step 3→ Value of Z—*Find the value of 'Z' by putting the value of each basic and non-basic variable in the Objective Function.*

Step 4→ Initial Simplex Table—*Draw the Initial Simplex Table as follows:*

Contribution per unit		C_i →	C_1	C_2	0	0	Replacement
C_i	Variables	Quantity	x_1	x_2	S_1	S_2	Ratio Qty/value of key column
C_1	S_1	....	....	....	1	0	
C_2	S_2	....	....	....	0	1	
Total Contribution	Z_j	0	0*	0	....	....	
Opportunity Cost	$(C_i\text{-}Z_j)$		C_1	C_2	0	0	

* **Note:** *The value in the Z_j Row for x_1 variable is computed by the formula = $C_1x_1 + C_2x_1$. The values in the Z_j Row in the column for other variables are computed by the same formula as stated.*

Step 5→ ***Key Column*** – *Mark the Column having* **maximum positive value** *in $(C_i - Z_j)$ row by ↑ sign representing the Opportunity Cost or Loss of not introducing one unit of the variable of that column. This Column is also known as Key Column. This column indicates the selection of* ***incoming variable*** *in the Next Simplex Table.*

Step 6→ ***Replacement Ratio***–*Find out Replacement Ratio (also known as Key Ratio) by dividing value in the Quantity Column of each row by corresponding Key Column value. Replacement Ratio represents how much quantum of variable can be produced based on that row taking the Key Column value.*

Step 7→ ***Key Row***—*Mark the Row having* ***minimum non-negative*** *Replacement Ratio by → sign. Minimum Replacement Ratio ensures that no basic variable will ever be negative. (This can be verified by putting higher Replacement Ratio in all constraints). This Row is known as Key Row. This row indicates the selection of* ***outgoing variable*** *from the Current Simplex Table.*

Step 8→ ***Key Element***—*Encircle the* ***element at the intersection*** *of Key Row and Key Column. This value is known as Key Element or Pivot Element.*

Step 9→ *Replace the outgoing variable by the incoming variable with its contribution per unit, i.e.,* C_i *in the first Column for Contribution Per Unit.*

Step 10→ *New Values of Key Row—Calculate the New Values of the Key Row as under:*

$$\text{New Values of Key Row} = \frac{\text{Old Values of Key Row}}{\text{Key Element}}$$

Step 11→ **New Values of Non-Key Row**—*Calculate the New Values of Other Rows (i.e. Non-Key Rows) as under:*

A	Old Values						
B	New values of Key Row						
C	Key Column Element						
D	Product of B&C						
E	New Values (A–D)						

Step 12→ *Draw another Simplex Table based on new values of each row.*

Step 13→ *Repeat Steps 4 to 12 till all values in* $(C_i - Z_j)$ *row becomes zero or negative which indicates that any further introduction of additional unit of the variable having negative value in* $(C_i - Z_j)$ *row will have negative contribution towards Objective Function [no effect in case of zero in* $(C_i - Z_j)$ *row]. This is also known as condition for optimal solution.*

Step 14→ **Optimal Solution**—*Find Optimal Solution from the Final Simplex Table, i.e., the value of Z and quantity of Non-basic Variables.*

$$\text{Value of } Z = C_i .(\text{Qty of } x_i) + C_j (\text{Qty of } x_j)$$

PROBLEM 3.1

Use simplex method to solve the following L P problem:

Max Z. = $6x_1 + 8x_2$

Subject to Constraints:

$$2x_1 + 3x_2 \leq 16$$
$$4x_1 + 2x_2 \leq 16$$

Solution

Step 1→ Formulation of LP problem after introducing slack variables:

Max. Z = $6x_1 + 8x_2 + 0S_1 + 0S_2$

Subject to constraints:

$$2x_1 + 3x_2 + S_1 = 16$$

$$4x_1 + 2x_2 + S_2 = 16$$

$$x_1, x_2, S_1, S_2 \geq 0$$

Step 2→ Preparing Initial Simplex Table:

Simplex Table I

Contribution per unit C_j →			6	8	0	0	Replacement Ratio
↓ C_i	Variable	Qty	x_1	x_2	S_1	S_2	Qty/Value of Key Column
0	S_1	16	2	[3]	1	0	$\frac{16}{3} = 5.33$ ←
0	S_2	16	4	2	0	1	$\frac{16}{2} = 8$
Total Contribution (Z_j)			0	0	0	0	
Opportunity Loss ($C_i - Z_j$)			6	8	0	0	

↑ Key Column   Key Element   Kew Row ←

Hence, the outgoing variable is S_1 and the incoming variable is x_2

Step 3→ Replacing the outgoing variable (S_1) by incoming variable (x_2) together with its contribution per unit.

Step 4→ Calculating the new values of Key Row as under:

$$\text{New Values of Key Row} = \frac{\text{Old Values of Key Row}}{\text{Key Element}}$$

$$= \frac{16}{3} \quad \frac{2}{3} \quad \frac{3}{3} \quad \frac{1}{3} \quad \frac{0}{3}$$

Step 5→ Calculating the new values of other Rows (i.e. Non-key Row) as under:

A	Old Values	16	4	2	0	1
B	New Values of Key Row	$\frac{16}{3}$	$\frac{2}{3}$	1	$\frac{1}{3}$	0
C	Key Column Element	2	2	2	2	2
D	Product of B & C	$\frac{32}{3}$	$\frac{4}{3}$	2	$\frac{2}{3}$	0
E	New Values (A − D)	$\frac{16}{3}$	$\frac{8}{3}$	0	$-\frac{2}{3}$	1

Step 6→ Preparing Second Simplex Table

Simplex Table II

Contribution per unit C_i →			6	8	0	0	Replacement Ratio
C_i ↓	Variable	Qty	x_1	x_2	S_1	S_2	Qty/Value of Key Column
8	x_2	$\frac{16}{3}$	$\frac{2}{3}$	1	$\frac{1}{3}$	0	$\frac{16/3}{2/3} = 8$
0	S_2	$\frac{16}{3}$	$\boxed{\frac{8}{3}}$ ←	0	$-\frac{2}{3}$	1	$\frac{16/3}{8/3} = 2$ ←
Total Contribution (Z_j)			5.33	8	$\frac{8}{3}$	0	
Opportunity Loss ($C_i - Z_j$)			– 67	0	$-\frac{8}{3}$	0	
			↑ Key Column		Key Element		Key Row

Step 7→ Replacing the outgoing variable (S_2) by incoming variable (x_1) together with its contribution per unit.

Step 8→ Calculating the new values of Key Row as under:

$$\text{New Values of Key Row} = \frac{\text{Old Values of Key Row}}{\text{Key Element}}$$

$$= \frac{16/3}{8/3} \quad \frac{8/3}{8/3} \quad \frac{0}{8/3} \quad \frac{-2/3}{8/3} \quad \frac{1}{8/3}$$

$$= 2 \quad 1 \quad 0 \quad -\frac{1}{4} \quad \frac{2}{3}$$

Step 9→ Calculation of the New Values of Non Key Rows as under:

A	Old Values	$\frac{16}{3}$	$\frac{2}{3}$	1	$\frac{1}{3}$	0
B	New Values of Key Row	2	1	0	$\frac{-1}{4}$	$\frac{3}{8}$
C	Key Column Element	$\frac{2}{3}$	$\frac{2}{3}$	$\frac{2}{3}$	$\frac{2}{3}$	$\frac{2}{3}$
D	Product of B & C	$\frac{4}{3}$	$\frac{2}{3}$	0	$\frac{1}{-6}$	$\frac{1}{4}$
E	New Values (A – D)	4	0	1	$\frac{1}{2}$	$-\frac{1}{4}$

Step 10→ Preparing Simplex Table III

Simplex Table III

Contribution per unit C_i →			6	8	0	0
↓ C_i	Variable	Quantity	x_1	x_2	S_1	S_2
8	x_2	4	0	1	$\frac{1}{2}$	$-\frac{1}{4}$
6	x_1	2	1	0	$-\frac{1}{4}$	$\frac{3}{8}$
Total Contribution (Z_j)		44	6	8	2.5	.25
Opportunity Loss ($C_i - Z_j$)			0	0	–2.5	–.25

Optimal Solution : Since, the values of $C_i - Z_j$ are ≤ 0, the solution is optimal at $x_1 = 2$ and $x_2 = 4$. The optimal value of $Z = 2 \times 6 + 4 \times 8$ = Rs. 44.

PRACTICAL STEPS INVOLVED IN SOLVING MINIMISATION PROBLEMS (WHERE ALL CONSTRAINTS HAVE "≥" TYPE INEQUALITIES).

Step 1→ *Deduct Non-negative Surplus Variables (say S_1, S_2, etc.) (also known as Basic Variables) in each constraint to convert inequalities into equations. Suppose the values of Surplus Variables exceed the values of Non-basic Variables; in such case, the total of Left Hand Side of the equation will become negative which is false; hence, we also add Non-negative Artificial Variables (say A_1, A_2, etc.) (also known as Basic Variables) in each constraint to satisfy the equations. We assume that the conribution of each Artificial Variable towards the Objective Function is infinitely large, say 'M'.*

Step 2→ *Assuming the value of each Non-basic Variable and Surplus Variable equal to 'zero', calculate the value of each Artificial Variable from the equations.*

Step 3→ *Find the value of 'Z' by putting the value of each basic and non-basic variable in the Objective Function.*

Step 4→ *Draw the Initial Simplex Table as given below:*

Contribution per unit	C_i →		C_1	C_2	0	0	M	M	Replacement
(C_i)	Variables	Quantity	x_1	x_2	S_1	S_2	A_1	A_2	Ratio Qty/Value of column
M	A_1	....	....	....	–1	0	1	0	
M	A_2	....	....	....	0	–1	0	1	
Total Contribution	Z_j	....	....	....	M	M	M	M	
Opportunity Cost ($C_i - Z_j$)			.....	....	–M	–M	0	0	

Note: *The value in the Z_j row for x_1 variable is computed by the formula = $C_1.x_1 + C_2.x_1$. In otherwords, all the values in Z_j Row and ($C_i - Z_j$) Row are computed in the same manner as in the case of Maximisation Problems.*

Step 5→ ***Key Column*** – *Mark the Column having* ***Minimum Value*** *in ($C_i - Z_j$) row by ↑ sign representing the Opportunity Cost or Loss of not introducing one unit of the variable of that column. This Column is also known as Key Column. This column indicates the selection of* ***incoming variable*** *in the Next Simplex Table.*

Step 6→ ***Replacement Ratio*** – *Find out the Replacement Ratio (also known as Key Ratio) by dividing value in the Quantity Column of each row by corresponding Key Column value. Replacement Ratio represents how much quantum of variables can be produced based on that row taking the Key Column value.*

Step 7→ ***Key Row*** – *Mark the Row having* ***Minimum Non-Negative*** *Replacement Ratio by → sign. Minimum Replacement Ratio ensures that no basic variable will ever be negative. (This can be verified by putting higher Replacement Ratio in all constraints). This Row is known as Key Row. This row indicates the selection of* ***outgoing variable*** *from the current simplex table.*

Step 8→ ***Key Element –*** *Encircle the* ***element at the intersection*** *of Key Row and key column. This value is known as Key Element or Pivot Element.*

Step 9→ *Replace the outgoing variable by the incoming variable together with its contribution per unit.*

Step 10→ *Calculate the New Values of the Key Row as under:*

$$\text{New values of key row} = \frac{\text{Old Value of Key Row}}{\text{Key Element}}$$

Step 11→ *Calculate the New Values of other rows (i.e. Non-key rows) as under:*

A Old Values
B New Values of Key Row
C Key Column Element
D Product of B & C
E New Values (A – D)

Step 12→ *Draw another Simplex Table based on new values of each row.*

Step 13→ *Repeat Steps 4 to 12 till all values in ($C_i - Z_j$) row becomes zero or positive which indicates that any further introduction of additional unit of the variable having positive value in ($C_i - Z_j$) row will have negative contribution towards Objective Function [no effect in case of zero in ($C_i - Z_j$) row]. This is also known as condition for optimal solution.*

Step 14→ *Find Optimal Solution from the Final Simplex Table, i.e., the values of Z and quantity of Non-basic Variables.*

PROBLEM 3.2

Use Simplex Method to solve the following LP problem:

Minimize $Z = 3x_1 + 2.5x_2$

Subject to constraints:

$$2x_1 + 4x_2 \geq 40$$
$$-5x_1 - 2x_2 \leq -50$$
$$x_1, x_2 \geq 0$$

Solution

Step 1→ Formulation of LP problem after introducing Slack and Artificial Variables:

Minimize $3x_1 + 2.5x_2 - 0S_1 - 0S_2 + MA_1 + MA_2$

Subject to constraints:

$$2x_1 + 4x_2 - S_1 + A_1 = 40$$
$$5x_1 + 2x_2 - S_2 + A_2 = 50$$

Step 2→ Preparing Initial Simplex Table I

Simplex Table I

Contribution per unit		C_i →	3	2.5	0	0	M	M	Replacement
↓ C_i	Variable	Quantity	x_1	x_2	S_1	S_2	A_1	A_2	Ratio Qty/Value of Key Column
M	A_1	40	2	4	–1	0	1	0	$\frac{40}{2}$ =20
M	A_2	50	[5] ←	2	0	–1	0	1	$\frac{50}{2}$ =25 ←
Total Contribution	(Z_j)	90M	7M	6M	–M	–M	M	M	
Opportunity Loss	$(C_i - Z_j)$		3–7M ↑	2.5–6M	M	M	0	0	

Key Column   Key Element   Key Row

Step 3→ Replacing the outgoing variable (A_2) by incoming variable (x_1) together with its contribution per unit.

Step 4→ Calculating the New Values of Key Row as under:

$$\text{New Value of Key Row} = \frac{\text{Old Value of Key Row}}{\text{Key Element}}$$

$$= \frac{50}{5} \quad \frac{5}{5} \quad \frac{2}{5} \quad \frac{0}{5} \quad -\frac{1}{5} \quad \frac{0}{5} \quad \frac{1}{5}$$

$$= 10 \quad 1 \quad \frac{2}{5} \quad 0 \quad -\frac{1}{5} \quad 0 \quad \frac{1}{5}$$

Step 5→ Calculation of the New Values of other Non Key Row:

A	Old Values	40	2	4	–1	0	1	0
B	New Values of Key Row	10	1	$\frac{2}{5}$	0	$-\frac{1}{5}$	0	$\frac{1}{5}$
C	Key Column Element	2	2	2	2	2	2	2
D	Product of B & C	20	2	$\frac{4}{5}$	0	$-\frac{2}{5}$	0	$\frac{2}{5}$
E	New Values (A – D)	20	0	$\frac{16}{5}$	–1	$\frac{2}{5}$	1	$-\frac{2}{5}$

Step 6→ Preparing Second Simplex Table II.

Simplex Table II

Contribution per unit	$C_i \rightarrow$		3	2.5	0	0	M	M	Replacement
↓ C_i	Variable	Quantity	x_1	x_2	S_1	S_2	A_1	A_2	Ratio Qty/Value of Key Column
M	A_1	20	0	$\boxed{\frac{16}{5}}$ ←	–1	$\frac{2}{5}$	1	$-\frac{2}{5}$	$\frac{20}{16/5} = 20$ ←
3	x_1	10	1	$\frac{2}{5}$	0	$-\frac{1}{5}$	0	$\frac{1}{5}$	$\frac{10}{2/5} = 25$
Total Contribution	(Z_j)	20M+30	3	$\frac{16M+6}{5}$	–M	$\frac{2M}{5} - \frac{3}{5}$	M	$-\frac{2}{5}M + \frac{3}{5}$	
Opportunity Loss	$(C_i - Z_j)$		0	$25 - \frac{16M+6}{5}$ ↑	M	$\frac{3}{5} - \frac{2M}{5}$	0	$M + \frac{2}{5}M - \frac{3}{5}$	

Key Coloumn Key Element Key Row

Step 7→ Replacing the outgoing variable (A_1) by incoming variable (x_2) together with its contribution per unit.

Step 8→ Calculating the New Values of Key Row as under:

$$\text{New Value of Key Row} = \frac{\text{Old Value of Key Row}}{\text{Key Element}}$$

$$= \frac{20}{16/5} \quad \frac{0}{16/5} \quad \frac{16/5}{16/5} \quad \frac{-1}{16/5} \quad \frac{2/5}{16/5} \quad \frac{1}{16/5} \quad \frac{-2/5}{16/5}$$

$$= 6.5 \quad 0 \quad 1 \quad -\frac{5}{16} \quad \frac{1}{8} \quad \frac{5}{16} \quad -\frac{1}{8}$$

Step 9→ Calculation of the New Values of Non Key Row:

A	Old Values	10	1	$\frac{2}{5}$	0	$-\frac{1}{5}$	0	$\frac{1}{5}$
B	New Values of Key Row	6.25	0	1	$-\frac{5}{16}$	$\frac{1}{8}$	$\frac{5}{16}$	$-\frac{1}{8}$
C	Key Column Element	$\frac{2}{5}$	$\frac{2}{5}$	$\frac{2}{5}$	$\frac{2}{5}$	$\frac{2}{5}$	$\frac{2}{5}$	$\frac{2}{5}$
D	Product of B & C	$\frac{20}{8}$	0	$\frac{2}{5}$	$-\frac{1}{8}$	$\frac{2}{40}$	$\frac{1}{8}$	$-\frac{2}{40}$
E	New Values (A – D)	7.5	1	0	$\frac{1}{8}$	$-\frac{1}{4}$	$-\frac{1}{8}$	$\frac{1}{4}$

Step 10→ Preparing Simplex Table III.

Simplex Table III

Contribution per unit C_i →			3	2.5	0	0	M	M
↓ C_i	Variable	Quantity	x_1	x_2	S_1	S_2	A_1	A_2
2.5	x_2	6.25	0	1	$-\frac{5}{16}$	$\frac{1}{8}$	$\frac{5}{16}$	$-\frac{1}{8}$
3	x_1	7.5	1	0	$\frac{1}{8}$	$-\frac{1}{4}$	$-\frac{1}{8}$	$\frac{1}{4}$
Total Contribution(Z_j)		38.125	3	2-5	-.40625	-.4375	.40625	.4375
Opportunity Loss (C_i–Z_j)			0	0	.40625	.4375	M-.40625	M-.4375

Optimal Solution: Since all $C_i - Z_j$ are ≥ 0, the table provides the optimal solution, i.e. $x_1 = 7.5$, and $x_2 = 6.25$. The optimal value of $Z = 7.5 \times 3 + 6.25 \times 2.5 = 38.125$.

PRACTICAL STEPS INVOLVED IN SOLVING MAXIMISATION PROBLEMS (WHERE ANY CONSTRAINT HAS "≥" OR "=" SIGN).

Step 1→

(a) ***Add*** *Non-negative Slack Variables in case of constraints having "≤" sign as usual in case of Maximisation Problems.*

(b) ***Deduct*** *Surplus Variables (say S_1, S_2) and Artificial Variables (say A_1, S_1) in case of constraints having "≥" sign as in case of Minimisation Problems.*

(c) ***Add*** *Artificial Variables (say A_1, S_1) in case of constraints having "=" sign. However, the contribution of Artificial Variables will be deducted in the Objective Function.*

Step 2→ *Follow steps 2 to 14 (given on Page 3.1 & 3.2) as usual in case of Maximisation Problems to obtain the Solution to the given problem.*

PROBLEM 3.3

Use Simplex Method to solve the following LP Problem:

Maximize $Z = 30x_1 + 20x_2$

Subject to constraints:

$$-x_1 - x_2 \geq -8$$
$$-6x_1 - 4x_2 \leq -12$$
$$5x_1 + 8x_2 = 20$$
$$x_1, x_2 \geq 0$$

Solution

Step 1→ Formulation of LP problem after introducing slack and artificial variables:

Max. $Z = 30x_1 + 20x_2 + 0S_1 + 0S_2 - MA_1 - MA_2$

Subject to constraints:

$$x_1 + x_2 + S_1 = 8$$
$$6x_1 + 4x_2 - S_2 + A_1 = 12$$
$$5x_1 + 8x_2 + A_2 = 20$$

Step 2→ Preparing Initial Simplex Table I:

Simplex Table I

Contribution per unit C_j →			30	20	0	0	–M	–M	Replacement
↓ C_i	Variable	Quantity	x_1	x_2	S_1	S_2	A_1	A_2	Ratio Qty/Value of Key Column
0	S_1	8	1	1	1	0	0	0	$\frac{8}{1}=8$
–M	A_1	12	6	4	0	–1	1	0	$\frac{12}{4}=3$
–M	A_2	20	5	[8] ←	0	0	0	1	$\frac{20}{8}=2.50$ ←
Total Contribution(Z_j)		–32M	–11M	–12M	0	M	–M	–M	
Opportunity Loss (C_j–Z_j)			30+11M	20+12M ↑	0	0	0	0	

Key Coloumn — Key Element — Key Row

Hence the outgoing variable is A_2 and the incoming variable is x_2.

Step 3→ Replacing the outgoing variable (A_2) by incoming variable (x_2) together with its contribution per unit.

Step 4→ Calculating the New Values of Key Row as under:

$$\text{New Values of Key Row} = \frac{\text{Old Value of Key Row}}{\text{Key Element}}$$

$$= \frac{20}{8} \quad \frac{5}{8} \quad \frac{1}{8} \quad \frac{0}{8} \quad \frac{0}{8} \quad \frac{0}{8} \quad \frac{1}{8}$$

Step 5→ Calculation of the New Values of Other Non Key Rows:

I[st] Non Key Row:

A	Old Values	8	1	1	1	0	0	0
B	New Values of Key Row	2.50	$\frac{5}{8}$	1	0	0	0	$\frac{1}{8}$
C	Key Column Element	1	1	1	1	1	1	1
D	Product of B & C	2.50	$\frac{5}{8}$	1	0	0	0	$\frac{1}{8}$
E	New Values (A – D)	5.50	$\frac{3}{8}$	0	1	0	0	$-\frac{1}{8}$

IInd Non Key Row:

A	Old Values	12	6	4	0	–1	1	0
B	New Values of Key Row	2.50	$\frac{5}{8}$	1	0	0	0	$\frac{1}{8}$
C	Key Column Element	4	4	4	4	4	4	4
D	Product of B & C	10	2.50	4	0	0	0	.50
E	New Values (A – B)	2	3.50	0	0	–1	1	$-\frac{1}{2}$

Step 6→ Preparing Second Simplex Table II.

Simplex Table II

Contribution per unit C_i →			30	20	0	0	–M	–M	Replacement
↓ C_i	Variable	Quantity	x_1	x_2	S_1	S_2	A_1	A_2	Ratio Qty/Value of Key Column
0	S_1	5.50	$\frac{3}{8}$	0	1	0	0	$-\frac{1}{8}$	$\frac{55}{3/8} = 14.67$
–M	A_1	2	[3.50] ←	0	0	–1	–1	$\frac{1}{-2}$	$\frac{2}{35} = 5.71$ ←
20	x_2	2.50	$\frac{5}{8}$	1	0	0	0	$\frac{1}{8}$	$\frac{2.5}{5/8} = 4$
Total Contribution(Z_j)		50-2M	12.50-3.50M	20	0	M	M	M+2.50	
Opportunity Loss (C_i–Z_j)			17.50+3.50M	0	0	–M	0	–2.50	
			↑ Key Coloumn		Key Element				Key Row

Hence, the outgoing variable is A_1 and the incoming variable is x_1.

Step 7→ Calculating the New Values of Key Row as under:

$$\text{New Values of Key Row} = \frac{\text{Old Values of Key Row}}{\text{Key Element}}$$

$$= \frac{4}{7} \quad 1 \quad 0 \quad 0 \quad -\frac{2}{7} \quad -\frac{2}{7} \quad -\frac{1}{7}$$

Step 8→ Calculation of the New Values of Non Key Rows:

I^st Non Key Row:

A	Old Values	5.50	$\frac{3}{8}$	0	1	0	0	$-\frac{1}{8}$
B	New Values of Key Row	$\frac{4}{7}$	1	0	0	$-\frac{2}{7}$	$-\frac{2}{7}$	$-\frac{1}{7}$
C	Key Column Element	$\frac{3}{8}$	$\frac{3}{8}$	$\frac{3}{8}$	$\frac{3}{8}$	$\frac{3}{8}$	$\frac{3}{8}$	$\frac{3}{8}$
D	Product of B & C	$\frac{3}{14}$	$\frac{3}{8}$	0	0	$-\frac{3}{28}$	$-\frac{3}{28}$	$-\frac{3}{56}$
E	New Values (A – D)	$\frac{74}{14}$	0	0	1	$\frac{3}{28}$	$\frac{3}{28}$	$-\frac{1}{14}$

IInd Non key Row:

A	Old Values	2.50	$\frac{5}{8}$	1	0	0	0	$\frac{1}{8}$
B	New Values of Key Row	$\frac{4}{7}$	1	0	0	$-\frac{2}{7}$	$-\frac{2}{7}$	$-\frac{1}{7}$
C	Key Column Element	$\frac{5}{8}$	$\frac{5}{8}$	$\frac{5}{8}$	$\frac{5}{8}$	$\frac{5}{8}$	$\frac{5}{8}$	$\frac{5}{8}$
D	Product of B & C	$\frac{5}{14}$	$\frac{5}{8}$	0	0	$-\frac{5}{28}$	$-\frac{5}{28}$	$-\frac{5}{56}$
E	New Values (A – D)	$\frac{30}{14}$	0	1	0	$\frac{5}{28}$	$\frac{5}{28}$	$\frac{3}{14}$

Step 9→ Preparing Simplex Table III.

Simplex Table III

Contribution per unit C_j →			30	20	0	0	–M	–M	Replacement
↓ C_i	Current Variable	Quantity	x_1	x_2	S_1	S_2	A_1	A_2	Ratio Qty/Value of Key Column
0	S_1	$\frac{37}{7}$	0	0	1	$\frac{3}{28}$	$\frac{3}{28}$	$-\frac{1}{14}$	$\frac{37/7}{3/28}=\frac{148}{3}$
30	x_1	$\frac{4}{7}$	1	0	0	$-\frac{2}{7}$	$-\frac{2}{7}$	$-\frac{1}{7}$	$\frac{4/7}{-2/7}=\frac{148}{3}$
20	x_2	$\frac{15}{7}$	0	1	0	$\boxed{\frac{5}{28}}$ ←	$\frac{5}{28}$	$\frac{3}{14}$	$\frac{15/7}{5/28}=12$ ←
Total Contribution(Z_j)		60	30	20	0	$-\frac{20}{28}$	$-\frac{20}{7}$	0	
Opportunity Loss ($C_j - Z_j$)			0	0	0	$\frac{20}{28}$ ↑	$-M+\frac{20}{28}$	–M	

Key Coloumn Key Element Key Row

Hence, the outgoing variable is x_2 and the incoming variable is S_2.

Step 10→ Replacing the outgoing variable (x_2) by incoming variable (S_2) together with its contribution per unit.

Step 11→ Calculating the New Values of Key Row as under:

$$\text{New Values of Key Row} = \frac{\text{Old Values of Key Row}}{\text{Key Element}}$$

$$= \quad 12 \quad 0 \quad \frac{28}{5} \quad 0 \quad 1 \quad 1 \quad \frac{6}{5}$$

Step 12→ Calculation of the New Values of Non Key Rows:

I[st] Non Key Row:

A	Old Values	$\frac{37}{7}$	0	0	1	$\frac{3}{28}$	$\frac{3}{28}$	$-\frac{1}{14}$
B	New Values of Key Row	12	0	$\frac{28}{5}$	0	1	1	$\frac{6}{5}$
C	Key Column Element	$\frac{3}{28}$	$\frac{3}{28}$	$\frac{3}{28}$	$\frac{3}{28}$	$\frac{3}{28}$	$\frac{3}{28}$	$\frac{3}{28}$
D	Product of B & C	$\frac{9}{7}$	0	0	$\frac{3}{5}$	$\frac{3}{28}$	$\frac{3}{28}$	$\frac{3}{70}$
E	New Values (A – D)	4	0	0	$\frac{2}{5}$	0	0	$-\frac{4}{35}$

IInd Non Key Row:

A	Old Values	$\frac{4}{7}$	1	0	0	$-\frac{2}{7}$	$-\frac{2}{7}$	$\frac{1}{7}$
B	New Values of Key Row	12	0	$\frac{28}{5}$	0	1	1	$\frac{6}{5}$
C	Key Column Element	$-\frac{2}{7}$	$-\frac{2}{7}$	$-\frac{2}{7}$	$-\frac{2}{7}$	$-\frac{2}{7}$	$-\frac{2}{7}$	$-\frac{2}{7}$
D	Product of B & C	$-\frac{24}{7}$	0	$-\frac{8}{5}$	0	$-\frac{2}{7}$	$-\frac{2}{7}$	$-\frac{12}{35}$
E	New Values (A – D)	4	1	$\frac{8}{5}$	0	0	0	$\frac{17}{35}$

Step 13→ Preparing Simplex Table IV.

Simplex Table IV

Contribution per unit C_j →			30	20	0	0	–M	–M
↓ C_i	Variable	Quantity	x_1	x_2	S_1	S_2	A_1	A_2
0	S_1	4	0	0	$\frac{2}{5}$	0	0	$\frac{4}{35}$
30	x_1	4	1	$\frac{8}{5}$	0	0	0	$\frac{17}{35}$
0	S_2	12	0	$\frac{28}{5}$	0	1	1	$\frac{6}{5}$
Total Contribution(Z_j)		120	30	48	0	0	0	$\frac{102}{7}$
Opportunity Loss ($C_j - Z_j$)			0	–28	0	0	–M	$-M - \frac{102}{7}$

Optimal Solution: Since all $C_j - Z_j$ are ≤ 0 the solution is optimum at $x_1 = 4$ and $x_2 = 0$. Thus, the value of $Z = 4 \times 30 = 120$.

PRACTICAL STEPS INVOLVED IN SOLVING MINIMISATION PROBLEMS (WHERE ANY CONSTRAINT HAS "≤" SIGN OR "=" SIGN)

Step 1→

*(a) **Deduct** Non-negative Surplus Variables and **Add** Artificial Variables in case of constraints having "≥" sign as usual in case of Minimisation Problems.*

*(b) **Add** Surplus Variables and Artificial Variables in case of constraints having "≤" sign as in case of Maximisation Problems.*

*(c) **Add** Artificial Variables in case of constraints having "=" sign.*

***Step 2→** Follow Steps 2 to 14 (given on Page 3.5 and 3.6) as usual in case of Minimisation Problems to obtain the Solution to the given problem.*

PROBLEM 3.4

Use Simplex Method to solve the following LP problem:

Minimize $Z = 30x_1 + 20x_2$

Subject to constraints:

$$-x_1 - x_2 \geq -8$$
$$-6x_1 - 4x_2 \leq -12$$
$$5x_1 + 8x_2 = 20$$
$$x_1, x_2 \geq 0$$

Solution

Step 1→ Formulation of problem after introducing slack variables:

$$-x_1 - x_2 \geq -8 \text{ or } x_1 + x_2 \leq 8$$
$$-6x_1 - 4x_2 \leq -12 \text{ or } 6x_1 + 4x_2 \geq 12$$

Minimize$Z = 30x_1 + 20x_2 - 0S_1 - 0S_2 + MA_1 + MA_2$

Subject to constraints:

$$x_1 + x_2 + S_1 = 8$$
$$6x_1 + 4x_2 - S_2 + A_1 = 12$$
$$5x_1 + 8x_2 + A_2 = 20$$

Step 2→ Preparing Initial Simplex Table I:

Simplex Table I

Contribution per unit C_i →			30	20	0	0	–M	–M	Replacement
↓ C_i	Variable	Quantity	x_1	x_2	S_1	S_2	A_1	A_2	Ratio Qty/Value of Key Column
0	S_1	8	1	1	1	0	0	0	$\frac{8}{1} = 8$
M	A_1	12	6	4	0	–1	1	0	$\frac{12}{4} = 3$
M	A_2	20	5	[8] ←	0	0	0	1	$\frac{28}{8} = 2.5$ ←
Total Contribution (Z_j)			11M	12M	0	–M	M	M	
Opportunity Loss $(C_i - Z_j)$			30–11M	20–12M	0	M	0	0	
				↑ Key column	Key Element				Key Row

Step 3→ Replacing the outgoing variable (A_2) by incoming variable (x_2) together with its contribution per unit.

Step 4→ Calculating the New Values of Key Row as under:

$$\text{New Values of Key Row} = \frac{\text{Old Value of Key Row}}{\text{Key Element}}$$

$$= \frac{20}{8} \quad \frac{5}{8} \quad \frac{1}{8} \quad \frac{0}{8} \quad \frac{0}{8} \quad \frac{0}{8} \quad \frac{1}{8}$$

$$= 2.5 \quad .625 \quad 1 \quad 0 \quad 0 \quad 0 \quad .125$$

Step 5→ Calculation of the New Values of Non Key Rows:

I[st] Non Key Row:

A Old Values	8	1	1	1	0	0	0
B New Values of Key Row	2.5	.625	1	0	0	0	.125
C Key Column Element	1	1	1	1	1	1	1
D Product of B & C	2.5	.625	1	0	0	0	.125
E New Values (A – D)	5.5	.375	0	1	0	0	–.125

IInd Non Key Row:

A Old Values	12	6	4	0	–1	1	0
B New Values of Key Row	2.5	.625	1	0	0	0	.125
C Key Column Element	4	4	4	4	4	4	4
D Product of B & C	10	2.5	4	0	0	0	.5
E New Values (A – D)	2	3.5	0	0	–1	1	–.5

Step 6→ Preparing Second Simplex Table II.

Simplex Table II

Contribution per unit C_i →			30	20	0	0	–M	–M	Replacement
↓ C_i	Variable	Quantity	x_1	x_2	S_1	S_2	A_1	A_2	Ratio Qty/Value of Key Column
20	x_2	2.5	.625	1	0	0	0	.125	$\frac{2.5}{.625} = 4$
0	S_1	5.5	.375	0	1	0	0	–.125	$\frac{5.5}{.375} = 14.67$
M	A_1	2	**[3.5]** ←	0	0	–1	1	–.5	$\frac{2}{3.5} = .57$ ←
Total Contribution (Z_j)			12.5+3.5M	20	0	–M	M	.32-.5M	
Opportunity Loss (C_i – Z_j)			17.5-3.5M	0	0	M	0	1.5M-.32	

↑ Key Column — Key Element — Key Row

Step 7→ Replacing the outgoing variable (A_1) by incoming variable (x_1) together with its contribution per unit.

Step 8→ Calculating the New Values of Key Row as under:

$$\text{New Values of Key Row} = \frac{\text{Old Value of Key Row}}{\text{Key Element}}$$

$$= \frac{2}{3.5} \quad \frac{3.5}{3.5} \quad \frac{0}{3.5} \quad \frac{0}{3.5} \quad \frac{-1}{3.5} \quad \frac{1}{35} \quad \frac{-5}{3.5}$$

$$= .571 \quad 1 \quad 0 \quad 0 \quad .28 \quad -.28 \quad -.4$$

Step 9→ Calculation of the new value of Non Key Rows:

I[st] Non Key Row:

A	Old Values	2.5	.625	1	0	0	0	.125
B	New Values of Key Row	.571	1	0	0	-.28	.28	–.14
C	Key Column Element	.625	.625	.625	.625	.625	.625	.625
D	Product of B & C	.356	.625	0	0	–0.175	.175	–.0875
E	New values (A – D)	2.14	0	1	0	.175	–.175	.2125

IInd Non Key Row:

A	Old Values	5.5	.375	0	1	0	0	–.125
B	New Values of Key Row	.571	1	0	0	–.28	.28	–.14
C	Key Column Element	.375	.375	.375	.375	.375	.375	.375
D	Product of B & C	.21	.375	0	0	–.105	.105	–.0525
E	New values (A – D)	5.285	0	0	1	.105	–.105	–.0725

Step 10→ Preparing Simplex Table III.

Simplex Table III

Contribution per unit C_i →			30	20	0	0	–M	–M
↓ C_i	Variable	Quantity	x_1	x_2	S_1	S_2	A_1	A_2
30	x_1	.571	1	0	0	–.28	.28	–.14
20	x_2	2.14	0	1	0	.175	–.175	.2125
0	S_1	5.285	0	0	1	.105	–.105	–0.0725
Total Contribution (Z_j)			30	20	0	–5	5	0
Opportunity Loss (C_i – Z_j)			0	0	0	5	M–5	M

Optimal Solution: Since all $C_i - Z_j$ are ≥ 0, the table provides the optimal solution, i.e. x_1 = .571 and x_2 = 2.14. The optimal value of Z = (.571 × 30) + (2.14 × 20) = 59.93.

PRACTICAL STEPS INVOLVED IN FORMULATING DUAL PROBLEM FROM THE PRIMAL PROBLEM

The practical steps involved in formulating dual problem from the primal problem are as follows:

Step 1→ *Ensure that in case of a maximization problem all constraints are of '≤' type or in case of a minimization problem, all constraints are of '≥' type.*

If not, adopt the following procedure:

In case of Maximisation Problem

Sign used in Constraints	*Procedure*
1. '≤' type	No change is required.
2. '≥' type	Convert the '≥' type inequality into '≤' type by changing the signs of all values appearing on left hand side and right hand side, (*e.g.* '+' sign into '–' sign, '–' sign into '+' sign).
3. '=' type	(a) Convert equality into two inequalities - one having '≥' sign and the other having '≤' sign. (b) Convert '≥' type inequality into ≤ type inequality by the changing the sign of all values.

In case of Minimization Problem

Sign used in Constraints	*Procedure*
1. '≤' type	Convert '≤' type inequality into '≥' type by changing the signs of all values appearing on left hand side and right hand side. (*e.g.* '+' sign into '–' sign, '–' sign into '+' sign).
2. '≥' type	No change in required.
3. '=' type	(a) Convert equality into two inequalities - one having '≥' sign and the other having '≤' sign. (b) Convert '≤' type inequality into '≥' type by changing the sign of all values.

Step 2→ *Restate the primal problem after taking Step 1.*

Step 3→ ***Change of Objective*** *– If the primal problem is a maximization problem, the dual problem will be a minimization problem. If the primal problem is a minimization problem, the dual problem will be a maximization problem.*

Step 4→ ***Number of Decision Variables in Dual Problem*** *– The number of decision variables in the dual problem is equal to the number of constraints in the primal problem.*

Step 5→ ***Coefficient of Decision Variables in Objective Function Dual Problem*** *– The constraints of the primal problem which appear on the right hand side of the constraints of the primal problem become the coefficients of the decision variables in objective function of the dual problem.*

Step 6→ ***Numbers of Constraints in Dual Problem*** – *The number of constraints in the decision problem is equal to the number of variables in the primal problem.*

Step 7→ *The coefficients of the constraints of the primal problem which appear from left to right are placed from top to bottom in the consraints of the dual problem.*

Step 8→ ***Change of Type of Constraint*** – *If the primal problem has 'less than or equal to' (≤) type constraints, the dual problem will have 'greater than or equal to' (≥) type constraints. If the primal problem has 'greater than or equal to' (≥) type constraints, the dual problem will have 'less than or equal to' (≤) type constraints.*

Step 9→ ***Right hand Side of the Constraints of Dual Problem*** – *The coefficients of objective function of the primal problem appear on the right hand side of the constraints of the dual problem.*

Step 10→ *Non-negativity restriction will also apply to decision variables of dual problem.*

TUTORIAL NOTES:

(i) *The maximum value of the objective function of the primal problem is the minimum value of the objective function of the dual problem.*

(ii) *If the primal problem is in the standard form, the solution of the dual problem can be obtained by multiplying the values of the slack variables in the final Simplex Table by the values ($C_i - Z_i$) appearing on the right hand side of the constraints of the primal problem.*

(iii) *The value of dual variable is referred to as the shadow price or imputed price of a resource. This is the highest price the manufacturer would be willing to pay for the resource. The shadow price of a resource is the unit price that is equal to the increase in profit to be realised by one additional unit of the resource.*

PROBLEM 3.5

Find the dual of the following problem:

Maximize $Z = 30x_1 + 20x_2$

Subject to constraints:

$$-x_1 - x_2 \geq -8 \qquad \text{I}$$

$$-6x_1 - 4x_2 \leq -12 \qquad \text{II}$$

$$5x_1 + 8x_2 = 20 \qquad \text{III}$$

$$x_1, x_2 \geq 0$$

Solution

Step 1→ *Restating Equality III as two inequalities:*

$$5x_1 + 8x_2 \leq 20 \qquad \text{IV}$$

$$5x_1 + 8x_2 \geq 20 \qquad \text{V}$$

Step 2→ *Converting '≥' type inequality into '≤' type*

$$x_1 + x_2 \leq 8$$

$$-5x_1 - 8x_2 \leq -20$$

Step 3→ *Now, restating the primal as below:*

Maximize $Z = 30x_1 + 20x_2$

Subject to constraints:

$$x_1 + x_2 \leq 8$$

$$-6x_1 - 4x_2 \leq -12$$
$$-5x_1 - 8x_2 \leq -20$$
$$5x_1 + 8x_2 \leq 20$$
$$x_1, x_2 \geq 0$$

Step 4→ *Now formulating the dual as below:*

Minimize $Z = 8y_1 - 12y_2 - 20y_3 + 20y_4$

Subject to constraints:

$$y_1 - 6y_2 - 5y_3 + 5y_4 \geq 30$$
$$y_1 - 4y_2 - 8y_3 + 8y_4 \geq 20$$
$$y_1 \text{ to } y_4 \geq 0 \text{ (non negativity constraint)}$$

PROBLEM 3.6

Find the dual of the following problem:

Minimize $Z = 30x_1 + 20x_2$

Subject to constraints:

$$-x_1 - x_2 \geq -8 \quad \text{I}$$
$$-6x_1 - 4x_2 \leq -12 \quad \text{II}$$
$$5x_1 + 8x_2 = 20 \quad \text{III}$$
$$x_1, x_2 \geq 0$$

Solution

Step 1→ *Restating equality III as two inequalities:*

$$5x_1 + 8x_2 \leq 20 \quad \text{IV}$$
$$5x_1 + 8x_2 \geq 20 \quad \text{V}$$

Step 2→ *Converting '≤' type inequality into '≥' type*

$$6x_1 + 4x_2 \geq 12$$
$$-5x_1 - 8x_2 \geq -20$$

Step 3→ *Now, Restating the primal as below:*

Minimize $Z = 30x_1 + 20x_2$

Subject to constraints:

$$-x_1 - x_2 \geq -8$$
$$6x_1 + 4x_2 \geq 12$$
$$-5x_1 - 8x_2 \geq -20$$
$$5x_1 - 8x_2 \geq 20$$
$$x_1, x_2 \geq 0$$

Step 4→ *Now the dual will be formulated as below:*

Maximize $Z = -8y_1 + 12y_2 - 20y_3 + 20y_4$

Subject to constraints:

$$-y_1 + 6y_2 - 5y_3 + 5y_4 \leq 30$$
$$-y_1 + 4y_2 - 8y_3 + 8y_4 \leq 20$$
$$y_1 \text{ to } y_4 \geq 0 \quad \text{(Non-negativity constraint)}$$

PROBLEM 3.7

Formulate the dual for the following linear program:

Maximise $100x_1 + 90x_2 + 40x_3 + 60x_4$

Subject to $6x_1 + 4x_2 + 8x_3 + 4x_4 \leq 140$

$10x_1 + 10x_2 + 2x_3 + 6x_4 \leq 120$

$10x_1 + 12x_2 + 6x_3 + 2x_4 \leq 50$

$x_1, x_2, x_3, x_4, \geq 0$

(Only formulation is required. Please do not solve.) ***(June, 2009)***

Solution

Dual:

Minimise $140y_1 + 120y_2 + 50y_3$

Subject to $6y_1 + 10y_2 + 10y_3 \geq 100$

$4y_1 + 10y_2 + 12y_3 \geq 90$

$8y_1 + 2y_2 + 6y_3 \geq 40$

$4y_1 + 6y_2 + 2y_3 \geq 60$

$y_1, y_2 y_3 y_4 \geq 0$

PROBLEM 3.8

The following is a linear programming problem. You are required to set up the initial simplex tableau. (Please do not attempt further iterations or solution):

Maximise $100x_1 = 80x_2$

Subject to $3x_1 + 5x_2 \leq 150$

$x_2 \leq 20$

$8x_1 + 5x_2 \leq 300$

$x_1 + x_2 \geq 25$

$x_1, x_2 \geq 0$ ***(Nov., 2009)***

Solution

Under the usual notations where S_1, S_2, S_3 are Slack Variables, A_4 = Artificial Variable S_4 = Surplus Variable, we have,

Maximise $Z = 100x_1 + 80x_2 + 0S_1 + 0S_2 + 0S_3 + 0S_4 - M\ A_4$.

Subject to $3x_1 + 5x_2 + S_1 = 150$

$x_2 + S_2 = 20$

$8x_1 + 5x_2 + S_3 = 300$

$x_1 + x_2 + - S_4 + A_4 = 25$

		x_1	x_2	S_1	S_2	S_3	S_4	A_4		
Basis	C_1	100	80	0	0	0	0	–M		
	C_B									
S_1	0	3	5	1	0	0	0	0	150	√
S_2	0	0	1	0	1	0	0	0	20	√
S_3	0	8	5	0	0	1	0	0	300	√
A_4	–M	1	1	0	0	0	–1	1	25	√
Z_j		–M	–M	0	0	0	M	–M	–25M	√
$C_j - Z_j$		100+M	80+M	0	0	0	–M	0		√

PROBLEM 3.9

Given below is the relevant portion of the first iteration of a linear program under the simplex method, using the usual notations.

			X_1	X_2	S_1	S_2	S_3
Quantity	*Basic Variable*	*Contribution Per unit*	*50*	*40*	*0*	*0*	*0*
150	S_1	0	3	5	1	0	0
20	S_2	0	0	1	0	1	0
296	S_3	0	8	5	0	0	1

(i) Write the initial linear program with the objective function and the in equations.

The following questions are to be answered independent of each other and based on the iteration given above:

(ii) What is the opportunity cost of bringing one unit of x_1 into the solution?

(iii) If we bring 4 units of x_1 into the solution, by how much will the basic variables changes?

(iv) What will be the change in the value of the objective function if 4 units of x_2 are brought into the solution?

(v) What will be the quantity of the incoming variable?

Solution

(i) Maximize $Z = 50x_1 + 40x_2$

Subject to

$$3x_1 + 5x_2 \leq 150$$
$$x_2 \leq 20$$
$$8x_1 + 5x_2 \leq 296$$
$$x_1, x_2 \geq 0$$

(ii) Opportunity Cost of bringing one unit of x_1 into the solution is Rs. 40, (i.e. the contribution lost on not bringing one unit of the next best choice, which is x_2.

(iii)

Change in basic variable per unit of x_1	*Change in basic variables for 4 units of x_1*	*Implication*
3	12	S_1 will be reduced by 12
0	0	S_2 will not be impacted
8	32	S_3 will be reduced by 32 units if we bring 4 units of x_1 into the solution

(iv) Objective function value will increase by 4 × 40 = Rs 160 if we bring in 4 units of x_2 into the solution.

(v) x_1 having highest contribution will be the incoming variable. Maximum no of units of x_1 that can come in = Maximum ratio, which is minimum of (150/3, 20/0, 296/8) = Minimum of (150/3, 20/0, 296/8) = Minimum of (50, ∞, 37). Hence quantity of incoming variable x_1 is 37 units.

PRACTICAL STEPS INVOLVED IN SOLVING MINIMISATION PROBLEMS

Step 1 → ***Dummy Row/Column:*** *See whether Number of Rows are equal to Number of Column. If yes, problem is balanced one; if not, then add a Dummy Row or Column to make the problem a balanced one by alloting zero value or specific value (if any given) to each cell of the Dummy Row or Column, as the case may be.*

Step 2 → ***Row Subtraction:*** *Subtract the minimum element of each row from all elements of that row.*

Note: *If there is zero in each row,there is no need for row substraction.*

Step 3 → ***Column Subtraction:*** *Subtract the minimum element of each column from all elements of that column.*

Note: *If there is zero in each column, there is no need for column substraction.*

Step 4 → ***Minimum No. of Horizontal and/or Vertical Lines:*** *Draw minimum number of Horizontal and/or Vertical Lines to cover all zeros.*

To draw minimum number of lines the following procedure may be followed:

1. *Select a row containing exactly one uncovered zero and draw a vertical line through the column containing this zero and repeat the process till no such row is left.*
2. *Select a column containing exactly one uncovered zero and draw a horizontal line through the row containing the zero and repeat the process till no such column is left.*

Step 5 → ***Subtraction/Addition of Minimum Uncovered Element:*** *If the total lines covering all zeros are equal to the size of the matrix of the Table, we have got the optimal solution; if not,* ***subtract*** *the minimum uncovered element from all uncovered elements and* ***add*** *this element to all elements at the intersection point of the lines covering zeros.*

Step 6 → ***Repeat Steps 4 and 5*** *till minimum number of lines covering all zeros is equal to the size of the matrix of the Table.*

Step 7 → ***Assignment:*** *Select a row containing exactly one unmarked zero and surround it by ' 'and draw a vertical line through the column containing this zero. Repeat this process till no such row is left; then select a column containing exactly one unmarked zero and surround it by ' ' and draw a horizontal line through the row containing this zero and repeat this process till no such column is left.*

Note: *If there are more than one unmarked zero in any row or column, it indicates that an alternative solution exists. In this case, select any one arbitrarily and pass two lines horizontally and vertically.*

Step 8 → *Add up the value attributable to the allocation which shall be the minimum value.*

Step 9 → ***Alternate Solution:*** *If there are more than one unmarked zero in any row or column, select the other one (i.e., other than the one selected in Step 7) and pass two lines horizontally and vertically. Add up the value attributable to the allocation which shall be the minimum value.*

PROBLEM 4.1

To stimulate interest and provide an atmosphere for intellectual discussion, a finance faculty in a management school decides to hold special seminars on four contemporary topics - leasing, portfolio management, private mutual funds, swaps, and options. Such seminars should be held once per week in the afternoons. However, scheduling these seminars (one for each topic, and not more than one seminar per afternoon) has to be done carefully so that the number of students unable to attend is kept to a minimum. A careful study indicates that the number of students who cannot attend a particular seminar on a specific day is as follows:

	Leasing	*Portfolio Management*	*Private Mutual funds*	*Swaps and Options*
Monday	50	40	60	20
Tuesday	40	30	40	30
Wednesday	60	20	30	20
Thursday	30	30	20	30
Friday	10	20	10	30

Required: Find an optimal schedule of the seminars. Also find out the total number of students who will be missing at least one seminar.

Solution

Step 1 → Introducing a dummy topic to make the problem balanced one by alloting zero students.

	Leasing	*Portfolio Management*	*Private Mutual funds*	*Swaps and Options*	*Dummy*
Monday	50	40	60	20	0
Tuesday	40	30	40	30	0
Wednesday	60	20	30	20	0
Thursday	30	30	20	30	0
Friday	10	20	10	30	0

Step 2 → ***Column Subtraction:*** Subtracting the minimum element of each column from all elements of that column. Since there is zero in each row, there is no need for row subtraction. Drawing minimum number of lines to cover all zeros.

	Leasing	*Portfolio Management*	*Private Mutual funds*	*Swaps and Options*	*Dummy*
Monday	40	20	50	0	0
Tuesday	30	10	30	10	0
Wednesday	50	0	20	0	0
Thursday	20	10	10	10	0
Friday	0	0	0	10	0

Since the number of lines (4) ≠ order of matrix (5), we will have to take step to increase the number of zeros.

Step 3 → Subtracting the minimum uncovered element (10 in this case) from all uncovered elements and adding it to all elements at the intersection point of the above lines and then drawing minimum number of lines to cover all zeros.

	Leasing	*Portfolio Management*	*Private Mutual funds*	*Swaps and Options*	*Dummy*
Monday	30	20	40	0	0
Tuesday	20	10	20	10	0
Wednesday	40	0	10	0	0
Thursday	10	10	0	10	0
Friday	0	10	0	20	10

Since number of lines drawn (5) = order of matrix (5), the above matrix will provide the optimal solution.

Step 4 → ***Assignment:*** Selecting a row containing exactly one unmarked zero and surrounding it by '□' and draw a vertical line through the column containing this zero. Repeating this process till no such row is left : then selecting a column containing exactly one unmarked zero and surrounding it by '□' and drawing a horizontal line through the row containing this zero and repeating the process till no such column is left.

	Leasing	*Portfolio Management*	*Private Mutual funds*	*Swaps and Options*	*Dummy*
Monday	30	20	40	[0]	0
Tuesday	20	10	20	10	[0]
Wednesday	40	[0]	10	0	0
Thursday	10	10	[0]	10	0
Friday	[0]	10	0	20	10

Step 5 → Computing minimum number of Students:

Day	*Seminar*	*No. of Students*
Monday :	Swaps and options	20
Tuesday :	No seminar	0
Wednesday :	Portfolio Management	20
Thursday :	Pvt. Mutual funds	20
Friday :	Leasing	10
		70

Thus, the total number of students who will be missing at least one seminar = 70

PROBLEM 4.2

A factory is going to modify of a plant layout to install four new machines M1, M2, M3 and M4. There are 5 vacant place J, K, L, M and available. Because of limite space machine M2 cannot be placed at L and M3 cannot be placed at J. The cost of locating machine to place in Rupees is shown below:

(Rs)

	J	K	L	M	N
M1	18	22	30	20	22
M2	24	18	–	20	18
M3	–	22	28	22	14
M4	28	16	24	14	16

Required: Determine the optimal assignment schedule in such a manner that the total cost are kept at a minimum,

Solution

Dummy machine (M5) is inserted to make it a balanced cost matrix and assume its installation cos to zero. Cost of install at cell M3 (J) and M2 (L) is very high marked as é.

	J	K	L	M	N
M1	18	22	30	20	22
M2	24	18	é	20	18
M3	é	22	28	22	14
M4	28	16	24	14	16
M5 (Dummy)	0	0	0	0	0

Step 1 → *Subtract the minimum element of each row from each element of that row*

	J	K	L	M	N
M1	0	4	12	2	4
M2	6	0	é	2	0
M3	é	8	14	8	0
M4	14	2	10	0	2
M5 (Dummy)	0	0	0	0	0

Step 2 → *Subtract the minimum element of each column from each element of that column*

	J	K	L	M	N
M1	0	4	12	2	4
M2	6	0	é	2	0
M3	é	8	14	8	0
M4	14	2	10	0	2
M5 (Dummy)	0	0	0	0	0

Step 3 → *Draw lines to connect the zero as under:*

	J	*K*	*L*	*M*	*N*
M1	0	4	12	2	4
M2	6	0	6	2	0
M3	6	8	14	8	0
M4	14	2	10	0	2
M5 (Dummy)	0	0	0	0	0

There are five lines which are equal to the order of the matrix. Hence the solution is optimal. We may proceed to make the assignment as under:

	J	*K*	*L*	*M*	*N*
M1	[0]	4	12	2	4
M2	6	[0]	é	2	0
M3	é	8	14	8	[0]
M4	14	2	10	[0]	2
M5 (Dummy)	0	0	[0]	0	0

The following is the assignment which keeps the total cost at minimum:

Machines	*Location*	*Cost Rs.*
M1	J	18
M2	K	18
M3	N	14
M4	M	14
M5 (Dummy)	L	0
Total		64

PROBLEM 4.3

Five swimmers are eligible to compete in a relay team which is to consist of four swimmers swimming four different swimming styles; back stroke, breast stroke, free style and butterfly. The time taken for the five swimmers—Anand, Bhaskar, Chandru, Dorai and Easwar—to cover a distance of 100 meters in various swimming styles are given below in minutes: seconds. Anand swims the back stroke in 1 : 09, the breast stroke in 1 : 15, and has never competed in the free style or butterfly. Bhaskar is a free style specialist averaging 1 : 01 for the 100 meters but can also swim the breast stroke in 1 : 16 and butterfly in 1 : 20. Chandru swims all styles - back stroke 1 : 10, butterfly 1 : 12, free style 1 : 05, and breast stroke 1 : 20. Dorai swims only the butterfly 1 : 11 while Easwar swims the back stroke 1 : 20, the breast stroke 1 : 16, the free style 1 : 06 and the butterfly 1 : 10. Which swimmer should be assigned to which swimming style? Who will not be in the relay?

Solution

Step 1 → Let us first create the assignment matrix with time expressed in seconds and Introducing a dummy to make the problem a balanced one by alloting zero.

	Back Stroke	*Breast Stroke*	*Free style*	*Butterfly*	*Dummy*
Anand	69	75	—	—	0
Bhaskar	—	76	61	80	0
Chandru	70	80	65	72	0
Dorai	—	—	—	71	0
Easwar	80	76	66	70	0

Step 2 → ***Column Subtraction:*** Subtracting the minimum element of each column from all elements of that column. Since there is zero in each row, there is no need for row subtraction. Drawing minimum number of Lines to cover all zeros.

	Back Stroke	*Breast Stroke*	*Free style*	*Butterfly*	*Dummy*
Anand	0	0	—	—	0
Bhaskar	—	1	0	10	0
Chandru	1	5	4	2	0
Dorai	—	—	—	1	0
Easwar	11	1	5	0	0

Since the number of lines (4) ≠ order of matrix (5), we will have to take step to increase the number of zeros.

Step 3 → Subtracting the minimum uncovered element (1 in this case) from all uncovered elements and adding it to all elements at the intersection point of the above lines and then drawing minimum numbers of lines to cover all zeros.

	Back Stroke	*Breast Stroke*	*Free style*	*Butterfly*	*Dummy*
Anand	0	0	—	—	1
Bhaskar	—	1	0	10	1
Chandru	0	4	3	1	0
Dorai	—	—	—	0	0
Easwar	11	1	5	0	1

Since the number of lines drawn (5) = the order of the matrix (5), the above matrix will provide the optimal solution.

Step 4 → *Assignment:* Selecting a row containing exactly one unmarked zero and surrounding it by '□' and draw a vertical line through the column containing this zero. Repeating this process till no such row is left; then selecting a column containing exactly one unmarked zero and surrounding it by '□' and draw a horizontal line through the row containing this zero and repeating the process till no such column is left.

	Back Stroke	*Breast Stroke*	*Free style*	*Butterfly*	*Dummy*
Anand	0	[0]	—	—	1
Bhaskar	0	1	[0]	10	1
Chandru	[0]	4	3	1	0
Dorai	—	—	—	0	[0]
Easwar	11	1	5	[0]	1

Step 5 → Computing minimum time:

	Time
Anand will be in Breast Stroke	75 seconds
Bhaskar will be in Free stroke	61 seconds
Chandru will be in Back stroke	70 seconds
Dorai will not participate (dummy)	00 seconds
Easwar will be in Butterfly	70 seconds
Total minimum time in the relay	276 (or 4 minutes 36 sec.)

Dorai will be out of the relay.

PROBLEM 4.4

Four Operators O_1, O_2, O_3 and O_4 are available to a manager who has to get four jobs J_1, J_2, J_3 and J_4 done by assigning one job to each operator. Given the time needed by different operators for different jobs in the matrix below:

	J_1	J_2	J_3	J_4
O_1	12	10	10	8
O_2	14	12	15	11
O_3	6	10	16	4
O_4	8	10	9	7

(i) How should manager assign the jobs so that the total time needed for all four jobs is minimum?

(ii) If job J_2 is not to be assigned to operator O_2, what should be the assignment over how much additional total time will be required?

Solution

Step 1 → *Row subtraction:* Subtracting the minimum element of each row from all elements of that row.

Operators	Job J_1	J_2	J_3	J_4
O_1	4	2	2	0
O_2	3	1	4	0
O_3	2	6	12	0
O_4	1	3	2	0

Step 2 → *Column Subtraction:* Subtracting the minimum element of each column from all element of that column and drawing minimum number of lines to cover all zeros.

Operators	Job J_1	J_2	J_3	J_4
O_1	3	1	0	0
O_2	2	0	2	0
O_3	1	5	10	0
O_4	0	2	0	0

Since the number of lines drawn (4) = order of matrix (4), the above matrix will provide the optimal solution.

Step 3 → *Assignment:* Selecting a row containing exactly one unmarked zero and surrounding it by ' ' and draw a vertical line through the column containing this zero. Repeating this process till no such row is left; they selecting a column containing exactly one unmarked zero and surrounding it by ' ' and draw a horizontal line through the row containing this zero and repeating the process till no such column is left.

Operators	Job J_1	J_2	J_3	J_4
O_1	3	1	[0]	0
O_2	2	[0]	2	0
O_3	1	5	10	[0]
O_4	[0]	2	0	0

Step 4 → Computing the Minimum Time:

	Time
Operator O_1 is assigned to Job J_3	10
Operator O_2 is assigned to Job J_2	12
Operator O_3 is assigned to Job J_4	4
Operator O_4 is assigned to Job J_1	8
Total	34

(ii) Step 1 → If Job J_2 is not be assigned to operator O_2 then put a '–' in the cell to obtain the following matrix.

Operators	Job			
	J_1	J_2	J_3	J_4
O_1	12	10	10	8
O_2	14	—	15	11
O_3	6	10	16	4
O_4	8	10	9	7

Step 2 → ***Row Subtraction:*** Subtracting the minimum element of each row from all elements of that row.

Operators	Job			
	J_1	J_2	J_3	J_4
O_1	4	2	2	0
O_2	3	—	4	0
O_3	2	6	12	0
O_4	1	3	2	0

Step 3 → ***Column Subtraction:*** Subtracting the minimum element of each column from all elements of that column and drawing minimum number of lines to cover all zeros.

Operators	Job			
	J_1	J_2	J_3	J_4
O_1	3	0	0	0
O_2	2	—	2	0
O_3	1	4	10	0
O_4	0	1	0	0

Since the number of lines = 3 and order of matrix = 4, we will have to take step to increase the number of zeros.

Step 4 → Subtracting the minimum uncovered element (1 in this case) from all uncovered elements and adding it to all elements at the intersection point of the above lines and then drawing minimum number of lines to cover all zeros.

Operators	Job			
	J_1	J_2	J_3	J_4
O_1	3	0	0	1
O_2	1	—	1	0
O_3	0	3	9	0
O_4	0	1	0	1

Since the number of lines drawn (4) = order of matrix (4), the above matrix will provide the optimal solution.

Step 5 → ***Assignment:*** Selecting a row containing exactly one unmarked zero and surrounding it by ' ' and draw a vertical line through the column containing this zero. Repeating this process till no such row is left; then selecting a column containing exactly one unmarked zero and surrounding it by '•' and draw a horizontal line through the row containing this zero and repeating the process till no such column is left.

Operators	Job			
	J_1	J_2	J_3	J_4
O_1	3	[0]	0	1
O_2	1	—	1	[0]
O_3	[0]	3	9	0
O_4	0	1	[0]	1

Step 6 → Computing minimum Time:

	Time
Operator O_1 is assigned Job J_2	10
Operator O_2 is assigned Job J_4	11
Operator O_3 is assigned Job J_1	6
Operator O_4 is assigned Job J_3	9
Total	36

Additional Total Time Required = 36 − 34 = 2 units of time.

PROBLEM 4.5 [Assignments of Job to Typists]

A solicitor firm employs typists on hourly piece basis for their daily work. There are five typists for service and their charges and speeds are different. According to an earlier understanding only one job is given to one typist and the typist is paid for full hours even if he works for a fraction of an hour. Find the least cost allocation for the following data:

Typist	*Rate per hour (Rs.)*	*No. of pages Typed/hour*	*Job*	*No. of Pages*
A	5	12	P	199
B	6	14	Q	175
C	3	8	R	145
D	4	10	S	298
E	4	11	T	178

Solution

Step 1 → The following matrix gives the cost incurred if the typist (i = A, B, C, D, E) executes the job (j = P, Q, R, S, T) which is calculated by following formula:

$$= \frac{\text{Total No. of Pages}}{\text{No. of pages typed/hour}} \text{ (Rounded off to next integer) } \updownarrow \text{ Rate per hour (Rs.)}$$

Typist	*Job*				
	P	*Q*	*R*	*S*	*T*
A	85	75	65	125	75
B	90	78	66	132	78
C	75	66	57	114	69
D	80	72	60	120	72
E	76	64	56	112	68

Step 2 → *Row Subtraction:* Subtracting the minimum element of each row from all elements of that row.

Typist	Job				
	P	*Q*	*R*	*S*	*T*
A	20	10	0	60	10
B	24	12	0	66	12
C	18	9	0	57	12
D	20	12	0	60	12
E	20	8	0	56	12

Step 3 → *Column Subtraction:* Subtracting the minimum element of each column from all the elements of that column and then drawing the minimum number of lines to cover all zeros.

Typist	Job				
	P	*Q*	*R*	*S*	*T*
A	2	2	0	4	0
B	6	4	0	10	2
C	0	1	0	1	2
D	2	4	0	4	2
E	2	0	0	0	2

Since the number of lines = 4 and order of matrix = 5, we will have to take step to increase the number of zeros.

Step 4 → Subtracting the minimum uncovered element (2 in this case) from all uncovered elements and adding it to all elements at the intersection point of the above lines and then drawing minimum number of lines to cover all zeros.

Typist	Job				
	P	*Q*	*R*	*S*	*T*
A	2	2	2	4	0
B	4	2	0	8	0
C	0	1	2	1	2
D	0	2	0	2	0
E	2	0	2	0	2

Since number of lines = 4 and order of matrix = 5, we will have to take step to increase the number of zeros.

Step 5 → Subtracting the minimum uncovered element (1 in this case) from all uncovered elements and adding it to all elements at the intersection point of the above lines and then drawing the minimum number of lines to cover all zeros.

Typist	Job				
	P	*Q*	*R*	*S*	*T*
A	2	1	2	3	0
B	4	1	0	7	0
C	0	0	2	0	2
D	0	1	0	1	0
E	3	0	3	0	3

Step 6 → *Assignment:* Selecting a row containing exactly one unmarked zero and surrounding it by '□' and draw a vertical line thorough the column containing this zero. Repeating this process till no such row is left; then selecting a column containing exactly one unmarked zero and surrounding it by '□' and draw a horizontal line through the row containing this zero and repeating the process till no such column is left.

Typist	*Job*				
	P	*Q*	*R*	*S*	*T*
A	2	1	2	3	[0]
B	4	1	[0]	7	0
C	0	[0]	2	0	2
D	[0]	1	0	1	0
E	3	0	3	[0]	3

Step 7 → Computing minimum cost:

Typist	*Job*		*Cost (Rs.)*
A	T	:	75
B	R	:	66
C	Q	:	66
D	P	:	80
E	S	:	112
	Total	Rs.	399

Alternate Solution:

Typist	*Job*				
	P	*Q*	*R*	*S*	*T*
A	2	1	2	3	[0]
B	4	1	[0]	7	0
C	0	0	2	[0]	2
D	[0]	1	0	1	0
E	3	[0]	3	0	3

Minimum cost:

Typist	*Job*	*Cost (Rs.)*
A	T	75
B	R	66
C	S	114
D	P	80
E	Q	64
	Total	399

PROBLEM 4.6 [Assignment of Rooms]

Welldone Company has taken the third floor of a multistoreyed building for rent with a view to locate one of their zonal offices. There are five main rooms in this floor to be assigned to five managers. Each room has its own advantages and disadvantages. Some have windows, some are closer to the washrooms or to the canteen or secretarial pool. The rooms are of all different sizes and shapes. Each of the five manages were asked to rank their room preferences amongst the rooms 301, 302, 303, 304 and 305. Their preferences were recorded in a table as indicated below.

Manager				
M_1	M_2	M_3	M_4	M_5
302 303 304	302 304 305 301	303 301 304 305 302	302 305 304 303	301 302 304

Most of the managers did not list all the five rooms since they were not satisified with some of these rooms and they have left off these from the list. Assuming that their preferences can be quantified by numbers, find out as to which manager should be assigned to which rooms so that their total preference ranking is a minimum.

Solution

Step 1 → Formulating the preference ranking assignment problem.

	Managers				
Rooms No.	M_1	M_2	M_3	M_4	M_5
301	—	4	2	—	1
302	1	1	5	1	2
303	2	—	1	4	—
304	3	2	3	3	3
305	—	3	4	2	—

Step 2 → ***Row Subtraction:*** Subtracting the minimum element of each row from all elements of that row. Since there is zero in each column, there is no need for column subtraction. Drawing the minimum number of lines to cover all zeros.

	Managers				
Rooms No.	M_1	M_2	M_3	M_4	M_5
301	—	3	1	—	0
302	0	0	4	0	1
303	1	—	0	3	—
304	1	0	1	1	1
305	—	1	2	0	—

Since number of lines = 5 and order of matrix = 5, the above matrix will provide the optimal solution.

Step 3 → *Assignment:* Selecting a row containing exactly one unmarked zero and surrounding it by '□' and draw a vertical line thorough the column containing this zero. Repeating this process till no such row is left; then selecting a column containing exactly one unmarked zero and surrounding it by '□' and draw a horizontal line through the row containing this zero and repeating the process till no such column is left.

	Managers				
Rooms No.	M_1	M_2	M_3	M_4	M_5
301	—	3	1	—	[0]
302	[0]	0	4	0	1
303	1	—	[0]	3	—
304	1	[0]	1	1	1
305	—	1	2	[0]	—

Step 4 → Computing minimum ranking

The assignment is given below:

			Ranking
M_1	→	Room No 302	1
M_2	→	Room No 304	2
M_3	→	Room No 303	1
M_4	→	Room No 305	2
M_5	→	Room No 301	1
			7

Thus, the total minimum ranking is 7.

PROBLEM 4.7

A machine operator processes five types of items on his machine each week, and must choose a sequences for them. The set-up cost per change depends on the item presently on the machine and the set-up to be made, according to the following table:

	To item				
For item	*A*	*B*	*C*	*D*	*E*
A	—	4	7	3	4
B	4	—	6	3	4
C	7	6	—	7	5
D	3	3	7	—	7
E	4	4	5	7	—

If he processes each type of item once and only once each week, how should he sequence the items on his machine in order to minimize the total set-up cost?

Solution

Step 1 → *Row Subtraction:* Subtracting the minimum element of each row from all elements of that row.

For item	To item A	B	C	D	E
A	—	1	4	0	1
B	1	—	3	0	1
C	2	1	—	2	0
D	0	0	4	—	4
E	0	0	1	3	—

Step 2 → *Column Subtraction:* Subtracting the minimum element of each column from all elements of that column and drawing minimum number of lines to cover all zeros.

For item	To item A	B	C	D	E
A	—	1	3	0	1
B	1	—	2	0	1
C	2	1	—	2	0
D	0	0	3	—	4
E	0	0	0	3	—

Since number of lines = 4 and order of matrix = 5, we will have to take step to increase the number of zeros.

Step 3 → Subtracting the minimum uncovered element (1 in this case) from all the uncovered elements and adding it to all the elements at the intersection point of the above lines and drawing minimum number of Lines to cover all zeros.

For item	To item A	B	C	D	E
A	—	0	2	0	0
B	0	—	1	0	0
C	2	1	—	3	0
D	0	0	3	—	4
E	0	0	0	4	—

Since the number of lines (5) = order of matrix (5), the above matrix will provide Optimal Solution.

Step 4 → *Assignment:* Selecting a row containing exactly one unmarked zero and surrounding it by '□' and draw a vertical line through the column containing this zero. Repeating this process till no such row is left; then selecting a column containing exactly one unmarked zero and surrounding it by '□' and draw a horizontal line through the row containing this zero and repeating the process till no such column is left.

For item	*To item*				
	A	*B*	*C*	*D*	*E*
A	—	0	2	[0]	0
B	[0]	—	1	0	0
C	2	1	—	3	[0]
D	0	[0]	3	—	4
E	0	0	[0]	4	—

Step 5 → Computing Minimum Set-up cost

Item	*Item*	*Cost (Rs.)*
A	D	3
B	A	4
C	E	5
D	B	3
E	C	5
	Total	**20**

Alternative Solution:

For item	*To item*				
	A	*B*	*C*	*D*	*E*
A	—	[0]	2	0	0
B	0	—	1	[0]	0
C	2	1	—	3	[0]
D	[0]	0	3	—	4
E	0	0	[0]	4	—

Minimum Set-up cost:

Item	*Item*	*Cost (Rs.)*
A	B	4
B	D	3
C	E	5
D	A	3
E	C	5
	Total	20

PROBLEM 4.8

A large engineering workshop has five shops. Hitherto, they have been fabricating five different types of components, one in each shop. Fabrication of one of these components is to be discontinued. Since the firm will follow the policy one shop-one component, one of the shops will be closed down. Data on the number of units to be manufactured and the unit costs are given below. Recommend an optimal plan as to which component should be produced in which shop and which of the shops be closed down. [Matrix elements are cost of fabrication in Rupees per unit.]

		C_1	C_2	C_3	C_4
S	S_1	6	7	5	8
H	S_2	7	6	5	9
O	S_3	8	7	6	9
P	S_4	8	9	4	8
S	S_5	9	8	6	7
Number of units (000)		8	6	4	5

Solution

This is an Assignment Problem, since each shop will produce only one component.

Because the number of units of the components differ the total cost of fabrication has to be taken into account instead of just the unit cost.

Total cost = Unit cost × No. of units.

Step 1 → Since there are five shops but only four components, a dummy component C_5 [with 0 costs] has to be included to balance the AP.

	C_1	C_2	C_3	C_4	C_5
S_1	48	42	20	40	0
S_2	56	36	20	45	0
S_3	64	42	24	45	0
S_4	64	54	16	40	0
S_5	72	48	24	35	0

Step 2 → ***Column Subtraction:*** Subtracting the minimum element of each column from all elements of that column and drawing the minimum number of lines to cover all zeros.

	C_1	C_2	C_3	C_4	C_5
S_1	0	6	4	5	0
S_2	8	0	4	10	0
S_3	16	6	8	10	0
S_4	16	18	0	5	0
S_5	24	12	8	0	0

Since number of lines drawn (5) = order of matrix = (5), the above matrix will provide optimal solution.

Step 3 → ***Assignment:*** Selecting a row containing exactly one unmarked zero and surrounding it by '□' and draw a vertical line through the column containing this zero. Repeating this process till no such row is left; then selecting a column containing exactly one unmarked zero and surrounding it by '□' and draw a horizontal line through the row containing this zero and repeating the process till no such column is left.

	C_1	C_2	C_3	C_4	C_5
S_1	0	6	4	5	0
S_2	8	0	4	10	0
S_3	16	6	8	10	0
S_4	16	18	0	5	0
S_5	24	12	8	0	0

Step 4 → Computing the Minimum:

Shop	*Component*	*Cost (Rs. 000)*
S_1	C_1	48
S_2	C_2	36
S_3	C_5	0 Shop to be closed down
S_4	C_3	16
S_5	C_4	35
	Total cost	135

PROBLEM 4.9 [Flight Scheduling]

Sohil Airlines, operating seven days a week, serves three cities A, B, and C according to the schedule shown in the following table. The layover cost per stop is roughly proportional to the square of the layover time. How should planes be assigned the flights so as to minimize the total layover cost?

Flight No. and Index	*From*	*Departure*	*To*	*Arrival*
A_1 B	A	09 A.M.	B	Noon
A_2 B	A	10 A.M.	B	01 P.M.
A_3 B	A	03 P.M.	B	06 P.M.
A_4 C	A	08 P.M.	C	Midnight
A_5 C	A	10 P.M.	C	02 A.M.
B_1 A	B	04 A.M.	A	07 A.M.
B_2 A	B	11 A.M.	A	02 P.M.
B_3 A	B	03 P.M.	A	06 P.M.
C_1 A	C	07 A.M.	A	11 A.M.
C_2 A	C	03 P.M.	A	07 P.M.

Solution

Assumption:

1. Any plane flying from a station must come back within 24 hours for scheduled trip.
2. Any plane starting from A for B must avail the next opportunity to come back to A.
3. It is not possible for any plane to make more than 2 trips, i.e., going and coming back.
4. Five planes will be operating on the line.

Step 1 → Let us first consider the cost matrix associated with the flights connecting A and C. Any plane through C_1A must return back to C by evening route A_4C or A_5C. At station A the layover for A_4C is 9 hours (11 A.M.–8 P.M.) while at station C, the layover for C_1A is 7 hours (Midnight–7 A.M.). Thus, the layover cost for route C_1A - A_4C is $9^2 + 7^2 = 130$ units. Similarly, the other route costs can be computed and the following cost matrix is obtained:

Table 1

	A_4 C	A_5 C
C_1A	130	146
C_2A	226	178

Step 2 → We now consider the cost associated with the flights connecting A and B. Any plane through the route A_1B cannot return by B_2A, because reaching B at noon, the plane has to return back the next day at 11 A.M. Thus we may consider the cost associated with this flight to be very high say M, to avoid this possibility. The costs for other trips between A and B are easily computed, and the following cost matrix is obtained:

Table 2

	B_1 A	B_2 A	B_3 A
A_1B	260	M	234
A_2B	234	M	260
A_3B	164	290	M

Finding optimal solution for Table 1

Step 3 → ***Row Subtraction:*** Subtracting the minimum element of each row from all elements of that row and drawing a minimum number of lines to cover all zeros.

	A_4 C	A_5 C
C_1A	0	16
C_2A	48	0

Since number of lines (2), = order of matrix = (2), the above matrix will provide optimal solution for table 1.

Step 4 → ***Assignment:*** Selecting a row containing exactly one unmarked zero and surrounding it by '□' and draw a vertical line thorough the column containing this zero. Repeating this process till no such row is left; then selecting a column containing exactly one unmarked zero and surrounding it by '□' and draw a horizontal line through the row containing this zero and repeating the process till no such column is left.

	A_4C	A_5C
C_1A	0	16
C_2A	48	0

Finding Solution for Table 2

Step 1 → *Row Subtraction:* Subtracting the minimum element of each row from all elements of that row and drawing the minimum number of lines to cover all zeros.

	$B_1 A$	$B_2 A$	$B_3 A$
A_1B	26	M	0
A_2B	0	M	26
A_3B	0	126	M

Since number of lines = 2, and order of matrix = 3, we will have to take step to increase the number of zeros.

Step 2 → Subtracting the minimum uncovered element (26 in this case) from all uncovered elements and adding it to all elements at the intersection point of the above lines and drawing a minimum number of lines to cover all zeros.

	$B_1 A$	$B_2 A$	B_3A
A_1B	52	M	0
A_2B	0	M	0
A_3B	0	100	M

Since number of lines (3), = order of matrix (3), the above matrix will provide optimal solution for Table 2.

Step 3 → *Assignment:* Subtracting a row containing exactly one unmarked zero and surrounding it by '•' and draw a vertical line thorough the column containing this zero. Repeating this process till no such row is left; then selecting a column containing exactly one unmarked zero and surrounding it by '•' and draw a horizontal line through the row containing this zero and repeating the process till no such column is left.

	$B_1 A$	$B_2 A$	$B_3 A$
A_1B	52	M	0
A_2B	0	M	0
A_3B	0	0	M

Step 4 → So, Optimal Route Schedule for 5 planes is as follows:

Plane No.	*Departure Route*	*Arrival Route*
1	A_1B	B_3A
2	A_2B	B_1A
3	A_3B	B_2A
4	C_1A	A_4C
5	C_2A	A_5C

PROBLEM 4.10 [Flight Scheduling]

XYZ airline operating 7 days a week has given the following time-table. Crews must have a minimum layover of 5 hours between flights. Obtain the pairing flights that minimizes layover time away from home. For any given pairing the crew will be based at the city that results in the smaller layover.

Flight Number	*Depart.*	*Arrive*	*Flight Number*	*Depart.*	*Arrive*
A_1	6 AM	8 AM	B_1	8 AM	10 AM
A_2	8 AM	10 AM	B_2	9 AM	11 AM
A_3	2 PM	4 PM	B_3	2 PM	4 PM
A_4	8 PM	10 PM	B_4	7 PM	9 PM

Solution

Step 1 → *Formulation of Assignment Problem:*

To begin with, let us first assume that the crew is based at Chennai. The flight A_1, which starts from Chennai at 6 AM, reaches Mumbai at 8 AM. The schedule time for the flight at Mumbai is 8 AM. Since the minimum layover time for crew is 5 hours, this flight can depart only on the next day i.e. the layover time will be 24 hours. Similarly, layover times for other flights are also calculated and given in the following tables.

Table 1: Layover Time in hours at Mumbai

Flight No.	B_1	B_2	B_3	B_4
A_1	24	25	6	11
A_2	22	23	28	9
A_3	16	17	22	27
A_4	10	11	16	21

Table 2: Layover Time in hours at Chennai

Flight No.	B_1	B_2	B_3	B_4
A_1	20	19	14	9
A_2	22	21	16	11
A_3	28	27	22	17
A_4	10	9	28	23

Now since the crew can be based at either of the places, minimum layover times can be obtained for different flight numbers by selecting the corresponding lower value out of the above two tables. The resulting table is given below:

Table 3: Minimum Layover Time between Flights

	Flight No.			
Flight No.	B_1	B_2	B_3	B_4
A_1	20	19	6	9
A_2	22	21	16	9
A_3	16	17	22	17
A_4	10	9	16	21

Step 2 → Subtracting the minimum element of each row from all the elements of that row, we get the following matrix. Since there is a zero in each column, there is no need to perform column reduction and drawing the minimum number of lines to cover all zeros.

Flight No.	Flight No.			
	B_1	B_2	B_3	B_4
A_1	14	13	0	3
A_2	13	12	7	0
A_3	0	1	6	1
A_4	1	0	7	12

Since the minimum number of lines to cover all zeros is four which is equal to the order of the matrix, the above table will give the optimal solution.

Step 3 → ***Assignment:*** Subtracting a row containing exactly one unmarked zero and surrounding it by '□' & draw a vertical line thorough the column containing this zero. Repeating this process till no such row is left; then selecting a column containing exactly one unmarked zero and surrounding it by '□' and draw a horizontal line through the row containing this zero and repeating the process till no such column is left.

Flight No.	Flight No.			
	B_1	B_2	B_3	B_4
A_1	14	13	[0]	3
A_2	13	12	7	[0]
A_3	[0]	1	6	1
A_4	1	[0]	7	12

Step 4 → Computing the Minimum Layover Time :

From Flight No.	*To Flight No.*	*Layover time*
A_1	B_3	6
A_2	B_4	9
A_3	B_1	16
A_4	B_2	9
		40 hours

PROBLEM 4.11 [Flight Scheduling]

A trip from Madras to Bangalore takes six hours by bus. A typical time table of the bus service in both directions is given below:

Departure from Madras	*Route Number*	*Arrival at Bangalore*	*Arrival at Madras*	*Route Number*	*Departure from Bangalore*
06.00	a	12.00	11.30	1	05.30
07.30	b	13.30	15.00	2	09.00
11.30	c	17.30	21.00	3	15.00
19.00	d	1.00	00.30	4	18.30
00.30	e	06.30	06.00	5	00.00

The cost of providing this service by the transport company depends upon the time spent by the bus crew (driver and conductor) away from their places in addition to service times. There are five crews. There is a constraint that every crew should be provided with more than 4 hours of rest before the return trip again and should not wait for more than 24 hours of rest before the return trip again. The company has residential facilities for the crew of Madras as well as at Bangalore. Find which line of service be connected with which other line so as to reduce the waiting time to the minimum.

Solution

Step 1 → *Formulation of Assignment Problem:* As the service time is constant for each line it does not appear directly in the computation. If the entire crew resides at Madras then the waiting times in hours at Bangalore for different route connections are given in the following Table :

Table 1 : Layover Time in Hours at Bangalore

Route	*1*	*2*	*3*	*4*	*5*
a	17.5	21	—	6.5	12
b	16	19.5	—	5	10.5
c	12	15.5	21.5	—	6.5
d	4.5	8	14	17.5	23
e	23	—	8.5	12	17.5

If Route a is combined with Route 1, the crew after arriving at Bangalore at 12 Noon start at 5.30 next morning. Thus the waiting time is 17.5 hours. Some of the assignments are infeasible. Route 3 leaves Bangalore at 15.00 hours. Thus the crew of Route a reaching Bangalore at 12 Noon are unable to take the minimum stipulated rest of four hours if they are asked to leave by Route 3. Hence a_3 is an infeasible assignment. Similarly other infeasible assignments have been markd with '–'.

Similarly, if the crew are assumed to reside at Bangalore then the waiting times of the crew in hours at Madras for different route combinations are given in Table 2.

Table 2 : Layover Time in hours at Madras

Route	*1*	*2*	*3*	*4*	*5*
a	18.5	15	9	5.5	24
b	20	16.5	10.5	7	-
c	24	20.5	14.5	11	5.5
d	7.5	4	22	18.5	13
e	13	9.5	-	24	18.5

As the crew can be asked to reside either at Madras or at Bangalore, minimum waiting time from the above operation can be computed for different route combination by choosing the minimum of the two waiting times. This is presented in Table 5. The asterisk marked waiting times indicates that the crew are based at Madras, otherwise they are based at Bangalore.

Table 3 : Minimum Layover Time in Hours

Route	*1*	*2*	*3*	*4*	*5*
a	17.5	15	9	5.5	12
b	16	16.5	10.5	5	10.5
c	12	15.5	14.5	11	5.5
d	4.5	8	14	17.5	13
e	13	9.5	8.5	12	17.5

Step 2 → *Row Subtraction:* Subtracting the minimum element of each row from all the elements of that row.

Route	1	2	3	4	5
a	12.00	9.5	3.5	0	6.5
b	11.00	11.5	5.5	0	5.5
c	6.5	10.00	9.0	5.5	0
d	0	3.5	9.5	13.0	8.5
e	4.5	1.0	0	3.5	9.0

Step 3 → *Column Subtraction:* Subtracting the minimum element of each column of the above matrix from all the elements of that column and then drawing the minimum number of line to cover all zeros.

Route	1	2	3	4	5
a	12.00	8.5	3.5	0	6.5
b	11.00	10.5	5.5	0	5.5
c	6.5	9.0	9.0	5.5	0
d	0	2.5	9.5	13.0	8.5
e	4.5	0	0	3.5	9.0

Since number of lines drawn (4) and order of matrix (5), we will have to take the step to increase the no. of zeros.

Step 4 → Subtracting the minimum uncovered element (3.5 in this case) from all the uncovered elements and adding to the elements at the intersection points and then drawing the minimum number of lines to cover all zeros.

Route	1	2	3	4	5
a	8.5	5.0	0	0	3.0
b	7.5	7.0	2.0	0	2
c	6.5	9.0	9.0	9.0	0
d	0	2.5	9.5	16.5	8.5
e	4.5	0	0	7.0	9.0

Since number of lines drawn (5) = order of matrix (5), the above matrix will provide the optimal solution.

Step 5 → *Assignment:* Subtracting a row containing exactly one unmarked zero and surrounding it by '☐' and draw a vertical line thorough the column containing this zero. Repeating this process till no such row is left; then selecting a column containing exactly one unmarked zero and surrounding it by '☐' and draw a horizontal line through the row containing this zero and repeating the process till no such column is left.

Route	1	2	3	4	5
a	8.5	5.0	[0]	[0]	3.0
b	7.5	7.0	2.0	0	2
c	6.5	9.0	9.0	9.0	[0]
d	[0]	2.5	9.5	16.5	8.5
e	4.5	[0]	0	7.0	9.0

Step 6 → Computing the Minimum Layover Time

Route to be Paired	*Residence of the Crew*	*Waiting time*
a – 3	Bangalore	9
b – 4	Madras	5
c – 5	Bangalore	5.5
d – 1	Madras	4.5
e – 2	Bangalore	9.5

The minimum total waiting time is thus 33.5 hours.

PRACTICAL STEPS INVOLVED IN SOLVING MAXIMISATION PROBLEMS

Step 1 → ***Dummy/Row/Column*** *See whether Number of Rows are equal to Number of Columns. If yes, problem is a balanced one; if not, then add a Dummy Row or Column to make the problem a balanced one by alloting zero value or specific value (if any given) to each cell of the Dummy Row or Column, as the case may be.*

Step 2 → *Derive* ***Profit Matrix*** *by deducting Cost from Revenue.*

Step 3 → *Derive* ***Loss Matrix*** *by deducting all elements from the largest element.*

Step 4 → *Follow the same Steps 2 to 9 as involved in solving Minimisation Problems.*

PROBLEM 4.12

Imagine yourself to be the Executive Director of a 5-star Hotel which has four banquet halls that can be used for all functions including weddings. The halls were all about the same size but the facilities in each hall differed. During a heavy marriage season, 4 parties approached you to reserve a hall for the marriage to be celebrated on the same day. These marriage parties were told that the first choice among these 4 halls would cost Rs. 10,000 for the day. They were also required to indicate the second, third and fourth preferences and the price that they would be willing to pay. Marriage party A & D indicated that they won't be interested in Halls 3 & 4. Other particulars are given in the following table:

	Revenue per Hall			
Marriage Party	*1*	*2*	*3*	*4*
A	10,000	9,000	X	X
B	8,000	10,000	8,000	5,000
C	7,000	10,000	6,000	8,000
D	10,000	8,000	X	X

Where *X* indicated that the party does not want that hall.

Required: Decide on an allocation that will maximise the revenue to your hotel.

Solution

Step 1 → Deriving loss matrix by deducting all events from the largest element (10,000)

	Loss Matrix/Hall			
Marriage Party	*1*	*2*	*3*	*4*
A	0	1000	X	X
B	2000	0	2000	5000
C	3000	0	4000	2000
D	0	2000	X	X

Step 2 → *Column Subtraction:* Subtracting the minimum element of each column from all elements of that column and drawing the minimum number of lines to cover all zeros.

	Loss Matrix/Hall			
Marriage Party	*1*	*2*	*3*	*4*
A	0	1000	X	X
B	2000	0	0	3000
C	3000	0	2000	0
D	0	2000	X	X

Since Number of Lines = 3 and Order of Matrix = 4, the above matrix will provide the optimal solution.

Step 3 → Subtracting the minimum uncovered element (1000 in this case) from all uncovered elements and adding it to all elements at the intersection points of the above lines and drawing the minimum number of lines to cover all zeros.

	Loss Matrix/Hall			
Marriage Party	*1*	*2*	*3*	*4*
A	0	0	X	X
B	3000	0	0	3000
C	4000	0	2000	0
D	0	1000	X	X

Since number of lines (4) = order of matrix (4), the above matrix will provide the optimal solution.

Step 4 → *Assignment:* Selecting a row containing exactly one unmarked zero and surrounding it by '□' and draw a vertical line thorough the column containing this zero. Repeating this process till no such row is left; then selecting a column containing exactly one unmarked zero and surrounding it by '□' and draw a horizontal line through the row containing this zero and repeating the process till no such column is left.

	Loss matrix/Hall			
Marriage Party	*1*	*2*	*3*	*4*
A	0	[0]	X	X
B	3000	0	[0]	3000
C	4000	0	2000	[0]
D	[0]	1000	X	X

Step 5 → Computing maximum:

		Revenue
Marriage Party	A – Hall 2	9,000
Marriage Party	B – Hall 3	8,000
Marriage Party	C – Hall 4	8,000
Marriage Party	D – Hall 1	10,000
	Total	35,000

PROBLEM 4.13 [Assignment of Batting Positions]

The captain of a cricket team has to allot five middle batting positions to five batsmen. The average runs scored by each batsman at these positions are as follows:

	Batting positions				
Batsman	*I*	*II*	*III*	*IV*	*V*
P	40	40	35	25	50
Q	42	30	16	25	27
R	50	48	40	60	50
S	20	19	20	18	25
T	58	60	59	55	53

(i) Find the assignment of batsmen to positions, which would give the maximum number of runs.

(ii) If another batsman 'U' with the following average runs in batting positions as given below:

Batting position:	I	II	III	IV	V
Average runs:	45	52	38	50	49

Is added to the team, should he be included to play in the team ? If so, who will be replaced by him?

Solution

Step 1 → Deriving Loss Matrix by deducting all elements from the largest element (60).

	Batting positions				
Batsman	*I*	*II*	*III*	*IV*	*V*
P	20	20	25	35	10
Q	18	30	44	35	33
R	10	12	20	0	10
S	40	41	40	42	35
T	2	0	1	5	7

Step 2 → *Row Subtraction:* Subtracting the minimum element of each row from all elements of that row.

	Batting positions				
Batsman	*I*	*II*	*III*	*IV*	*V*
P	10	10	15	25	0
Q	0	12	26	17	15
R	10	12	20	0	10
S	5	6	5	7	0
T	2	0	1	5	7

Step 3 → *Column Subtraction:* Subtracting the minimum element of each column from all elements of that column and drawing minimum number of lines to cover all zeros.

Batting positions					
Batsman	*I*	*II*	*III*	*IV*	*V*
P	10	10	14	25	0
Q	0	12	25	17	15
R	10	12	19	0	10
S	5	6	4	7	0
T	2	0	0	5	7

Since number of lines = 4 and order of matrix = 5, we will have to take step to increase the number of zeros.

Step 4 → Subtracting the minimum uncovered element (in this case 4) from all uncovered elements and adding it to all elements at the intersection point of the above lines and drawing minimum number of lines to cover all zeros.

Batting positions					
Batsman	*I*	*II*	*III*	*IV*	*V*
P	6	6	10	25	0
Q	0	12	25	21	19
R	6	8	15	0	10
S	1	2	0	7	0
T	2	0	0	9	11

Since the number of lines drawn (5) = order of matrix (5), the above matrix will provide the optimal solution.

Step 5 → *Assignment:* Selecting a row containing exactly one unmarked zero and surrounding it by '□' and draw a vertical line thorough the column containing this zero. Repeating this process till no such row is left; then selecting a column containing exactly one unmarked zero and surrounding it by '□' and draw a horizontal line through the row containing this zero and repeating the process till no such column is left.

Batting positions					
Batsman	*I*	*II*	*III*	*IV*	*V*
P	6	6	10	25	[0]
Q	[0]	12	25	21	19
R	6	8	15	[0]	10
S	1	2	[0]	7	0
T	2	[0]	0	9	11

Step 6 → Computing Maximum Runs:

Batsman	*Batting positions*	*Runs*
P	V	50
Q	I	42
R	IV	60
S	III	20
T	II	60
	Total	232

Part (ii)

Step 1 → Including Batsman U in Initial Table. **Introducing a Dummy batting position** to make the problem a balanced one by alloting zero.

	Batting positions					
Batsman	*I*	*II*	*III*	*IV*	*V*	*VI*
P	40	40	35	25	50	0
Q	42	30	16	25	27	0
R	50	48	40	60	50	0
S	20	19	20	18	25	0
T	58	60	59	55	53	0
U	45	52	38	50	49	0

Step 2 → Deriving Loss Matrix by deducting all elements from the largest element (60).

	Batting positions					
Batsman	*I*	*II*	*III*	*IV*	*V*	*VI*
P	20	20	25	35	10	60
Q	18	30	44	35	33	60
R	10	12	20	0	10	60
S	40	41	40	42	35	60
T	2	0	1	5	7	60
U	15	8	22	10	11	60

Step 3 → ***Row Subtraction:*** Subtracting the minimum element of each row from all elements of that row.

	Batting positions					
Batsman	*I*	*II*	*III*	*IV*	*V*	*VI*
P	10	10	15	25	0	50
Q	0	12	26	17	15	42
R	10	12	20	0	10	60
S	5	6	5	7	0	25
T	2	0	1	5	7	60
U	7	0	14	2	3	52

Step 4 → *Column Subtraction:* Subtracting the minimum element of each column from all element of that column and drawing minimum number of Lines to cover all zeros.

	Batting positions					
Batsman	*I*	*II*	*III*	*IV*	*V*	*VI*
P	10	10	14	25	0	25
Q	0	12	25	17	15	17
R	10	12	19	0	10	35
S	5	6	4	7	0	0
T	2	0	0	5	7	35
U	7	0	13	2	3	27

Since number of lines (6) = order of matrix (6), the above matrix will provide the optimal solution.

Step 5 → *Assignment:* Selecting a row containing exactly one unmarked zero and surrounding it by '□' and draw a vertical line through the column containing this zero. Repeating this process till no such row is left; then selecting a column containing exactly one unmarked zero and surrounding it by '□' and draw a horizontal line through the row containing this zero and repeating the process till no such column is left.

	Batting positions					
Batsman	*I*	*II*	*III*	*IV*	*V*	*VI*
P	10	10	14	25	[0]	25
Q	[0]	12	25	17	15	17
R	10	12	19	[0]	10	35
S	5	6	4	7	0	[0]
T	2	0	[0]	5	7	35
U	7	[0]	13	2	3	17

Step 6 → Computing Maximum Runs:

Batsman	*Batting Positions*	*Runs*
P	V	50
Q	I	42
R	IV	60
S	VI (dummy)	-
T	III	59
U	II	52
	Total	263

∴ Batsman S will be replaced by Batsman U.

PROBLEM 4.14 [Assignment of New Methods]

A production manager wants to assign one of the five new methods to each of the four operations. The following table summarises the weekly output in units:

Operator	Weekly Output				
	M_1	M_2	M_3	M_4	M_5
A	4	6	11	16	9
B	5	8	16	19	9
C	9	13	21	21	13
D	6	6	9	11	7

Cost per unit in Rs. 10, Selling Price per unit Rs. 35. Find the maximum profit per month.

Solution

Note: Since Profit per unit (Rs 25 i.e., Rs 35 – Rs 10) is same the given problem can be solved using minimization technique.

Step 1 → Introducing a Dummy Operator to make the problem a balanced one by alloting zero output.

Operator	Methods				
	M_1	M_2	M_3	M_4	M_5
A	4	6	11	16	9
B	5	8	16	19	9
C	9	13	21	21	13
D	6	6	9	11	7
Dummy	0	0	0	0	0

Step 2 → Deriving Loss Matrix by subtracting all elements from the largest element (21).

Operator	Methods				
	M_1	M_2	M_3	M_4	M_5
A	17	15	10	5	12
B	16	13	5	2	12
C	12	8	0	0	8
D	15	15	12	10	14
Dummy	21	21	21	21	21

Step 3 → ***Row Subtraction:*** Subtracting the minimum element of each row from all elements of that row and then drawing the minimum number of lines to cover all zeros.

Operator	Methods				
	M_1	M_2	M_3	M_4	M_5
A	12	10	5	0	7
B	14	11	3	0	10
C	12	8	0	0	8
D	5	5	2	0	4
Dummy	0	0	0	0	0

Since number of lines = 3 and order of matrix = 5, we will have to take step to increase the number of zeros.

Step 4 → Subtracting the minimum uncovered element (4 in this case) from all uncovered elements and adding it to all elements at the intersection point of the above lines and drawing minimum number of lines to cover all zeros.

Operator	Methods				
	M_1	M_2	M_3	M_4	M_5
A	8	6	5	0	3
B	10	7	3	0	6
C	8	4	0	0	4
D	1	1	2	0	0
Dummy	0	0	4	4	0

Since the number of lines = 4 and order of matrix = 5, we will have to take step to increase the number of zeros.

Step 5 → Subtracting the minimum uncovered element (3 in this case) from all uncovered elements and adding it to all elements at the intersection point of the above lines and drawing minimum number of lines to cover all zeros.

Operator	Methods				
	M_1	M_2	M_3	M_4	M_5
A	5	3	2	0	0
B	7	4	0	0	3
C	8	4	0	0	3
D	1	1	2	3	0
Dummy	0	0	4	7	0

Since the number of lines = 4 and order of matrix = 5, we will have to take step to increase the number of zeros.

Step 6 → Subtracting the minimum uncovered elements (1 in this case) from all uncovered elements and adding it to all elements at the intersection point of the above lines and drawing minimum number of lines to cover all zeros.

Operator	Methods				
	M_1	M_2	M_3	M_4	M_5
A	4	2	2	0	0
B	6	3	0	0	3
C	7	3	0	3	4
D	0	0	2	3	0
Dummy	0	0	5	8	1

Since number of lines (5) = order of matrix (5), the above matrix will provide optimal Solution.

Step 7 → ***Assignment:*** Selecting a row containing exactly one unmarked zero and surrounding it by '□' and draw a vertical line thorough the column containing this zero. Repeating this process till no such row is left; then selecting a column containing exactly one unmarked zero and surrounding it by '□' and draw a horizontal line through the row containing this zero and repeating the process till no such column is left.

Operator	Methods M_1	M_2	M_3	M_4	M_5
A	4	2	2	0	[0]
B	6	3	0	[0]	3
C	7	3	[0]	3	4
D	[0]	0	2	3	0
Dummy	0	[0]	5	8	1

Step 8 → Computing Optimal Output per month and Maximum Profit:

Operators	Methods	Units Per week	Units Per month
A	M_5	9	36
B	M_4	19	76
C	M_3	21	84
D	M_1	6	24
Dummy	M_2	0	0
	Total Output	55	220

Total sales Revenue for the month @ Rs. 35 per unit	7,700
Less: Total Production Cost for the month @ Rs. 10 per unit	(2,200)
Maximum Profit	5,500

Alternative Solution:

Operator	Methods M_1	M_2	M_3	M_4	M_5
A	4	2	2	0	[0]
B	6	3	0	[0]	3
C	7	3	[0]	3	4
D	0	[0]	2	3	0
Dummy	[0]	0	5	8	1

Operators	Methods	Units Per week	Units Per month
A	M_5	9	36
B	M_4	19	76
C	M_3	21	84
D	M_2	6	24
Dummy	M_1	0	0
	Total Output	55	220

Total sales Revenue for the month @ Rs. 35 per unit	7,700
Less: Total Production Cost for the month @ Rs. 10 per unit	(2,200)
Maximum Profit	5,500

PROBLEM 4.15

The cost matrix giving selling cost per unit of a product by salesman A, B, C and D in regions R_1, R_2, R_3 and R_4 is given below:

	A	*B*	*C*	*D*
R_1	4	12	16	8
R_2	20	28	32	24
R_3	36	44	48	40
R_4	52	60	64	56

(i) Assign one salesman to one region to minimise the selling cost.

(ii) If the selling price of the product is Rs. 2000 per unit and variable cost excluding the selling cost given in the table is Rs. 100 per unit, find the assignment that would maximise the contribution.

(iii) What other conclusion can you make form the above?

Solution

4	12	16	8
20	28	32	24
36	44	48	40
52	60	64	56

Subtracting minimum element – each row.

0	8	12	4
0	8	12	4
0	8	12	4
0	8	12	4

Subtracting minimum element – each column.

0	0	0	0
0	0	0	0
0	0	0	0
0	0	0	0

Minimum no. of lines to cover all zeros = 4 = order of matrix. Hence optional assignment is possible.

$$\text{Minimum cost} = 4 + 28 + 56 = 136.$$

$$= AR_1 + BR_2 + CR_3 + DR_4$$

Since all zeros, the are 24 solution to the assignment problem

Viz.	A	B	C	D	
	R_1	R_2	R_3	R_4	
	R_2	R_3	R_4	R_1	
	R_3	R_4	R_1	R_2	
	R_4	R_1	R_2	R_3	
	R_1	R_3	R_4	R_2	etc.

A can be assigned in 4 ways, B in 3 ways for each of A's 4 ways.

(ii) SP – VC = 100 Rs

	A	*B*	*C*	*D*
R_1	96	88	84	92
R_2	80	72	68	76
R_3	64	56	52	60
R_4	48	40	36	44

Subtracting the highest term

0	8	12	4
16	24	28	20
32	40	44	36
48	56	60	52

Subtracting minimum term of each row

0	8	12	4
0	8	12	4
0	8	12	4
0	8	12	4

Which is the same as the earlier matrix

Maximum contribution = Rs. (96 + 72 + 52 + 44) = Rs. 264.

Alternative Solution:

Maximization of contribution is same as minimizing cost. Hence, same assignments as in (i) will be optional solution

Maximum Contribution Rs. (400 – 136) = Rs 264

(iii) (a) The relative cost of assigning person i to region r does not change by addition or subtraction of a constant from either a row, or column or all elements of the matrix.

(b) Minimizing cost is the same as maximizing contribution. Hence, the assignment solution will be same applying point (i) above.

(c) Many zero's represent many feasible least cost assignment. Here, all zeros mean maximum permutation of a 4 × 4 matrix, viz. 4 × 3 × 2 × 1 = 24 solutions are possible.

PROBLEM 4.16 [Assignment of Machines]

A company is faced with the problem of assigning 4 machines to 6 different jobs (one machine to one job only). The profits are estimated as follows:

Job	Machine			
	A	*B*	*C*	*D*
1	3	6	2	6
2	7	1	4	4
3	3	8	5	8
4	6	4	3	7
5	5	2	4	3
6	5	7	6	4

Required: Solve the problem to maximize the total profits.

Solution

Step 1 → Introducing Dummy machines to make the problem a balanced one by alloting zero profit.

	A	*B*	*C*	*D*	*E*	*F*
1	3	6	2	6	0	0
2	7	1	4	4	0	0
3	3	8	5	8	0	0
4	6	4	3	7	0	0
5	5	2	4	3	0	0
6	5	7	6	4	0	0

Step 2 → Derive Loss Matrix by deducting all elements from the largest element (8)

	A	*B*	*C*	*D*	*E*	*F*
1	5	2	6	2	8	8
2	1	7	4	4	8	8
3	5	0	3	0	8	8
4	2	4	5	1	8	8
5	3	6	4	5	8	8
6	3	1	2	4	8	8

Step 3 → *Row Subtraction:* Subtracting the minimum element of each row from all elements of that row.

	A	*B*	*C*	*D*	*E*	*F*
1	3	0	4	0	6	6
2	0	6	3	3	7	7
3	5	0	3	0	8	8
4	1	3	4	0	7	7
5	0	3	1	2	5	5
6	2	0	1	3	7	7

Step 4 → *Column Subtraction:* Subtracting the minimum element of each column from all elements of that column and drawing minimum number of lines to cover all zeros.

	A	B	C	D	E	F
1	3	0	3	0	1	1
2	0	6	2	3	2	2
3	5	0	2	0	3	3
4	1	3	3	0	2	2
5	0	3	0	2	0	0
6	2	0	0	3	2	2

Since number of lines = 5 and order of matrix = 6, we will have to take step to increase the number of zeros.

Step 5 → Subtracting the minimum uncovered element (1 in this case) from all uncovered elements and adding it to all elements at the intersection point of the above lines and drawing minimum number of Lines to cover all zeros.

	A	B	C	D	E	F
1	3	0	3	0	0	0
2	0	6	2	3	1	1
3	5	0	2	0	2	2
4	1	3	3	0	1	1
5	1	4	1	3	0	0
6	2	0	0	3	1	1

Since number of lines (6), = order of matrix (6), the above matrix will provide Optimal Solution.

Step 6 → *Assignment:* Selecting a row containing exactly one unmarked zero and surrounding it by '□' and draw a vertical line thorough the column containing this zero. Repeating this process till no such row is left; then selecting a column containing exactly one unmarked zero and surrounding it by '□' and draw a horizontal line through the row containing this zero and repeating the process till no such column is left.

	A	B	C	D	E	F
1	3	0	3	0	0	0
2	0	6	2	3	1	1
3	5	0	2	0	2	2
4	1	3	3	0	1	1
5	1	4	1	3	0	0
6	2	0	0	3	1	1

Step 7 → Computing Maximum Profit:

Job	*Machine*	*Profit (Rs.)*
1	E	0
2	A	7
3	B	8
4	D	7
5	F	0
6	C	6
	Total	28

Alternative Solution:

	A	*B*	*C*	*D*	*E*	*F*
1	3	0	3	0	0	0
2	0	6	2	3	1	1
3	5	0	2	0	2	2
4	1	3	3	0	1	1
5	1	4	1	3	0	0
6	2	0	0	3	1	1

Computing Maximum Profit:

Job	*Machine*	*Profit (Rs.)*
1	F	0
2	A	7
3	B	8
4	D	7
5	E	0
6	C	6
	Total	28

PROBLEM 4.17 [Assignment of Production]

A firm is contemplating the introduction of three products 1, 2 and 3, in it's plants A, B and C. Only a single product is decided to be introduced in each of the plants. The unit cost of producing ith product in jth plants, is given in the following matrix:

	Plant		
Product	*A*	*B*	*C*
1	8	12	—
2	10	6	4
3	7	6	6

(i) How should the products be assigned so that the total unit cost is minimised?

(ii) If the quantity of different products is as follows, then what assignment shall minimise the aggregate production cost?

Product	*Quantity (in units)*
1	2,000
2	2,000
3	10,000

(iii) It is expected that the selling prices of the products produced by different plants would be different; as shown in the following table:

	Plant		
Product	*A*	*B*	*C*
1	15	18	—
2	18	16	10
3	12	10	8

Assuming that the quantities mentioned in (ii) above would be produced and sold, how should the products be assigned to the plants to obtain maximum profits ?

Solution

Part (i)

Step 1 → *Row Subtraction:* Subtracting the minimum element of each row from all elements of that row. Since there is zero in each column, there is no need for column subtraction. Drawing minimum number of lines to cover all zeros.

	Plant		
Product	*A*	*B*	*C*
1	0	4	—
2	6	2	0
3	1	0	0

Since number of lines (3) = order of matrix (3), the above matrix will provide the optimal Solution.

Step 2 → *Assignment:* Selecting a row containing exactly one unmarked zero and surrounding it by '□' and draw a vertical line thorough the column containing this zero. Repeating this process till no such row is left; then selecting a column containing exactly one unmarked zero and surrounding it by '□' and draw a horizontal line through the row containing this zero and repeating the process till no such column is left.

	Plant		
Product	*A*	*B*	*C*
1	[0]	4	—
2	6	2	[0]
3	1	[0]	0

Step 3 → Computing Minimum Unit Cost:

Products	*Plants*	*Units Cost (Rs.)*
1	A	8
2	C	4
3	B	6
	Total	18

Part (ii)

Step 1 → Deriving Total Production Cost Matrix by multiplying Quantity Matrix by Unit Cost Matrix.

Product	*Plant* A	B	C
1	16,000	24,000	—
2	20,000	12,000	8,000
3	70,000	60,000	60,000

Step 2 → ***Row Subtraction:*** Subtracting the minimum element of each row from all elements of that row. Since there is zero in column, there is no need for column subtraction. Drawing minimum number of lines to cover all zeros.

Product	*Plant* A	B	C
1	0	8,000	—
2	12,000	4,000	0
3	10,000	0	0

Since number of lines (3) and order of matrix (3), the above matrix will provide the optimal solution.

Step 3 → ***Assignment:*** Selecting a row containing exactly one unmarked zero and surrounding it by '□' and draw a vertical line thorough the column containing this zero. Repeating this process till no such row is left; then selecting a column containing exactly one unmarked zero and surrounding it by '□' and draw a horizontal line through the row containing this zero and repeating the process till no such column is left.

Product	*Plant* A	B	C
1	[0]	8,000	—
2	12,000	4,000	[0]
3	10,000	[0]	0

Step 4 → Computing Minimum Cost

Products	Plants	Units Cost (Rs.)
1	A	16,000
2	C	8,000
3	B	60,000
	Total	84,000

Part (iii)

Step 1 → Deriving Sales Matrix by following formula:

Sale = Units × Selling Price Per Unit

	Plant		
Product	A	B	C
1	30,000	36,000	—
2	36,000	32,000	20,000
3	1,20,000	1,00,000	80,000

Step 2 → Deriving Profit Matrix by deducting Cost from revenue by the following formula:

Profit = Total Sales – Total Cost

	Plant		
Product	A	B	C
1	14,000	8,000	—
2	16,000	20,000	12,000
3	50,000	40,000	20,000

Step 3 → Deriving Loss Matrix by deducting all elements from the largest element (50,000).

	Plant		
Product	A	B	C
1	36,000	42,000	—
2	34,000	30,000	38,000
3	0	10,000	30,000

Step 4 → *Row Subtraction:* Subtracting the minimum element of each row from all elements of that row.

	Plant		
Product	A	B	C
1	0	6,000	—
2	4,000	0	8,000
3	0	10,000	30,000

Step 5 → ***Column Subtraction:*** Subtracting minimum element of each column from all elements of that column and drawing minimum number of Lines to cover all zeros.

	Plant		
Product	*A*	*B*	*C*
1	0	6,000	—
2	4,000	0	0
3	0	10,000	22,000

Since number of lines = 2 and order of matrix = 3, we will have to take step to increase the number of zeros.

Step 6 → Subtracting the minimum uncovered element (6,000 in this case) from all uncovered elements and adding it to all elements at the intersection point of the above lines and drawing minimum number of lines to cover all zeros.

	Plant		
Product	*A*	*B*	*C*
1	0	0	—
2	10,000	0	0
3	0	4,000	16,000

Since number of lines (3) and order of matrix (3), the above matrix will provide the optimal solution..

Step 7 → ***Assignment:*** Selecting a row containing exactly one unmarked zero and surrounding it by '□' and draw a vertical line thorough the column containing this zero. Repeating this process till no such row is left; then selecting a column containing exactly one unmarked zero and surrounding it by '□' and draw a horizontal line through the row containing this zero and repeating the process till no such column is left.

	Plant		
Product	*A*	*B*	*C*
1	0	0	—
2	10,000	0	0
3	0	4,000	16,000

Step 7 → Computing Maximum Profit:

Products	*Plants*	*Profit (Rs.)*
1	B	8,000
2	C	12,000
3	A	50,000
	Total	70,000

PROBLEM 4.18 [Assignment of Sales Territory]

A manufacturing company has four zones A, B, C, D and four sales engineers P, Q, R, S respectively for assignment. Since the zones are not equally rich in sales potential, therefore it is estimated that a particular engineer operating in a particular zone will bring the following sales:

Zone A	:	4,20,000
Zone B	:	3,36,000
Zone C	:	2,94,000
Zone D	:	4,62,000

The engineers are having different sales ability. Working under the same conditions, their yearly sales are proportional to 14, 9, 11 and 8 respectively. The criteria of maximum expected total sales is to be met by assigning the best engineer to the richest zone, the next best to the second richest zone and so on.

Required: Find the optimum assignment and the maximum sales.

Solution

Step 1 → Deriving Revenue Matrix.

Sales Engineer	*Proportion*	*Index taking B as base*
P	14	1
Q	9	$\frac{9}{14}$
R	11	$\frac{11}{14}$
S	8	$\frac{8}{14}$

The problem here is to find the optimum assignment in thefollowing sales table so as to maximise the total sales of the company.

Territory Engineer	*Zones (Sales in thousands of rupees)*			
	I	*II*	*III*	*IV*
P	$420 \times 1 = 420$	$336 \times 1 = 336$	$294 \times 1 = 294$	$462 \times 1 = 462$
Q	$420 \times \frac{9}{14} = 270$	$336 \times \frac{9}{14} = 216$	$294 \times \frac{9}{14} = 189$	$462 \times \frac{9}{14} = 297$
R	$420 \times \frac{11}{14} = 330$	$336 \times \frac{11}{14} = 264$	$294 \times \frac{11}{14} = 231$	$462 \times \frac{11}{14} = 363$
S	$420 \times \frac{8}{14} = 240$	$336 \times \frac{8}{14} = 192$	$294 \times \frac{8}{14} = 168$	$462 \times \frac{8}{14} = 264$

Step 2 → Deriving Loss Matrix by deducting all elements from the largest element (462).

Sales Engineer	*Zones (Loss in thousands of rupees)*			
	A	***B***	***C***	***D***
P	42	126	168	0
Q	192	246	273	165
R	132	198	231	99
S	222	270	294	198

Step 3 → ***Row Subtraction:*** Subtracting the minimum element of each row from all elements of that row.

Sales Engineer	*Zones (Loss in thousands of rupees)*			
	A	***B***	***C***	***D***
P	42	126	168	0
Q	27	81	108	0
R	33	99	132	0
S	24	72	96	0

Step 4 → ***Column Subtraction:*** Subtracting the minimum element of each column from all elements of that column and drawing minimum number of lines to cover all zeros.

Sales Engineer	*Zones (Loss in thousands of rupees)*			
	A	*B*	*C*	*D*
P	18	54	72	0
Q	3	9	12	0
R	9	27	36	0
S	0	0	0	0

Since number of lines = 2 and order of matrix = 4, we will have to take step to increase the number of zeros.

Step 5 → Subtracting the minimum uncovered element (in this case 3) from all uncovered elements and adding it to all elements at the intersection point of the above lines and drawing minimum number of lines to cover all zeros.

Sales Engineer	*Zones (Loss in thousands of rupees)*			
	A	*B*	*C*	*D*
P	15	51	69	0
Q	0	6	9	0
R	6	24	33	0
S	0	0	0	3

Since number of lines = 3 and order of matrix = 4, we will have to take step to increase the number of zeros.

Step 6 → Subtracting the minimum uncovered element (in this case 6) from all uncovered elements and adding it to all elements at the intersection point of the above lines and drawing minimum number of lines to cover all zeros.

Sales Engineer	Zones (Loss in thousands of rupees)			
	A	B	C	D
P	15	45	63	0
Q	0	0	3	0
R	6	18	27	0
S	6	0	0	9

Since number of lines = 3 and order of matrix = 4, we will have to take step to increase the number of zeros.

Step 7 → Subtracting the minimum uncovered element (in this case 6) from all uncovered elements and adding it to all elements at the intersection point of the above lines and drawing minimum number of lines to cover all zeros.

Sales Engineer	Zones (Loss in thousands of rupees)			
	A	B	C	D
P	9	39	57	0
Q	0	0	3	6
R	0	12	21	0
S	6	0	0	15

Since the minimum number of lines drawn to cover all the zeros is 4 which is equal to the order of the matrix. Hence, the above table will give the optimum assignment.

Step 8 → ***Assignment:*** Selecting a row containing exactly one unmarked zero and surrounding it by '•' and draw a vertical line thorough the column containing this zero. Repeating this process till no such row is left; then selecting a column containing exactly one unmarked zero and surrounding it by '•' and draw a horizontal line through the row containing this zero and repeating the process till no such column is left.

Sales Engineer	Zones (Loss in thousands of rupees)			
	A	B	C	D
P	9	39	57	[0]
Q	0	[0]	3	6
R	[0]	12	21	0
S	6	0	[0]	15

Step 9 → Computing the Maximum Sales:

Engineers	Zones	Sales (in Rs.)
P	D	4,62,000
Q	B	2,16,000
R	A	3,30,000
S	C	1,68,000
		11,76,000

It can be seen from the above assignments that the best engineer P is assigned to the richest zone D, the next best engineer R is assigned to second richest zone A, the next best engineer Q is assigned to zone B and so on. Hence, the optimum assignment matches the company's criteria of achieving the maximum expected total sales.

PROBLEM 4.19 [Preparation of Production and Profit Matrix]

A firm produces four products. There are four operators who are capable of producing any of these four products. The processing time varies from operator to operator. The firm records 8 hours a day and allows 30 minutes for lunch. The processing time in minutes and the profit for each of the products are given below:

	Products			
Operators	*A*	*B*	*C*	*D*
1	15	9	10	6
2	10	6	9	6
3	25	15	15	9
4	15	9	10	10
Profit (Rs) per unit	8	6	5	4

Find the optimal assignment of products to operators.

Solution

Step 1 → *Deriving Production Matrix:* The firm records 8 hours a day and allows 30 minutes for lunch, hence the net working time available per day is 7 hours and 30 minutes i.e. 450 minutes. The number of units of each product which could be produced in 450 minutes by the four operators is calculated in the table given below by using the formula (i.e. 450 Minutes/ Processing time).

	Products			
Operators	*A*	*B*	*C*	*D*
1	30	50	45	75
2	45	75	50	75
3	18	30	30	50
4	30	50	45	45
Profit per unit	8	6	5	4

Step 2 → Deriving Profit Matrix by multiplying output by profit per unit

	Profit matrix in Rs. of Products			
Operators	*A*	*B*	*C*	*D*
1	240	300	225	300
2	360	450	250	300
3	144	180	150	200
4	240	300	225	180

Step 3 → Deriving Loss Matrix by deducting all the elements from the largest element (450)

	Loss matrix in Rs. of Products			
Operators	*A*	*B*	*C*	*D*
1	210	150	225	150
2	90	0	200	150
3	306	270	300	250
4	210	150	225	270

Step 4 → *Row Subtraction:* Subtracting the minimum element of each row from all elements of that row.

	Loss matrix in Rs. of Products			
Operators	*A*	*B*	*C*	*D*
1	60	0	75	0
2	90	0	200	150
3	56	20	50	0
4	60	0	75	120

Step 5 → *Column Subtraction:* Subtracting the minimum element of each column from all elements of that column and drawing minimum number of lines to cover all zeros.

	Loss matrix in Rs. of Products			
Operators	*A*	*B*	*C*	*D*
1	4	0	25	0
2	34	0	150	150
3	0	20	0	0
4	4	0	25	120

Since number of lines = 3 and order of matrix = 4, we will have to take step to increase the number of zeros.

Step 6 → Subtracting the minimum uncovered element (in this case 4) from all uncovered elements and adding it to all elements at the intersection point of the above lines and drawing minimum number of lines to cover all zeros.

	Loss matrix in Rs. of Products			
Operators	*A*	*B*	*C*	*D*
1	0	0	21	0
2	30	0	146	150
3	0	24	0	4
4	0	0	21	120

Step 7 → *Assignment:* Selecting a row containing exactly one unmarked zero and surrounding it by '□' and draw a vertical line thorough the column containing this zero. Repeating this process till no such row is left; then selecting a column containing exactly one unmarked zero and surrounding it by '□' and draw a horizontal line through the row containing this zero and repeating the process till no such column is left.

Operators	Loss matrix in Rs. of Products			
	A	B	C	D
1	0	0	21	[0]
2	30	[0]	146	150
3	0	24	[0]	4
4	[0]	0	21	120

Step 8 → Computing the Maximum Profit:

Operator	Product	Profit (Rs.)
1	D	300
2	B	450
3	C	150
4	A	240
	Total	Rs. 1,140

PROBLEM 4.20

A manager was asked to assign tasks to operators (one task per operator only) so as to minimize the time taken. He was given the matrix showing the hours taken by the operators for the tasks.

First, he preformed the row minimum operation. Secondly, he did the column minimum operation. Then, he realized that there were 4 tasks and 5 operators. At the third step he introduced the dummy row and continued with his fourth step of drawing lines to cover zeros. He drew 2 vertical lines (under operator III and operator IV) and two horizontal lines (aside task T_4 and dummy task T_5). At step 5, he performed the necessary operation with the uncovered element, since the number of lines was less than the order of the matrix. After this, his matrix appeared as follows:

Operators

Tasks	*I*	*II*	*III*	*IV*	*V*
T_1	4	2	5	0	0
T_2	6	3	3	0	3
T_3	4	0	0	0	1
T_4	0	0	5	3	0
T_5 (dummy)	0	0	3	3	0

(i) What was the matrix after step II ? Based on such matrix, ascertain (ii) and (iii) given below.

(ii) What was the most difficult task for operators I, II and V?

(iii) Who was the most efficient operators?

(iv) If you are not told anything about the manager's errors, which operator would be denied any task? Why?

(v) Can the manager go ahead with his assignment to correctly arrive at the optional assignment, or should he start afresh after introducing the dummy task at the beginning?

Solution

	01	02	03	04	05
(given)					
T_1	4	2	5	0	0
T_2	6	3	3	0	3
T_3	4	0	0	0	1
T_4	0	0	5	3	0
T_5	0	0	3	3	0
(dummy)					

Junction values at dummy = 3.3 was the minimum uncovered element.

Previous step was

7	5	5	0	3
9	6	3	0	6
7	3	0	0	4
0	0	2	0	0
0	0	0	0	0

(i) At step II the matrix was:

7	5	5	0	3
9	6	3	0	6
7	3	0	0	4
0	0	2	0	0

(ii) For Operator 1, Most difficult task will be indicated by hours = T_2

Operator II T_2

Operator V T_2

(iii) Most efficient operator = Operator 4

(iv) If the Manager's mistake was not known,

4	2	5	0	(88)
6	3	3	(88)	3
4	0	(88)	0	1
0	0	5	3	0
0	0	3	3	0

We continue the assignment; $T_1 — 0_5$, $T_2 – 0_4$, $T_3 – 0_3$ are fixed.

Between T_4 and T_5, 0_1 or 0_2 Can be allotted.

So, other 0_1 or 0_2 can be denied the job.

(v) Yes, the Manager can go ahead with the optimal assignment.

Row minimum is not affected by when the dummy was introduced.

Column minimum was affected. But in the process, more zeros were generated to provide better solution.

PROBLEM 4.21

A city corporation has decided to carry out road repairs on 4 main roads in the city.

The Government has agreed to make a special grant of Rs 50 lacs towards the cost with the condition that the repairs should be carried out at lowest cost. Five contractors have sent their bids. Only road will be awarded to one contractor. The bids are given below:

	Cost of Repairs (Rs in lacs)				
	Road	*R_1*	*R_2*	*R_3*	*R_3*
Contractors	C_1	9	14	19	15
	C_2	7	17	20	19
	C_3	9	18	21	18
	C_4	10	12	18	19
	C_5	10	15	21	16

You are informed that C_2 should get R_1 and C_4 should get R_2 to minimize costs,

(i) What is the minimum cost allocation?

(ii) How much is the minimum discount that the eliminated contractor should offer for meriting a contract?

(iii) Independent of (ii) above, if the corporation can negotiate to get a uniform discount rate from each contractor, what is the minimum rate of discount so that the cost is within the grant amount?

Solution

(i) There are 5 rows and 4 columns hence insert a dummy column R_5.

1. C_2 has been allocated to R_1

2. C_4 has been allocated to R_2. Hence the assignment is restricted to

	R_3	R_4	R_5
C_1	19	15	0
C_3	21	18	0
C_5	21	16	0

Column Minimum

	R_3	R_4	R_5
C_1	0	0	0
C_3	2	3	0
C_5	2	1	0

	R_3	R_4	R_5
C_1	0	0	1
C_3	1	2	0
C_5	1	0	0

Hence C_1 has been allotted to R_3, C_3 to R_5 and C_5 to R_4.

Hence the Minimum cost is = 7 + 12 + 19 + 16 + 0 = 54 Lacs

(ii) C_3 should reduce 2 lacs for R_1, 6 lacs for R_2, 2 lacs for R_3 and 2 lacs for R_4

Minimum Discount = 2 Lacs for any of R_1, R_3, R_4

(iii) Minimum rate of Discount (54 – 50) = 4/54 = 7.41%

5 TRANSPORTATION PROBLEMS

PRACTICAL STEPS INVOLVED IN SOLVING TRANSPORTATION PROBLEMS OF MINIMIZATION TYPE

Step 1 → ***Dummy Origin/Destination:*** *See whether Total Requirements are equal to Total Availability; if yes, go to Step 2; if not, introduce a Dummy Origin/Destination, as the case may be, to make the problem a balanced one, taking Transportation Cost per unit as zero for each Cell of Dummy Origin/Destination or as otherwise indicated.*

↓

Step 2 → ***Initial Feasible Solution:*** *Find Initial Feasible Solution by following either the Least Cost Method (or LCM) or North-West Corner Method (or NWCM) or Vogel's Approximation Method (or VAM), (Refer to page 5.2, 5.3 and 5.4).*

Note: *Unless otherwise stated, Use VAM.*

↓

Step 3 → ***Introduction of Infinitely Small Quantity 'e':*** *After obtaining the Initial Feasible Solution Table, see whether Total Number of Allocations are equal to "m + n - 1",; if yes, go to Step 4; if not, introduce an infinitely small quantity 'e' to the Least Cost Independent Cell. (i.e., for which no Loop can be formed).*

Note : *Introduce as many number of 'e' as the total number of allocated cells falls below "m + n -1".*

↓

Step 4 → ***Optimality Test:*** *Carry out the Optimality Test on the Initial Solution Table to find out the optimal solution. (Refer to page 5.27).*

Step 5 → ***Minimum Cost:*** *Calculate the Total Minimum Cost =* $\Sigma (X_{ij} \updownarrow C_{ij})$,

where, X *= Units Allocated to a Cell;*

C *= Shipping Cost per Unit of a Cell;*

i *= Row Number;*

j *= Column Number*

FINDING INITIAL (OR BASIC) FEASIBLE SOLUTION

In general, any basic feasible solution of a transportation problem with **m origins** (such as factories) and **n destinations** (such as warehouses) should have '*m + n - 1*' non zero basic variables.

A transport problem is said to be a degenerate transport problem if it has a basic feasible solution with number of non zero basic variables less than $m + n - 1$.

According to Mustafit, "A degenerate basic feasible solution in a transportation problem exists if and only if some partial sum of availabilities (row) is equal to a partial sum of requirements (column)".

Initial feasible solution can be obtained by any of the following three methods:

Method I	:	Least Cost Method (or LCM)
Method II	:	North-West Corner Method (or NWCM)
Method III	:	Vogel's Approximation Method (or VAM)

Let us discuss these methods one by one as under:

METHOD I : Least Cost Method (or LCM)

The practical steps involved in the Least Cost Method are given below:

Step 1 → *Make maximum possible Allocation to the **Least Cost Cell** depending upon the demand/supply for the Column/Row containing that Cell. In case of Tie in the Least Cost Cells, make allocation to the Cell by which maximum demand or capacity is exhausted.*

↓

Step 2 → *Make allocation to the **Second Lowest Cost Cell** depending upon the remaining demand/supply for the Row/Column containing that Cell.*

↓

Step 3 → *Repeat the above Steps till all Rim Requirements are exhausted, i.e., entire demand and supply is exhausted.*

PROBLEM 5.1 [Introduction of Dummy Origin in Case of Contribution Matrix]

Find the basic feasible solution by Least Cost Method.

	W_1	W_2	W_3	W_4	*Supplies*
F_1	48	60	56	58	140
F_2	45	55	53	60	260
F_3	50	65	60	62	360
Demand	200	320	250	210	

Note: Cell entries are the unit contributions.

Solution

Step 1→ Introducing a Dummy factory with zero profit per unit as the total demand is not equal to total supply in order to make the problem balanced one.

	W_1	W_2	W_3	W_4	*Supplies*
F_1	48	60	56	58	140
F_2	45	55	53	60	260
F_3	50	65	60	62	360
F_4	0	0	0	0	220
Demand	200	320	250	210	

Step 2→ Deriving Loss Matrix by deducting each element from the maximum element (i.e. 65) in order to use minimisation technique and finding initial feasible solution by LCM.

	W_1	W_2	W_3	W_4	*Supplies*
F_1	17	5	9 [140]	7	140
F_2	20	10	12 [90]	5 [170]	260
F_3	15	0 [320]	5	3 [40]	360
F_4	65 [200]	65	65 [20]	65	220
Demand	200	320	250	210	

METHOD II : North-West Corner Method (or NWCM)

The practical steps involved in the North-West Corner Method are given below:

Step 1→ *Make maximum possible* ***allocation to the Upper-Left Corner Cell*** *(also known as North-West Corner Cell) in the First Row depending upon the availability of supply for that Row and demand requirement for the Column containing that Cell.*
Note: *Unit transportation cost is completely ignored.*

↓

Step 2→ *Move to the* ***Next Cell of the First Row*** *depending upon remaining supply for that Row and the demand requirement for the next Column. Go on till the Row total is exhausted.*

↓

Step 3→ *Move to the the next Row and make allocation to the Cell below the Cell of the preceding Row in which the last allocation was made and follow Steps 1 and 2.*

↓

Step 4→ *Follow Steps 1 to 3 till all Rim requirements are exhausted, i.e., the entire demand and supply is exhausted.*

PROBLEM 5.2 [Introduction of Dummy Origin in Case of Contribution Matrix]

Find initial feasible solution by North West Corner Method in Problem 5.1.

Solution

Initial Feasible Solution by North West Corner Method (NWCM)

	W_1	W_2	W_3	W_4	*Supplies*
F_1	17 [140]	5	9	7	140
F_2	20 [60]	10 [200]	12	5	260
F_3	15	0 [120]	5 [240]	3	360
F_4	65	65	65 [10]	65 [210]	220
Demand	200	320	250	210	

METHOD III : Vogel's Approximation Method (or VAM)

The practical steps involved in Vogel's Approximation Method (*or VAM*) are given below:

Step 1 → ***Row Difference:*** *Find the difference between Smallest and Second Smallest element of each Row, representing the Opportunity Cost of not making the allocation to the Smallest Element Cell, and write the difference on the right-hand side of the concerned Row. In case of tie between two smallest elements, the difference should be taken as zero.*

Step 2 → ***Column Difference:*** *Find the difference between Smallest and Second Smallest element of each column, representing the Opportunity Cost of not making the allocation to the Smallest Element Cell, and write the difference below the concerned Column. In case of tie between two smallest elements, the difference should be taken as zero.*

Step 3 → ***Largest Difference:*** *Mark the Largest Difference amongst all Differences by an arrow indicating the allocation to be made to the row/column having largest difference. Allocate maximum possible quantity to the Least Cost Cell of the Selected row/column depending upon the quantity available. In case of tie between the Differences, select the row or column having least cost cell. However, in case of tie even in case of Least Cost, make allocation to that Cell by which maximum requirements are exhausted.*

Step 4 → *Shade the Row/Column whose availability or requirement is exhausted so that it shall not be considered for any further allocation.*

Step 5 → *Repeat Step 1 and 4 till entire demand and supply is exhausted.*

Step 6 → *Draw the Initial Feasible Solution Table obtained after the above steps.*

PROBLEM 5.3 [Introduction of Dummy Origin in Case of Contribution Matrix]

Find initial feasible solution by VAM in Problem 5.1.

Solution

Initial Feasible Solution by Vogel's Approximation Method (VAM)

	W_1	W_2	W_3	W_4	*Supplies*	D_1	D_2	D_3	D_4	D_5
F_1	17	5	9 [140]	7	140	2	2	8	8	—
F_2	20	10	12 [50]	5 [210]	260	5	7	8	8	8
F_3	15	0 [320]	5 [40]	3	360	3	2	10	—	—
F_4	65 [200]	65	65 [20]	65	220	0	0	0	0	0
Dem.	200	320	250	210						
D_1	2	5	4	2						
D_2	2	—	4	2						
D_3	2	—	4	—						
D_4	3	—	3	—						
D_5	45	—	53	—						

INTRODUCING AN INFINITELY SMALL QUANTITY 'e' IN CASE THE TOTAL NUMBER OF ALLOCATION IS LESS THAN "M + N - 1"

PROBLEM 5.4 [Case when Total Number of Allocations < M + N - 1]

Find the initial basic feasible solution by VAM. Is the number of allocation equal to 'M + N – 1'? If no, how will you deal with this situation?

	W_1	W_2	W_3	W_4	*Supplies*
F_1	1	2	4	4	6
F_2	4	3	2	0	8
F_3	0	2	2	1	10
Demand	4	6	8	6	

Note: Cell entries are the unit transportation costs.

Solution

Initial Feasible Solution by Vogel's Approximation Method

	W_1	W_2	W_3	W_4	Supplies	D_1	D_2	D_3
F_1	1	2 [6]	4	4	6	1	1	2
F_2	4	3	2 [2]	0 [6]	8	2	1	1
F_3	0 [4]	2	2 [6]	1	10	1	2	0
Dem.	4	6	8	6				
D_1	1	0	0	1				
D_2	1	0	0	—				
D_3	—	0	0	—				

Since Allocations are 5 which is less than m + n – 1 (i.e. 4 + 3 – 1 = 6), an infinitestimally small allocation e is placed in the least cost and independent cell in such a way that no loop can be formed by the allocated cells (includes the one in which *e* to be allocated)

There are two least cost cells (1, 1) & (3, 4)

Suppose, *e* is allocated in cell (3, 4)

	W_1	W_2	W_3	W_4
F_1	1	2 [6]	4	4
F_2	4	3	2 [2]	0 [6]
F_3	0 [4]	2	2 [6]	1 [e]

Since loop can be formed after allocating '*e*' in the cell (3, 4), '*e*' should not be allocated here.

Let us allocate '*e*' in the cell (1, 1)

	W_1	W_2	W_3	W_4	Supplies
F_1	1 [e]	2 [6]	4	4	6
F_2	4	3	2 [2]	0 [6]	8
F_3	0 [4]	2	2 [6]	1	10
	4	6	8	6	

APPLICATION OF OPTIMALITY TEST

The practical steps involved in Optimality Test are given below :

Step 1 → ***U_i & V_j:*** *Compute "U_i" and "V_j" for all Rows and Columns respectively on the basis of Allocated Cells such that $C_{ij} = U_i + V_j$ after taking any U_i or $V_j = 0$, where C_{ij} = Shipping Cost per unit of Occupied Cell;*

i = Row Number;

j = Column Number;

U_i = Shipping Cost per unit of Supplying Station; and

V_j = Shipping Cost per unit of Receiving Station

Note: *While taking any U_i or $V_j = 0$, that row or column which is having maximum allocated cells, should preferably be selected.*

↓

Step 2 → ***Opportunity Cost for Unallocated Cells:*** *Compute Opportunity Cost, (say OC), for Unallocated Cells where $OC = C_{ij} - (U_{ij} + V_{ij})$.*

↓

Step 3 → ***Loop:*** *If 'OC' of each cell is either positive or zero, Initial Feasible Solution is the Optimal Solution. However, if 'OC' for any Cell is negative, Initial Feasible Solution is not optimal. In that case, Find Closed Loop (explained on page 5.9) for the Cell having negative 'OC' and transfer entire quantity from the Allocated Cell having minimum quantity, that is covered by that Loop amongst all Allocated Cells covered by that Loop, to the Unallocated Cell having negative 'OC' (the procedure to transfer the quantity has been explained on page 5.9).*

Note: *The above procedure will be followed even in case 'OC' of any Unallocated Cell is "zero" and 'OC' of other Unallocated Cells is positive to get Alternate Solution.*

↓

Step 4 → ***Infinitely Small Quantity 'e':*** *See whether total number of allocated cells after Step 3 is equal to "m + n −1"; if yes, go to step 5, if not introduce an infinitely small quantity 'e' to the Least Cost Independent Cell, i.e., for which no Loop can be formed.*

Note: *Introduce as many number of 'e' as the total number of Allocated Cells falls below "m + n − 1".*

↓

Step 5 → *Repeat Steps 1 to 4 till 'OC' of all Unallocated Cells is positive.*

PROBLEM 5.5 [When the Number of Allocation is Less Than 'm + n - 1']

Test the following initial solution for optimality

	W_1	W_2	W_3	W_4	Supplies
F_1	1 [e]	2 [6]	4	4	6
F_2	4	3	2 [2]	0 [6]	8
F_3	0 [4]	2	2 [6]	1	10
Demand	4	6	8	6	

Note: Cell entries are transportation costs per unit.

Solution

Step 1 → : *Calculation of U_i and V_j on the basis of costs of allocated cells*

	W_1	W_2	W_3	W_4	U_i
F_1	1	2			$U_0 = 0$
F_2			2	0	$U_1 = -1$
F_3	0		2		$U_2 = -1$
V_j	$V_0 = 1$	$V_1 = 2$	$V_2 = 3$	$V_3 = 1$	

Step 2 → C_{ij} *Matrix of Costs for unallocated cells*

	W_1	W_2	W_3	W_4
F_1			4	4
F_2	4	3		
F_3		2		1

Step 3 → $U_i + V_j$ *Matrix for unallocated Cells*

	W_1	W_2	W_3	W_4
F_1			3	1
F_2	0	1		
F_3		1		0

Step 4 → Δ_{ij} *Matrix where* $\Delta_{ij} = C_{ij} - (U_i + V_j)$

	W_1	W_2	W_3	W_4
F_1			1	3
F_2	4	2		
F_3		1		1

Step 5 → *Since all Δ_{ij} are positive the above solution is optimal. The optimal solution is given below:*

Factory	*Warehouse*	*Qty.*	*Cost per Unit*	*Total cost*
F_1	W_3	6	2	12
F_2	W_3	2	2	4
F_2	W_4	6	0	0
F_3	W_1	4	0	0
F_3	W_3	6	2	12
				28

LOOPING AND REALLOCATION MATRIX

The practical steps involved in the Looping are given below:

Step 1 → ***Most Negative Opportunity Cost Cell:*** *Put a 'Tick' mark in the most negative Opportunity Cost Cell.*
In case of tie, any one may be selected arbitraily, preferably select that one with which corners points are minimum.

↓

Step 2 → ***Draw Loop:*** *Draw at least four lines in the form of a rectangle covering at least four Cells out of which One Cell will be the ticked Cell and the rest will be the Allocated Cells. This is called 'Loop'. In other words all the corners (except the starting corner which lies in most negative unallocated cell) of the Loop will lie in the allocated cells.*

↓

Step 3 → ***Putting '+' & '–' Signs:*** *Put '+' sign on ticked cell and '–' sign on the next allocated corner cell covered by the loop and '+' sign on the next to next allocated corner cell covered by the loop and so on.*
In other words, '+' or '–' sign should be put in each allocated corner cell in alternative order.

↓

Step 4 → ***Transfer of Entire Quantity:*** *Transfer the entire quantity from the Least Allocated Cell (i.e. cell having the least quantity) which has '–', to the Cells containing '+' and deduct the transferred quantity from the other cell containing '–'.*
Note: *A Loop can even contain more than Four Cells; however, Number will always remain 'even'. In that case, one Cell will be the Unallocated Cell having most negative Opportunity Cost and the Others will be the Allocated Cells.*

PROBLEM 5.6 [When there is a Tie between the Two Most Negative Cells]

Prepare a reallocation matrix from the following information:

Initial Allocation Matrix

	1	2	3	4
A	3		6	1
B		4		
C		6		
D				5
E	10	e		

Δ_{ij} (Cell Evaluation) Matrix

	1	2	3	4
A		16		
B	20		35	–8
C	40		20	7
D	13	18	33	
E			10	–8

Solution

Step 1 →Ticking one of the most negative cells (B, 4) and (E, 4) of cell evaluation matrix from where looping is to be started and putting θ quantity therein and drawing lines in such a way that turning point of the line is in the allocated cells. Let us first tick (B, 4) cell.

	1	2	3	4
A	3+		6	1–
B		4–		+
C		6		
D				5
E	10–	e+		

Step 2 → Calculating new quantity of each corner of the loop after subtracting from and adding to 1 quantity (being the least one in negative corner cells) to each of the loop corner quantity.

Corner (B, 4) = 0 + 1 = 0
Corner (A, 4) = 1 – 1 = 0
Corner (A, 1) = 3 + 1 = 4
Corner (E, 1) = 10 – 1= 9
Corner (E, 2) = e + 1 = 1
Corner (B, 2) = 4 – 1 = 3

Step 3 → Now Reallocation Matrix becomes as under:

	1	2	3	4
A	4		6	
B		3		1
C		6		
D				5
E	9	1		

Alternative Solution: Let us tick (E, 4) cell.

Step 1 → Ticking the another most negative cell (E, 4) of cell evaluation matrix from where looping is to be started and putting θ quantity therein and drawing lines in such a way that turning point of the line is in the allocated cells.

	1	*2*	*3*	*4*
A	3+		6	1−
B		4		
C		6		
D				5
E	10−	e		θ +

Step 2 → Calculating new quantity of each corner of the loop after subtracting from and adding to 1 quantity (being the least one in negative corner cells) to each of the loop corner quantity.

Corner (E, 4) = 0 + 1 = 0
Corner (A, 4) = 1 − 1 = 0
Corner (A, 1) = 3 + 1 = 4
Corner (E, 1) = 10 − 1 = 9

Step 3 → Now Reallocation Matrix becomes as under:

	1	*2*	*3*	*4*
A	4		6	
B		4		
C		6		
D				5
E	9	e		1

PROBLEM 5.7 [Use of High Cost Where there is Restriction on Transfer]

Solve the following transportation problem:

GODOWNS

		1	*2*	*3*	*4*	*5*	*6*	*Stock Available*
FACTORY	1	7	5	7	7	5	3	60
	2	9	11	6	11	—	5	20
	3	11	10	6	2	2	8	90
	4	9	10	9	6	9	12	50
Demand		60	20	40	20	40	40	

Note: It is not possible to transport any quantity from factory 2 to godown 5.
Required: State whether the solution derived by you is unique.

Solution

Step 1 → Finding Initial Feasible Solution by following the Vogel's Approximation Method (or VAM).

Factory	*Godowns* 1	2	3	4	5	6	*Availability*	*Diff.*
1	7	5 (20)	7	7	5	3 (40)	60/40/0	2/4/0
2	9 (10)	11	6 (10)	11	∞	5	20/10/0	1/3
3	11	10	6 (30)	2 (20)	2 (40)	8	90/70/30/0	0/4/2/5
4	9 (50)	10	9	6	9	12	50/0	3/0
Demand	60/50/0	20/0	40/10/0	20/0	40/0	40/0		
Diff.	2	5	0/1	4	3	2		

Step 2 → Since the total number of allocations is less than "M + N – 1" allocations, let us introduce an infinitely small quantity 'e' to the least cost independent cell to make the total number of allocations equal to "M + N – 1" allocations.

Let us calculate "U_i's" and "V_j's" for all rows and columns respectively on the basis of allocated cells such that $C_{ij} = U_i + V_j$ assuming $U_1 = 0$,

Let us calculate Δ_{ij} (Opportunity Cost), for unallocated cells where $\Delta_{ij} = C_{ij} - (U_{ij} + V_{ij})$.

U_i & V_j Matrix

						U_i
	5				3	–2
9		6			5 (e)	0
		6	2	2		0
9						0
V_j 9	7	6	2	2	5	

C_{ij} Matrix for Unallocated Cells

7		7	7	5	
	11		11	∞	
11	10				8
	10	9	6	9	12

$U_i + V_j$ Matrix for Unallocated cells

						U_i
7		4	0	0		-2
	7		2			0
9	7				5	0
	7	6	2	2	5	0
V_j 9	7	6	2	2	5	

$\Delta_{ij} = C_{ij} - (U_i + V_j)$ Matrix

0		3	7	5	
	4		9		
2	3				3
	3	3	4	7	7

Step 3 → Since all Δ_{ij} are positive, the above solution is optimal. The optimal solution is given below:

Factory	to Godown	Unit	Cost	Value (Rs.)
1	2	20	5	100
1	6	40	3	120
2	1	10	9	90
2	3	10	6	60
3	3	30	6	180
3	4	20	2	40
3	5	40	2	80
4	1	50	9	450
			Total cost Rs.	1120

Note: Since one of Δ_{ij} is zero, the above solution is not unique. Hence an alternative solution exists. The alternative solution can be found by taking any cell with zero Δ_{ij} as the basic cell.

Students may find that the alternate solution is as given below:

Factory	to Godown	Unit	Cost	Value (Rs.)
1	1	10	7	70
1	2	20	5	100
1	6	30	3	90
2	3	10	6	60
2	6	10	5	50
3	3	30	6	180
3	5	40	2	80
3	4	20	2	40
4	1	50	9	450
			Total Cost	Rs. 1120

PROBLEM 5.8

Consider the following data for the transportation problem:

Factory	Destination			Supply to be exhausted
	(1)	(2)	(3)	
A	5	1	7	10
B	6	4	6	80
C	3	2	5	15
Demand	75	20	50	

Since there is not enough supply, some of the demands at the three destinations may not be satisfied. For the unsatisfied demands, let the penalty costs be rupees 1, 2 and 3 for destinations (1), (2) and (3) respectively.

Find the optimal allocation that minimizes the transportation and penalty costs

Solution

Step 1 → *Formulating the Transportation Problem.*

Since demand (= 75 + 20 + 50 = 145) is greater than supply (= 10 + 80 + 15 = 105) by 40 units, the given problem is an unbalanced one. We introduce a dummy factory with a supply of 40 units. It is given that for the unsatisfied demands, the penalty cost is rupees 1, 2 and 3 for destinations (1), (2) and (3) respectively. Hence, the transportation problem becomes:

Factory	Destination (1)	(2)	(3)	Supply to be exhausted
A	5	1	7	10
B	6	4	6	80
C	3	2	5	15
Dummy	1	2	3	40
Demand	75	20	50	

Step 2 → Finding Initial Feasible Solution by following the Vogel's Approximation Method (or VAM).

Factory	Destination (1)	(2)	(3)	Supply	Differences
A	5	1 [10]	7	10/0	4 - -
B	6 [20]	4 [10]	6 [50]	80/70/50/0	2 2 2
C	3 [15]	2	5	15/0	1 1 1
Dummy	1 [40]	2	3	40/0	11 -
Demand	75/35/20/0	20/10/0	50/0		
Difference	2 2 3	1 0 2	2 2 1		

Step 3 → ***Optimality Test:*** Since the total number of allocations is equal to "M+N–1" allocations, the initial solution is straight away tested for optimality.

Let us calculate "Ui's" and "Vj's" for all rows and columns respectively on the basis of allocated cells such that $C_{ij} = U_i + V_j$ assuming $U_1 = 0$,

Let us calculate Δ_{ij} (Opportunity Cost), for unallocated cells where $\Delta_{ij} = C_{ij} - (U_{ij} + V_{ij})$.

U_i & V_j Matrix

			U_i
	1		–3
6	4	6	0
3			–3
1			–5
V_j 6	4	6	

C_{ij} Matrix for Unallocated Cells

5		7
	2	5
	2	3

$U_i + V_j$ Matrix of unallocated cells U_i

			U_i
3		3	–3
			0
	1	3	–3
	–1	1	–5
V_j	6	4	6

$\Delta_{ij} = C_{ij} - (U_i + V_j)$ Matrix

2		4
	1	2
	3	2

Step 4 → Since all Δ_{ij} are positive, the above solution is optimal. The optimal solution is given below:

Factory	*Destination*	*Units*	*Cost*	*Total Cost*	
A	(2)	10	Re 1	Rs. 10	Transportation cost
B	(1)	20	Rs. 6	Rs. 120	
B	(2)	10	Rs. 4	Rs. 40	
B	(3)	50	Rs. 6	Rs. 300	
C	(1)	15	Rs. 3	Rs. 45	
Dummy	(1)	40	Re 1	Rs. 40	Penalty cost
				Rs. 555	

PROBLEM 5.9 [How to deal with cost in fractions and fixed price for destinations]

A company produces a small component for all industrial products and distributes it to five wholesalers at a fixed price of Rs.2.50 per unit. Sales forecasts indicate that monthly deliveries will be 3,000, 3,000, 10,000, 5,000 and 4,000 units to wholesalers 1, 2, 3, 4 and 5 respectively. The monthly production capabilities are 5,000, 10,000, 12,500 at plants 1, 2 and 3 respectively. The direct costs of production of each unit are Rs. 1.00, Re. 0.90 and Re. 0.80 at plants 1, 2 and 3 respectively. The transportation costs of shipping a unit from a plant to a wholesaler are given below:

		Wholesaler				
		1	*2*	*3*	*4*	*5*
	1	0.05	0.07	0.10	0.15	0.15
Plant	2	0.08	0.06	0.09	0.12	0.14
	3	0.10	0.09	0.08	0.10	0.15

Find how many components each plant supplies to each wholesaler in order to maximize profit.

Solution

Since the total capacity of plants is more than the supply to the wholesalers by a quantity 27500 units – 25000 units = 2500 units, so the problem is an unbalanced transportation problem. Introduce a dummy wholesaler supplying 2500 units such that the transportation costs plus the production cost from various plants to this destination are assumed to be zero. Also, the direct costs of production of each unit are given as Re.1, Re.0.90 and Re.0.80 at plants 1, 2 and 3 respectively. The modified balanced transportation problem is now obtained as follows:

		1	*2*	*3*	*4*	*5*	*Dummy*	*Capacity*
	1	1.05	1.07	1.10	1.15	1.15	0	5000
Plant	2	0.98	0.96	0.99	1.02	1.04	0	10000
	3	0.90	0.89	0.88	0.90	0.95	0	12500
		3000	3000	10000	5000	4000	2500	

For simplicity in computations multiply all direct cost *plus* transportation costs in the above table by 100, and consider 100 units = 1 unit of items. Hence, the simplified cost table becomes:

		1	*2*	*3*	*4*	*5*	*Dummy*	*Capacity*
	1	105	107	110	115	115	0	50
Plant	2	98	96	99	102	104	0	100
	3	90	89	88	90	95	0	125
Supply		30	30	100	50	40	25	3

Let us now apply Vogel's Approximation method to find the initial basic feasible solution.

	Wholesaler							
Plant	*1*	*2*	*3*	*4*	*5*	*Dummy*	*Capacity*	*Difference*
1	[25] 105	107	110	115	115	[25] 0	50/25/0	105/2/2/2/5/10
2	[5] 98	[30] 96	[25] 99	102	[40] 104	0	100/70/4/5/5	96/2/2/2/1/6
3	90	89	[75] 88	[50] 90	95	0	125/75/0	88/1/–
Supply	30/25/0	30/0	100/25/0	50/0	40/0	25/0		

Diff.						
	8	7	11	12	9	0
	8	7	11	12	9	–
	8	7	11	–	9	–
	7	11	11	–	11	–
	7	–	11		11	

The initial basic feasible solution as obtained by VAM is given below:

	Wholesaler						
Plant	*1*	*2*	*3*	*4*	*5*	*Capacity*	*Difference*
1	[25] 105	107	110	115	115	25 0	50
2	[5] 98	[30] 96	[25] 99	120	[40] 104	0	100
3	99	98	[75] 88	[50] 90	95	0	120
Supply		30	30	100	50	40	25

We now apply the optimally test to find whether the initial solution found above is optimal or not. The number of allocations is 8 which is equal to the required m + n – 1 (=8) allocations. Also, these allocations are independent. Hence, both the conditions of optimality test are satisfied.

Let us now introduce u_i's, (1 = 1, 2, 3) and v_j's, (j = 1, 2, 3, ... 6) such that $\Delta_{ij} = c_{ij} - (u_i + v_j)$ for allocated cells. We assume that $u_2 = 0$ and remaining u_i's, v_js and Δ_{ij}'s are calculated as below:

Plant	Wholesaler 1	2	3	4	5	Dummy	u_i's
1	[25] 105	4 107	4 110	7 115	4 115	[25] 0	7
2	[5] 98	[30] 96	[25] 99	[1] 102	[40] 104	7 0	0
3	3 90	4 89	[75] 88	[50] 90	2 95	18 0	−11
v_j	98	96	99	101	104	−7	

Since all Δ_{ij}'s for non-basic cells are positive, therefore, the solution obtained above is an optimal one. The allocation of plant to wholesaler and their (transportation cost + direct production cost) is given below:

Plant	Warehouse	No. of units	Cost per unit (Rs.)	Total cost Rs.
1 →	1	2500	1.05	2625
2 →	1	500	0.98	490
2 →	2	3000	0.96	2880
2 →	3	2500	0.99	2475
2 →	5	4000	0.104	4160
3 →	3	7500	0.88	6600
3 →	4	5000	0.90	4500
				23730

Since the company distributes the component at a fixed price of Rs.2.50 per unit to all five wholesalers, the profit is given by

Profit = Rs. 2.50 × 22500 – Rs. 23,730 = Rs. 56,250 – Rs. 23,730 = Rs. 32,520

(**Note:** The problem has been solved using the cost matrix. However, it can be solved using the profit matrix first and then converting it to minimization problem).

PROBLEM 5.10

The following table shows all the necessary information on the available supply to each warehouse, the requirement of each market and the unit transportation cost from each warehouse to each market:

		Market I	II	III	IV	Supply
Warehouse	A	5	2	4	3	22
	B	4	8	1	6	15
	C	4	6	7	5	8
Requirement		7	12	17	9	

The shipping clerk has worked out the following schedule from his experience:

12 Units from A to II

1 Unit from A to III

9 Units from A to IV

15 Units from B to III

7 Units from C to I and

1 Unit from C to III.

You are required to answer the following:

(i) Check and see if the clerk has the optimal schedule;

(ii) Find the optimal schedule and minimum total shipping cost; and

(iii) If the clerk is approached by a carrier of route C to II, who offers to reduce his rate in the hope of getting some business, by how much should the rate be reduced before the clerk should consider giving him an order?

Solution

(i) The shipping clerk has worked out the following schedule as initial solution:

		Market				
		I	*II*	*III*	*IV*	*Supply*
	A	5	12 2	1 4	9 3	22
Warehouse	B	4	8	15 1	6	15
	C	7 4	6	1 7	5	8
Requirement		7	12	17	9	

The initial solution is tested for optimality. The total number of independent allocations is 6 which is equal to the desired (m + n – 1) allocations. We introduce u_i's (I = 1, 2, 3) and v_j's (j = 1, 2, 3, 4) such that $\Delta_{ij} = c_{ij} - (u_i + v_j)$. Let us assume $u_i = 0$, remaining u_1's and v_1's are calculated as below:

	I	II	III	IV	u_i
A	4	12	1 +θ	9 –θ	0
	5	2	4	3	
B	6	9	15	6	–3
	4	8	1	6	
C	7	1	1 –θ	–1 θ	3
	4	6	7	5	
v_j	1	2	4	3	

Since one of the Δ_{ij}'s is negative, the schedule worked out by the clerk is not the optimal solution.

(ii) Introduce in the cell with -ve Δ_{ij} [i.e. the cell (C, IV)], an assignment θ. The value of θ and the reallocated solution as obtained from above is given below. The value of u_i's, v_j's are also calculated.

$$\theta = \min(9 - \theta = 0 \;\&\; 1 - \theta = 0) = 1$$

	I	II	III	IV	u_i
A	3	12	2	8	0
	5	2	4	3	
B	5	9	15	6	–3
	4	8	1	6	
C	7	2	1	1	2
	4	6	7	5	
v_j	2	2	4	3	

Since all Δ_{ij}'s for non basic cells are positive, the solution as calculated in the above table is optimal solution. The supply of units from each warehouse to markets, along with the transportation cost is given below:

Warehouse	*Market*	*Units unit(Rs.)*	*Cost per Cost(Rs.)*	*Total*
A	II	12	2	24
A	III	2	4	8
A	IV	8	3	24
B	III	15	1	15
C	I	7	4	28
C	IV	1	5	5
			Minimum Total Shipping Cost	= 104

(iii) If the clerk wants to consider the carrier of route C to II for giving an order, then his transportation cost must be less than the cost of carrier of routes C to I and C to IV i.e. his transportation cost should be at the most Rs. 3 per unit. If the carrier C to II brings down his cost to Rs. 3, he will get an order for 1 unit, and the schedule will be:

Warehouse	*Market*	*Units unit(Rs.)*	*Cost per Cost(Rs.)*	*Total*
A	II	11	2	22
A	III	2	4	8
A	IV	9	3	27
B	III	15	1	15
C	I	7	4	28
C	II	1	3	3
			Minimum Total Shipping Cost	= 103

and the Total Shipping Cost will be Rs. 103

PROBLEM 5.11

A particular product is manufactured in factories A, B, C and D; and is sold at centres 1, 2 and 3. The cost in Rs. of product per unit and capacity in kg per unit time of each plant is given below:

Factory	*Cost (Rs.) per unit*	*Capacity (kg) per unit*
A	12	100
B	15	20
C	11	60
D	13	80

The sale price in Rs. per unit and the demand in kg per unit time are as follows:

Sales centre	*Sale Price (Rs.) per unit*	*Demand (kg) per unit*
1	15	120
2	14	140
3	16	60

Required: Find the optimal sales distribution.

Solution

Step 1 → Deriving profit matrix by equation (i.e. Selling Price – Cost) and Introducing a Dummy factory with zero profit per unit as the total demand is not equal to total supply in order to make the problem balanced one.

Factory	*Sales Centres*			*Capacity (kg) per unit*
	1	*2*	*3*	
A	3	2	4	100
B	0	–1	1	20
C	4	3	5	60
D	2	1	3	80
Dummy	0	0	0	60
Demand (kg)	120	140	60	320

Step 2 → Deriving Loss Matrix by deducting each element from the maximum element (i.e. 5) in order to use minimisation technique and Finding Initial Feasible Solution by VAM.

Factory	*Sales Centre*			*Capacity*	*Difference*
	1	*2*	*3*		
A	2 [100]	3	1	100/0	1 1 -
B	5	6 [20]	4	20/0	1 1 1
C	1	2	0 [60]	60/0	1 - -
D	3 [20]	4 [60]	2	80/60/0	1 1 1
Dummy	5	5 [60]	5	60/0	0 0 0
Demand	120/20/0	140/120/60/0	60/0		
Difference	1	1	1		
	1	1	—		
	2	1	—		

Step 3 → Since the total number of allocations is less than "M + N – 1" allocations, let us introduce an infinitely small quantity 'e' to the least cost independent cell to make the total number of allocations equal to "M + N – 1" allocations.

Let us calculate "U_i's" and "V_j's" for all rows and columns respectively on the basis of allocated cells such that $C_{ij} = U_i + V_j$ assuming $U_1 = 0$,

Let us calculate Δ_{ij} (Opportunity Cost), for unallocated cells where $\Delta_{ij} = C_{ij} - (U_i + V_{ij})$.

U_i & V_j Matrix

			U_i
2		e 1	3
	6		6
		0	2
3	4		4
	5		5
V_j: –1	0	–2	

C_{ij} Matrix for Unallocated cells

	3	
5		4
1	2	
		2
5		5

$U_i + V_j$ Matrix

			U_i
	3		3
5		4	6
1	2		2
		2	4
4		3	5
V_j: –1	0	–2	

$\Delta_{ij} = C_{ij} - (U_i + V_j)$ Matrix

	0	
0		0
0	0	
		0
1		2

Step 4 → Since all Δ_{ij} are positive, the above solution is optimal. The optimal solution is given below:

From Factory	*To Sales Centre*	*Quantity*	*Profit per unit (Rs.)*	*Total Profit (Rs.)*
A	1	100	3	300
B	2	20	–1	–20
C	3	60	5	300
D	1	20	2	40
D	2	60	1	60
Dummy	2	60	0	0
			Total Profit =	680

Note: *Since some of Δ_{ij} are zero, the above solution is not unique. Hence an alternative solution exists. The alternative solution can be found by taking any cell with zero Δ_{ij} as the basic cell.*

PROBLEM 5.12

A company has four factories situated in four different locations in the country and four sales agencies located in four other locations in the country. The cost of production (Rs. per unit), the sale price (Rs. per unit), shipping cost (Rs. per unit) in the cells of matrix, monthly capacities and monthly requirements are given below:

Factory	*Sales Agency*				*Monthly Capacity (Units)*	*Cost of Production*
	1	*2*	*3*	*4*		
A	7	5	6	4	10	10
B	3	5	4	2	15	15
C	4	6	4	5	20	16
D	8	7	6	5	15	15
Monthly Requirements (Units)	8	12	18	22		
Sales Price	20	22	25	18		

Find the monthly production and distribution schedule which will maximize profit.

Solution

Step 1 →Deriving Profit Matrix below by equation:

Profit = Sales Price − Cost of Production − Shipping Cost

Factory	*Sales Agency*				*Monthly Capacity (units)*
	1	*2*	*3*	*4*	
A	3	7	9	4	10
B	2	2	6	1	15
C	0	0	5	−3	20
D	−3	0	4	−2	15
Monthly Requirements	8	12	18	22	

Step 2 → Deriving Loss Matrix by deducting each element from the maximum element (i.e. 9) in order to use minimisation technique and Finding Initial Feasible Solution VAM.

(Allocations shown in brackets.)

Factory	*Sales Agency*				*Monthly Capacity*	*Difference*
	1	2	3	4		
A	6	2 [10]	0	5	10/0	2/3-
B	7	7	3	8 [15]	15/0	4/0/0-
C	9 [2]	9	4 [18]	12	20/2/0	5/0/0/0
D	12 [6]	9 [2]	5	11 [7]	15/13/6/0	4/2/2/2
Monthly Requirement	8/6/0	12/2/0	18/0	22/7		
Difference	1/2/2/3	5/2/2/0	3 - - -	3/4/4/1		

Step 3 → Since the total number of allocations is equal to "M + N – 1" allocations, the initial solution is straight away tested for optimality.

Let us calculate "U_i's" and "V_j's" for all rows and columns respectively on the basis of allocated cells such that $C_{ij} = U_i + V_j$ assuming $U_3 = 0$,

Let us calculate Δ_{ij} (Opportunity Cost), for unallocated cells where $\Delta_{ij} = C_{ij} - (U_{ij} + V_{ij})$.

U_i & V_j Matrix

				U_i
	2			–7
			8	–3
9		4		–3
12	9		11	0
V_j: 12	9	7	11	

C_{ij} Matrix for Unallocated cells

6		0	5
7	7	3	
	9		12
		5	

$U_i + V_j$ Matrix

				U_i
5		0	4	–7
9	6	4		–3
	6		8	–3
		7		0
V_j: 12	9	7	11	

$\Delta_{ij} = C_{ij} - (U_i + V_j)$ Matrix

1		0	1
–2	5	–1	
	3		4
		–2	

Step 4 → Since all Δ_{ij} are not positive, the above solution is not optimal. Let us place a small allocation θ in the cell with most negative Δ_{ij} and form a loop including this cell and test the solution for optimality. Next improved solution as obtained from above is shown below which is tested for optimality. The value of "U_i's", "V_j's" and Δ_{ij} are also calculated.

Looping Matrix

	10		
			15
2+		18–	
–6	2	θ +	

Reallocation Matrix

	10		
			15
8		12	
θ	2	6	7

U_i & V_j Matrix

				U_i
	2			–7
			8	–3
9		4		–1
	9	5	11	0
V_j: 10	9	5	11	

C_{ij} Matrix for Unallocated cells

6		0	5
7	7	3	
	9		12
12			

$U_i + V_j$ Matrix

				U_i
3		−2	4	−7
7	6	2		−3
	8		10	−1
10				0
V_j: 10	9	5	11	

$\Delta_{ij} = C_{ij} - (U_i + V_j)$ Matrix

3		2	1
	0	1	1
	1		2
	2		

Step 5 → Since all Δ_{ij} are positive, the above solution is optimal. The optimal solution is given below:

Factory	*Sales Agency*	*Profit*
A	2	10 x Rs 7 = Rs. 70
B	4	15 x Rs 1 = Rs. 15
C	1	8 x Rs 0 = Rs. 0
C	3	12 x Rs 5 = Rs. 60
D	2	2 x Rs 0 = Rs. 0
D	3	6 x Rs 4 = Rs. 24
D	4	7 x Rs −2 = Rs. −14
	Total	= Rs. 155

Note: Since one of Δ_{ij} is zero, the above solution is not unique. Hence an alternative solution exists. The alternative solution can be found by taking cell with zero Δ_{ij} as the basic cell.

PROBLEM 5.13

ABC Enterprises is having three plants manufacturing dry-cells, located at different locations. Production cost differs from plant to plant. There are five sales offices of the company located in different regions of the country. The sales prices can differ from region to region. The shipping cost from each plant to each sales office and other data are given by following table:

Production Data Table

Production cost per unit	*Max. Capacity in No. of units*	*Plant No.*
20	150	1
22	200	2
18	125	3

Shipping Costs Table

	Sales Office 1	*Sales Office 2*	*Sales Office 3*	*Sales Office 4*	*Sales Office 5*
Plant 1	1	1	5	9	4
Plant 2	9	7	8	3	6
Plant 3	4	5	3	2	7

Demand & Sales Prices

	Sales Office 1	Sales Office 2	Sales Office 3	Sales Office 4	Sales Office 5
Demand	80	100	75	45	125
Sales Price	30	32	31	34	29

Find the production and distribution schedule most profitable to the company.

Solution

Step 1 → Deriving the Profit Matrix by equation (i.e. Profit = Selling Price – Cost of Production – Shipping Cost) and Introducing a Dummy Sales Office with zero profit per unit as the total demand is not equal to total supply in order to make the problem balanced one.

9	11	6	5	5	0	150
–1	3	1	9	1	0	200
8	9	10	14	4	0	125
80	100	75	45	125	50	475

Step 2 → Deriving Loss Matrix by deducting each element from the maximum element (i.e. 14) in order to use minimisation technique and finding the initial feasible solution by VAM.

Plant / *Sales Centre*

	1	2	3	4	5	6	*Capacity*	*Difference*
1	5 (50)	3 (100)	8	9	9	14	150	2 2 2 4 - -
2	15	11	13	5 (45)	13 (105)	14 (50)	200	6 2 2 2 1 1
3	6 (30)	5	4 (75)	0	10 (20)	14	125	1 1 1 4 4 4
Demand	80	100	75	45	125	50		
Diff.	1	2	4	5	1	0		
	1	2	4	-	1	0		
	1	2	-	-	1	0		
	1	-	-	-	1	0		
	9	-	-	-	3	0		
	-	-	-	-	3	0		

Step 3 → Since the total number of allocations is equal to "M + N – 1" allocations, the initial solution is straightaway tested for optimality.

Let us calculate "U_i's" and "V_j's" for all rows and columns respectively on the basis of allocated cells such that $C_{ij} = U_i + V_j$ assuming $U_3 = 0$,

Let us calculate Δ_{ij} (Opportunity Cost), for unallocated cells where $\Delta_{ij} = C_{ij} - (U_{ij} + V_{ij})$.

U_i & V_j Matrix

						U_i
5	3					–4
			5	13	14	0
6		4		10		–3
9	7	7	5	13	14	V_j

C_{ij} Matrix for Unallocated cells

		8	9	9	14
15	11	13			
	5		0		14

$U_i + V_j$ Matrix / U_i

						U_i
		3	1	9	10	−4
9	7	7				0
	4		2		11	−3
V_j: 9	7	7	5	13	14	

$\Delta_{ij} = C_{ij} - (U_i + V_j)$ Matrix

		5	8	0	4
6	4	6			
	1		-2		3

Step 4 → Since all Δ_{ij} are not positive, the above solution is not optimal. Let us place a small allocation θ in the cell with most negative Δ_{ij} and form a loop including this cell and test the solution for optimality. Next improved solution as obtained from above is shown below which is tested for optimality. The value of "U_i's", "V_j's" and Δ_{ij} are also calculated.

Looping Matrix

50	100				
			45−	105+	50
30		75	θ+	20−	

Reallocation Matrix

50	100				
			25	125	50
30		75	20		

U_i & V_j Matrix

						U_i
5	3					−6
			5	13	14	0
6		4	0			−5
V_j: 11	9	9	5	13	14	

C_{ij} Matrix for Unallocated cells

		8	9	9	14
15	11	13			
	5			10	14

$U_i + V_j$ Matrix

						U_i
		3	−1	7	8	−6
11	9	9				0
	4			8	9	−5
V_j: 11	9	9	5	13	14	

$\Delta_{ij} = C_{ij} - (U_i + V_j)$ Matrix

		5	10	2	6
4	2	4			
	1			2	5

Step 5 → Since all Δ_{ij} are positive, the above solution is optimal. The optimal solution is given below:

Plant	*Sales Office*	*Units*	*Profit per unit*	*Profit*
1	1	50	9	450
1	2	100	11	1100
2	4	25	9	225
2	5	125	1	125
2	Dummy	50	0	0
3	1	30	8	240
3	3	75	10	750
3	4	20	14	280
			Total	3,170

PROBLEM 5.14 [Maximizing Billing of Assignment]

A leading firm has three auditors. Each auditor can work upto 160 hours during the next month, during which time three projects must be completed. Project 1 will take 130 hours, project 2 will take 140 hours, the project 3 will take 160 hours. The amount per hour that can be billed for assigning each auditor to each project is given below:

Auditor	*Project*		
	1 *Rs.*	*2* *Rs.*	*3* *Rs.*
1	1,200	1,500	1,900
2	1,400	1,300	1,200
3	1,600	1,400	1,500

Required: Formulate this as a transportation problem and find the optimal solution. Also find out the maximum total billings during the next month.

Solution

Step 1 → Introducing a Dummy Project with zero amount per unit as the total hours required is not equal to total hours available in order to make the problem balanced one and divide by Rupees by 100 to ease computations.

Auditor	*Project*			*Dummy*	*Time*
	1 *Rs.*	*2* *Rs.*	*3* *Rs.*	*Rs.*	*available (hours)*
1	12	15	19	0	160
2	14	13	12	0	160
3	16	14	15	0	160
Time required (hrs)	130	140	160	50	480

Step 2 → Deriving Loss Matrix by deducting each element from the maximum element (i.e. 19) in order to use minimisation technique and Finding Initial Feasible Solution VAM.

Auditor	*Project*			*Dummy*	*Time available*	*Difference*
	1	*2*	*3*			
1	7	4	0 (160)	19	160/0	4/-/-/-
2	5	6 (110)	7	19 (50)	160/50/0	1/1/13/13
3	3 (130)	5 (30)	4	19	160/30/0	1/2/14/-
Time Required	130/0	140/110/0	160/0	50/0		
Difference	2/2/-/-	1/1/1/1	4/-/-	0/0/0		

Step 3 → Since the total number of allocations is less than "M + N – 1" allocations, let us introduce an infinitely small quantity 'e' to the least cost independent cell to make the total number of allocations equal to "M + N – 1" allocations.

Let us calculate "U_i's" and "V_j's" for all rows and columns respectively on the basis of allocated cells such that $C_{ij} = U_i + V_j$ assuming $U_1 = 0$,

Let us calculate Δ_{ij} (Opportunity Cost), for unallocated cells where $\Delta_{ij} = C_{ij} - (U_{ij} + V_{ij})$.

U_i & V_j Matrix

				U_i
		0	19	−4
	6		19	1
		e		
3	5	4		0
V_j: 3	5	4	18	

C_{ij} Matrix for Unallocated cells

7	4		19
5		7	
			19

$U_i + V_j$ Matrix

-1	1		14	−4
4		5		1
			18	0
3	5	4	18	

$\Delta_{ij} = C_{ij} - (U_i + V_j)$ Matrix

8	3		5
1		2	
			1

Step 4 → Since all Δ_{ij} are positive, the above solution is optimal. The optimal solution is given below:

Auditor	*Project*	*Billing amount (Rs.)*
1	3	160 × Rs. 1900 = 3,04,000
2	2	110 × Rs. 1300 = 1,43,000
3	1	130 × Rs. 1600 = 2,08,000
3	2	30 × Rs. 1400 = 42,000
	Total billing	= 6,07,000

PROBLEM 5.15

A company has four factories F_1, F_2, F_3 and F_4 manufacturing the same product. Production and raw material costs differ from factory to factory, and are given in the following table in the first two rows. The transportation costs from the factories to sales depots S_1, S_2, S_3 are also given.

The last two columns in the table give the sale price and the total requirement at each depot. The production capacity of each factory is given in the last row.

		F_1	F_2	F_3	F_4	Sales Price per unit	Requirements in units
Production cost/unit		15	18	14	13		
Raw material cost/unit		10	9	12	9		
Transportation Cost per unit :	S_1	3	9	5	4	34	80
	S_2	1	7	4	5	32	120
	S_3	5	8	3	6	31	150
		10	150	50	100		

Determine the most profitable production and distribution schedule and the corresponding profit. The surplus production should be taken to yield zero profit.

Solution

Step 1 → Deriving the profit matrix below by the following equation:

Profit = Sales Price − Product Cost − Raw Material Cost − Transportation Cost.

	F_1	F_2	F_3	F_4	
S_1	6	−2	3	8	80
S_2	6	−2	2	5	120
S_3	1	−4	2	3	150
	10	150	50	100	

Step 2 → Introducing a Dummy factory with zero profit per unit as the total demand is not equal to total supply in order to make the problem balanced one.

	F_1	F_2	F_3	F_4	*Dummy*	
S_1	6	−2	3	8	0	80
S_2	6	−2	2	5	0	120
S_3	1	-4	2	3	0	150
	10	150	50	100	40	

Step 3 → Deriving Loss Matrix by deducting each element from the maximum element (i.e. 8) in order to use minimisation technique.

	F_1	F_2	F_3	F_4	*Dummy*	
S_1	2	10	5	0	8	80
S_2	2	10	6	3	8	120
S_3	7	12	6	5	8	150
	10	150	50	100	40	

Step 4 → Finding Initial Feasible Solution by following the Vogel's Approximation Method (or VAM).

							Diff
	2	10	5	0 [80]	8	80/0	2
	2 [10]	10 [40]	6 [50]	3 [20]	8	120/110/90/40/0	1/3*/2*/2
	7	12 [110]	6	5	8 [40]	150/110/0	1/1/2/4*
Av.	10/0	150/40/0	50/0	100/20/0	40/0		
	0/5	0/2	1/0	3/2*	0/0		

Step 5 → Since the total number of allocations is equal to "M + N − 1" allocations, the initial solution is straight away tested for optimality.

Let us calculate "U_i's" and "V_j's" for all rows and columns respectively on the basis of allocated cells such that $C_{ij} = U_i + V_j$ assuming $U_1 = 0$,

Let us calculate Δ_{ij} (Opportunity Cost), for unallocated cells where $\Delta_{ij} = C_{ij} - (U_{ij} + V_{ij})$.

U_i & V_j Matrix

					U_i
			0		−3
2	10	6	3		0
	12			8	2
2	10	6	3	6	V_j

C_{ij} Matrix for Unallocated cells

2	10	5		8
				8
7		6	5	

$U_i + V_j$ Matrix

					U_i
−1	7	3		3	−3
				6	0
4		8	5		2
2	10	6	3	6	V_j

$\Delta_{ij} = C_{ij} - (U_i + V_j)$ Matrix

3	3	2		5
				2
3		-2	0	

Step 6 → Since all Δ_{ij} are not positive, the above solution is not optimal. Let us place a small allocation θ in the cell with most negative Δ_{ij} and form a loop including this cell and test the solution for optimality. Next improved solution as obtained from above is shown below which is tested for optimality. The value of "U_i's", "V_j's" and Δ_{ij} are also calculated.

Looping Matrix

			80	
10	40+	50–	20	
	110–	θ+		40

Reallocation Matrix

			80	
10	90		20	
	60	50		40

U_i & V_j Matrix

					U_i
			0		−3
2	10		3		0
	12	6		8	2
2	10	4	3	6	V_j

C_{ij} Matrix for Unallocated cells

2	10	5		8
		6		8
7			5	

$U_i + V_j$ Matrix

					U_i
−1	7	1		3	−3
		4		6	0
4			5		2
2	10	4	3	6	V_j

$\Delta_{ij} = C_{ij} - (U_i + V_j)$ Matrix

3	3	4		5
		2		2
3			0	

Step 6 → Since all Δ_{ij} are positive, the above solution is optimal. The optimal solution is given below:

Sales Department	*Factory*	*Qty*	*Profit per Unit (Rs.)*	*Total Profit (Rs.)*
S_1	F_4	80	8	640
S_2	F_1	10	6	60
S_2	F_2	90	−2	−180
S_2	F_4	20	5	100
S_3	F_2	60	−4	−240
S_3	F_3	50	2	100
			Total	480

Note: Since one of Δ_{ij} is zero, the above solution is not unique. Hence an alternative solution exists. The alternative solution can be found by taking cell with zero Δ_{ij} as the basic cell.

PROBLEM 5.16 [Portfolio Problem]

XYZ and Co. provided the following data seeking your advice on optimum investment strategy:

Investment Made at the Beginning of year	*Net Return Data (in Paise) of Selected Investments*				*Amount Available (Lacs)*
	P	*Q*	*R*	*S*	
1	95	80	70	60	70
2	75	65	60	50	40
3	70	45	50	40	90
4	60	40	40	30	30
Maximum Investment (Lacs)	40	50	60	60	—

The following additional information are also provided :

— P, Q, R and S represent the selected investments.

— The company has decided to have four years investment plan.

— The policy of the company is that amount invested in any year will remain so until the end of the fourth year.

— The values (Paise) in the table represent net return on investment of one Rupee till the end of the planning horizon (for example, a Rupee invested in Investment P at the beginning of year I will grow to Rs. 1.95 by the end of the fourth year, yielding a return of 95 paise).

Using the above, determine the optimum investment strategy.

Solution

Step 1 → Introducing a Dummy Investment with zero return per unit as the total demand is not equal to total supply in order to make the problem balanced one.

Year	*Net Return data (in paise) of investment*					*Amount Available*
	P	*Q*	*R*	*S*	*Dummy*	
1	95	80	70	60	0	70
2	75	65	60	50	0	40
3	70	45	50	40	0	90
4	60	40	40	30	0	30
Maximum Investment	40	50	60	60	20	

Step 2 → Deriving Loss Matrix by deducting each element from the maximum element (i.e. 95) in order to use minimisation technique and then finding Initial Feasible Solution by VAM.

(Allocations are shown in brackets.)

Year	*Loss Matrix-Investment type* P	Q	R	S	Dummy	*Amount available*	*Difference*
1	[40] 0	[30] 15	25	35	95	70/30/0	15/10 —
2	20	[20] 30	[20] 35	45	95	40/20/0	10/5/5/10
3	25	50	[40] 45	[50] 55	95	90/50/0	20/5/5/ 10/40
4	35	55	55	[10] 65	[20] 95	30/20/0	20/0/ 0/10/30
Maximum Investment	40/0	50/20/0	60/40/0	60/10/0	20/0		
Difference	20	15	10	10	0		
	—	15	10	10	0		
	—	20	10	10	0		
	—	—	10	10	0		

Step 3 → Since the total number of allocations is equal to "M + N – 1" allocations, the initial solution is straight away tested for optimality.

Let us calculate "U_i's" and "V_j's" for all rows and columns respectively on the basis of allocated cells such that $C_{ij} = U_i + V_j$ assuming $U_4 = 0$,

Let us calculate Δ_{ij} (Opportunity Cost), for unallocated cells where $\Delta_{ij} = C_{ij} - (U_{ij} + V_{ij})$.

U_i & V_j Matrix

					U_i
0	15				–35
	30	35			–20
		45	55		–10
			65	95	0
V_j: 35	50	55	65	95	

C_{ij} Matrix for Unallocated cells

		25	35	95
20			45	95
25	50			95
35	55	55		

$U_i + V_j$ Matrix

					U_i
		20	30	60	–35
15			45	75	–20
25	40			85	–10
35	50	55			0
V_j: 35	50	55	65	95	

$\Delta_{ij} = C_{ij} - (U_i + V_j)$ Matrix

		5	5	35
5			0	20
0	10			10
0	5	0		

Step 4 → Since all Δ_{ij} are positive, the above solution is optimal. The optimal solution is given below:

Year A	*Investment* Strategies B	*Investment* C	*Return* D	*Total Return* E = C × D
1	P	40	0.95	38
1	Q	30	0.80	24
2	Q	20	0.65	13
2	R	20	0.60	12
3	R	40	0.50	20
3	S	50	0.40	20
4	S	10	0.30	3
				130

Note: Since some of Δ_{ij} are zero, the above solution is not unique. Hence the alternative solution exist. The alternative solution can be found by taking any cell with zero Δ_{ij} as the basic cell.

PROBLEM 5.17 [Portfolio Problem]

A company wishes to determine an investment strategy for each of the next four years. Five investment types have been selected, investment capital has been allocated for each of the coming four years, and maximum investment levels have been established for each investment type. An assumption is that amounts invested in any year will remain invested until the end of the planning horizon of four years. The following table summarises the data for this problem. The values in the body of the table represent net return on investment of one rupee upto the end of the planning horizon. For example, a rupee invested in investment type B at the beginning of year 1 will grow to Rs. 1.90 by the end of the fourth year, yielding a net return of Re. 0.90.

Investment made At the beginning Of year	*Investment Type*					*Rupees available (in 000's)*
	A	*B* *NET*	*C* *RETURN*	*D* *DATA*	*E*	
1	0.80	0.90	0.60	0.75	1.00	500
2	0.55	0.65	0.40	0.60	0.50	600
3	0.30	0.25	0.30	0.50	0.20	750
4	0.15	0.12	0.25	0.35	0.10	800
Maximum Rupees Investment (in 000's)	750	600	500	800	1,000	

The objective in this problem is to determine the amount to be invested at the beginning of each year in an investment type so as to maximise the net rupee return for the four-year period.

Solve the above transportation problem and get an optimal solution. Also calculate the net return on investment for the planning horizon of four year period.

Solution

Step 1 → Introducing a Dummy Variable with zero net rupee return as the total amount available is not equal to total investment in order to make the problem balanced one and expressing the Net Return Data in Paise.

Years	*Net Return Data (Re.)*					*Available Rs. (in 000's)*
	A	*B*	*C*	*D*	*E*	
1	80	90		75	100	500
2	55	65	40	60	50	600
3	30	25	30	50	20	750
4	15	12	25	35	10	800
Dummy	0	0	0	0	0	1000
Maximum rupees Investment in ('000)	750	600	500	800	1000	3650

Step 2 → Deriving Loss Matrix by deducting each element from the maximum element (i.e. 1.00) in order to use minimisation technique.

Years	*Net Return Data (Re.)*					*Available Rs. (in 000's)*
	A	*B*	*C*	*D*	*E*	
1	020	010	040	025	0	500
2	045	035	060	040	050	600
3	070	075	070	050	080	750
4	085	088	075	065	090	800
Dummy	100	100	100	100	100	1000
Maximum rupees Investment in ('000)	750	600	500	800	1000	3650

Step 3 → Finding Initial Feasible Solution VAM.

Years	A	B	C	D	E	Rs. available (000's)	Difference
1	20	10	40 [500]	25	0	500/0	10 - - - -
2	45	35 [600]	60	40	50	600/0	5 5 - - -
3	70	75	70	50 [750]	80	750/0	20 20 20 - -
4	85 [250]	88	75 [500]	65 [50]	90	800/750	10 10 10 10 10
Dummy	100 [500]	100	100	100	100 [500]	1000/500/00	0 0 0 0

Maximum 750/ 600/0 1000/0 800/ 500/
Rupee invest- 500/0 50/0 500/0
ment in ('000)

Differences				
25	25	20	15	50
25	40	10	10	30
15	-	5	15	10
15	-	25	35	10
15	-	25	-	10

Step 4 → Since the total number of allocations is less than "M + N – 1" allocations, let us introduce an infinitely small quantity 'e' to the least cost independent cell to make the total number of allocations equal to "M + N – 1" allocations.

Let us calculate "U_i's" and "V_j's" for all rows and columns respectively on the basis of allocated cells such that $C_{ij} = U_i + V_j$ assuming $U_1 = 0$,

Let us calculate Δ_{ij} (Opportunity Cost), for unallocated cells where $\Delta_{ij} = C_{ij} - (U_{ij} + V_{ij})$.

U_i & V_j Matrix

						U_i
		e				
		10			0	–85
		35				–60
				50		–15
	85		75	65		0
	100				100	15
V_j	85	95	75	65	85	

C_{ij} Matrix for Unallocated cells

20		40	25	
45		60	40	50
70	75	70		80
	88			90
	100	100	100	

$U_i + V_j$ Matrix

						U_i
	0		–10	–20		–85
	25		15	5	25	–60
	70	80	60		70	–15
		95			85	0
		110	90	80		15
V_j	85	95	75	65	85	

$\Delta_{ij} = C_{ij} - (U_i + V_j)$ Matrix

20		50	45	
20		45	35	25
0	–5	10		10
	–7			5
	–10	10	20	

Step 5 → Since all Δ_{ij} are not positive, the above solution is not optimal. Let us place a small allocation θ in the cell with most negative Δ_{ij} and form a loop including this cell and test the solution for optimality. Next improved solution as obtained from above is shown below which is tested for optimality. The value of "U_i's", "V_j's" and Δ_{ij} are also calculated.

Looping Matrix

	e–			+500
	600			
			750	
250		500	50	
500	+θ	500		-500

Reallocation Matrix

				500
	600			
			750	
250		500	50	
500	e			500

U_i & V_j Matrix

						U_i
					0	*–85*
		35				*–50*
				50		*–15*
	85		75	65		*0*
	100	100			100	*15*
V_j	*85*	*85*	*75*	*65*	*85*	

C_{ij} Matrix for Unallocated cells

20	10	40	25	
45		60	40	50
70	75	70		80
	88			90
		100	100	

U_i + V_j Matrix

						U_i
	0	0	–10	20		*–85*
	35		25	15	35	*–50*
	70	70	60		70	*–15*
		85			85	*0*
			90	80		*15*
Vj	*85*	*85*	*75*	*65*	*85*	

$\Delta_{ij} = C_{ij} - (U_i + V_j)$ Matrix

20	10	50	5	
10		35	25	15
0	5	10		10
	3			5
		10	20	

Step 6 → Since all Δ_{ij} are positive, the above solution is optimal. The optimal solution is given below:

In the year	*Investment type*	*Amount (in 000's)*	*Net Return per Re.*	*Total Return*
1	E	500	1.00	500.0
2	B	600	.65	390.0
3	D	750	.50	375.0
4	A	250	.15	37.5
4	C	500	.25	125.0
4	D	50	.35	17.5
			Total	1,445.0

Note: Since one of Δ_{ij} is zero, the above solution is not unique. Hence an alternative solution exists. The alternative solution can be found by taking cell with zero Δ_{ij} as the basic cell.

PROBLEM 5.18

TULSIAN LTD requests you to find optimal solution using the following data:

Factories *Item (per unit)*	F_1	F_2	F_3	F_4	*Sales Price Per unit*	*Requirement*
Conversion Cost	0.15	0.18	0.14	0.13	—	—
Raw Material Cost	0.10	0.09	0.12	0.09	—	—
Transportation Cost S_1	0.03	0.09	0.05	0.04	0.34	80
S_2	0.01	0.07	0.04	0.05	0.32	120
S_3	0.05	0.0	0.03	0.06	0.31	150
Production Capacity	10	150	50	100	—	—

For the unsatisfied demands, let the penally costs be rupee 0.01, 0.02 and 0.03 for Sales Depots S_1, S_2 and S_3 respectively.

Solution

1. To simplity the computations let us multiply Costs and Sales Price in the above table by 100.
2. Profit = Sales Price – Conversion Cost – Raw Material Cost – Transportation Cost.
3. Since the requirement (= 350) is greater than the availability (=310 units), the given problem is an unbalanced one. Let us now convert it into balanced one by introducing a dummy factory with production (=350 – 310 = 40) units and penalty costs.
4. Hence, the balanced transportation profit matrix becomes as follows:

	Factories					
Sales Depots	F_1	F_2	F_3	F_4	*Dummy*	*Requirement*
S_1	6	–2	3	8	–1	80
S_2	6	–2	2	5	–2	120
S_3	1	–4	2	3	–3	150
Availability	10	150	50	100	40	

5. Let us now convert this Profit Matrix into Opportunity Loss Matrix so that standard minimisation transportation technique can be applied to it by subtracting all the elements of the above matrix from the highest element (=8) and apply Vogel's Approximation Method to find the Initial Feasible Solution. The resultant Loss Matrix is given below:

Now the remaining solution is same as given in problem 5.15

PROBLEM 5.19

Goods manufactured at 3 plants, A, B and C are required to be transported to sales outlets X, Y and Z. The unit costs of transporting the goods from the plants to the outlets are given below:

Plants / *Sales outlets*	*A*	*B*	*C*	*Total Demand*
X	3	9	6	20
Y	4	4	6	40
Z	8	3	5	60
Total supply	40	50	30	120

You are required to:

(i) Compute the initial allocation by North-West Corner Rule.
(ii) Compute the initial allocation by Vogel's approximation method and check whether it is optional.
(iii) State your analysis on the optionally of allocation under North-West conrner Rule and Vogel's Approximation method.

Solution

(i) Initial allocation under NW corner rule is as above.

Initial cost:

$20 \times 3 = 60$
$20 \times 4 = 80$
$20 \times 4 = 80$
$30 \times 3 = 90$
$30 \times 5 = 150$
$\quad\quad\quad\;\; 460$

(ii) Initial solution by VAM:

			Supply	Penalties		
20 (3)	– (9)	– (6)	20	3		
20 (4)	– (4)	20 (6)	40	0	0	2
(8)	50 (3)	10 (5)	60	2	2	2
40	50	30				
1	1	1				
4	1	1				
	1	1				

Initial cost:

$20 \times 3 = 60$
$20 \times 4 = 80$
$50 \times 3 = 150$
$20 \times 6 = 120$
$10 \times 5 = 100$
$\quad\quad\quad\;\; 460$

Checking for optimality

3			$u_1 = 0$
4		6	$u_2 = 1$
	3	5	$u_3 = 0$
$v_1 = 3$	$v_2 = 3$	$v_3 = 5$	

$u_i + v_i$

	3	5	0
	4		1
3			0
3	3	5	

$\Delta_{ij} = c_{ij} - (u_i + v_j)$

	6	1
	0	
5		

$\Delta_{ij} = c_{ij} - (u_i + v_j)$

Conclusion

The solution under VAM is optimal with a zero in R_2C_2 which means that the cell C_2R_2 which means that the cell C_2R_2 can come into solution, which will be another optimal solution. Under NWC rule the initial allocation had C_2R_2 and the total cost was the same Rs. 460 as the total cost under optimal VAM solution. Thus, in this problem, both methods have yielded the optimal solution under the 1st allocation. If we do an optimally test for the solution, we will get a zero for D_{ij} in C_3R_2 indicating the other optimal solution which was obtained under VAM.

PROBLEM 5.20

The cost per unit of transporting goods from the factories X, Y, Z destination. A, B and C, and the quantities demanded and supplied are tubulated below. As the company is working out the optimum logistics, the Govt.; has announced a fall in oil prices. The revised unit costs are exactly half the costs given in the table. You are required to evaluate the minimum transportation cost.

Destinations / *Factories*	*A*	*B*	*C*	*Supply*
X	15	9	6	10
Y	21	12	6	10
Z	6	18	9	10
Demand	10	10	10	30

Solution

(a) The problem may be treated as an assignment problem. The solution will be the same even if prices are halved. Only at the last stage, calculate the minimum cost and divide it by 2 to account for fall in oil prices.

	A	B	C
X	15	9	6
Y	21	12	6
Z	6	18	9

Subtracting Row minimum, we get

	A	B	C
X	9	3	0
Y	15	6	0
Z	0	12	3

Subtracting Column minimum,

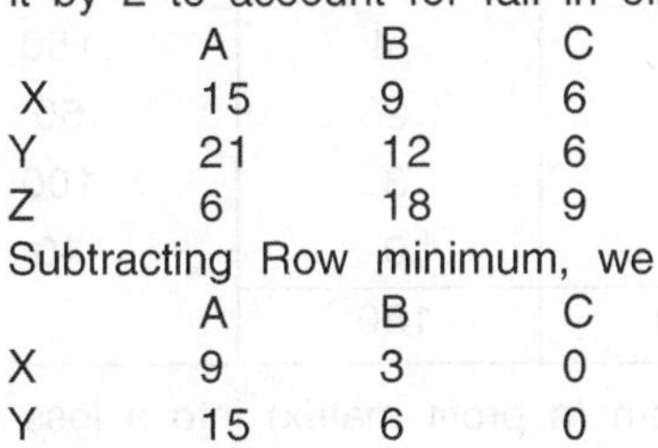

No of lines required to cut Zeros = 3

		Cost/u	*Units*	*Cost*	*Revised Cost being 50%*
Allocation:	X→B	9	10	90	45
	Y→C	6	10	60	30
	Z→A	6	10	60	30
				210	105

Minimum cost = 105 Rs.

PROBLEM 5.21

Following is the profit matrix based on four factories and three sales depots of the company:

		S_1	S_2	S_3	*Availability*
	F_1	6	6	1	10
Towns	F_2	–2	–2	–4	150
	F_3	3	2	2	50
	F_4	8	5	3	100
Requirement		80	120	150	

Determine the most profitable distribution schedule and the corresponding profit, assuming no profit in case of surplus production.

Solution

The given transportation problem is an unbalanced one and it is a maximisation problem. As a first step, we will balance this transportation problem, by adding a dummy factory, assuming no profit in case of surplus production.

Sales Depots

		S_1	S_2	S_3	*Availability*
	F_1	6	6	1	10
	F_2	–2	–2	–4	150
Factories	F_3	3	2	2	50
	F_4	8	5	3	100
	Dummy	0	0	0	40
	Requirement	80	120	150	

We shall now convert the above transportation problem (a profit matrix) into a loss matrix by subtracting all the elements from the highest value in the table i.e. 8. Thereafter, we shall apply the VAM find an initial solution.

Sales depots

		S_1	S_2	S_3	Availability	Diff.
	F_1	2	[10] 2	7	10/0	0.5--
	F_2	10	[40] 10	[110] 12	150/110/0	0222
Factories	F_3	5	[50] 6	6	50/0	1000
	F_4	[80] 0	[20] 3	5	100/20/0	322
	Dummy	8	8	[40] 8	40/0	0000
	Requirement	80/0	120/110/90/40/0	150		
	Diff.	2	1	1		
		–	1	1		
		–	3	1		
		–	2	2		

The initial solution obtained by VAM is given below.

Sales depots

		S_1	S_2	S_3
	F_1	2	[10] 2	7
	F_2	10	[40] 10	[110] 12
Factories	F_3	5	[50] 6	6
	F_4	[80] 0	[20] 3	5
	Dummy	8	8	40 8

The initial solution is tested for optimality. The total number of independent allocations is 7 which is equal to the desired (m + n – 1) allocations. We introduce u_i's (i = 1, 2 ... 5) and v_j's (j = 1, 2, 3) such that $\Delta_{ij} = c_{ij} - (u_i + v_j)$. Let us assume $u_2 = 0$, remaining u_i's, v_j's and Δ_{ij}'s are calculated below:

Sales Depots

		S_1	S_2	S_3	u_i
	F_1	3 / 2	10 / 2	3 / 7	–8
	F_2	3 / 10	40 +θ / 10	110 −θ / 12	0
Factories	F_3	2 / 5	50 −θ / 6	–2 +θ / 6	–6
	F_4	80 / 0	20 / 3	0 / 5	–7
	Dummy	5 / 8	2 / 8	40 / 8	–4
	v_j	7	10	12	

Since one of the Δ_{ij} is negative, the initial solution is not optimal. Let us introduce in the cell with –ve Δ_{ij} {i.e. the cell (F_3, S_3)}, an assignement θ. The value of θ and the reallocated solution as obtained from about is given below. The values of u_i's, v_j's and Δ_{ij}'s are also calculated.

$$\theta = \min \{(50 - \theta) = (110 - \theta) = 0\} = 50$$

Sales Depots

		S_1	S_2	S_3	u_i
	F_1	3 / 2	10 / 2	3 / 7	–8
	F_2	3 / 10	90 / 10	60 / 12	0
Factories	F_3	4 / 5	2 / 6	50 / 6	–4
	F_4	80 / 0	20 / 3	0 / 5	–7
	Dummy	11 / 8	2 / 8	40 / 8	–4
	v_j	7	10	12	

Since all D_{ij}'s for non basic cells are positive, the solution as calculated in the above table is optimal solution. The distribution schedule from factories to sales depots along with profit is given below:

Factory	*Sales depot*	*No. of units*	*Profit per unit*	*Total profit*
F_1	S_2	10	6	60
F_2	S_2	90	–2	–180
F_2	S_3	60	–4	–240
F_3	S_3	50	2	100
F_4	S_1	80	8	640
F_4	S_2	20	5	100
				480

(**Note:** Since one of the D_{ij}'s = 0, alternate schedule with a profit of Rs. 480 exists.)

PROBLEM 5.22

Three refineries with daily capacities of 6, 5 and 8 million gallons, respectively, supply three distribution areas with daily demands of 4, 8 and 7 million gallons, respectively. Gasoline is transported to the three distribution areas through a network of pipelines. The transportation cost is 10 cents per 1000 gallons per pipeline mile. Table gives the mileage between the refineries and the distribution areas. Refinery 1 is not connected to distribution area 3.

Price Per Million

City

	1	2	3	4
Plant	2	600	700	350
	3	320	300	350
	4	500	480	450

Mileage Chart for Problem 5

Distribution area

		1	2	3
	1	120	180	—
Refinery	2	300	100	80
	3	200	250	120

(a) Construct the associated transportation model.
(b) Determine the optimum shipping schedule in the network.

Solution

Initial solution by applying VAM.

From \ To	1	2	3	Total	D_1	D_2	D_3
1	12 [3]	18 [3]	m	6	6	6	6
2	30	10 [5]	8	5	2		
3	20 [1]	28	12 [7]	8	8	8	8
Total	4	8	7	19			
D_1	8	8	4				
D_2	8	10	m				
D_3	8	10	—				

As number of allocation is equal to 5(i.e. m + n – 1), solution obtained is initial feasible solution.

Checking solution for optimality by applying MODI methods.

From \ To	1	2	3	Total	v_i
1	3 12	3 18	m m–4	6	12
2	30 26	5 10	8 12	5	4
3	1 20	28 2	7 12	8	20
Total	4	8	7	19	
v_j	0	6	–8		

Since all Δ_{ij} are positive for unallocated cell therefore initial solution obtained is optimal one.

Refinery	*Distribution Area*	*Quantity*	*Total*
1	1	3	36
1	2	3	54
2	2	5	50
3	1	1	20
3	3	7	84
			244

PROBLEM 5.23

In Problem 5.22, suppose that the capacity of refinery 3 is 6 million gallons only and that distribution area 1 must receive all its demand. Additionally, any shortages at areas 2 and 3 will incur a penalty of 5 cents per gallon.

(a) Formulate the problem as a tranportation model.

(b) Determine the optimum shipping schedule.

Solution

Initial solution by applying VAM.

From \ To	1	2	3	Total	D_1	D_2	D_3	D_3
1	12 [4]	18 [2]	m	6	6	6	6	m–8
2	30	10 [5]	8	5	2	—	—	—
3	20	25 [3]	12 [6]	6	8	8	—	—
Dummy	m	50	50 [1]	2	0	0	0	0
Total	4	8	7	19				
D_1	8	8	4					
D_2	8	7	38					
D_3	m-12	32	m-50					
D_4	—	32	m-50					

As number of allocated cells is equal to 6 (i.e. m+n–1) hence solution obtained is initial pasible solution.

Now checking solution for aptionality.

From \ To	1	2	3	Total	v_i
1	12 [4]	18 [2]	m m–18	6	12
2	30 26	10 [5] –	8 + –2	5	4
3	20 14	25 [3] 13	12 [6]	6	6
Dummy	m m–44	50 + [1]	50 – [1]	2	44
Total	4	8	7	19	
v_j	0	6	6		

Checking the optimality by applying MODI method.

To / From	1	2	3	Total	u_i
1	4 12	2 18	m m–16	6	12
2	30 26	4 10	1 8	5	4
3	20 12	25 11	6 12	6	6
Dummy	m m–44	2 50	50	2	44
Total	4	8	7	19	
v_j	0	6	4		

Since all Δ_{ij} are positive, hence solution obtained is optimal one.
Hence optimal solution is

Refinery	*Distribution Area*	*Quantity*	*Total*
1	1	4	48
1	2	2	36
2	2	4	40
2	3	1	8
3	3	6	72
Dummy	2	2	100
			304

PROBLEM 5.24

Cars are shipped from three distribution centers to five dealers. The shipping cost is based on the mileage between the sources and the destinations, and is independent of whether the truck makes the trip with partial or full loads. Following table summarizes the mileage between the distribution centers and the dealers together with the monthly supply and emand figures given in *number* of cars. A full truckload includes 18 cars. The transportation cost per truck mile is Rs. 25.

(a) Formulate the problem as a tranportation model.

(b) Determine the optimal shipping schedule.

Mileage chart and Supply and Demand

		Dealer					
		1	2	3	4	5	Supply
Center	1	100	150	200	140	35	400
	2	50	70	60	65	80	200
	3	40	90	100	150	130	150
Demand		100	200	150	160	140	

Solution

To / From	1	2	3	4	5	Total	
1	2,500	3,750	5,000	3,500	875	23	400/18 R. off to next figure
2	1,250	1,750	1,500	1,625	2,000	12	2001/18 R. off to next figure
3	1,000	2,250	2,500	3,750	3,250	9	150/18 R. off to next figure
Total	6	12	9	9	8	44	
	100/18 R. off to next figure	200/18 R. off to next figure	150/18 R. off to next figure	160/18 R. off to next figure	190/18 R. off to next figure		

Initial Solution by Applying VAM

To / From	1	2	3	4	5	Total	D_1	D_2	D_3	D_3
1	2,500	[12] 3,750	[3] 5,000	3,500	[8] 875	23	1625	1625	1250	1250
2	1,250	1,750	[3] 1,500	[9] 1,625	2,000	12	250	250	250	250
3	[6] 1,000 1000	2,250	[3] 2,500	3,750 1125	3,250 4875	9	1250	1250	1250	250
Total	6	12	9	9	8	44				
D_1	250	500	1000	1875	1125					
D_2	250	500	1000	—	1125					
D_3	250	500	1000	—	—					
D_4	—	500	1000	—	—					

As number of allocations are equal to 7(i.e. m+n–1) so initial solution obtained is initial feasible solution.

Checking the solution for optimality by applying MODI method.

From \ To	1	2	3	4	5	Total	D_1	D_2	D_3	D_3
1	2,500	[12] 3,750	[3] 5,000	3,500	[8] 875	23	1625	1625	1250	1250
2	1,250	1,750	[3] 1,500	[9] 1,625	2,000	12	250	250	250	250
3	[6] 1,000 1000	2,250	[3] 2,500	3,750 1125	3,250 4875	9	1250	1250	1250	250
Total	6	12	9	9	8	44				

D_1	250	500	1000	1875	1125
D_2	250	500	1000	—	1125
D_3	250	500	1000	—	—
D_4	—	500	1000	—	—

Checking the solution for optimality by applying MODI method.

From \ To	1	2	3	4	5	Total	u_i
1	2,500 625	[12] − 3,750	5,000 1625	[3] + 3,500	[8] 875	23	875
2	1,250 1250	1,750 − 125	[6] + 1,500	[6] − 1,625	2,000 3000	12	−1000
3	[6] 1,000	+ 2,250 − 625	[3] − 2,500	3,750 1125	3,250 3250	9	0
Total	6	12	9	9	8	44	
v_j	1,000	2,875	2,500	2,625	0		

Checking the solution for optimality by applying MODI method

To / From	1	2	3	4	5	Total	u_i
1	2,500 0	− [9] 3,750	− 5,000 1625	+ [6] 3,500	[8] 875	23	875
2	1,250 625	1,750 −125	[9] + 1,500	[3] − 1,625	2,000 3000	12	−1,000
3	[6] 1,000	[3] 2,250	2,500 625	3,750 1750	3,250 3825	9	−625
Total	6	12	9	9	8	44	
v_j	1,625	2,875	2,500	2,625	0		

Checking the solution for optimality by applying MODI method.

To / From	1	2	3	4	5	Total	u_i
1	2,500 0	[6] 3,750	5,000 1500	[9] 3,500	[8] 875	23	875
2	1,250 750	[3] 1,750	[9] 1,500	[3] 1,625 125	2,000 3125	12	−1,125
3	[6] 1,000	[3] 2,250	2,500 500	3,750 1750	3,250 3875	9	−625
Total	6	12	9	9	8	44	
v_j	1,625	2,875	2,625	2,625	0		

As all Δ_{ij} are positive and zero, solution obtained is optimal one and also has an alternative solution since Δ_{ij} = 0.

Centre	*Dealer*	*No. of Trucks*	*No. of Cars*	*Cost*
1	2	6	100	22,500
1	4	9	160	31,500
1	5	8	140	7,000
2	2	3	50	5,250
2	3	9	150	13,500
3	1	6	100	6,000
3	2	3	150	6,750
				92,500

PROBLEM 5.25

The following matrix is a minimization problem for transportation cost The unit transportation costs are given at the right hand corners of the cells and the Δij values are encircled.

	D_1	D_2	D_3	Supply
F_1	3	4	4	500
F_2	9 (88)	6 300	7 (88)	300
F_3	4 (88)	6 (88)	5 200	200
Demand	300	400	300	1000

Find the optimum solution (s) and the minimum cost. *(May 2011)*

Solution

Δ_{ij} values are given for unallocated cells. Hece, no. of allocated cells = 5, which = 3 + 3 – 1 = no. of columns + no of rows – 1.

Allocating in other than Δ_{ij} cells.

Factory	S_1	D_2	D_3	Supply
	3 300	4 100	4 100	500
	9 (88)	6 300	7 (88)	300
	4 (88)	6 (88)	5 200	200
	300	400	300	1000

This solution is optional since Δ_{ij} are non-ve. For the other optional solution, which exists since Δ_{ij} = 0 at R_3 C_1, this cell should be brought in with a loop: R_2 C_1 – R_1 C_1 – R_1 C_3 – R_3 C_3.

Working Notes:

Step I : R_1C_1 (Minimum of 300, 500)

Step II: R_2C_2 (Minimum of 300, 400)

Step III: R1C2 balance of C_2 Total: 100, R_1 Total = 100

Step IV: R_1C_3 100 (balance of C_3 Total = 200)

Step V: R_3C_3 200

Solution I

−100				+100
	300	100	100	
		300		
+100	(88)		200	−100

Solution II

200	100	200
	300	
100		100

	Solution I	*Solution II*
Cost:	3 × 300 = 900	3 × 200 = 600
	4 × 100 = 400	4 × 100 = 400
	4 × 100 = 400	4 × 200 = 800
	6 × 300 = 1,800	6 × 300 = 1,800
	5 × 200 = 1,000	5 × 100 = 500
		4 × 100 = 400
Minimum Cost	4,500	4,500

PROBLEM 5.26

A company has three plants located at A, B and C. The production of these plants is absorbed by four distribution centres located at X, Y, W and Z, the transportation cost per unit has been shown in small cells in the following table:

Factories \ *Distribution Centres*	*X*	*Y*	*W*	*Z*	*Supply (Units)*
A	6	9	13	7	6000
B	6	10	11	5	6000
C	4	7	14	8	6000
Demand (Units)	4000	4000	4500	5000	17500 \ 18000

Find the optimum solution of the transportation problem by applying Vogel's Approximation Method. ***(Nov., 2010)***

Solution

Step 1: Initilal Allocatlon based on Least cost cells corresponding to highest differences

	X	*Y*	*W*	*Z*	*Dummy*	*Total*
A		2,000	3,500		500	6,000
B			1,000	5,000		6,000
C	4,000	2,000				6,000
Total	4,000	4,000	4,500	5,000	500	18,000

Step 2: Δ_{ij} Matrix values for Unallocated cells

	X	*Y*	*W*	*Z*	*Total*
A	0			0	
B	2	3			2
C			3	3	2

All Δ_{ij} values > 0. Therefore initial allocation is optimal.

Step 3: Optimal Transportation Cost

	Units	*Costs involved*	*Total*
A to Y	2,000	9	18,000
A to W	3,500	13	45,500
B to W	1,000	11	11,000
B to Z	5,000	5	25,000
C to X	4,000	4	16,000
C to Y	2,000	7	14,000
			Total Minimum Cost = 1,29,500

Note: Since there are zeroes in the Δ_{ij} Matrix alternate solutions exist.

6 CRITICAL PATH METHOD — DRAWING NETWORK

NETWORK (OR ARROW DIAGRAM)

A network is a graphical representation of inter-relationship of the various activities of a project. While drawing network, the following rules must be kept in mind.

1. An activity cannot occur untill all activities leading to it are complete.
2. No activity can start untill its tail event is reached.

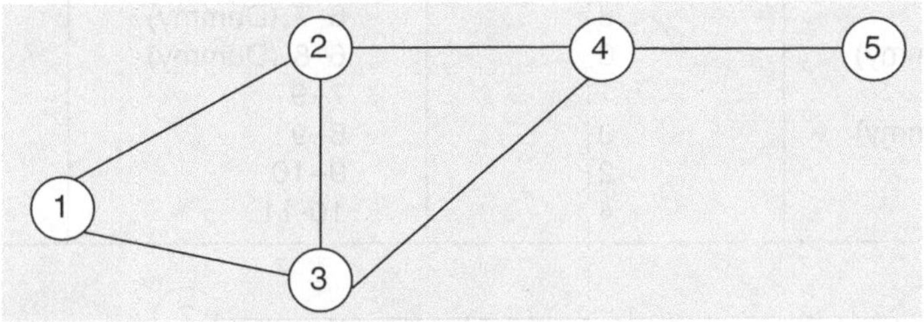

Activity	Head Event	Tail Event
1 – 2	2 (Burst Event)	1 (Burst Event)
1 – 3	3 (Merge Event)	1 (Burst Event)
2 – 3	3 (Merge Event)	2 (Burst Event)
2 – 4	4 (Merge Event)	2 (Burst Event)
3 – 4	4 (Merge Event)	3
4 – 5	5	4

The aforesaid graphical representation showing the inter-relationships of the various activities of a project is called '**Network**'.

WORKING METHODOLOGY OF CRITICAL PATH ANALYSIS

The working methodology of Critical Path Analysis (CPA) which includes both CPM and PERT, consists of following five steps:

Step 1: *Analyse and breakdown the project in terms of specific activities and/or events.*
Step 2: *Determine the interdependence and sequence of specific activities and prepare a network.*
Step 3: *Assign estimate of time, cost or both to all the activities of the network.*
Step 4: *Identify the longest or critical path through the network.*
Step 5: *Monitor, evaluate and control the progress of the project by replanning, rescheduling and reassignment of resources.*

CONVENTIONS FOLLOWED IN DRAWING NETWORK

The conventions followed in drawing a network are as follows:

1. Draw the arrow directing from left to right, that is, time and progress of the project flows from left to right.
2. As far as possible avoid drawing arrows that cross each other. Where ever crossing of arrows is unavoidable, bridging may be done.
3. An activity is always bounded by two events, called the start event and the end event. No event should hang loosely on the network.
4. Each node should be numbered without ambiguity. The numbers are assigned to events in such a way that the number assigned to the ending event of an activity is greater than the number assigned to the beginning event of that activity.

PROBLEM 6.1

Draw a network from the following activity and find a critical path and duration of project.

Activity	*Duration (Days)*	*Activity*	*Duration (Days)*
1–2	3	5–6	7
1–3	8	6–7 (Dummy)	0
2–4 (Dummy)	0	6–8 (Dummy)	0
2–7	1	7–9	5
3–4 (Dummy)	0	8–9	6
3–8	2	9–10	8
4–5	4	10-11	9

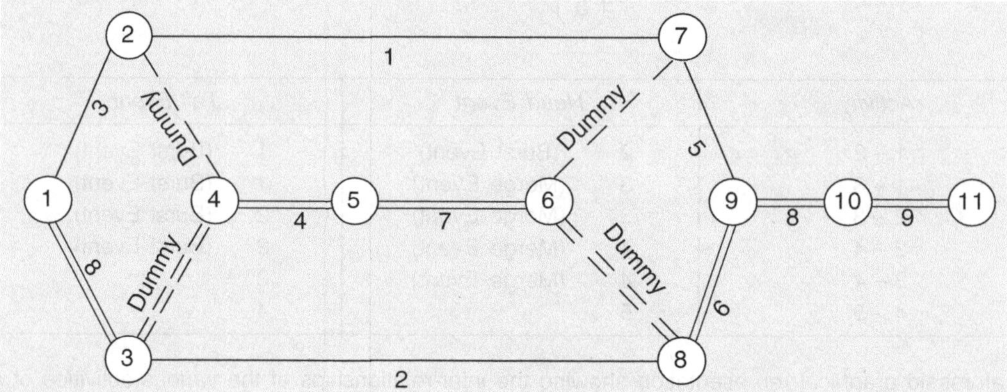

Solution

Various Paths	*Duration of Paths*
1 – 2 – 7 – 9 – 10 – 11	(3 + 1 + 5 + 8 + 9) = 26
1 – 2 – 4 – 5 – 6 – 7 – 9 – 10 – 11	(3 + 0 + 4 + 7 + 0 + 5 + 8 + 9) = 36
1 – 2 – 4 – 5 – 6 – 8 – 9 – 10 – 11	(3 + 0 + 4 + 7 + 0 + 6 + 8 + 9) = 37
1 – 3 – 8 – 9 – 10 – 11	(8 + 2 + 6 + 8 + 9) = 33
1 – 3 – 4 – 5 – 6 – 7 – 9 – 10 – 11	(8 + 0 + 4 + 7 + 0 + 5 + 8 + 9) = 41
1 – 3 – 4 – 5 – 6 – 8 – 9 – 10 – 11	(8 + 0 + 4 + 7 + 0 + 6 + 8 + 9) = 42

Hence the critical path is 1 – 3 – 4 – 5 – 6 – 8 – 9 – 10 – 11 with duration of 42 days.

PROBLEM 6.2

Draw a network for the following activity and find a critical path and total project duration.

Activity	*Duration (Days)*	*Activity*	*Duration (Days)*
1–2	3.3	4–5	11
2–3	6.7	5–6 (Dummy)	0
2–4	3.0	5–7	4.0
3–4 (Dummy)	0	6–7	6.0
3–6	7.7		

Solution

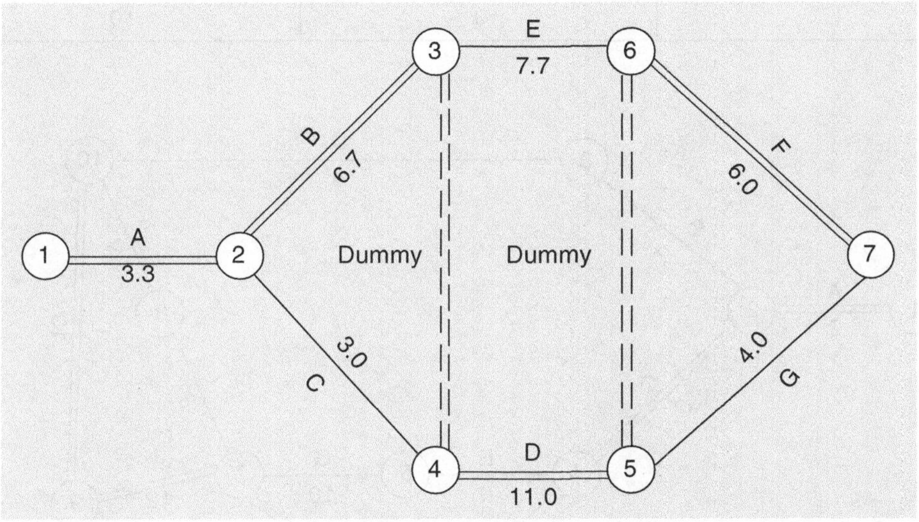

Various Paths	*Duration of Paths*
1 – 2 – 3 – 4 – 5 – 6 – 7	[3.3 + 6.7 + 0 + 11 + 0 + 6] = 27 days
1 – 2 – 3 – 6 – 7	[3.3 + 6.7 + 7.7 + 6] = 23.7 days
1 – 2 – 3 – 4 – 5 – 7	[3.3 + 6.7 + 0 + 11 + 4] = 25 days
1 – 2 – 4 – 5 – 6 – 7	[3.3 + 3 + 11 + 0 + 6] = 23.3 days
1 – 2 – 4 – 5 – 7	[3.3 + 3 + 11 + 4] = 21.3 days

Thus, the critical path is 1-2-3-4-5-6-7 or A-B-D-F and the expected project completion time is 27 days.

PROBLEM 6.3

Construct a PERT Diagram from the following information, and determine the critical path.

Activity	*Immediate Predecessor*	*Duration (Days)*
A	—	2
B	A	4
C	A	6
D	B	8
E	C	6
F	C	10
G	E	10
H	F	14
I	G,H	8
J	G, H	12
K	I	4
L	J	10

Solution

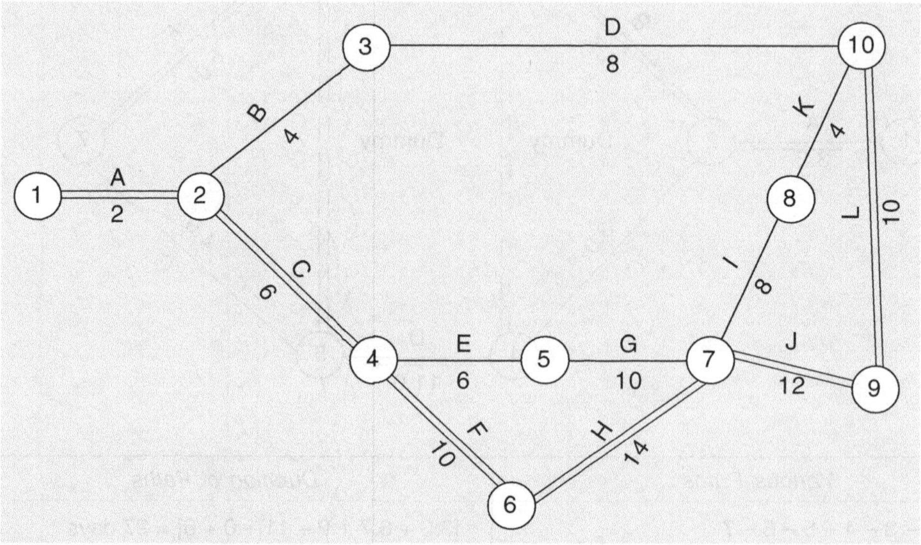

Various Paths	*Duration of Paths*
1 – 2 – 3 – 10	2 + 4 + 8 = 14
1 – 2 – 4 – 5 – 7 – 8 – 10	2 + 6 + 6 + 10 + 8 + 4 = 36
1 – 2 – 4 – 5 – 7 – 9 – 10	2 + 6 + 6 + 10 + 12 + 10 = 46
1 – 2 – 4 – 6 – 7 – 8 – 10	2 + 6 + 10 + 14 + 8 + 4 = 44
1 – 2 – 4 – 6 – 7 – 9 – 10	2 + 6 + 10 + 14 + 12 + 10 = 54

Hence the critical path is 1 – 2 – 4 – 6 – 7 – 9 – 10 i.e. (A – C – F – H – J – L) with project duration of 54 days.

PROBLEM 6.4

Draw a network from the following activity and find a critical path and duration of project.

Activity	*Immediate Predecessor*	*Duration (Days)*
A	—	3
B	—	8
C	A, B	4
D	B	2
E	A	1
F	C	7
G	E, F	5
H	D, F	6
I	G, H	8
J	I	9

Solution

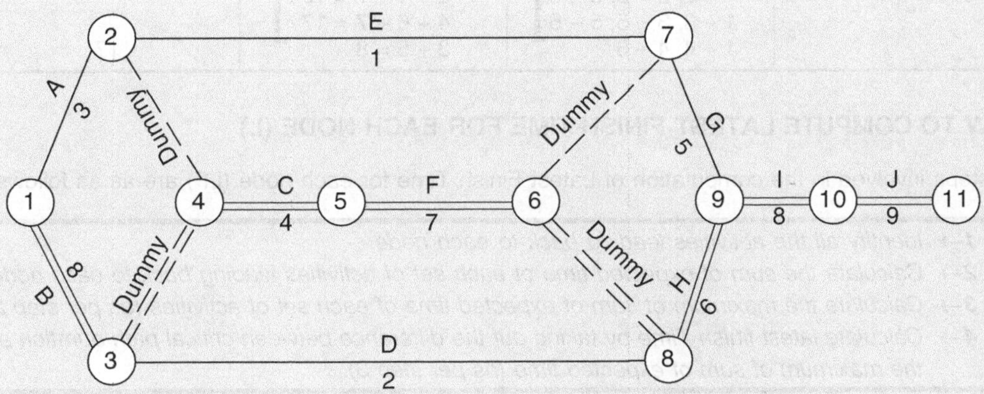

Various Paths	*Duration of Paths*
1 – 2 – 7 – 9 – 10 – 11	(3 + 1 + 5 + 8 + 9) = 26
1 – 2 – 4 – 5 – 6 – 7 – 9 – 10 – 11	(3 + 0 + 4 + 7 + 0 + 5 + 8 + 9) = 36
1 – 2 – 4 – 5 – 6 – 8 – 9 – 10 – 11	(3 + 0 + 4 + 7 + 0 + 6 + 8 + 9) = 37
1 – 3 – 8 – 9 – 10 – 11	(8 + 2 + 6 + 8 + 9) = 33
1 – 3 – 4 – 5 – 6 – 7 – 9 – 10 – 11	(8 + 0 + 4 + 7 + 0 + 5 + 8 + 9) = 41
1 – 3 – 4 – 5 – 6 – 8 – 9 – 10 – 11	(8 + 0 + 4 + 7 + 0 + 6 + 8 + 9) = 42

Hence the critical path is 1 – 3 – 4 – 5 – 6 – 8 – 9 – 10 – 11 (B – C – F – H – I – J) with duration of 42 days.

HOW TO COMPUTE EARLIEST START TIME FOR EACH NODE (E)

The steps involved in the computation of Earliest Start Time for each node (E) are as follows:

Step 1→ *Identify all the activities leading to each node.*
Step 2→ *Calculate the sum of expected Time of each set of activities leading to each node.*
Step 3→ *Calculate the maximum of the sum of expected time of each set of activities (as per step 2).*

The aforesaid calculations may be presented in the form of following table:

Table Showing the Computation of Earliest Start Time (E)

Node	*Activities leading to Node*	*Sum of Expected time*	*ES (being the Maximum of expected time)*
1	–	0	0
2	1 – 2	2	2
3	1 – 3	4	4
4	1 – 4	3	3
5	1 – 2, 2 – 5]	2 + 1 = 3]	
	1 – 3, 3 – 5]	4 + 6 = 10]	10
6	1 – 2, 2 – 5, 5 – 6]	2 + 1 + 7 = 10]	
	1 – 3, 3 – 5, 5 – 6]	4 + 6 + 7 = 17]	
	1 – 4, 4 – 6	3 + 5 = 8	17

HOW TO COMPUTE LATEST FINISH TIME FOR EACH NODE (L)

The steps involved in the computation of Latest Finish Time for each node (LF) are as as follows:

Step 1→ *Identify all the activities leading back to each node.*
Step 2→ *Calculate the sum of expected time of each set of activities leading back to each node.*
Step 3→ *Calculate the maximum of sum of expected time of each set of activities (as per step 2).*
Step 4→ *Calculate latest finish Time by taking out the difference between critical path duration and the maximum of sum of expected time (as per step 3).*

The aforesaid calculations may be presented in the form of following table:

Table Showing the Computation of Latest Finish Time (L)

Node (1)	*Activities leading back to Node* (2)	*Sum of Expected time* (3)	*Max. of sum of Expected time* (4)	*LF (17 - Col. 4)* (5)
6	–	0	0	17
5	6 – 5	7	7	10
4	6 – 4	5	5	12
3	6 – 5, 5 – 3	7 + 6 = 13	13	4
2	6 – 5, 5 – 2	7 + 1 = 8	8	9
1	6 – 5, 5 – 2, 2 – 1	7 + 1 + 2 = 10		
	6 – 5, 5 – 3, 3 – 1	7 + 6 + 4 = 17		
	6 – 4, 4 – 1	5 + 3 = 8	17	0

PROBLEM 6.5

The monthly maintenance work in a machine shop consists of 10 steps A to J. The inter-relationship between them are identified by event numbers:

Steps	*Event Numbers*	*Duration (Days)*
A	1–2	3
B	2–3	5
C	2–4	8
D	3–5	4
E	3–6	2
F	4–6	9
G	4–7	3
H	5–8	12
I	6–8	10
J	7–8	6

(a) Draw a Network.
(b) Compute early and late start and finish time for each activity.
(c) How much slack does Activity (3–5), Activity (4–6) and Activity (7–8) have?
(d) Identify the critical path and critical activities.
(e) If Activity (2–3) takes 8 days instead of 5 days what will be the project completion time ?
(f) Identify the activities that have a free slack.

Solution

(a) **Network**

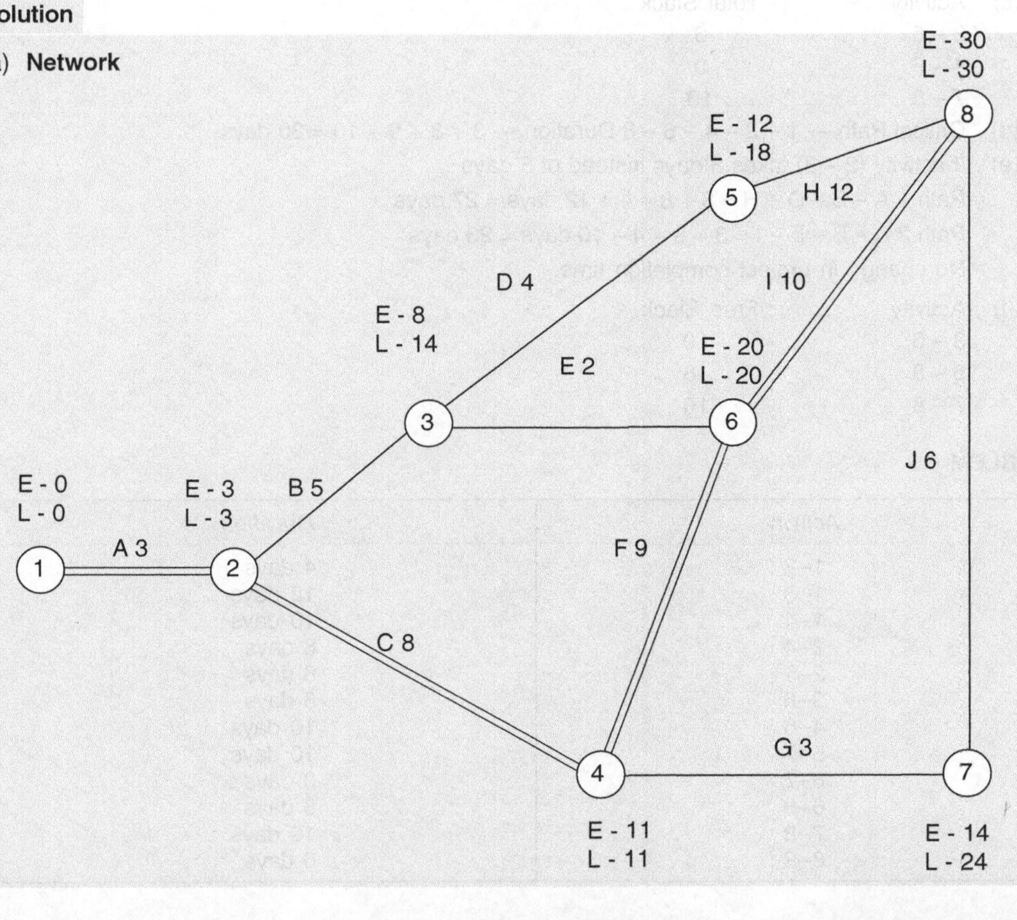

Various Paths	*Duration of Paths*
1 – 2 – 3 – 5 – 8	(3 + 5 + 4 + 12) = 24
1 – 2 – 3 – 6 – 8	(3 + 5 + 2 + 10) = 20
1 – 2 – 4 – 6 – 8	(3 + 8 + 9 + 10) = 30
1 – 2 – 4 – 7 – 8	(3 + 8 + 3 + 6) = 20

Hence the critical path is 1 – 2 – 4 – 6 – 8 (A – C – F – I) with duration of 30 days.

(b) Early and Late Start & Finish Time

	1 *i-j*	*2* *D*	*3* *ES*	*4* *LF*	*5* *EF* *(2 + 3)*	*6* *LS* *(4 – 2)*	*7* *Total float* *(6 – 3)*	*8* *HES*	*9* *Free float* *(7 – 8)*	*10* *TES*	*11* *IF* *(9 – 10)*
A	1 – 2	3	0	3	3	0	0	0	0	0	0
B	2 – 3	5	3	14	8	9	6	6	0	0	0
C	2 – 4	8	3	11	11	3	0	0	0	0	0
D	3 – 5	4	8	18	12	14	6	6	0	6	0
E	3 – 6	2	8	20	10	18	10	0	10	6	4
F	4 – 6	9	11	20	20	11	0	0	0	0	0
G	4 – 7	3	11	24	14	21	10	10	0	0	0
H	5 – 8	12	12	30	24	18	6	0	6	6	0
I	6 – 8	10	20	30	30	20	0	0	0	0	0
J	7 – 8	6	14	30	20	24	10	0	10	10	0

(c)

Activity	Total Slack
3 – 5	6
4 – 6	0
7 – 8	10

(d) Critical Path — 1 – 2 – 4 – 6 – 8 Duration — 3 + 8 + 9 + 10 = 30 days

(e) If activity (2 – 3) takes 8 days instead of 5 days

Path 1 A – B – D – H = 3 + 8 + 4 + 12 days = 27 days

Path 2 A – B – E – I = 3 + 8 + 4 + 10 days = 23 days

No change in project completion time.

(f)

Activity	Free Slack
3 – 6	10
5 – 8	6
7 – 8	10

PROBLEM 6.6

Activity	*Duration*
1–2	4 days
1–3	12 days
1–4	10 days
2–4	8 days
2–5	6 days
3–6	8 days
4–6	10 days
5–7	10 days
6–7	0 days
6–8	8 days
7–8	10 days
8–9	6 days

With the help of the activities given above draw a network. Determine its critical path, earliest start time, earliest finish time, latest start time, latest finish time, total float, free float and independent float.

Solution

The network based on the activities is as follows:

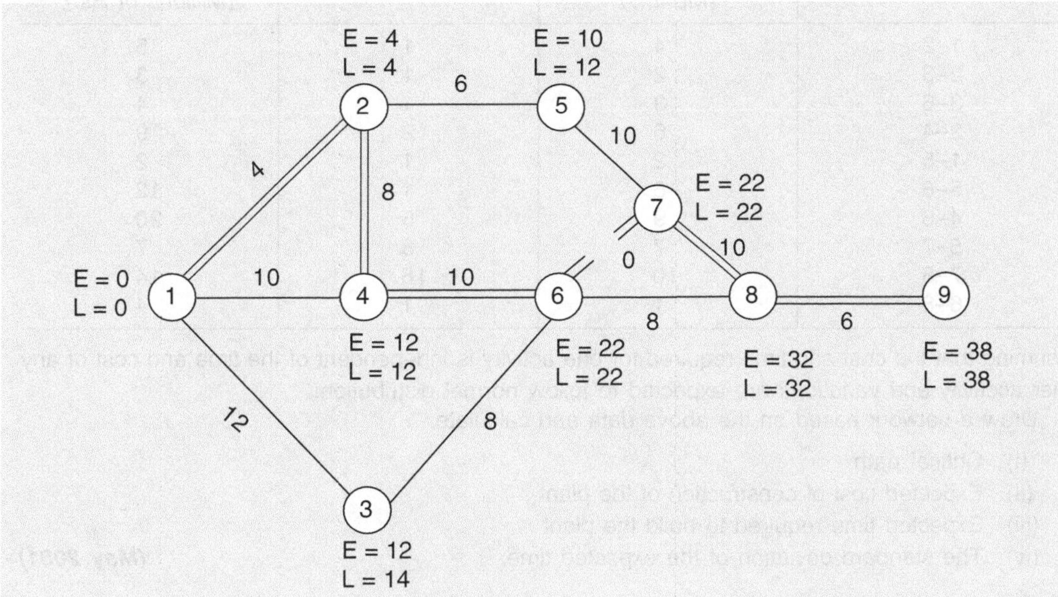

The time estimates and floats are calculated as below:

1 *Activity*	2 *D*	3 *ES*	4 *LF*	5=(2+3) *EF*	6=4−2 *LS*	7=(6−3) *Total Float*	8 *HES*	9=(7−8) *Free Float*	10 *TES*	11=(9−10) *IF*
1 - 2	4	0	4	4	0	0	0	0	0	0
1 - 3	12	0	14	12	2	2	2	0	0	0
1 - 4	10	0	12	10	2	2	0	2	0	2
2 - 4	8	4	12	12	4	0	0	0	0	0
2 - 5	6	4	12	10	6	2	2	0	0	0
3 - 6	8	12	22	20	14	2	0	2	2	0
4 - 6	10	12	22	22	12	0	0	0	0	0
5 - 7	10	10	22	20	12	2	0	2	2	0
6 - 7	0	22	22	22	22	0	0	0	0	0
6 - 8	8	22	32	30	24	2	0	2	0	2
7 - 8	10	22	32	32	22	0	0	0	0	0
8 - 9	6	32	38	38	32	0	0	0	0	0

Critical Path is represented by 1 - 2 - 4 - 6 - 7 - 8 - 9.

PROBLEM 6.7

Consider the schedule of activities and related information as given below, for the construction of a Plant:

Activity	*Expected Time (Months)*	*Variance*	*Expected Cost (Millions of Rs.)*
1–2	4	1	5
2–3	2	1	3
3–6	3	1	4
2–4	6	2	9
1–5	2	1	2
5–6	5	1	12
4–6	9	5	20
5–7	7	8	7
7–8	10	16	14
6–8	1	1	4

Assuming that the cost and time required for one activity is independent of the time and cost of any other acctivity and variations are expected to follow normal distribution.

Draw a network based on the above data and calculate:

(i) Critical path
(ii) Expected cost of construction of the plant
(iii) Expected time required to build the plant
(iv) The standard deviation of the expected time. ***(May 2001)***

Solution

The required network is drawn below:

(i) From the above network, it can be noted that the critical path is 1 – 2 – 4 – 6 – 8.
(ii) Expected cost of construction of the plant = (5 + 3 + 4 + 9 + 2 + 12 + 20 + 7 + 14 + 4) millions of Rs. = Rs. 80 millions
(iii) Expected time required to build the plant = 4 + 6 + 9 + 1 = 20 months
(iv) It is given that the time required for one activity is independent of the time and cost of any other activity and various are expected to follow normal distribution, the S.D.
Hence, the variance of the expected time is determined by summing the variance of critical activities and is = 1 + 2 + 5 + 1 = 9.
Standard Deviation of the expected time = $\sqrt{9}$ = 3 months.

PROBLEM 6.8

The following information is available:

Activity		*No. of days*	*No. of men required per day*
D	2–6	6	3
E	3–5	4	2
F	5–6	1	3
G	4–6	1	8

(i) Draw the network and find the critical path.
(ii) What is the peak requirement of Manpower? On which day(s) will this occur?
(iii) If the maximum labour available on any day is only 10, when can the project be completed? ***[CA (May 2008)]***

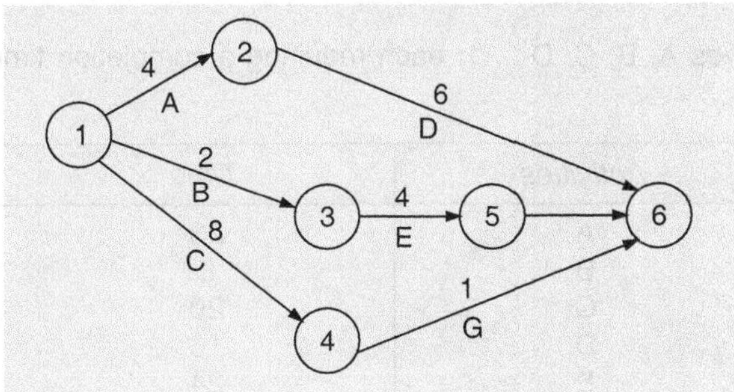

Path	Days
AD	10 → CP
BEF	7
CG	9

Critical Path = 1 – 2 – 6

i.e. AD = 10 days.

Peak requirement is 11 men, required on days 7 and 9.

If only 10 men are available on any day, shift F, G to days 10 and 11 and the project can be completed in 11 days.

Day	1	2	3	4	5	6	7	8	9	10	11	12	13	14
	A_2	A_2	A_2	A_2										
					D_3	D_3	D_3	D_3	D_3	D_3				
	B_3	B_3	E_2	E_2	E_2	E_2								
							F_3							
	C_5	C_5	C_5	C_5	C_5	C_5	C_5	C_5						
									G_8					
	10	10	9	9	10	10	11	8	11	3				
If s/o shift										F_3	G_8			
New														

PROBLEM 6.9

Given that a project involves A, B, C, D ... 1; each requiring a completion time, in days, as per the following table.

Activities	*Time*
A	23
B	8
C	20
D	16
E	24
F	18
G	19
H	4
I	10

Given that activity A precedes activities D and E; activities B and D precede aactivity F, activity C precedes activity G; activities B and G precedes activity H, and activities F and G precede activity 1, draw the network and calculate:

(i) Total float
(ii) Free float
(iii) Independent float
(iv) Critical path
(v) Project completion time

Solution

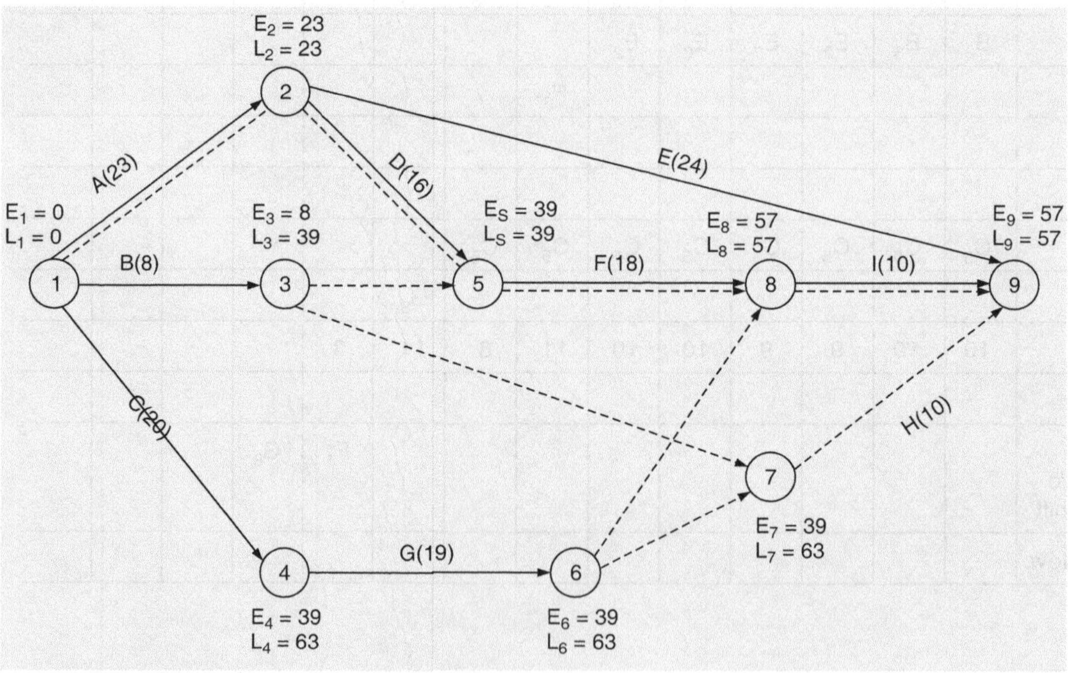

Critical path = A – D – F – I
Total duration of the project = 67 day.

Calculation of Total Float, Free Float and Independent Float

Activity (1)	Duration (2)	Earlier start (3)	Latest Finish (4)	Earliest Finish (5) = (2) + (3)	Total Float (6) = (4) – (5)	Head Even slack (interfering float (7)	Free Float (8) = (6) – (7)	Tail event slack (9)	Independent float (10) = (8) – (9)
A(1–2)	23	0	23	23	0	0	0	0	0
B(1–3)	8	0	39	8	31	31	0	0	0
C(1–4)	20	0	38	20	18	18	0	0	0
D(2–5)	16	23	39	39	0	0	0	0	0
E(2–9)	24	23	67	47	20	0	20	0	20
F(5–8)	15	39	57	57	0	0	0	0	0
G(4–6)	19	20	57	39	18	18	0	18	0
H(7–9)	4	39	67	43	24	0	24	24	0
I(8–9)	10	57	67	67	0	0	0	0	0

PROBLEM 6.10

The activities involved in a candle light chair service are lasted in the following table construct the project network.

Activity	Predecessor(s)	Duration (days)
A: Select music	—	2
B: Learn music	A	14
C: MaPe copies and buy books	A	14
D: Tryouts	B, C	3
E: Rehearsals	D	70
F: Rent candelabra	D	14
G: Decorate candelabra	F	1
H: Set up decorations	D	1
I: Order chair robe stoles	D	7
J: Check up public address system	D	7
K: Select music tracks	J	14
L: Set up public address system	K	1
M: Final Rehearsal	E, G, L	1
N: Chair Party	H, M	1
O: Find program	I, N	1

Required: Draw the network and calculate

(i) Total float

(ii) Free float

(iii) Independent float

(iv) Critical path

Solution

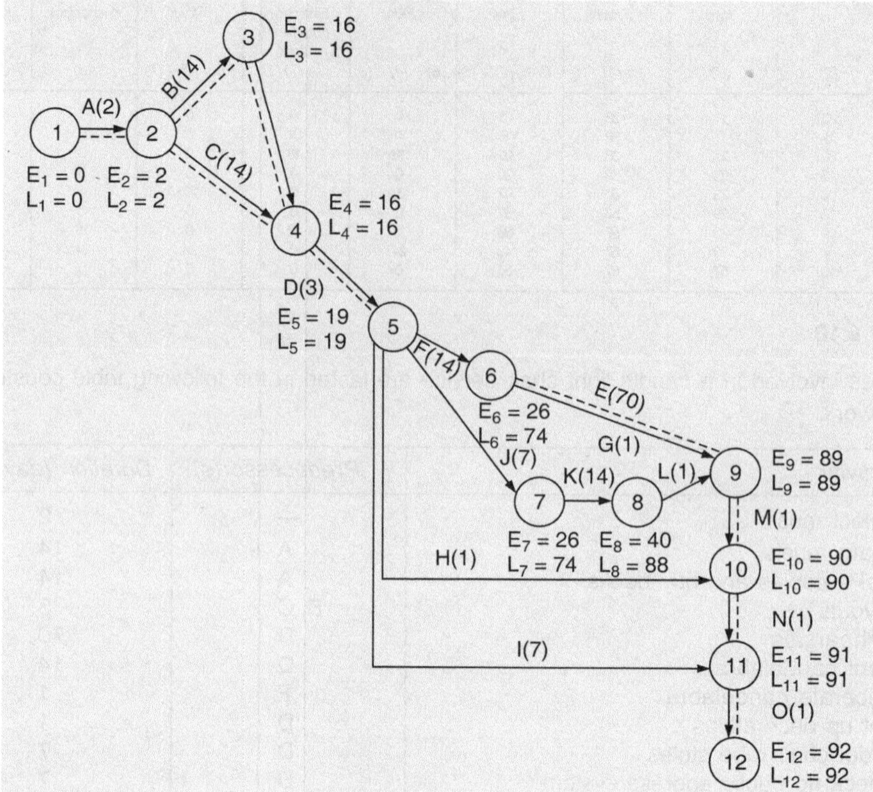

Critical path = A – B – C – D – E – M – N – O

Calculation of floats

Activity	*Duration*	*Earlier start*	*Latest Finish*	*Earliest Finish*	*Total Float*	*Head Even slack (interfering float*	*Free Float*	*Tail event slack*	*Independent float*
(1)	*(2)*	*(3)*	*(4)*	*(5) = (2) + (3)*	*(6) = (4) – (5)*	*(7)*	*(8) = (6) – (7)*	*(9)*	*(10) = (8) – (9)*
A(1–2)	2	0	2	2	0	0	0	0	0
B(2–3)	14	2	16	16	0	0	0	0	0
C(2–4)	14	2	16	16	0	0	0	0	0
D(4–5)	3	16	19	19	0	0	0	0	0
E(5–9)	70	19	89	89	0	0	0	0	0
F(5–6)	14	19	88	33	55	55	0	0	0
G(6–9)	1	33	89	34	55	0	55	55	0
H(5–10)	1	19	90	20	70	0	70	0	70
I(5–11)	7	19	91	26	65	0	65	0	65
J(5–7)	7	19	74	26	48	48	0	48	0
K(7–8)	14	26	88	40	48	48	0	48	0
L(8–9)	1	40	89	41	48	0	48	0	48
M(9–10)	1	89	90	90	0	0	0	0	0
N(10–11)	1	90	91	91	0	0	0	0	0
O(11–12)	1	91	92	92	0	0	0	0	0

PROBLEM 6.11

A cabinet manufacturing company is planning to introduce a new model of cabinets which requires to following tasks.

Task	Description	Tasetime (minutes)
A	Prepare the wheels	10
B	Mount the wheels	5
C	Assemble the wheels	15
D	Attach the top	11
E	Attach the base	10
F	Insert the brackets	5
G	Insert the shelves	5
H	Attach the doors	10
I	Attach the back panel	10
J	Point the unit	15

The wheels are mainted after they are prepared. The base cannot be attached until the sides are assembled and the wheels mounted. The top cannot be attached not the brackets inserted after the brackets are installed. The back panel is attached after the base and top are attached. The doors are attached after the shelves are inserted and the top and base are attached. The unit is painted after the back and doors are attached.

(i) Identify the immediate predecessors of each task and draw the network.

(ii) Find the cretical path and list the critical activities.

(iii) Obtain the earliest and latest start and completion times of all the activities and their total, free and independent floats.

Solution

Activities	Predecessor
A	—
B	A
C	—
D	C
E	B, C
F	C
G	F
H	G, D, E
I	D, E
J	H, I

Network

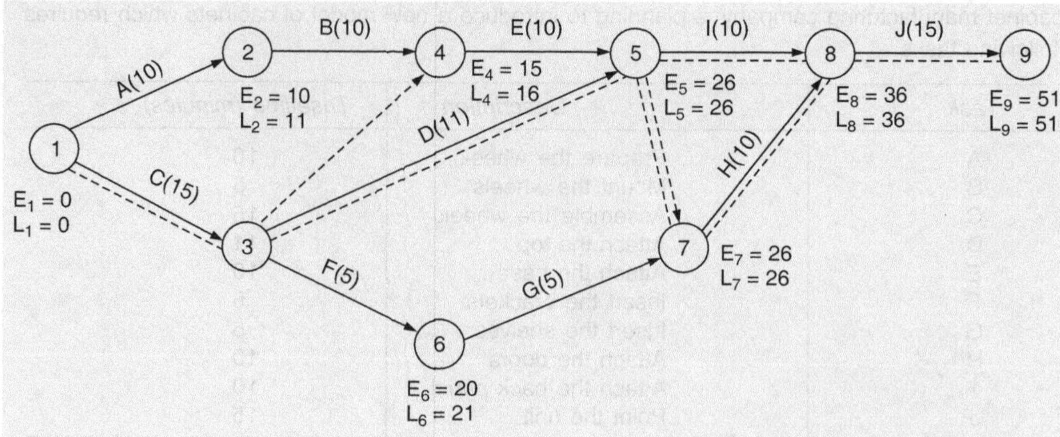

Activity (1)	Duration (2)	Earlier start (3)	Latest Finish (4)	Earliest Finish (5) = (2) + (3)	Total Float (6) = (4) – (5)	Head Even slack (interfering float (7)	Free Float (8) = (6) – (7)	Tail event slack (9)	Independent float (10) = (8) – (9)
A(1–2)	10	0	11	10	1	1	0	0	0
B(2–4)	5	10	16	15	1	1	0	1	0
C(1–3)	15	0	15	15	0	0	0	0	0
D(3–5)	11	15	26	26	0	0	0	0	0
E(4–5)	10	15	26	25	1	0	1	1	0
F(3–6)	5	15	21	20	1	1	0	0	0
G(6–7)	5	20	26	25	1	0	1	1	0
7H(7–8)	10	26	36	36	0	0	0	0	0
I(5–8)	10	26	36	36	0	0	0	0	0
J(8–9)	10	36	51	51	0	0	0	0	0

Critical path – C – D – H – I – J
Project Duration = 51 days

PROBLEM 6.12

The number of days of total float (TF), earliest start times (EST) and duration in days are given for some of the following activities:

Activity	*TF*	*EST*	*Duration*
1-2	0	0	
1-3	0		
1-4	5		
2-4	0	4	
2-5	1		5
3-6	2	12	
4-6	0	12	
5-7	3		
6-7		23	
6-8	2		
7-8	0	23	
8-9		30	6

(i) Draw the network.

(ii) List the paths with their corresponding durations and state when the project can be completed.

Solution

(a)

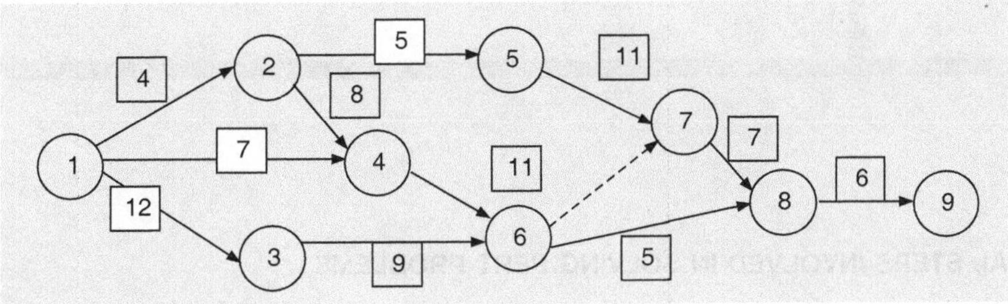

Network Diagram: 6-7 dummy

6-8-9 and 7-8-9

1-2-5-7 and 1-2-4-6

1-4-6 and 1-3-6

Activity	*Duration*	*Early Start*	*Late Start*	*Late Finish*	*Total Float*
1-2	4	0	0	4	0
1-3	12	0	2	14	0
1-4	7	0	5	12	5
2-4	8	4	4	12	0
2-5	5	4	8	13	1
3-6	9	12	14	23	2
4-6	11	12	12	23	0
5-7	11	9	12	23	3
6-7	0	23	23	23	0
6-8	5	23	25	30	2
7-8	7	23	23	30	0
8-9	6	30	30	36	0

Path	*Duration*
1-2-5-7-8-9	32
1-2-4-6-7-8-9	36
1-2-4-6-8-9	34
1-4-6-7-8-9	31
1-4-6-8-9	29
1-3-6-7-8-9	34
1-3-6-8-9	32

PERT

PRACTICAL STEPS INVOLVED IN SOLVING PERT PROBLEMS

The practical steps involved in solving PERT problems are given below:

Step 1→ *Prepare a table showing Expected Duration and Variance for each activity of the project:*

Activity		*Estimated Duration*			*Standard Deviation*	*Variance*
		Optmistic	*Pessimistic*	*Most Likely Expected*		
$i - j$	t_o	t_p	t_m	t_e	σ	σ^2

Where, Expected Duration $(t_e) = \dfrac{(t_0 + t_p + 4t_m)}{6}$

Standard Deviation $(\sigma) = \dfrac{(t_p - t_0)}{6}$

Variances (σ^2) = Square of standard deviation

Step 2→ *Draw a Project Network of Activities (or Jobs) based upon Expected Duration of the Activities.*

Step 3→ *Find out the Critical Path.*

Step 4→ *Find out the Total Expected Duration of the Project based upon the Network. This is also the Average Duration (or $\overline{X}$) of the Project.*

Step 5→ *Find out the Standard Deviation of the Project by following formula:*

$\sigma = \sqrt{(\text{Sum of Variances of Critical Path Activities})}$

Step 6→ *Calculate the Probability of completing the Project, if required, within a particular time period, say X, as follows:*

(i) *Calculate the value of Z as follows:*

$$Z = \frac{X - \bar{X}}{\sigma} \quad \text{or} \quad Z = \frac{T_1 - T_2}{\sigma} \quad \text{where, } X = T_1 = \text{Expected Duration}$$

$$\bar{X} = T_2 = \text{Critical Path Duration}$$

(ii) *Find out the Probability for the value of Z from the Normal Variate Table as follows:*

If the value of Z is positive *P = 0.50 + Probability for Z from the Table.*
If the value of Z is negative *P = 0.50 − Probability for Z from the Table.*

Step 7→ *Calculate the Expected Time of completion of the Project at a given probability, if required, as follows:*

(i) *Find out the value of Z from the Normal Variate Table for the given Probability after deducting 0.50 from the Probability.*

(ii) *Put the value of Z in the formula given in Step 6 and find out the value of X, i.e. the Expected Time of completion of the Project at the given Probability.*

PROBLEM 7.1

Tulsian Ltd., has undertaken a project which has an expected duration of 15 days with a variance of 9 days.

Calculate:

(a) The probability that the project will be completed on or before 12 days.
(b) The probability that the project will be completed on or before 18 days.
(c) The probability that the project will not be completed on or before 12 days.
(d) The probability that the project will not be completed on or before 18 days.
(e) The probability that the project will be completed in not less than 3 days earlier than expected.
(f) The probability that the project will be completed in not more than 3 days later than expected.
(g) The probability that the project will take more than 12 days, but not more than 18 days.
(h) The probability that the project will be completed not before 12 days but before 18 days.
(i) The probability that the company has to pay a maximum penalty of Rs. 15,000 if there is a penalty of Rs. 5,000 per day if duration of project extend beyond expected duration.
(j) The probability that the company has to pay a minimum penalty of Rs. 20,000 if there is penalty of Rs. 5,000 per day if duration extend beyond expected duration.

Solution

(a) $Z = \frac{X - \bar{X}}{\sigma} = \frac{12 - 5}{3} = -1 \; (\sigma^2 = 9 \text{ or } \sigma = 3)$

Area lying between $Z = 0$ and $Z = -1$ is equal to 0.3413
Hence $P(x \leq 12) = 0.50 - 0.3413 = .1587$ or 15.87%

(b) $Z = \frac{X - \bar{X}}{\sigma} = \frac{18 - 15}{3} = 1$

Area lying between $Z = 0$ and $Z = 1$ is equal to 0.3413
Hence $P(x \leq 18) = .50 + .3413 = .8413$ or 84.13%

(c) $P(x > 12) = 1 - P(x \leq 12) = 1 - .1587 = 84.13$ or 84.13%
(d) $P(x > 18) = 1 - P(x \leq 18) = 1 - .8413 = .1587$ or 15.87%
(e) Same solution as given in Case (a).
(f) Same solution as given in Case (b).
(g) $P(12 < x \leq 18) = .8413 - .1587 = .6826$ or 68.26%
(h) $Z = \dfrac{11-15}{3} = 1.33$

$P(x \leq 11) = .50 - .4082 = .0918$

$Z = \dfrac{17-15}{3} = .667$

Area lying between $Z = 0$ and $Z = .667$ is equal to .2486
$P(x \leq 17) = .5 + .2486 = .7486$
$P(11 < x \leq 17) = .7486 - .0918 = .6568$ *or* 65.68%

(i) $P(x \leq 18) = .8413$
$P(x \leq 15) = .5000$
$P(15 < x \leq 18) = .8413 - .5000 = .3413$ *or* 34.13%

(j) $P(x \leq 18) = .8413$
$P(x > 18) = 1 - .8413 = .1587$ *or* 15.87%

PROBLEM 7.2

A project has the following activities and characteristics.

Activity	*Estimated Duration in Weeks*		
i – j	*Optimistic*	*Most Likely*	*Pessimistic*
1 – 2	1	1	7
1 – 3	1	4	7
1 – 4	2	2	8
2 – 5	1	1	1
3 – 5	2	5	14
4 – 6	2	5	8
5 – 6	3	6	15

Required:

(a) Find expected time and variance.
(b) Draw the project network.
(c) Find total float.
(d) Find expected project length and activities on the critical path.
(e) Determine the variance and Standard Deviation of critical path.
(f) Determine the probability that project will be completed:

(i) At least 3 weeks earlier than expected;
(ii) Not more than 3 weeks than expected;

(g) If the project due date is 18 weeks, what is probability of meeting and non-meeting the due date at 90% level?
(h) Within how many weeks would you expect the project to be completed with probability of 0.99?
(i) Find the event variances. (For both Tail and Head Event)
(j) The contract specifies a Rs. 5,000 per week penalty for each week the completion of the project extends beyond 17 weeks. What is the probability that this company will have to pay a maximum penalty of Rs. 15,000.

Solution

(a) Expected duration on the basis of the assumption that the activity follows beta distribution, has been calculated with the help of the following formulae:

Activity	$t_e = \dfrac{t_0 + 4t_m + t_p}{6}$	$Variance = \left(\dfrac{t_p - t_0}{6}\right)^2$
1 – 2	$\dfrac{1+4\times1+7}{6}=2$	$\left(\dfrac{7-1}{6}\right)^2=1$
1 – 3	$\dfrac{1+4\times4+7}{6}=4$	$\left(\dfrac{7-1}{6}\right)^2=1$
1 – 4	$\dfrac{2+4\times2+8}{6}=3$	$\left(\dfrac{8-2}{6}\right)^2=1$
2 – 5	$\dfrac{1+4\times1+1}{6}=1$	$\left(\dfrac{1-1}{6}\right)^2=0$
3 – 5	$\dfrac{2+4\times4+14}{6}=6$	$\left(\dfrac{14-2}{6}\right)^2=4$
4 – 6	$\dfrac{2+4\times5+8}{6}=6$	$\left(\dfrac{8-2}{6}\right)^2=1$
5 – 6	$\dfrac{3+4\times6+15}{6}=7$	$\left(\dfrac{15-3}{6}\right)^2=4$

Activity 1	*Duration* 2	*ES* 3	*LF* 4	*EF* 5 = 2 + 3	*LS* 6 = 4 – 2	*TF* 7 = 6 – 3
1 - 2	2	0	9	2	7	7
1 - 3	4	0	4	4	0	0
1 - 4	3	0	12	3	9	9
2 - 5	1	2	10	3	9	7
3 - 5	6	4	10	10	4	0
4 - 6	5	3	17	8	12	9
5 - 6	7	10	17	17	10	0

(b) The network is drawn as follows:

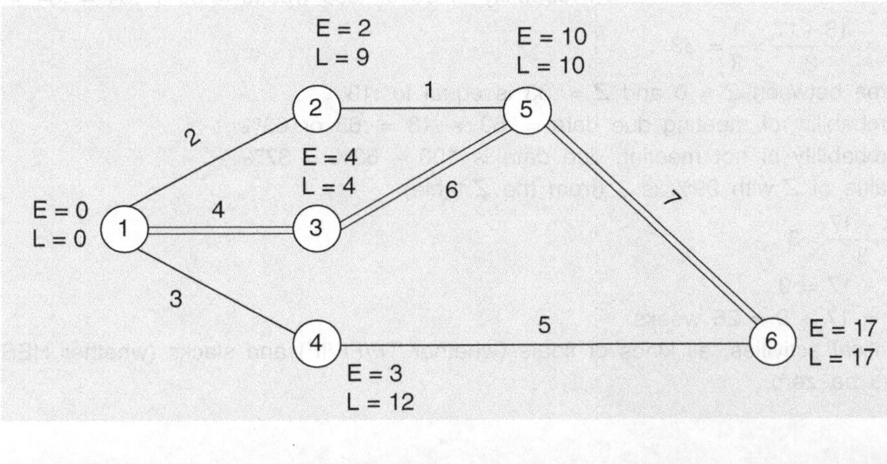

Various Paths	*Duration of Paths*
1 – 2 – 5 – 6	2 + 1 + 7 = 10
1 – 3 – 5 – 6	4 + 6 + 7 = 17
1 – 4 – 6	3 + 5 = 8

Hence the critical Path is 1 – 3 – 5 – 6 with duration of 17 weeks.

(c) Expected Project Length = 17 weeks

(d) Activities on Critical Path are 1 – 3, 3 – 5 & 5 – 6

(e) Variance and Standard Deviation of critical path

Activity	*Variance* $= \left(\frac{t_p - t_0}{6}\right)^2$
1 – 3	$\left(\frac{7-1}{6}\right)^2 = 1$
3 – 5	$\left(\frac{14-2}{6}\right)^2 = 4$
5 – 6	$\left(\frac{15-3}{6}\right)^2 = 4$
	$V_t\,(\sigma^2) \quad = 9$

S. D. $(\sigma) = \sqrt{\sigma^2} = \sqrt{9} = 3$

(f) (i) $$Z = \frac{X - \bar{X}}{\sigma}$$

where, X = Actual Duration = 14 and $\bar{X}$ = CPM Duration = 17

$$Z = \frac{14-17}{3} = -1$$

Area between $Z = 0$ and $Z = -1$ is equal to .34

Probability of 14 or less weeks = .50 – .34 = .16 or 16%

(ii) $$Z = \frac{20-17}{3} = 1$$

Area between $Z = 0$ and $Z = 1$ is equal to .34

= Probability of 20 or less weeks = 50 + .34 = .84 = 84%

(g) $$Z = \frac{18-17}{3} = \frac{1}{3} = .33$$

Area between $Z = 0$ and $Z = .33$ is equal to .13

Probability of meeting due date = .50 + .13 = .63 or 63%

Probability of not meeting due date is 100 – 63% = 37%

(h) Value of Z with 99% is 3 (from the Z table)

$$\frac{X-17}{3} = 3$$

X – 17 = 9

X = 17 + 9 = 26 weeks

Note: At critical activities, all kinds of floats (whether TF/FF/IF) and slacks (whether HES/TES) shall always be zero.

(i) **Calculation of Event variances for Earliest Time TE**

Event	*Activities on the Largest Path Leading to event No. 1, 2 .....6*	*Max. of Sum of variances of such activities*
1	None	0
2	1 – 2	1
3	1 – 3	1
4	1 – 4	1
5	1 – 2, 2 – 5, V = 1 + 0 = 1 1 – 3, 3 – 5 V = 1 + 4 = 5	5
6	1 – 3, 3 – 5, 5 – 6, V = 1 + 4 + 4 = 9 1 – 2, 2 – 5, 5 – 6, V = 1 + 0 + 4 = 5 1 – 4, 4 – 6, V = 1 + 1 = 2	9

Calculation of Event variances for Latest Time TL

Event	*Activities on Largest Path From it to last event 6 Of these activities*	*Sum of variances*
1	1 – 3, 3 – 5, 5 – 6	9
2	2 – 5, 5 – 6	4
3	3 – 5, 5 – 6	8
4	4 – 6	1
5	5 – 6	4
6	None	0

(j) $P(x \leq 17) = .50$

$$P(x \leq 20) = P\left(Z = \frac{20 - 17}{3}\right) \quad \text{or } P(Z \leq 1) = .84$$

$P(P7 < x \leq 20) = .84 - .50 = .34$ or 34%

PROBLEM 7.3

The following information is given:

Activity	(1–2)	(2–3)	(2–4)	(3–5)	(4–6)	(5–6)	(5–7)	(6–7)
Pessimistic time (in weeks)	3	9	6	8	8	0	5	8
Most likely time (in weeks)	3	6	4	6	6	0	4	5
Optimistic time (in weeks)	3	3	2	4	4	0	3	2

Required:

Draw the Network diagram for the above. Calculate :

(i) Variance to each activity.

(ii) Critical path and expected project length.

(iii) The probability that the project will be completed in 23 weeks.

Given that :

Z Value :	1.90	1.91	1.92	1.93	1.94
Probability :	0.9713	0.9719	0.9726	0.9732	0.9738

Solution

The required network is drawn below:

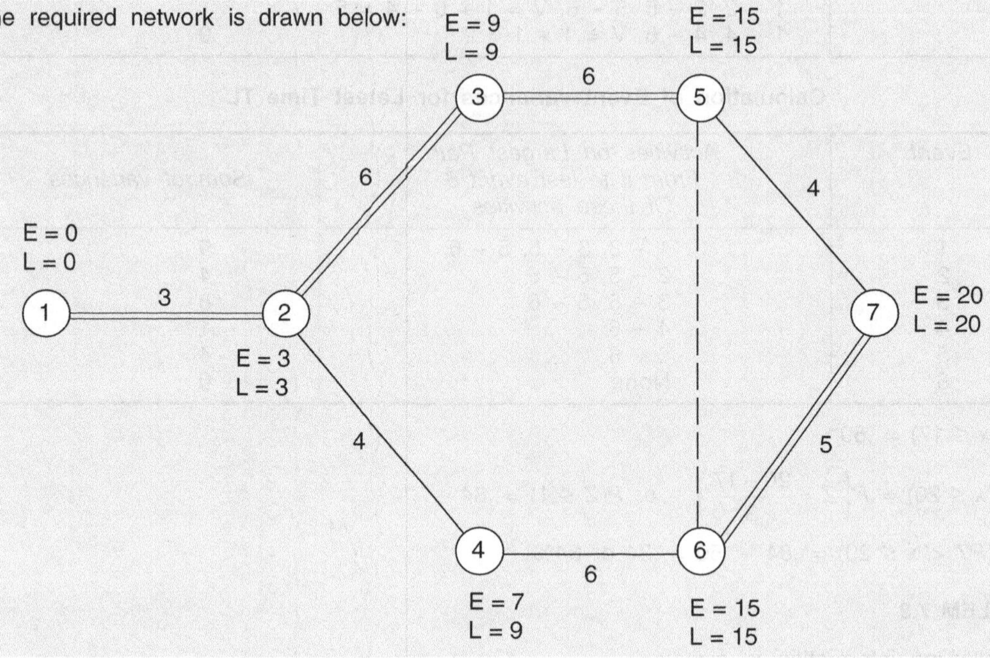

The expected time marked in the above network diagram for various activities is calculated in the table below:

Activities	*Optimistic* (t_o)	*Time(in weeks) Most likely* (t_m)	*Pessimistic* (t_p)	*Expected time (weeks)* $t_e = \frac{t_0 + 4t_m + t_p}{6}$	*Variance* $V_t = \left(\frac{t_p - t_0}{6}\right)^2$
1–2	3	3	3	3	0
2–3	3	6	9	6	1
2–4	2	4	6	4	4/9
3–5	4	6	8	6	4/9
4–6	4	6	8	6	4/9
5–6	0	0	0	0	0
5–7	3	4	5	4	1/9
6–7	2	5	8	5	1

Various Paths	*Duration of Paths*
1 – 2 – 3 – 5 – 7 – 10	3 + 6 + 6 + 4 = 19
1 – 2 – 3 – 5 – 6 – 7	3 + 6 + 6 + 0 + 5 = 20
1 – 2 – 4 – 6 – 7	3 + 4 + 6 + 5 = 18

Hence the critical path is 1 – 2 – 3 – 5 – 6 – 7 with duration of 20 weeks.

(i) Variance of each of the activities has been calculated in the last column of the above table.

(ii) Critical path is given by 1 – 2 – 3 – 5 – 6 – 7 and the expected project length is 20 weeks.

(iii) Variance of the critical path = σ^2 = 0 + 1 + 4/9 + 0 + 1 = 22/9 = 2.444

Mean = x = 20 weeks

To calculate the probability of completing the project in 23 weeks, we will first calculate the normal variate Z as below:

$$Z = \frac{D - \bar{x}}{\sigma} = \frac{23 - 20}{\sqrt{2.444}} = 1.92$$

$P(x \le 23) = P(z \le 1.92) = 0.9726$ (from the given table)

Thus the probability that the project will be completed in 23 weeks is 97.26%.

PROBLEM 7.4

Example shown below is a PERT network and related set of activity time:

i-j	*A*	*B*	*C*	*D*	*E*	*F*	*G*	*H*	*I*	*J*	*K*	*L*
t_o	10	12	8	4	0	12	6	9	4	0	5	9
t_m	13	15	11	7	0	18	12	12	6	0	8	12
t_p	22	18	20	16	0	36	18	27	8	0	11	33

Required:

(a) Determine the expected completion time of each activity.

(b) Determine the earliest expected completion time, the latest expected completion time and float of each activity.

(c) What is the total project completion time, and what are activities on the critical path?

(d) Determine S.D. of expected completion time for only those activities on the critical path.

(e) Determine the probability that the project will be completed within 41 weeks.

Solution

$$t_e = \frac{t_p + 4t_m + t_0}{6}; V_t = \left(\frac{t_p - t_0}{6}\right)^2$$

1 i-j	t_o	$4t_m$	t_p	2 t_e	3 ES	4 LF	5=3+2 EF	6=4-2 LS	7=6-3 TF	V_t	S.D.
1–2	10	52	22	14	0	31	14	17	17		
1–3	8	44	20	12	0	12	12	0	0	4	2
1–4	12	60	18	15	0	25	15	10	10		
2–6	4	28	16	8	14	39	22	31	17		
3–4	0	0	0	0	12	25	12	25	13		
3–5	12	72	36	20	12	32	32	12	0	16	4
3–7	6	48	18	12	12	32	24	20	8		
4–6	9	48	27	14	15	39	29	25	10		
5–6	4	24	8	6	32	39	38	33	1		
5–7	0	0	0	0	32	32	32	32	0	0	0
6–8	5	32	11	8	38	47	46	39	1		
7–8	9	48	33	15	32	47	47	32	0	16	4
									$\Sigma V_t = 36$		

Hence S.D. of the critical path $= \sqrt{36} = 6$

Probability of completing critical path in 41 weeks is computed below:

$$Z = \frac{41 - 47}{6} = -1$$

∴ Probability = 0.159

PROBLEM 7.5

A project consists of seven activities and the time estimates of the activities are furnished as under:

Activity	*Optimistic Days*	*Most likely Days*	*Pessimistic Days*
1-2	4	10	16
1-3	3	6	9
1-4	4	7	16
2-5	5	5	5
3-5	8	11	32
4-6	4	10	16
5-6	2	5	8

Required:

(i) Draw the network diagram.

(ii) Identify the critical path and its duration.

(iii) What is the probability that the project will be completed in 5 days earlier than the critical path duration?

(iv) What project duration will provide 95% confidence level of completion ($Z_{0.95}$ = 1.65)?

Given

Z	11.00	1.09	1.18	1.25	1.33
Probability	0.1587	0.1379	0.7190	0.1056	0.0918

(c) Calculation of expected time and variance of each activity:

Activity	*Optimistic Days*	*Most likely Days*	*Pessimistic Days*	*Expected Duration*	*Varian*
1-2	4	10	16	10	4
1-3	3	6	9	6	1
1-4	4	7	16	8	4
2-5	5	5	5	5	0
3-5	8	11	32	14	16
4-6	4	10	16	10	4
5-6	2	5	8	5	1

Paper-5: Cost Management

The network diagram is as under:

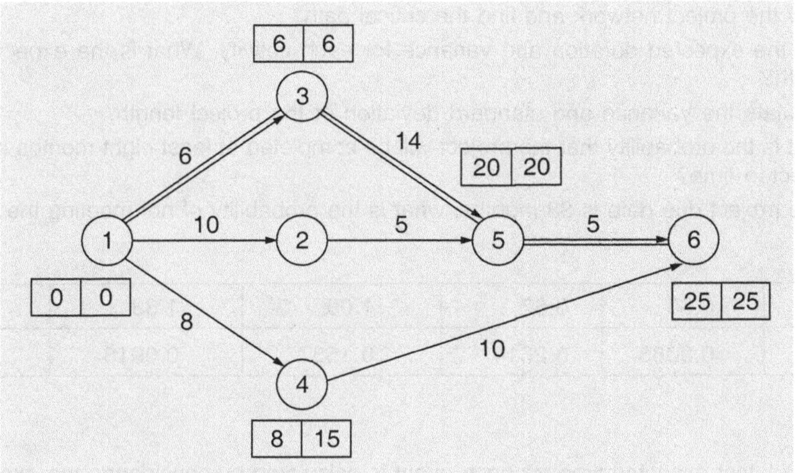

Critical Path:	1–3		3–5		5–6
Duration (days)	6		14		5 = 25 days
Standard deviation:	1	+	16	+	1 = 18
					$\sqrt{18} = 4.24$

Probability that the project will be completed five days earlier:

$$Z = \frac{20 - 25}{4.24} = -1.18.$$

According to probability values given in the question probability is 11.9%

To obtain 95% confidence level:

$$1.65 = \frac{X - 25}{4.24}$$

$$X - 25 = 6.996$$

$$X = 32 \text{ days}$$

PROBLEM 7.6

An Engineering Project has the following activities whose time estimates are listed below:

Activity	*Estimated duration (in months)*		
	Optimistic	*Most likely*	*Pessimistic*
1-2	2	2	14
1-3	2	8	14
1-4	4	4	16
3-5	4	10	28
4-6	4	10	16
5-6	6	12	30

(i) Draw the project network and find the critical path.

(ii) Find the expected duration and variance for each activity. What is the expected project length?

(iii) Calculate the variance and standard deviation of the project length.

(iv) What is the probability that the project will be completed at least eight months earlier than expected time?

(v) If the project due date is 38 months, what is the probability of not meeting the due date?

Given:

Z:	0.50	0.67	1.00	1.33	2.00
Prob.:	0.3085	0.2514	0.1587	0.0918	0.0228

(Nov 2001)

Solution

The earliest and latest expected time for each event is calculated by considering the expected time of each activity as shown in the table below:

Activity *(i – j)*	t_o	t_m	t_p	$t_e = (t_o + 4t_m + t_p)/6$	$\sigma^2 = \left(\frac{t_p - t_o}{6}\right)^2$
1-2	2	2	14	4	4
1-3	2	8	14	8	4
1-4	4	4	16	6	4
2-5	2	2	2	2	0
3-5	4	10	28	12	16
4-6	4	10	16	10	4
5-6	6	12	30	14	16

(a) The project network is drawn below:

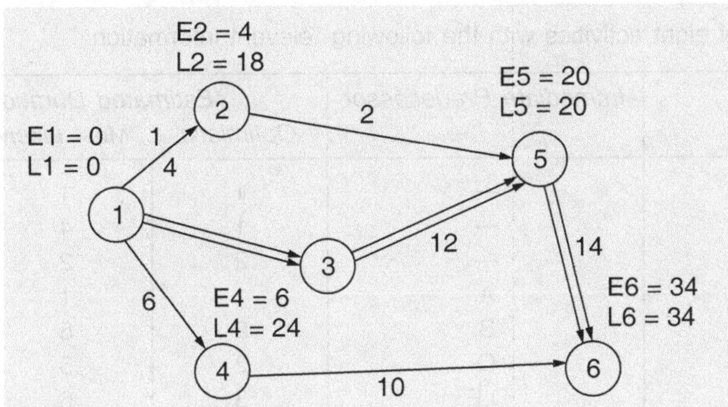

(i) Critical Path is: 1 – 3 – 5 – 6

(ii) The expected duration and variance of each activity is shown in the table above.

The expected project length is the sum of the duration of critical activities. Hence,

Expected project Length = 8 + 12 + 14 = 34 months

(iii) Variance of the project length Is the sum of the variances of critical activities,

Variance of project length = σ^2 * 4 + 16 + 18 = 38 months

Therefore, Standard Deviation = $\sigma = \sqrt{36} = 6$

(iv) Probability that the project will be completed at least 8 months earlier than the expected time of 34 months is given by

$$\text{Probability}\left[Z \leq \frac{T_s - T_e}{\sigma_e} = \frac{(34-8)-34}{6}\right] = \text{Prob. } [Z \leq -1.33]$$

But Z = –1.33 from the normal distribution table is 0.0918.

Students may please note that the values for the Prob. for a Z value correspond to the shaded area as shown In the diagram below:

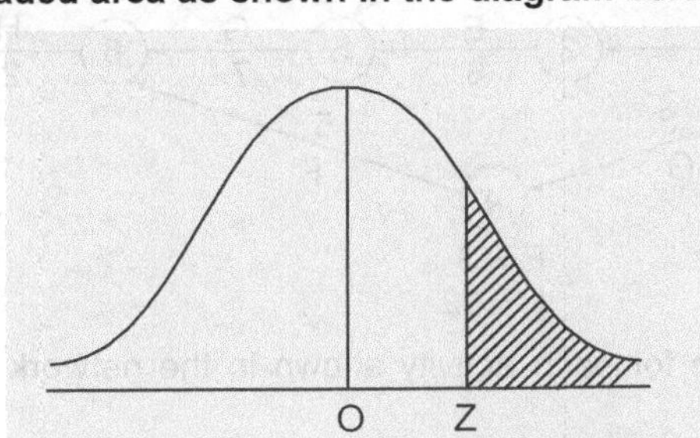

Thus, the probability of completing the project within 26 months is 9.18%.

(v) If the project due date is 38 months, then the probability of not meeting the due date is given by

$$\text{Prob.}\left[Z > \frac{T_s - T_e}{\sigma_e} = \frac{(38-34)}{6}\right] = \text{Prob.} [Z > 0.67]$$

But Z = 0.67 from the normal distribution is 0.2514.

Thus, the probability of not meeting the due date is 25.14%.

PROBLEM 7.7

A project consists of eight activities with the following relevant information:

Activity	*Immediate Predecessor*	*Estimated Duration (Days)*		
		Optimistic	*Most Likely*	*Pessimist! c*
A	—	1	1	7
B	—	1	4	7
C	—	2	2	8
D	A	1	1	1
E	B	2	5	14
F	C	2	5	8
G	D,E	3	6	15
H	F,G	1	2	3

(i) Draw the PERT network and find out the expected project completion time.

(ii) What duration will have 95% confidence for project completion ?

(iii) If the average duration for activity F increases to 14 days, what will be its effect on the expected project completion time which will have 95% confidence ?

(For standard normal Z = 1.645, area under the standard normal curve from 0 to Z = 0.45)

(May 1996)

Solution

(i) The required network is drawn below:

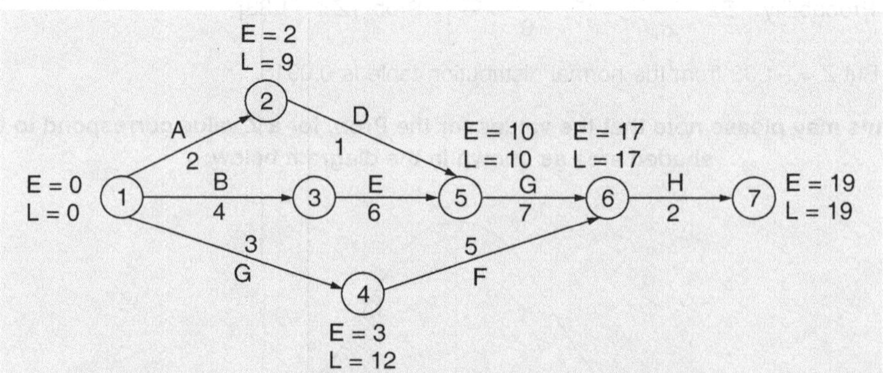

The expected time for each activity shown in the network above is calculated in the following table:

Activity		*Estimated Duration (Days)*			*Expected duration*	*Variance*
		Optimistic	*Most likely*	*Pessimistic*	*Γ*	*Γ*
A	1-2	1	1	7	2	1
B	1-3	1	4	7	4	1
C	1-4	2	2	8	3	1
D	2-5	1	1	1	1	0
E	3-5	2	5	14	6	4
F	4-6	2	5	8	5	1
G	5-6	3	6	15	7	4
H	6-7	1	2	3	2	1/9

The critical oath is oiven bv 1-3-5-6-7 or B-P-G-H and the exoected nroiect corrmletion

(ii) The variance for critical path is 1 + 4 + 4 + 1/9 = 82/9

Standard deviation of critical path = σ_{11} = 3.02(approx.).

To calculate the project duration which will have 95% chances of its completion, we utilise the given value of Z corresponding to 95% confidence which is 1.645.

Thus, Z = 1.645

or X = 1.645 × 3.02 + 19 = 23.97days ≅ 24days

Hence, 24 days of project completion time will have 95% probability of its completion.

(iii) If the average duration for activity Pancreases to 14 days, then the path 1 – 4 – 6 – 7 i.e., C – F – H will also become critical path with expected project completion time of 19 days. Now, activities C and F are also critical activities. Since we are given only the average duration for activity F, it is assumed that the variance for this activity is zero, Further, since PERT analysis is based on the assumption that the activities are independent in terms of their variance, therefore, standard deviation of critical paths can be computed as:

$$s = \sqrt{\frac{82}{9} + 1} = \sqrt{\frac{91}{9}} = 3.18$$

We now wish to calculate the expected project completion time that will have 95% confidence level,

P(Z < 1.645) = 0.95.

or X = 19 + 1.645 × 3.18 = 24,23 days.

Hence the project duration of 24,23 days will have 95% confidence of completion.

PROBLEM 7.8

A small project is composed of seven activities, whose time estimates are listed below. Activities are identified by their beginning (i) and ending (j) node numbers.

Activity	*Estimated duration (in days)*		
	Optimistic	*Most likely*	*Pessimistic*
1-2	2	2	14
1-3	2	8	14
1-4	4	4	16
2-5	2	2	2
3-5	4	10	28
4-6	4	10	16
5-6	6	12	30

(a) Draw the project network.

(b) Find the expected duration and variance for each activity. What is the expected project length?

(c) If the project due date is 38 days, what is the probability of meeting the due date?

Given:

z	0.50	0.67	1.00	1.33	2.00
P	0.3085	0.2514	0.1587	0.0918	0.0228

Solution

Activity (I – j)	Estimated durations (in days) a	m	b	$\frac{a+4m+b}{6}$	$\sigma^2 = \left(\frac{b-a}{6}\right)^2$
1-2	2	2	14	4	4
1-3	2	8	14	8	4
1-4	4	4	16	6	4
2-5	2	2	2	2	0
3-5	4	10	28	12	16
4-6	4	10	16	10	4
5-6	6	12	30	14	16

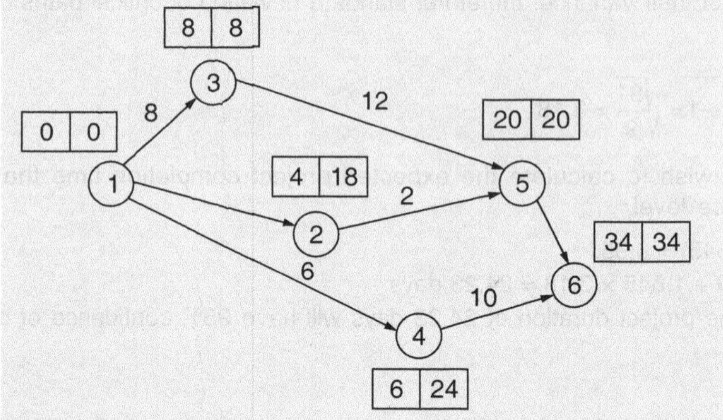

The critical path is 1 ... 3 ... 5 ... 6

(b) The expected duration of the project 8 + 12 + 14 = 34 days

(c) Variance of project length is s^2 = 4 + 16 + 16 = 36

The standard normal deviate is:

$$Z = \frac{\text{due date} - \text{expected date of completion}}{\sqrt{\text{variance}}}$$

$Z = \frac{26-34}{6} = \frac{8}{6} = -1.33$ probability of meeting the due date is 0.0918 or 9.18%

(d) When due date is 38 days

$Z = \frac{38-34}{6} = \frac{4}{6} = 0.67$. Probability meeting the date is 0.2515 or 25.14%.

PROBLEM 7.9 [Updating the Network]

Tulsian Ltd. Provides you the following network and information relating to progress of a project:

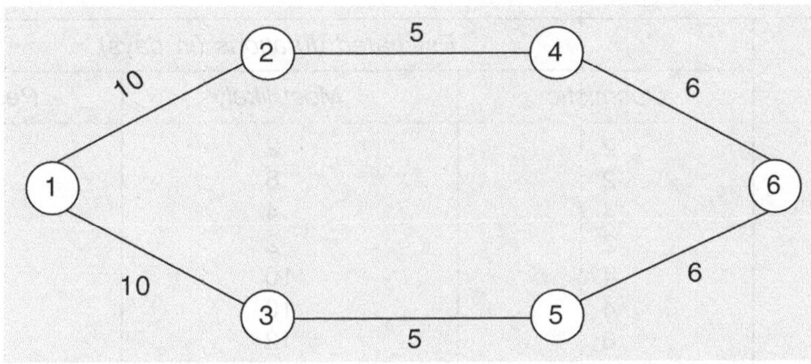

This project has been reviewed after 11 days and following situation has been noted:

1. Activity 1-2 has been completed and activity 2-4 has yet to start.
2. Activity 1-3 has not been started till now.
3. Activity 4-6 can be completed in 5 days instead of 6 days.
4. Due to some technical problem activity 5-6 will now take 8 days.

Required: Update the above network with revised duration.

Solution

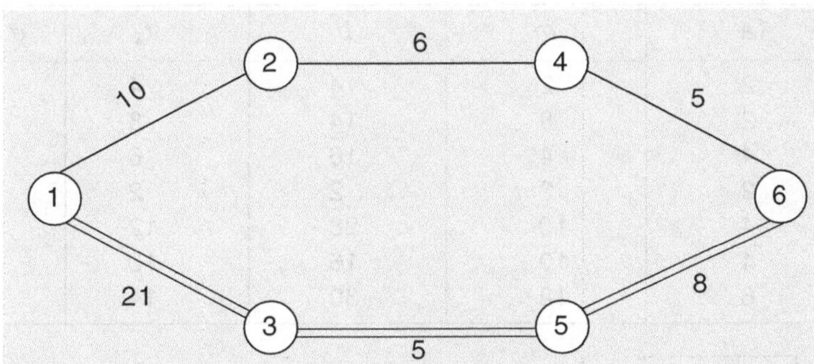

Activity	New Duration
2 – 4	11 + 5 – 10 = 6
1 – 3	10 + 11 = 21

PROBLEM 7.10

A small project is composed of seven activities, whose time estimates are listed below. Activities are identifies by their beginning (i) and ending (j) node numbers:

Activity	*Estimated durations (in days)*		
(i-j)	*Optimistic*	*Most likely*	*Pessimistic*
1-2	2	2	14
1-3	2	8	14
1-4	4	4	16
2-5	2	2	2
3-5	4	10	28
4-6	4	10	16
5-6	6	12	30

(a) Draw the project network.

(b) Find the expected duration and variance for each activity. What is the expected project length?

Given :

Z	0.50	0.67	1.00	1.33	2.00
P	0.3085	0.2514	0.1587	0.0918	0.0228

Solution

Activity Estimated Durations:

Activity Estimated Durations (days) $t_e = \dfrac{(a + 4m + b)}{6}$ Duration

Activity	*a*	*m*	*b*	t_e	$\sigma = [(b-a)/6]^2$
1-2	2	2	14	4	4
1-3	2	8	14	8	4
1-4	4	4	16	6	4
2-5	2	2	2	2	0
3-5	4	10	28	12	16
4-6	4	10	16	10	4
5-6	6	12	30	14	16

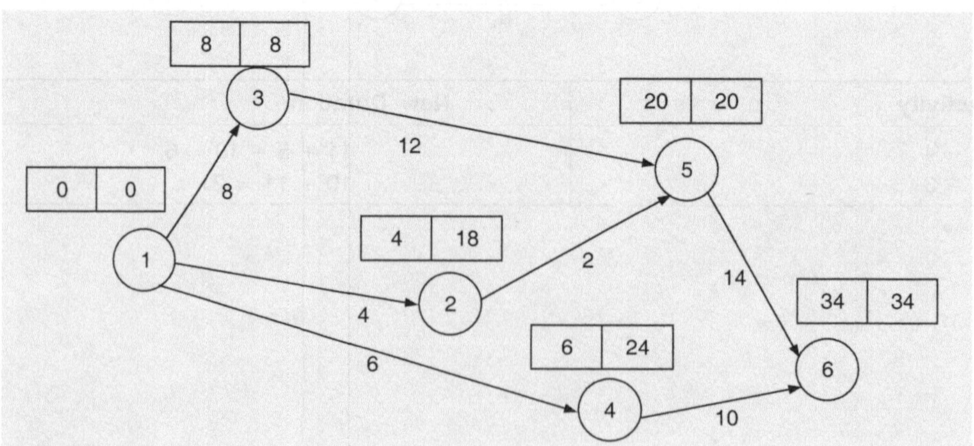

Critical Path is 1-3-5-6.

The expected project duration = 8 + 12 + 14 = 34 days

8 CRASHING, RESOURCE ALLOCATION AND SMOOTHING

PROBLEM 8.1

A project has the following time schedule.

Activity	Time in months	Activity	Time in months
1-2	2	3-7	5
1-3	2	4-6	3
1-4	1	5-8	1
2-5	4	6-9	5
3-6	8	7-8	4
		8-9	3

Required:

(i) Construct PERT Network and compute, (a) Total float for each activity, (b) Critical path and its duration.

(iii) Also find the minimum number of cranes the project must have for its activities 2 – 5, 3 – 7 and 8 – 9 without delaying the project. Then, is any change required in PERT Network? If so, indicate the same.

Solution

Table Showing the Calculation of Total Float

Activity (1)	Duration (2)	ES (3)	LS (4)	EF (5 = 2 + 3)	LF (6 = 4 – 2)	TF (7 = 6 – 3)
1-2	2	0	7	2	5	5
1-3	2	0	2	2	0	0
1-4	1	0	7	1	6	6
2-5	4	2	11	6	7	5
3-6	8	2	10	10	2	0
3-7	5	2	8	7	3	1
4-6	3	1	10	4	7	6
5-8	1	6	12	7	11	5
6-9	5	10	15	15	10	0
7-8	4	7	12	11	8	1
8-9	3	11	15	14	12	1

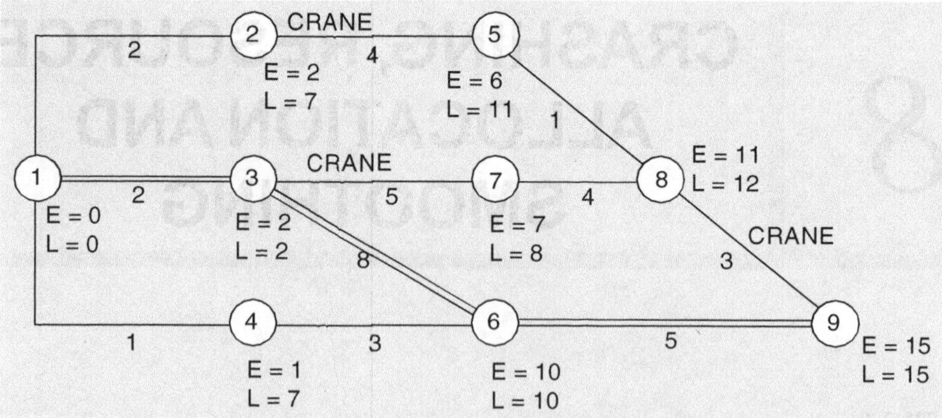

Various Paths	Duration of Paths
1 – 2 – 5 – 8 – 9	2 + 4 + 1 + 3 = 10
1 – 3 – 7 – 8 – 9	2 + 5 + 4 + 3 = 14
1 – 3 – 6 – 9	2 + 8 + 5 = 15
1 – 4 – 6 – 9	1 + 3 + 5 = 9

Hence the critical path is 1 – 3 – 6 – 9 with total project duration of 15 days.

Minimum No. Cranes

Finish	3 – 7	at	7	with one crane
Finish	2 – 5	at	7 + 4 = 11	with the same crane
Finish	5 – 8	at	11 + 1 = 12	without the crane
Finish	8 – 9	at	12 + 3 = 15	with the same crane.

Thus one crane is sufficient.

2 – 5, 5 – 8 and 8 – 9 start at 7, 11 and 12 respectively.

PROBLEM 8.2

The following table lists the activities of a maintenance project :

Activity	Duration (in months)
1–2	2
1–3	2
1–4	1
2–5	4
3–6	5
3–7	8
4–7	3
5–8	1
6–8	4
7–9	5
8–9	3

(i) Draw the project network.

(ii) Find the critical path and duration of the project.

(iii) Suppose we are required to employ a special piece of equipment on activities 1 – 3, 3 – 6, 2 – 5, 5 – 8 and 8 – 9, one at a time. Will it affect the duration of the project? Explain.

Solution

(i) The network for the given project is drawn below:

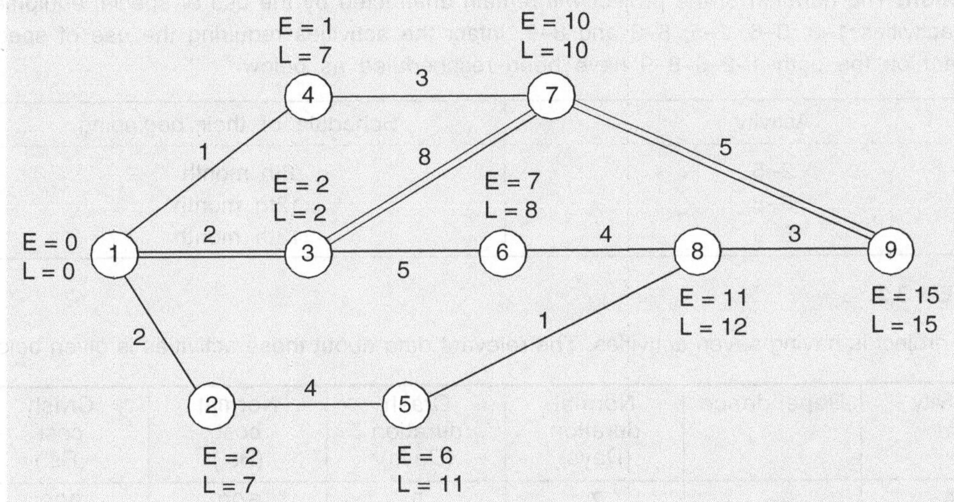

Various Paths	Duration of Paths
1 – 3 – 7 – 9	2 + 8 + 5 = 15
1 – 3 – 6 – 8 – 9	2 + 5 + 4 + 3 = 14
1 – 2 – 5 – 8 – 9	2 + 4 + 1 + 3 = 10
1 – 4 – 7 – 9	1 + 3 + 5 = 9

Hence the critical path is 1 – 3 – 7 – 9 with project duration of 15 days.

(ii) The critical path is 1 – 3 – 7 – 9 and the project duration is 15 months.

(iii) The time scaled version of the above network is drawn below :

Various paths are 1 – 3 – 7 – 9 of 15 months duration.
1 – 3 – 6 – 8 – 9 of 14 months duration.
1 – 2 – 5 – 8 – 9 of 10 months duration.
1 – 4 – 7 – 9 of 9 months duration.

Special equipment (SE) is required on activities 1 – 3; 3 – 6; 2 – 5; 5 – 8 and 8 – 9.

Step 1 → We are required to calculate new schedule of activities due to Special Equipment requirement on 1 – 3; 3 – 6; 2 – 5; 5 – 8; and 8 – 9 activities.
Activities on the paths 1 – 4 – 7 – 9; 1 – 3 – 7 – 9 will continue as per the existing schedule.

Step 2 → Special equipment is required from 3rd onwards on activities 3–6 and 2–5. The path 1–2–5–8–9 on which 2–5 lies has a total float of 5 months and if the activity 2–5 on this path is delayed by 5 months then during this period the activity 3–6 will be completed. Such a post-ponement of activity 2–5, 5–8 and 8–9 by 5 months will spare the special equipment to be used exclusively by the activity 3–6.

Step 3 → Activity 2–5 will start from 8th month and requires 4 months for its completion. Therefore the special equipment may now be utilised by the activity 2–5.

Step 4 → The activity 5–8 will start on the 12th month and requires one month for its completion. During this month special equipment can be utilised by this activity.

Step 5 → The activity 8–9 will start on the 13th month and requires 3 months to get completed by a utilising special equipment. The project will be completed by end of 15th month.

Conclusion: The duration of the project will remain unaffected by the use of special equipment on the activities 1–3; 3–6; 2–5; 5–8 and 8–9. Infact the activities requiring the use of special equipment on the path 1–2–5–8–9 have been rescheduled as below:

Activity	Schedule of their beginning
2–5	8th month
5–8	12th month
8–9	13th month

PROBLEM 8.3

A small project is having seven activities. The relevant data about these activities is given below:

Activity	Dependence	Normal duration (Days)	Crash duration (Days)	Normal cost (Rs.)	Crash cost (Rs.)
A	—	7	5	500	900
B	A	4	2	400	600
C	A	5	5	500	500
D	A	6	4	800	1,000
E	B, C	7	4	700	1,000
F	C, D	5	2	800	1,400
G	E, F	6	4	800	1,600

(i) Find out the normal duration and the minimum duration.
(ii) What is the percentage increase in cost to complete the project in 21 days?

Solution

The required network is drawn below:

Various Paths	Duration of Paths
1 – 2 – 4 – 6 – 7	7 + 4 + 7 + 6 = 24
1 – 2 – 3 – 4 – 6 – 7	7 + 5 + 0 + 7 + 6 = 25
1 – 2 – 3 – 5 – 6 – 7	7 + 5 + 0 + 5 + 6 = 23
1 – 2 – 5 – 6 – 7	7 + 6 + 5 + 6 = 24

(i) The critical path of the project is A → C → E → G or 1–2–3–4–6–7 with normal duration of 25 days.
The minimum duration of the project is 18 days.
(ii) The cost slope for various activities is given below:

Activity	Normal Duration	Crash duration	Normal cost (Rs.)	Crash cost (Rs.)	Cost slope (Rs.)
A (1-2)	7	5	500	900	$\frac{900-500}{7-5}=200$
B (2-4)	4	2	400	600	$\frac{600-400}{4-2}=100$
C (2-3)	5	5	500	500	N.A.
D (2-5)	6	4	800	1000	$\frac{1000-800}{6-4}=100$
E (4-6)	7	4	700	1000	$\frac{1000-700}{7-4}=100$
F (5-6)	5	2	800	1400	$\frac{1400-800}{5-2}=200$
G (6-7)	6	4	800	1600	$\frac{1600-800}{6-4}=400$
		Total	4,500		

Step 1 → Various paths of the network are given below:

1–2–3–4–6–7 with duration = 25 days
1–2–4–6–7 with duration = 24 days
1–2–3–5–6–7 with duration = 23 days
1–2–5–6–7 with duration = 24 days

In order to determine the cost of completing the project in 21 days, let us crash that activity on the critical path which has minimum cost slope. It can be seen that the minimum cost slope of Rs. 100 corresponds to activity E (4-6) and it lies on the critical path. Hence, we crash activity E (4-6) by 1 day at an additional cost of Rs. 100.

Step 2 → Various paths now are

1–2–3–4–6–7 with duration = 24 days
1–2–4–6–7 with duration = 23 days
1–2–3–5–6–7 with duration = 23 days
1–2–5–6–7 with duration = 24 days

An examination of the above four paths clearly points out that there are two critical paths namely viz 1–2–3–4–6–7 and 1–2–5–6–7, each with duration = 24 days. To reduce the project duration by three days more, there are following possible combinations of activities.

1. Crash activities 4 – 6 on the path 1–2–3–4–6–7 and 5 – 6 on the path 1–2–5–6–7 by one day each at an addition cost of Rs. 100 + Rs. 200 = Rs. 300
2. Crash activities 4 – 6 on path 1–2–3–4–6–7 and 2 – 5 on path 1–2–5–6–7 by one day each at an additional cost of Rs. 100 + Rs. 100 = RS. 200
3. Crash activity 1–2 by one day at an additional cost of Rs. 200.

It can be observed that the additional cost of reducing the project duration by one day in combination 2 as well as combination 3 is Rs. 200. Hence any of these two can be selected for crashing. However, since crashing activity 1–2 by 1 day reduces the duration of all the paths by 1 day, we will crash it by 1 day. The project duration becomes = 23 days at an additional cost = Rs. 200.

Step 3 → Crash activity 1 – 2 by 1 day further, it would reduce the project duration to 22 days at an additional cost = Rs. 200.

Step 4 → Activity 1 – 2 can not be crashed further. So we now select the combination of an additional cost of Rs. 100 + Rs. 100 = Rs. 200.

The project duration now becomes equal to 21 days.

Hence, in order to complete the project in 21 days, an additional cost of Rs. 100 + Rs. 200 + Rs.200 + Rs. 200 = Rs. 700 will be incurred.

The normal cost of completing the project in 25 days = Rs. 4500.

Hence, the percentage increase in cost to complete the project is 21 days

$$= \frac{\text{Rs. } 700}{\text{Rs. } 4500} \times 100 = 15.5\%$$

PROBLEM 8.4

The Arcot Machinery Company has been offered a contract to build delivery nine extruding presses to the Home Bottling Company. The contract price negotiated contingent upon meeting a specified delivery time, with a bonus offered for early delivery. The marketing department has established the following cost and time information.

Activity	Normal Time (Weeks) a	b	m	Normal Cost (Rs,)	CrashTime (weeks)	Crash Cost (Rs.)
1-2	1	5	3	5,000	1	9,000
2-3	1	7	4	8,000	3	14,000
2-4	1	5	3	4,000	2	6,000
2-5	5	11	8	5,000	7	6,000
3-6	2	6	4	3,000	2	5,000
4-6	5	7	6	2,000	4	3,600
5-7	4	6	5	10,000	4	14,000
6-7	1	5	3	7,000	1	10,600

Normal delivery time is 16 weeks for a contract price of Rs. 62,000.

On the basis of the calculated profitability for each delivery time specified in the following table, what delivery schedule do you recommend that the company should implement?

Contract Delivery Time (weeks)	Contract Amount (Rs.)
15	62,500
14	64,000
13	70,000
12	72,500

(Here a = t_o : Optimistic time, b = t_p : pessimistic time, m = t_m : Most likely time.)

Solution

Let us first calculate the expect duration of each activity.

Activity	Normal Time (weeks) a	b	m	Expected duration Rs.	Normal Cost (weeks)	Crash Time (Rs.)	Crash Cost	Cost Slope
1-2	1	5	3	3	5000	1	9000	2000
2-3	1	7	4	4	8000	3	14000	6000
2-4	1	5	3	3	4000	2	6000	2000
2-5	5	11	8	8	5000	7	6000	1000
3-6	2	6	4	4	3000	2	5000	1000
4-6	5	7	6	6	2000	4	3600	800
5-7	4	6	5	5	10000	4	14000	4000
6-7	1	5	3	3	7000	1	10600	1800

The network for the given problem is drawn below:

The critical path is 1-2-5-7 with total duration of 16 weeks. Cost of all activities is Rs. 44,000.

Contract price is Rs. 62,000 for normal delivery time of 16 weeks. Hence the profit is of Rs. 18000.

For calculating the most profitable delivery schedule, let us start crashing the activities on the critical path. Cost slopes for various activities are given in the above table.

Step 1 → The critical activity 2-5 has the least cost slope of Rs. 1,000, so we crash this activity by 1 day. Crashing cost is Rs. 1,000. The contract amount for delivery time of 15 weeks is Rs. 62,500

Profit = Rs. 62,500 – (Rs. 44,000 + Rs. 1,000)
= Rs. 62,500 – Rs. 45,000 = Rs. 17,500

Step 2 →Now there are two critical paths viz. 1-2-4-6-7 and 1-2-5-7 with duration of 15 weeks. So we crash activity 1-2 by 1 day at crash cost of Rs. 2,000. Project duration is 14 weeks.

Profit = Rs. 65,000 – Rs. (45,000 + 2,000) = Rs. 18,000.

Step 3 → We again crash activity 1-2 by 1 day. So the project duration is 13 weeks

Profit = Rs. 70,000 – (Rs. 47,000 + Rs. 2,000)
= Rs. 70,000 – Rs. 49,000 = Rs. 21,000

Step 4 → Now we crash activity 4-6 for path 1-2-4-6-7 at crash cost of Rs. 800 and activity 5-7 for path 1-2-5-7 at crash cost of Rs. 4,000. Project duration is now 12 weeks.

Profit = Rs. 72,500 – (Rs. 49,000 + Rs. 4000 + Rs. 800)
= Rs. 72,500 – Rs. 53,800 = Rs. 18,700

No further crashing is possible.

From step 3, it can be seen that the profit is maximum when the project duration is 13 weeks. Hence, the company should implement at the delivery schedule of 13 weeks at a contract amount of Rs. 70,000 to gain maximum profit of Rs. 21,000.

PROBLEM 8.5

A project with normal duration and cost along with crash duration and cost for each activity is given below:

Activity	Normal Time (Hrs.)	Normal Cost (Rs.)	Crash Time (Hrs.)	Crash Cost (Rs.)
1–2	5	200	4	300
2–3	5	30	5	30
2–4	9	320	7	480
2–5	12	620	10	710
3–5	6	150	5	200
4–5	0	0	0	0
5–6	8	220	6	310
6–7	6	300	5	370

Required:

(i) Draw network diagram and identify the critical path.

(ii) Find out the total float associated with each activity.

(iii) Crash the relevant activities systematically and determine the optimum project completion time and corresponding cost. **[June, 2009]**

Solution

(i) Network Diagram

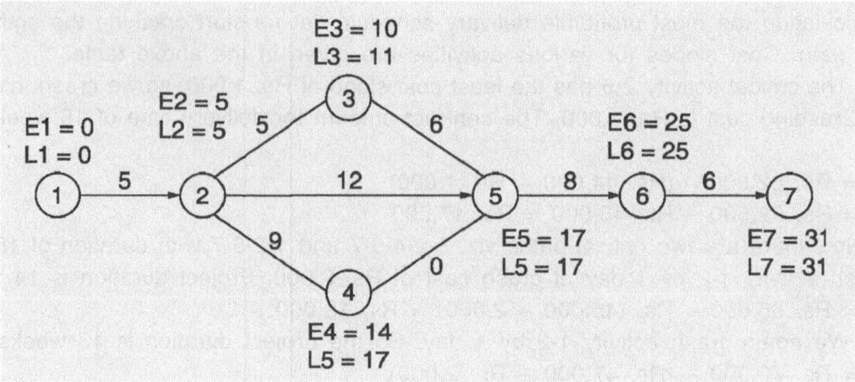

Path are 1-2-5-6-7 = 31 hours, this is critical path

1-2-3-5-6-7 = 30 hours

1-2-4-5-6-7 = 28 hours

(ii) Total Floats

Activity	Duration hours	Early start	Latest start	Early finish	Latest finish	Total float
1-2	5	0	0	5	5	0
2-3	5	5	6	10	11	1
2-4	9	5	8	14	17	3
2-5	12	5	5	17	17	0
3-5	6	10	11	16	17	1
4-5	0	14	17	14	17	3
5-6	8	17	17	25	25	0
6-7	6	25	25	31	31	0

(iii) Calculation of Crashing

Activity	Nt	Nc	Ct	Cc	Slop = (Cc-Nc)/(Nt-Ct)
1-2	5	200	4	300	100
2-3	5	30	5	30	0
2-4	9	320	7	480	80
2-5	12	620	10	710	45
3-5	6	150	5	200	50
4-5	0	0	0	0	0
5-6	8	220	6	310	45
6-7	6	300	5	370	70

The critical path activities are	1-2	2-5	5-6	6-7
Slope	100	45	45	70

Two activities cost slope cost is minimum (2-5 and 5-6) but activity 5-6 is common and critical, it also continuing so reduce by 2 hours, then reduce activity 2-5 by one hour.

	Activity	From-to	Project durations	Cost
I	5-6	8-6 hours	31-2 = 29	1840 + (2 × 45) + (29 × 50) = 3380
II	2-5	12-11	29-1 = 28	1840 + 90 + (1 × 45) + (28 × 50) = 3375

After this reduction now two paths are critical 1-2-3-5-6-7 = 28 and 1-2-5-6-7 = 28

So	1-2	3-5 2-5	6-7
Slope cost	100	50 + 45 = 95	70

As cost per hour for every alternative is greater than Rs. 50 (overhead cost per hour). Therefore, any reduction in the duration of project will increase the cost of project completion. Therefore, time for projects is 28 weeks, minimum cost is Rs. 3375.

PROBLEM 8.6

The normal time, crash time and crashing cost per day are given for the following network:

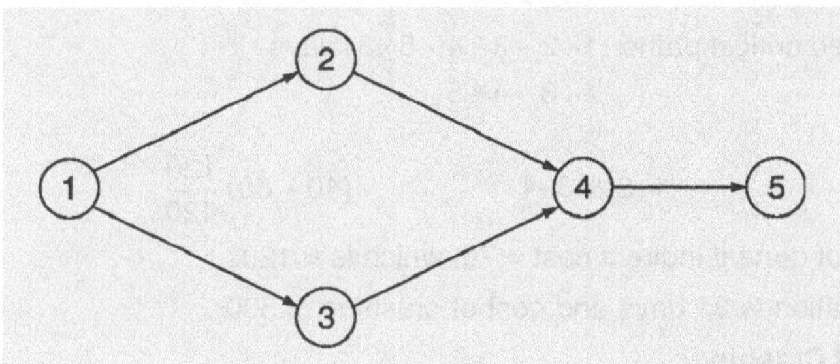

Activity	Normal time (days)	Crash time (days)	Crashing cost (Rs./day)
1-2	18	14	40
1-3	23	22	20
2-3	8	5	60
2-4	10	6	40
3-4	3	2	80
4-5	8	6	50

(i) Crash the project duration in steps and arrive at the minimum duration. What will be the critical path and the cost of crashing?

(ii) If there is an indirect cost of Rs. 70 per day, what will be the optimal project duration and the cost of crashing? **[Nov. 2008]**

Solution

(i) **Critical path**

1 – 2 – 4 – 5 37 days

Path	Normal	Crash
1 – 2 – 4 – 5	36	26
1 – 2 – 3 – 4 – 5	37	27
1 – 3 – 4 – 5	34	30

	Crash Activity	Days,	Cost
Step I	1–2	1	40
II	1–2	1	40
III	4–5	1	50
IV	4–5	1	50
V	2–3	1	60
VI	1–2&1–3	1	60 (40 + 20)
		6	300

Revised critical paths: 1 – 2 – 4 – 5, 1 – 2 – 3 – 4 – 5, 1 – 3 – 4 – 5 } 31 days

VII	1–2 & 3–4	$(40 + 80)\dfrac{120}{420}$	30 days

But VII is not done if indirect cost = 70, which is < 120.

(ii) Project duration is 31 days and cost of crashing is 300.

Working of Crashing:

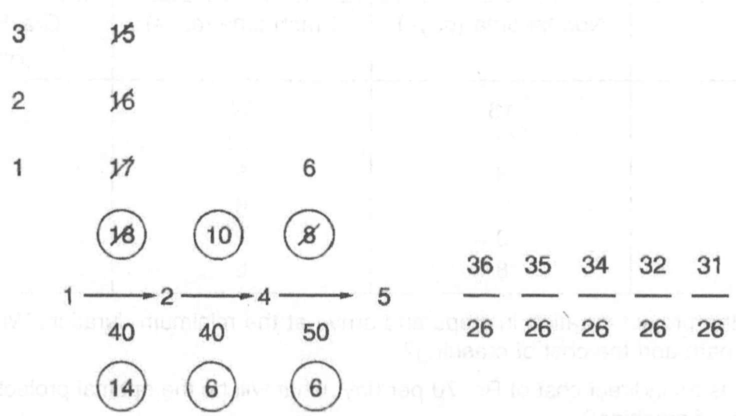

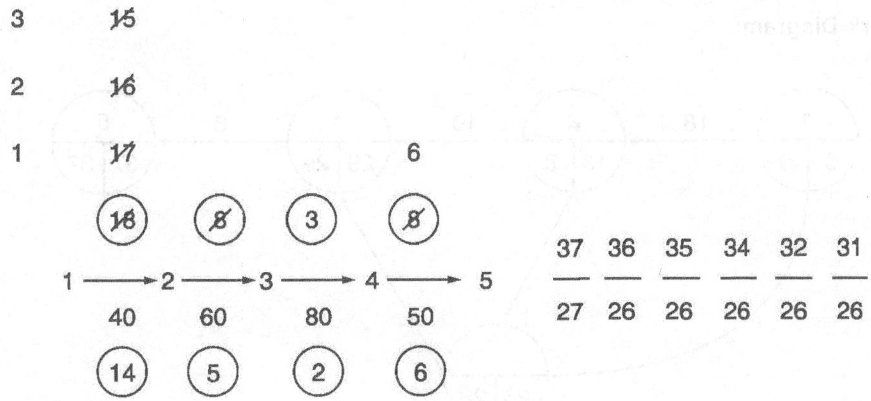

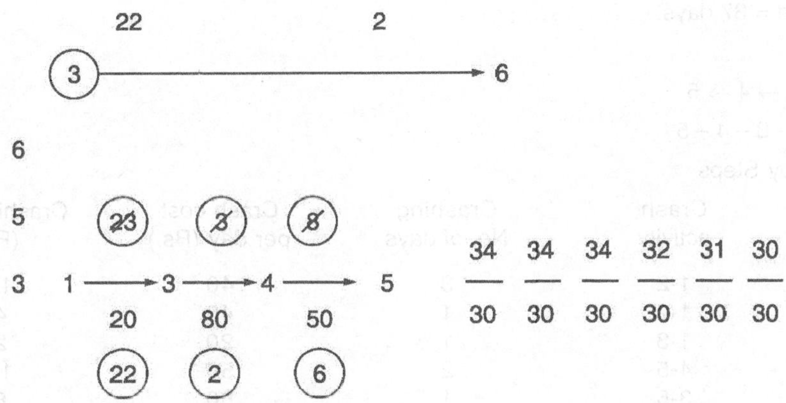

Critical Path: 1 – 2 – 3 – 4 – 5 (37 days) Crashing cost

(1) 1–2	1 day	40
(2) 1–2	1 day	40
(3) 4–5	2 days	100
(4) 2–3	1 day	60
(5) 1 – 2 &1 – 3	1 day (40 + 20)	60
		300

Revised critical path: 1–2–4–5
1–2–3–4–5
1–3–4–5

Duration 31 days

(**Note:** After each crashing a networking diagram has to be drawn and critical path has to be decided).

Alternative Solution:

(i) Network Diagram:

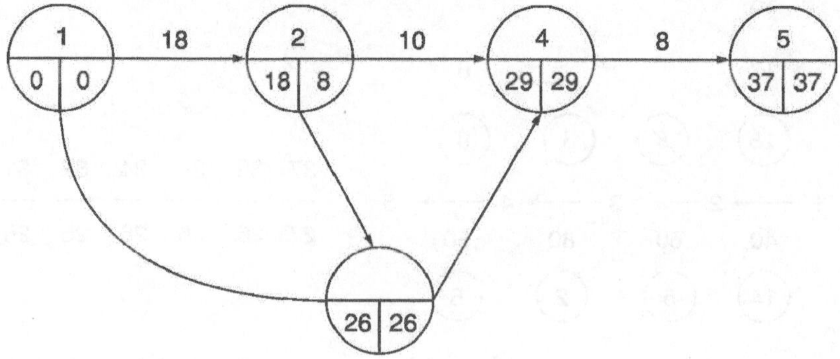

Project duration = 37 days.

Critical Paths:

(i) 1 → 3 → 4 → 5

(ii) 1 – 2 – 3 – 4 – 5

Crashing by Steps

	Crash activity	Crashing No. of days	Crash cost per day (Rs.)	Crashing cost (Rs.)
Step : 1	1-2	3	40	120
Step : 2	1-2	1	40	40
	1-3	1	20	20
Step : 3	4-5	2	50	100
Step : 4	3-5	1	80	80
				360

Revised Network

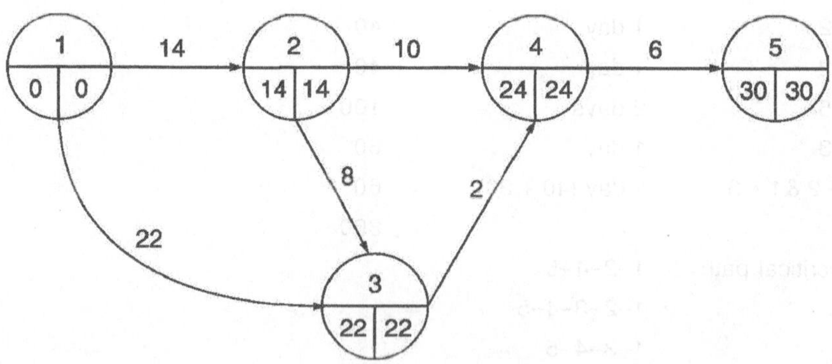

Effective crashing days = 7

Critical Paths:

(i) 1 – 2 – 4 – 5

(ii) 1 – 3 – 4 – 5

(iii) 1 – 2 – 3 – 4 – 5

Project duration = 30 days

Crashing cost = Rs. 360.

(ii) For optimal project duration, we have to consider indirect cost per day i.e. Rs. 70. The crashing cost of activity 3–4 is Rs. 80 which is higher than indirect cost per day. Hence, we may opt it out (Step 4).
In that case, project duration = 31 days.
Crashing cost = Rs. 280.
Saving in indirect cost = 6 × Rs. 70 = Rs. 420.

PROBLEM 8.7

A small project consists of jobs as given in the table below. Each job is listed with its normal time and a minimum or crash time (in days). The cost (in Rs. per day) of each job is also given:

Job (i–j)	Normal Duration (in days)	Minimum (crash) Duration (in days)	Cost of Crashing (Rs. per day)
1-2	9	6	20
1-3	8	5	25
1-4	15	10	30
2-4	5	3	10
3-4	10	6	15
4-5	2	1	40

(i) What is the normal project length and the minimum project length?

(ii) Determine the minimum crashing cost of schedules ranging from normal length down to, and includng the minimum length schedule. That is, if L = Length of the schedule, find the costs of schedules which are L, L – 1, L – 2 and so on.

(iii) Overhead costs total Rs. 60 per day. What is the optimum length schedule in terms of both crashing and overhead cost? List the schedule duration of each job for your solution.

(May 2002)

Solution

(i) The required network is given below:

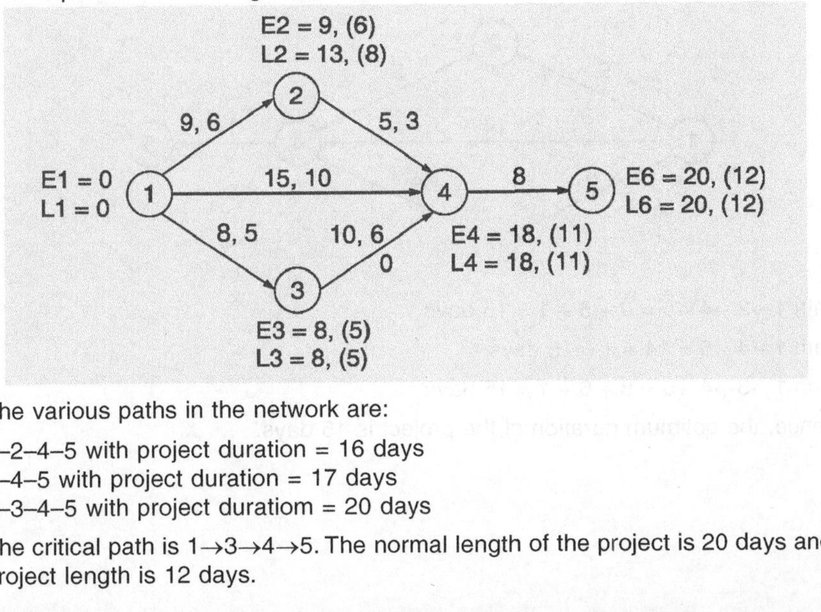

The various paths in the network are:

1–2–4–5 with project duration = 16 days
1–4–5 with project duration = 17 days
1–3–4–5 with project duratiom = 20 days

The critical path is 1→3→4→5. The normal length of the project is 20 days and minimum project length is 12 days.

(ii) Since the present schedule consumes more time than the minimum project length, the duration can be reduced by crashing some of the activities. Also, since the project duration is controlled by the activities lying on the critical path, the duration of some of te activities lying on critical path can be reduced. It is given that overhead cost is Rs. 60 per day.

Step I: First, the crashing cost of activity (3, 4) being minimum, the duration of this activity can be compressed from 10 days to 9 days. The total cost for 19 day's schedule = Rs. 15 + Rs. 19 × 60 = Rs. 1155.

Step II: Since the critical path remans unchanged, the duration of activity (3, 4) can be further reduced from 9 days to 8 days resulting in an additional cost of Rs. 15 so that total cost for 18 days schedule = Rs. 30 + Rs. 60 × 18 = Rs. 30 + Rs. 1080 = Rs. 1110.

Step III: Continue this procedure till the minimum project length schedule. The calculations are given below:

Normal Project length (days)	Job crashed	Crashing cost (Rs.)	Overhead cost @ Rs.60 days	Total cost (Rs.)
20		—	20 × 60	1200
19	3-4	1 × 15 = 15	19 × 60	1155
18	3-4	2 × 15 = 30	18 × 60	1110
17	3-4	3 × 15 = 45	17 × 60	1065
16	4-5	3 × 15 + 1 × 40 = 85	16 × 60	1045
15	3-4, 1-4	4 × 15 + 1 × 40 + 1 × 30 = 130	15 × 60	1030
14	1-3, 1-4, 2-4	130 + 1 × 30 + 1 × 25 + 1 × 10 = 195	14 × 60	1035
13	1-3, 1-4, 2-4	195 + 1 × 25 + 1 × 30 +1 × 10 = 260	13 × 60	1040
12	1-3, 1-4, 1-2	260 + 25 + 30 + 20 = 335	12 × 60	1055

(ii) Since the total cost starts increasing from 14 days duration onwards, the minimum total cost of Rs. 1,030 for the optimum project duration of 15 days occurs for optimum duration of each job as given below:

Job :	(1, 2)	(1, 3)	(1, 4)	(2, 4)	(3, 4)	(4, 5)
Optimum: duration (day)	9	8	14	5	6	1

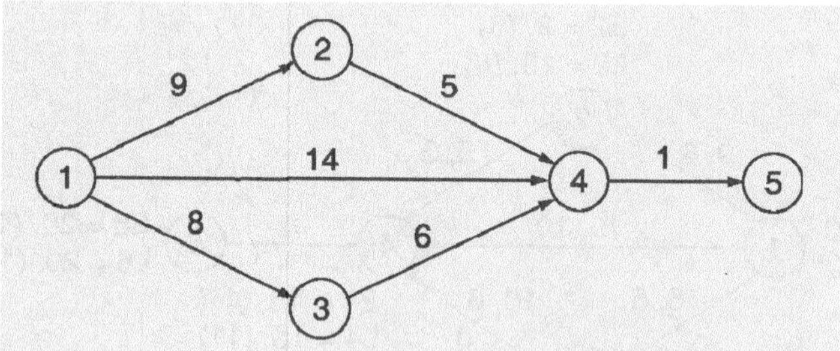

Path 1→2→4→5 = 9 + 5 + 1 = 15 days

Path 1→4→5 = 14 + 1 = 15 days

Path 1→3→4→5 = 8 + 6 + 1 = 15 days

Hence, the optimum duration of the project is 15 days.

PROBLEM 8.8

The data for a project are

Activity	Preceding Activity	Time (in weeks)		Cost (in Rs.)	
		Normal	Crash	Normal	Crash
A	—	3	2	18,000	19,000
B	—	8	6	600	1,000
C	B	6	4	10,000	12,000
D	B	5	2	4,000	10,000
E	A	13	10	3,000	9,000
F	A	4	4	15,000	15,000
G	F	2	1	1,200	1,400
H	C, E, G	6	4	3,500	4,500
I	F	2	1	7,000	8,000

(a) Draw the project network diagram and find the critical path.

(b) If a deadline of 17000 Rs. is imposed for completion of the project, what activities will be crashed, what would be the additional costs and what would be the critical activities of the network after crashing?

Solution

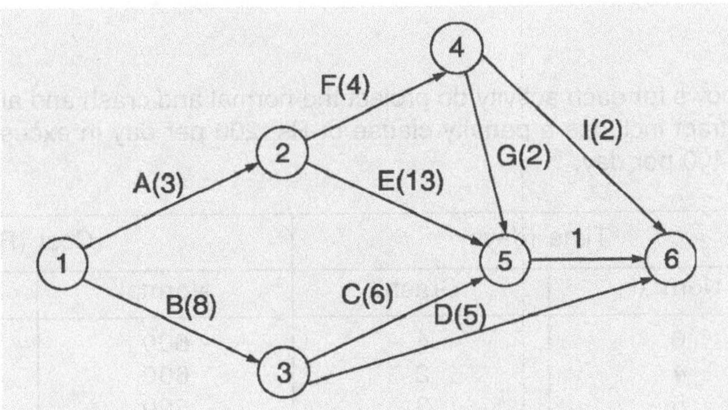

Critical path = A – E – H

Project duration = 22 weeks.

(ii) Calculation of incremental cost of crashing

Activity	Nodes	Normal cost	Crash cost	Cost	NO. of week crashed	Incremental cost of crashing per week
A	1-2	18,000	19,000	1,000	1	1,000
B	1-3	600	1,000	400	2	200
C	3-5	10,000	12,000	2,000	2	1,000
D	3-6	4,000	10,000	6,000	3	2,000
E	2-5	3,000	9,000	6,000	3	2,000
F	2-4	15,000	15,000	0	0	—
G	4-5	1,200	1,400	200	1	200
H	5-6	3,500	4,500	1,000	2	500
I	4-6	7,000	8,000	1,000	1	1,000

Various path	Duration
A–F–I	2
A–E–H	22 (Critical path)
A–F–G–H	15
A–B–C–H	20
B–D	13

Crashing	Critical path	Option	Cost involved	Suction after crashing
(1)	A-E-H	H (2 day)	1,000	20
(2)	A-E-H	A (1 day)	1,000	19
(3)	A-E-H	E (1 day)	2,000	18
(4)	A–E–H	E (1 day)	2,000	
	B-C-H	B (1 day)	200	17
			6,200	

∴ Crashing cost = 6,200

Normal cost = 62,300

Total cost = Normal cost + crashing cost = 68,500

PROBLEM 8.9

The following table shows for each activity do project the normal and crash and also the normal and crash costs. The contract includes a penalty clause of Rs. 200 per day in excess of 19 days. The overhead cost is Rs. 400 per day.

Activity	Time (days)		Cost (Rs.)	
	Normal	Crash	Normal	Crash
1–2	6	4	600	1,000
1–3	4	2	600	1,400
2–4	5	3	500	1,500
2–5	3	1	450	650
3–5	6	4	900	2,000
4–5	8	4	800	3,000
5–6	4	2	400	1,000
6–7	3	2	450	800

(i) Draw the project network and determine the critical path.

(ii) Find the cost of completing the project is normal time.

(iii) Crash the project activities and determine the cost of completing the project in minimum time.

(iv) What is the optimal duration of the project and what is the cost involved.

Solution

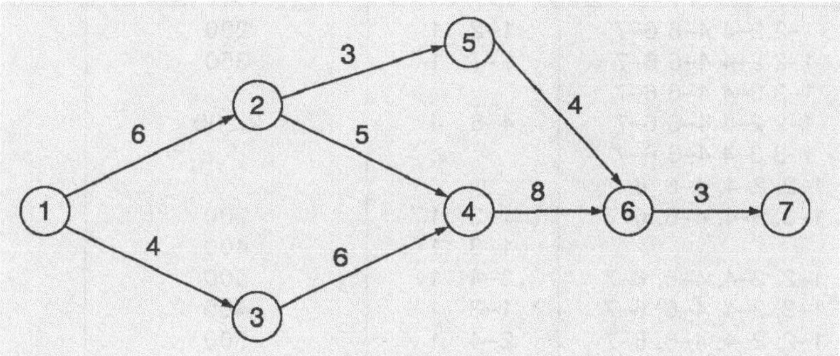

(i) Various path Duration

1–2–5–6–7	16	
1–3–4–6–7	21	
1–2–4–6–7	22	(Critical path)

(ii) Cost of completing the project in normal time

Project cost = 4,700

Overhead cost = 400 × 22 = 8,800

Penalty = 200 (22 – 19) = 600

Total 14,100

(iii) Cost of completing the project in minimum time

Calculation of incremental cost of crashing

Activity	Crash cost	Crash days	Incremental cost of crashing per day
1-2	400	2	200
1-3	800	2	400
2-4	1,000	2	500
2-5	200	2	100
3-4	1,100	2	550
4-6	2,200	4	550
5-6	600	2	300
6-7	350	1	350

Crashing	Critical paths	Path to be crashed	Day cost crashed involved	Duration
(1)	1–2 2–4 4–6 6–7	1–2 1	200	21
(2)	1–2 2–4 4–6 6–7	6–7 1	350	20
	1–3 3–4 4–6 6–7			
(3)	1–2 2–4 4–6 6–7	4–6 4	2,200	16
	1–3 3–4 4–6 6–7			
(4)	1–2, 2–4, 4–6, 6–7			
	1–3, 3–4, 4–6, 6–7	1–2 1	200	
		1–3 1	400	15
(5)	1–2, 2–4, 4–6, 6–7	2–4 1	500	
	1–3, 3–4, 4–6, 6–7	1–3 1	400	14
(6)	1–2, 2–4, 4–6, 6–7	2–4 1	500	
	1–3, 3–4, 4–6, 6–7	3–4 1	550	13
(7)	1–2, 2–4, 4–6, 6–7	No more		
	1–3, 3–4, 4–6, 6–7	crashing		
	1–2, 2–5, 5–6, 6–7	possible		

Total crashing cost = 5,300

Cost of completing the project in minimum time

Normal cost	= 4,700
Crashing cost	= 5,300
Overhead cost	= 5,200
Penalty	= 0
Total	15,200

(iv) **Optimal Duration of Project**

No. of days is which project is completed	Overhead cost	Penalty	Normal cost	Crash cost	Total
22	8,800	600	4,700	0	14,100
21	8,400	400	4,700	200	13,700
20	8,000	200	4,700	550	13,450
19*	7,600	0	4,700	1,100	13,400
18	7,200	0	4,700	1,650	13,550
17	6,800	0	4,700	2,200	13,700
16	6,400	0	4,700	2,750	13,850
15	6,000	0	4,700	2,750	14,050
14	5,600	0	4,700	3,350	14,550
13	5,200	0	7,700	5,300	15,200

Optimum duration of the project is 19 days and the cost involved is Rs. 13,400.

PROBLEM 8.10

The following network gives the duration in days for each activity:

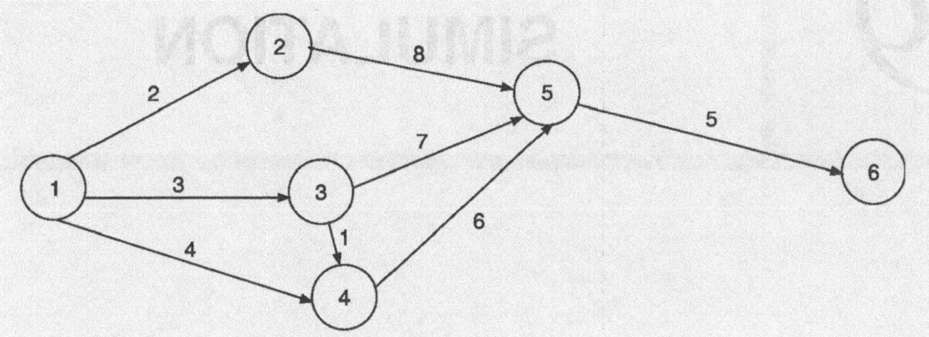

(i) You are required to list the critical paths.

(ii) Given that each activity can be crashed by a maximum of one day, choose to crash any four activities so that the project duration is reduced by 2 days. **(Nov., 2009)**

Solution

Critical Paths	Duration
(i) 1-2-5-6	2 + 8 + 5 =15
(ii) 1-3-5-6	3 + 7 + 5 =15
(iii) 1-4-5-6	4 + 6 + 5 =15
(iv) 1-3-4-5-6	3 + 1+ 6 + 5 =15

(i) Choose 5-6, common path;

Crash by 1 day

(ii) Choose: 1 – 2,1 – 3,1 – 4

Or

(iii) Choose: 1 – 2, 3 – 5,4 – 5

Or

(iv) Choose: 2 – 5 , 3 – 5,4 – 5

Or

(v) Choose: 1 – 3,1 – 4, 2 – 5

9 SIMULATION

PRACTICAL STEPS IN THE SIMULTATION PROCESS

Although simulations vary in complexity from situation to situation, in general one would have to go through the following steps:

Step 1→ *Define the problem or system you inteneded to simulate.*

Step 2→ *Formulate the model you intend to use.*

Step 3→ *Test the model and Compare its behaviour with the behaviour of the actual problem.*

Step 4→ *Identify and collect the data needed to test the model.*

Step 5→ *Run the Simulation*

Step 6→ *Analyze the resuls of the simulation and, if desired, change the solution you are evaluating.*

Step 7→ *Rerun the Simulation to test the new solution.*

Step 8→ *Validate the simulation; this involves increasing the chances of the inferences you may draw about the real situation from running the simulation to become valid.*

MONTE CARLO SIMULATION

The Monte Carlo method is the earliest method of simulation. It employs random numbers and is used to solve problems that depend upon probability, where physical experimentation is impractable and the creation of a mathematical formula impossible. It is a method of simulation by the sampling technique. That is, first of all, the probability distribution of the variable under consideration is determined; then a set of random numbers is used to generate a set of values that have the same distributional characteristics as the actual experience it is designed to simulate. The steps involved in carrying out Monte Carlo Simulation are:

Step 1→ *Select the measure of effectiveness of the problem, that is, what element is used to measure success in improving the system modelled. This is the element one wants to maximise or minimise. For example, this might be idle time of a service facility, or inventory shortages per period.*

Step 2→ *Identify the variables which influence the measure of effectiveness significantly. For example, the number of service facilities in operation or the number of units in inventory and so on.*

Step 3→ *Determine the proper cumulative probability distribution of each variable selected under Step (2) plot these, with the probability on the vertical axis and the values of variables on horizontal axis.*

Step 4→ *Get a set of random numbers.*

Step 5→ *Consider each random number as a decimal value of the cumulative probability distribution. With the decimal, enter the cumulative distribution plot from the vartical axis. Project this point horizontally, until it intersects cumulative probability distribution curve. Then project the point of intersection down into the vertical axis.*

Step 6→ *Record the value generated in Step (5) into the formula derived from the chosen measure of effectiveness. Solve and record the value. This value is the measure of effectiveness for that simulated value.*

Step 7→ *Repeat Steps (5) and (6) until sample is large enough for the satisfaction of the decision maker.*

PROBLEM 9.1 [Frequency Distribution of Probability Estimates]

The investment required for introducing a new product is Rs. 10,000. The probability estimates for variable cost selling price and annual sales volume are given below :

Selling price		*Variable cost*		*Annual volume*	
Value (Rs.)	*Probability*	*Value (Rs.)*	*Probability*	*Value (Rs.)*	*Probability*
3	0.20	1	0.20	4,000	0.20
4	0.60	2	0.50	6,000	0.50
5	0.20	3	0.30	8,000	0.30

Required: Simulate the situation by generating random number to find out selling price, variable cost and the annual sales volume. The random number schemes for the three factors are given below:

Selling price

Value	*Cumulative probability*	*Random number*
3	0.2	00-19
4	0.8	20-79
5	1.0	80-99

Variable cost

Value	*Cumulative probability*	*Random number*
1	0.2	00-19
2	0.7	20-69
3	1.0	70-99

Annual Sales volume

Value	*Cumulative probability*	*Random number*
4,000	0.2	00-19
6,000	0.7	20-69
8,000	1.0	70-99

Also prepare the frequency distribution of the Probability Estimates

Use the following sequence of Sixty random numbers (First 3 random numbers for the first trial etc.)

97, 95, 12, 02, 92, 75, 80, 67, 14, 66, 24, 72, 86, 76, 20, 55, 64, 82, 50, 02, 74, 29, 53, 08, 58, 16, 01, 51, 16, 69, 14, 55, 36, 86, 54, 35, 24, 23, 52, 39, 36, 99, 47, 41, 41, 60, 71, 41, 65, 88, 48, 44, 74, 11, 93, 10, 95, 20, 46, 36

Solution

Net Profit = (Selling price – Variable cost) ↕ Annual sales – Rs. 10,000 (being fixed cost)

Table : Simulation Work Sheet

	Selling price		*Variable cost*		*Annual volume*		*Net*
Observation No.	***Random No.***	***Value (Rs.)***	***Random No.***	***Value (Rs.)***	***Random No.***	***Value (units)***	***Profit (Rs.)***
1	97	5	95	3	12	4,000	–2,000
2	02	3	92	3	75	8,000	–10,000
3	80	5	67	2	14	4,000	2,000
4	66	4	24	2	72	8,000	6,000
5	86	5	76	3	20	6,000	2,000
6	55	4	64	2	82	8,000	6,000
7	50	4	2	1	74	8,000	14,000
8	29	4	53	2	08	4,000	–2,000
9	58	4	16	1	01	4,000	2,000
10	51	4	16	1	69	6,000	8,000
11	14	3	55	2	36	6,000	–4,000
12	86	5	54	2	35	6,000	8,000
13	24	4	23	2	52	6,000	2,000
14	39	4	36	2	99	8,000	6,000
15	47	4	41	2	41	6,000	2,000
16	60	4	71	3	41	6,000	–4,000
17	65	4	88	3	48	6,000	–4,000
18	44	4	74	3	11	4,000	–6,000
19	93	5	10	1	95	8,000	22,000
20	20	4	46	2	36	6,000	2,000

Total Profit = Rs. 50,000, Average Profit = Rs. 50,000/20 = Rs. 2,500

The results of 20 simulations are noted in the following table. We find that losses have occurred in some of the trials and the average profit = Rs. 2,500. The associated risk can be easily found out by taking the profitability figures and computing the associated probabilities.

Table Showing the Frequency Distribution of the Probability Estimates

Profit	*Frequency*	*Cumulative Frequency*	*Probability*
22,000	1	1	1/20
14,000	1	2	2/20
8,000	2	4	4/20
6,000	3	7	7/20
2,000	6	13	13/20
-2,000	2	15	15/20
-4,000	3	18	18/20
-6,000	1	19	19/20
-10,000	1	20	20/20

PROBLEM 9.2 [SIMULATING THE DEFECTED ITEMS]

The output of a production line is checked by an inspector for one or more of three different types of defects, called defects A, B and C. If defect A occurs, the item is scrapped. If defect B or C occurs, the item must be reworked. The time required to rework a B defect is 15 minutes and the time required to rework a C defect is 30 minutes. The probabilities of an A, B and C defects are .15, .20 and .10 respectively. For ten items coming off the assembly line, determine the number of items without any defects, the number scrapped and the total minutes of rework time. Use the following random numbers:

RN for defect A	48	55	91	40	93	01	83	63	47	52
RN for defect B	47	36	57	04	79	18	10	13	57	09
RN for defect C	82	95	18	96	20	8	56	11	52	03

Solution

Table I - Random Numbers Coding

Defect A			*Defect B*			*Defect C*		
Whether Defect Exists ?	*Cum. Prob.*	*Random numbers assigned*	*Whether Defect Exists ?*	*Cum. Prob.*	*Random numbers assigned*	*Whether Defect Exists ?*	*Cum. Prob.*	*Random numbers assigned*
Yes	0.15	00-14	Yes	0.20	00-19	Yes	0.10	00-09
No	1.00	15-99	No	1.00	20-99	No	1.00	10-99

Table II - Simulation Worksheet

Item No.	*RN for defect A*	*Whether defect exist or not*	*RN for defect B*	*Whether defect exist or not*	*RN for defect C*	*Whether defect exist or not*	*Which defect*	*Rework time (in minutes) exists*	*Remarks*
1	48	No	47	No	82	No	—	—	—
2	55	No	36	No	95	No	—	—	—
3	91	No	57	No	18	No	—	—	—
4	40	No	04	Yes	96	No	B	15	—
5	93	No	79	No	20	No	—	—	—
6	01	Yes	18	Yes	8	Yes	A, B, C	—	Scrap
7	83	No	10	Yes	56	No	B	15	—
8	63	No	13	Yes	11	No	B	15	—
9	47	No	57	No	52	No	—	—	—
10	52	No	09	Yes	03	Yes	B,C	15 + 30 = 45	—

During the simulated period,
No. of items without any defect = 5
No. of items scrapped = 1
No. of items required rework = 4
Total rework time required = 90 minutes

PROBLEM 9.3 [Penalty Cost for Excess & Short Output]

A company manufacturers 30 items per day. The sale of these items depends upon demand which has the following distribution:

Sales (Units)	*Probability*
27	0.10
28	0.15
29	0.20
30	0.35
31	0.15
32	0.05

The production cost and selling price of each unit are Rs. 40 and Rs. 50 respectively. Any unsold product is to be disposed off at a loss of Rs. 15 per unit. There is a penalty of Rs. 5 per unit if the demand is not met.

Required: Using the following random numbers estimate total profit/loss for the company for the next 10 days : 10, 99, 65, 99, 95, 01, 79, 11, 16,20

If the company decides to produce 29 items per day, what is the advantage or disadvantage to the company?

Solution

Table I - Random Number Coding

Sales (units)	*Probability*	*Cumulative Probability*	*Random numbers assigned*
27	0.10	0.10	00-09
28	0.15	0.25	10-24
29	0.20	0.45	25-44
30	0.35	0.80	45-79
31	0.15	0.95	80-94
32	0.05	1.00	95-99

Profit per unit = Selling Price per unit – Cost per unit
= Rs. 50 – Rs. 40 = Rs. 10 per unit

Table II - Simulation Work Sheet

(i) *Day*	*(ii)* *Random number*	*(iii)* *Estimated sale*	*(iv)* *Profit/Loss per day when production = 30 items per day*	*(v)* *Profit/Loss per day when production = 29 items per day*
1	10	28	28 × Rs. 10 – 2 × Rs. 15 = 250	28 × Rs. 10 – 1 × Rs. 15 = 265
2	99	32	30 × Rs. 10 – 2 × Rs. 5 = 290	29 × Rs. 10 – 3 × Rs. 5 = 275
3	65	30	30 × Rs. 10 = 300	29 × Rs. 10 – 1 × Rs. 5 = 285
4	99	32	30 × Rs. 10 – 2 × Rs. 5 = 290	29 × Rs. 10 – 3 × Rs. 5 = 275
5	95	32	30 × Rs. 10 – 2 × Rs. 5 = 290	29 × Rs. 10 – 3 × Rs. 5 = 275
6	01	27	27 × Rs. 10 – 3 × Rs. 15 = 225	27 × Rs. 10 – 2 × Rs. 15 = 240
7	79	30	30 × Rs. 10 = 300	29 × Rs. 10 – 1 × Rs. 5 = 285
8	11	28	28 × Rs. 10 – 2 × Rs. 15 = 250	28 × Rs. 10 – 1 × Rs. 15 = 265
9	16	28	28 × Rs. 10 – 2 × Rs. 15 = 250	28 × Rs. 10 – 1 × Rs. 15 = 265
10	20	28	28 × Rs. 10 – 2 × Rs. 15 = 250	28 × Rs. 10 – 1 × Rs. 15 = 265
Total Profit =			**Rs. 2,695**	**Rs. 2,695**

It is evident from this table that there is no additional profit or loss if the production is reduced to 29 items per day since the total profit remains unchanged i.e. Rs. 2,695.

PROBLEM 9.4 [Calculation of No. of Mopeds waiting in the factory and No. of Empty spaces on the Lorry]

A company manufactures around 200 mopeds. Depending upon the availability of raw materials and other conditions, the daily production has been varying from 196 mopeds to 204 mopeds, whose probability distribution is as given below :

Production/day:	196	197	198	199	200	201	202	203	204
Probability :	0.05	0.09	0.12	0.14	0.20	0.15	0.11	0.08	0.06

The finished mopeds are transported in a specially designed three storeyed lorry that can accomodate only 200 mopeds.

Required: Using the following 15 random numbers 82, 89, 78, 24, 53, 61, 18, 45, 04, 23, 50, 77, 27, 54, 10 simulate the process to find out:

(i) What will be the average number of mopeds waiting in the factory?

(ii) What will be the average number of empty space on the lorry.

Solution

Table I - Random Numbers Coding

Production per day	***Probability***	***Cumulative probability***	***Random number interval***
196	0.05	0.05	00-04
197	0.09	0.14	05-13
198	0.12	0.26	14-25
199	0.14	0.40	26-39
200	0.20	0.60	40-59
201	0.15	0.75	60-74
202	0.11	0.86	75-85
203	0.08	0.94	86-93
204	0.06	1.00	93-99

Table II - Simulation Worksheet

Random numbers *A*	*Daily production* *B*	*Capacity of lorry* *C*	*No. of Mopeds Waiting (Empty Space)* *D = B − C*	*Cumulative No. of mopeds waiting* *E*	*No. of empty spaces* *F*
82	202	200	2	2	0
89	203	200	3	5	0
78	202	200	2	7	0
24	198	200	(2)	5	0
53	200	200	0	5	0
61	201	200	1	6	0
18	198	200	(2)	4	0
45	200	200	0	4	0
04	196	200	(4)	0	0
23	198	200	(2)	0	2
50	200	200	0	0	0
77	202	200	2	2	0
27	199	200	(1)	1	0
54	200	200	0	1	2
10	197	200	(3)	-	-
				42	4

(i) Average No. of Mopeds waiting in the factory = 42/15 = 2.8 per day

(ii) Average No. of Empty spaces on the lorry = 4/15 = .267 per day

PROBLEM 9.5 [Simulating Process Time]

XYZ Scientific Equipment manufacturing company is engaged in producing different types of high class equipment for use in science laboratories. The company has two different assembly times to produce its most popular product. The processing time for each of the assembly lines is regarded as a random variable and is described by the following distributions:

Processing time (minutes)	*Assembly A_1*	*Assembly A_2*
20	0.20	0.10
21	0.40	0.15
22	0.20	0.40
23	0.15	0.25
24	0.05	0.10

Using the following random numbers, generate data on the process times for 15 units of the item and compute the expected process time for the product :

3441 7674 4349 4383 8311 1519 0236 4594 1554
0575 8900 8008 2874 2434 0993

For the purpose, read the numbers horizontally, taking the first two digits for the processing time on assembly A_1 and the last two digits for processing time on assembly A_2.

Solution

Table I : Random Number Coding

Time (mts.)	*Assembly A_1*			*Assembly A_2*		
	Prob.	*Cum. prob.*	*RN Interval*	*Prob.*	*Cum. Prob.*	*RN Interval*
20	0.20	0.20	00-19	0.10	0.10	00-09
21	0.40	0.60	20-59	0.15	0.25	10-24
22	0.20	0.80	60-79	0.40	0.65	25-64
23	0.15	0.95	80-94	0.25	0.90	65-89
24	0.05	1.00	95-99	0.10	1.00	90-99

The random numbers for the first unit are 34 and 41 respectively for the assemblies A1 and A2. From Table 2, we observe that the times corresponding to these are 22 and 21 minutes respectively. Thus the total time required for the unit is 43 minutes. In the same way, the times for the other 14 units are determined and shown in the last column of the table.

Table II : Simulation Worksheet

Unit	*Assembly A_1*		*Assembly A_2*		*Total time*
	R. Number	*Time*	*R. Number*	*Time*	*(mts.)*
1	34	21	41	22	43
2	76	22	74	23	45
3	43	21	49	22	43
4	43	21	83	23	44
5	83	23	11	21	44
6	15	20	19	21	41
7	02	20	36	22	42
8	45	21	94	24	45
9	15	20	54	22	42
10	05	20	75	23	43
11	89	23	00	20	43
12	80	23	08	20	43
13	28	21	74	23	44
14	24	21	34	22	43
15	09	20	93	24	44
				Total	**649**

Expected time = 649/15 = 43.27

PROBLEM 9.6

A d.p. manager estimates that the keypunch staff is idle 20% of the time and would like to take a work-sampling study that would be accurate within $\pm$ 4%. The manager wishes to have 95% confidence in the resulting study. How many observations should be taken? The demand and leadtime for a particular item have the distributions show below. Explain how the demand over the lead time could be generated using Monte Carlo simulation. Use the random numbers shown in your explanation.

Leadtime (week)	*Probability*	*Random Nos.*
2	0.25	38, 10, 41, 82
3	0.50	
4	0.25	

Demand items/week	Probability	Random Nos.
100	0.10	15, 51, 60, 30, 72
150	0.15	09, 40, 50, 84, 86
200	0.50	49, 32
250	0.15	
300	0.10	

Solution

$$n = \frac{Z^2 pq}{h^2} = \frac{1.96^2 \times 0.2 \times 0.8}{0.04^2} = 384 \text{ observations.}$$

Leadtime	Cumulative Probability	Random Number Interval
2	0.25	00 – 24
3	0.75	25 – 74
4	1.00	75 – 99

Therefore, leadtimes for the given random nos. are as follows in brackets: 38 (3), 10 (2), 41 (3), 82 (4).

Demand Items/week	Cumulative Probability	Random Number Interval
100	0.10	00 – 09
150	0.25	10 – 24
200	0.75	25 – 74
250	0.90	75 – 89
300	1.00	90 – 99

Therefore demands for the given random nos. are as follows in brackets : 15 (150), 51(200), 60(200), 30(200), 72(200), 02(100), 40(200), 50(200), 84(250), 76(250), 49(200), 32(200).

Leadtime	*Leadtime Demand*
3	150 + 200 + 200 = 550
2	200 + 200 = 400
3	100 + 200 + 200 = 500
4	250 + 250 + 200 + 200 = 900

PROBLEM 9.7 [Simulating the weather]

The occurrence of rain in a city on a day is dependent upon whether or not it rained on the previous day. If it rained on the previous day, the rain distribution is given by:

Event	Probability
No rain	0.50
1 cm. rain	0.25
2 cm. rain	0.15
3 cm. rain	0.05
4 cm. rain	0.03
5 cm. rain	0.02

If it did not rain the previous day, the rain distribution is given by :

Event	Probability
No rain	0.75
1 cm. rain	0.15
2 cm. rain	0.06
3 cm. rain	0.04

Simulate the city's weather for 10 days and determine by simulation the total days without rain as well as the total rainfall during the period. Use the following random numbers :

67 63 39 55 29 78 70 06 78 76

for simulation assume that for the first day of the simulation it had not rained the day before.

Solution

Table I - Random Number Coding (Rain on Previous Day)

Event	*Probability*	*Cumulative Probability*	*Random numbers assigned*
No rain	0.50	0.50	00-49
1 cm. rain	0.25	0.75	50-74
2 cm. rain	0.15	0.90	75-89
3 cm. rain	0.05	0.95	90-94
4 cm. rain	0.03	0.98	95-97
5 cm. rain	0.02	1.00	98-99

Table II - Random Number Coding (No Rain on previous day)

Event	*Probability*	*Cumulative Probability*	*Random numbers assigned*
No rain	0.75	0.75	00-74
1 cm. rain	0.15	0.90	75-89
2 cm. rain	0.06	0.96	90-95
3 cm. rain	0.04	1.00	96-99

Table III - Simulation Work Sheet

Day	*Random Numbers*	*Event*	
1	67	No rain	(from table 2)
2	63	No rain	(from table 2)
3	39	No rain	(from table 2)
4	55	No rain	(from table 2)
5	29	No rain	(from table 2)
6	78	1 cm. rain	(from table 2)
7	70	1 cm. rain	(from table 1)
8	06	No rain	(from table 1)
9	78	1 cm. rain	(from table 2)
10	76	2 cm. rain	(from table 1)

Hence, during the simulated period, it did not rain on 6 days out of 10 days. The

PROBLEM 9.8 [Simulating the Dentist's Clinic]

Dr. Strong is a dentist who schedules all her patients for 30 minutes appointments. Some of the patients take more or less than 30 minutes depending on the type of dental work to be done. The following summary shows the various categories of work, their probabilities and the time actually needed to complete the work :

Category	*Time required*	*Probability of category*
Filling	45 minutes	0.40
Crown	60 minutes	0.15
Cleaning	15 minutes	0.15
Extraction	45 minutes	0.10
Checkup	15 minutes	0.20

Simulate the dentist's clinic for four hours and determine the average waiting time for the patients as well as the idleness of the doctor. Assume that all the patients show up at the clinic at exactly their scheduled arrival time starting at 8.00 a.m. Use the following random numbers for handling the above problem :

40 82 11 34 25 66 17 79

Solution

Table I - Random Number Coding

Type	*Probability*	*Cumulative Probability*	*Random Numbers*
Filling	0.40	0.40	00-39
Crown	0.15	0.55	40-54
Cleaning	0.15	0.70	55-69
Extraction	0.10	0.80	70-79
Checkup	0.20	1.00	80-99

Table II - Simulation Work Sheet

Patient	*Scheduled Arrival*	*Random Number*	*Category*	*Service Time*
1	8.00	40	Crown	60 minutes
2	8.30	82	Checkup	15 minutes
3	9.00	11	Filling	45 minutes
4	9.30	34	Filling	45 minutes
5	10.00	25	Filling	45 minutes
6	10.30	66	Cleaning	15 minutes
7	11.00	17	Filling	45 minutes
8	11.30	79	Extraction	45 minutes

Now, let us simulate the dentist's clinic for four hours starting at 8.00 A.M.

Table showing the waiting times for the patients

A	*B*	*C*	*D*	*E = C + D*	*F = C − B*
Patient	*Arrival*	*Service Starts*	*Service Time*	*Service Ends*	*Waiting (Minutes)*
1	8.00	8.00	60 Minutes	9.00	0
2	8.30	9.00	15 Minutes	9.15	30
3	9.00	9.15	45 Minutes	10.00	15
4	9.30	10.00	45 Minutes	10.45	30
5	10.00	10.45	45 Minutes	11.30	45
6	10.30	11.30	15 Minutes	11.45	60
7	11.00	11.45	45 Minutes	12.30	45
8	11.30	12.30	45 Minutes	1.15	60
				Total	285

The average waiting time of a patient $= \frac{285}{5}$ 35.625 minutes.

The dentist was not idle during the entire simulated period.

PROBLEM 9.9

Ramu and Raju are workers on a two station assembly line. The distribution of activity times at their station is:

Time (in sec.)	10	20	30	40	50	60	70	80
Time freq. for Ramu :	4	6	10	20	40	11	5	4
Time freq. for Raju :	4	5	6	7	10	8	6	4

(a) Simulate operation of the line for 8 items using the random numbers : 06, 57, 47, 17, 43, 07, 27, 68 for Ramu and 26, 97, 76, 02, 02, 05, 16, 56 for Raju.

(b) Assuming Raju must wait until Ramu completes first item before starting work will he have to wait to process any of the other eight items. Explain your answer based upon your simulation.

Solution

Table I : Random Number Coding

For Ramu				*For Raju*			
Time in secs.	*Time frequency*	*cum. f*	*Random Number allotted*	*Frequency*	*cum. f*	*2* x cum. f*	*Random Number allotted*
10	4	4	00 - 03	4	4	8	00 - 07
20	6	10	04 - 09	5	9	18	08 - 17
30	10	20	10 - 19	6	15	30	18 - 29
40	20	40	20 - 39	7	22	44	30 - 43
50	40	80	40 - 79	10	32	64	44 - 63
60	11	91	80 - 90	8	40	80	64 - 79
70	5	96	91 - 95	6	46	92	80 - 91
80	4	100	96 - 100	4	50	100	92 - 100

*Cumulative frequencies for Raju are multiplied by 2 to make these from 100.

Table 2 : Stimulation Number Sheet

For Ramu		*For Raju*	
Random Nos.	*Processing* time*	*Random Nos.*	*Processing* time*
6	20	26	30
57	50	97	80
47	50	76	60
17	30	02	10
43	50	02	10
7	20	05	10
27	40	16	20
68	50	56	50

* This time corresponds to the time value of the random number corresponding to cumulative frequency value e.g., for Ramu in first row the random number is 6 which lies in the class of cum. freq. = 10 having time value equal to 20 sec. Similarly, processing time for Raju can be calculated.

Table 3 : Computation of Waiting time for Raju

	For Ramu		*For Raju*			
Item No.	*Processing time*	*Cum. time*	*Start time*	*Processing time*	*End. time*	*Waiting time*
1	20	20	20	30	50	—
2	50	70	70*	80	150	20
3	50	120	150	60	210	—
4	30	150	210	10	220	—
5	50	200	220	10	230	—
6	20	220	230	10	240	—
7	40	260	260*	20	280	20
8	50	310	310*	50	360	30

Thus Raju has to wait for items 2, 7 and 8.

* End time of current item of Ramu or end time of previous item of Raju whichever is higher has been taken as start time of current item for Raju.

PROBLEM 9.10

A process involves the production of a particular component which is then installed into an end product. The average production time for the component is 4 minutes and the following probability distribution has been derived from past observation :

Production time (Minutes)	*Probability*
2	0.10
3	0.25
4	0.40
5	0.10
6	0.10
7	0.05

The time taken to install a component is 3 minutes on the average with the following probability distribution:

Installation time (Minutes)	*Probability*
2	0.30
3	0.45
4	0.15
5	0.10

The system uses one operative for installation but the company is considering employing another operative on the installation process.

Required: Simulate 10 arrivals on the current system, using the following 2 digit random numbers:

20, 74, 94, 22, 90, 45, 44, 16, 04, 32, 03, 62, 61, 89, 01, 27, 49, 50, 90, 98.

Solution

Table I - Random Number Coding

Production time			Installation time		
Minutes	*Probability*	*R.N. allotted*	*Minutes*	*Probability*	*R.N. allotted*
2	0.10	00-09	2	0.30	00-29
3	0.25	10-34	3	0.45	30-74
4	0.40	35-74	4	0.15	75-89
5	0.10	75-84	5	0.10	90-99
6	0.10	85-94			
7	0.05	95-99			

Table II - Simulation Work Sheet

A.N.	*R.N.*	*A.T. (cum)*	*R.N.*	Installation			Minutes	
				Time	*Start*	*End*	*I.T.*	*W.T.*
1	20	3	03	2	3	5	3	—
2	74	7	62	3	7	10	2	—
3	94	13	61	3	13	16	3	—
4	22	16	89	4	16	20	—	—
5	90	22	01	2	22	24	2	—
6	45	26	27	2	26	28	2	—
7	44	30	49	3	30	33	2	—
8	16	33	50	3	33	36	—	—
9	04	35	90	5	36	41	—	1
10	32	38	98	5	41	46	—	3
						Total	**14**	**4**

PROBLEM 9.11 [Monte Carlo Simulation for Inventory Decision]

A book store wishes to carry 'Ramayana' in stock. Demand is probabilistic and replenishment of stock takes 2 days (i.e. if an order is placed on March 1, it will be delivered on March 3). The probabilities of demand are given below:

Demand (daily)	0	1	2	3	4
Probability	0.05	0.10	0.3	0.45	0.10

Each time an order is placed, the store incurs an ordering cost of Rs. 10 per order. The store also incurs a carrying cost of 50 paise per book per day which is calculated on the basis of stock at the end of each day.

The manager of the book store wishes to compare two options for his inventory decision.

Option A: Order 5 books when the inventory at the beginning of the day *plus* orders outstanding is less than 8 books.

Option B: Order 8 books when the inventory at the beginning of the day *plus* orders outstanding is less than 8 books.

Currently (beginning of 1st day) the store has a stock of 8 books plus 6 books ordered two days ago and expected to arrive next day.

Required: Using Monte Carlo Simulation for 10 cycles, recommend which option the manager should choose.

The two digit random nos. are given below:

89, 34, 78, 63, 61, 81, 39, 16, 13, 73

Solution

Table I : Random Number Coding

Demand	*Prob.*	*Cum. Prob.*	*Random Nos.*
0	0.05	0.05	00-04
1	0.10	0.15	05-14
2	0.30	0.45	15-44
3	0.45	0.90	45-89
4	0.10	1.00	90-99

Stock in hand = 8 and stock on order = 6 (expected next day)

Table II : Simulation Worksheet for option 'A'

A Random Number (given)	*B Sales*	*C Op. Stock*	*D Receipt*	*E = C + D − B Closing Stock on hand*	*F Orders out-standing*	*G = C + F Opening stock + orders o/s*	*H Order quantity*
89	3	8	—	5	6	14	—
34	2	5	6	9	6	11	—
78	3	9	—	6	—	9	—
63	3	6	—	3	—	6	*5
61	3	3	—	0	5	8	*5
81	3	0	5	2	5	5	*5
39	2	2	—	0	5	7	—
16	2	0	5	3	10	10	—
13	1	3	5	7	5	8	—
73	3	7	—	4	0	7	*5

*5 books have been ordered 4 times.

∴ Ordering cost = Rs. (4 × 10) = Rs. 40

Closing stock of 10 days = (5 + 9 + 6 + 3 + 2 + 3 + 7 + 4) = 39 books.

Closing cost @ Re. 0.5 per book/day = 39 × 0.5 = Rs. 19.5

Total cost for 10 days = Rs. (40 + 19.5) = Rs. 59.5

Table III : Simulation Worksheet for option 'B'

A Random Number (given)	B Sales	C Op. Stock	D Receipt	E = C + D - B Closing Stock on hand	F Orders out-standing	G = C + F Opening stock + orders o/s	H Order quantity
89	3	8	0	5	6	4	—
34	2	5	6	9	—	11	—
78	3	9	—	6	—	9	—
63	3	6	—	3	8	6	8
61	3	3	—	0	8	11	—
81	3	0	8	5	—	8	—
39	2	5	—	3	8	5	8
16	2	3	—	1	8	11	—
13	1	1	8	8	—	9	—
73	3	8	—	5	—	8	—

*8 books have been ordered two times when the inventory at the beginning of the day plus orders outstanding is less than 8.

∴ ordering cost = Rs. 2 × Rs. 10 = Rs. 20. (1)

Closing stock of 10 days = (5 + 9+ 6 + 3 + 5 + 3 + 1 + 8 + 5) = 45 books

Carrying cost @ Re. 0.5 per book per day

= (45 × Re. .5) = Rs. 22.50 (2)

∴ Total cost = Rs. (22.50 + 20) = Rs. 42.50

Since 'Option B' has lower cost than 'Option A', i.e., 42.50 < 59.50 the manager should choose option 'B'.

PROBLEM 9.12

The management has the following available data:

Quantity Demanded	Probability	Lead time (days)	Probability
0	0.10	2	0.20
1	0.45	3	0.65
2	0.30	4	0.15
3	0.15		

The management wants to ascertain its inventory cost if they wish to reord when the quantity on hand is 6 units and order each time a quantity of 12 units. The cost of ordering is Rs. 120, and the cost of holding the inventory per day in stock is Rs. 5 per unit. The management has found that when it runs out of stock, it cost Rs. 75 per unit. Simulate the situation for 15 days by using given random numbers.

Random No. for Sale (49, 67, 06, 30, 95, 01, 10, 70, 80, 66, 69, 76, 86, 56, 84)
Random No. for lead time (84, 79)

[Assume that opening stock is 10 units and sale is made at the beginning of day, and ordered quantity is also received at the beginning of the day and order is placed by checking opening stock at beginning of every day].

Solution

Statement showing Allocation of Random Numbers

(Demand)

Demand	*Probability*	*Cumulative Probability*	*Random Nos.*
0	0.10	0.10	0-9
1	0.45	0.55	10-54
2	0.30	0.85	55-84
3	0.15	1.00	85-99
Lead Time			
2	0.20	0.20	0-19
3	0.65	0.85	20-84
4	0.15	1.00	85-99

Table : Simulation of Demand and Lead Time for 15 Days

Day	*Stock On hand Beginning Of week*	*Demand Random No.*	*Quantity demanded*	*Quantity received*	*Stock on hand end of week*	*Inventory carrying costs*	*Stock Out Quantity*	*Lead Time Costs*	*Random No.*	*Lead Time period*
1	10	49	1	—	9	45				
2	9	67	2	—	7	35				
3	7	06	0	—	7	35				
4	7	30	1	—	6	30				
5	6	95	3	—	3	15			84	3
6	3	01	0	—	3	15				
7	3	10	1	—	2	10				
8	2	70	2	12	12	60				
9	12	80	2	—	10	50				
10	10	66	2	—	8	40				
11	8	69	2	—	6	30				
12	6	76	2	—	4	20			79	3
13	4	86	3	—	1	5				
14	1	56	2	—	—	—	1	75		
15	—	84	2	12	10	59				

For the simulated period of 15 days, the total inventory costs are:-

Inventory carrying costs = Rs. 440
Ordering costs (2 orders × 120) = Rs.240
Stock-out costs (1 stock-out) = Rs. 75
Total = Rs.755

PROBLEM 9.13

An Investment Corporation wants to study the investment projects based on three factors: market demand in units, price per unit *minus* cost per unit, and the investment required. These factors are felt to be independent of each other. In analysing a new consumer product, the corporation estimates the following probability distributions :

Annual Demand Units	Probability	(Price-Cost) per unit Rs.	Probability	Investment Rs.	Required Probability
25,000	0.05	3.00	0.10	27,50,000	0.25
30,000	0.10	5.00	0.20	30,00,000	0.50
35,000	0.20	7.00	0.40	35,00,000	0.25
40,000	0.30	9.00	0.20		
45,000	0.20	10.00	0.10		
50,000	0.10				
55,000	0.05				

Required: Using simulation process, repeat the trial 10 times, compute the return on investment for each trial taking these three factors into account. Approximately, what is the most likely return ?

Use the following random numbers for annual demand, (Price-Cost) and the investment required:

28, 57, 60, 17, 64, 20, 27, 58, 61, 30, 19, 07, 90, 02, 57,
28, 29, 83, 58, 41, 18, 67, 16, 71, 43, 68, 47, 24, 19, 97

Solution

Statement showing the Allocation of Random Numbers

Annual Demand

Events	Probabilities Probability	Cumulative Number	Random
25,000	0.05	0.05	0-4
30,000	0.10	0.15	5-14
35,000	0.20	0.35	15-34
40,000	0.30	0.65	35-64
45,000	0.20	0.85	65-84
50,000	0.10	0.95	85-94
55,000	0.05	1.00	95-99
Price- Cost			
3.00	0.10	0.10	0.-9
5.00	0.20	0.30	10-29
7.00	0.40	0.70	30-69
9.00	0.20	0.90	70-89
10.00	0.10	1.00	90-99
Investment			
27,50,000	0.25	0.25	0-24
30,00,000	0.50	0.75	25-74
35,00,000	0.25	1.00	75-99

Simulation Worksheet

Trials A	*Random Number for demand* B	*Simulated Demand* C	*Random No. for profit* D	*Simulated Profit* E	*Total Profit* F = C × E	*Random No. for investment* G	*Simulated Investment* H	*Return (in %)* I = F/H × 100
1	28	35,000	19	5.00	1,75,000	18	27,50,000	6.36
2	57	40,000	07	3.00	1,20,000	67	30,00,000	4.00
3	60	40,000	90	10.00	4,00,000	16	27,50,000	14.55
4	17	35,000	02	3.00	1,05,000	71	30,00,000	3.50
5	64	40,000	57	7.00	2,80,000	43	30,00,000	9.33
6	20	35,000	28	5.00	1,75,000	68	30,00,000	5.83
7	27	35,000	29	5.00	1,75,000	47	30,00,000	5.83
8	58	40,000	83	9.00	3,60,000	24	27,50,000	13.10
9	61	40,000	58	7.00	2,80,000	19	27,50,000	10.18
10	30	35,000	41	7.00	2,45,000	97	35,00,000	7.00

PROBLEM 9.14

A retailer deals in a perishable commodity. The dialy demand and supply are variables. The data for the past 500 days show the following demand and supply:

Supply		*Demand*	
Availability (kg.)	*No. of days*	*Demand (kg.)*	*No. of days*
10	40	10	50
20	50	20	110
30	190	30	200
40	150	40	100
50	70	50	40

Th retailer buys the commodity at Rs. 20 per kg and sells it at Rs. 30 per kg. Any commodity remains at the end of the day, has no saleable value. Moreover, the loss (unearned profit) on any unsatisfied demand is Rs. 8 per kg. Given the following pair of random numbers, simulate 6 days sales, demand and profit.

(31, 18); (63, 84); (15, 79); (07, 32); (43, 75); (81, 27)

The first random number in the pair is for supply and the second random number is for demand viz. in the first pair (31, 18), use 31 to simulate supply and 18 to simulate demand.

Solution

The demand and supply patterns yield the following prbability distribution. The numbers 00-99 are allocated in proportion to the probabilities associated with each event.

Availability (Kg)	*Prob*	*Com Prob*	*Random numbers allocated*	*Demand (Kg)*	*Prob.*	*Cum Prob.*	*Random number allocated*
10	0.08	0.08	00-07	10	0.10	0.10	00-09
20	0.10	0.18	08-17	20	0.22	0.32	10-31
30	0.38	0.56	18-55	30	0.40	0.72	32-71
40	0.30	0.86	56-85	40	0.20	0.92	72-91
50	0.14	1.00	86-99	50	0.08	1.00	92-99

Let us simulate the supply and demand for the next six days using the given random numbers in order to find the profit if the cost of the commodity is Rs. 20 per kg, the selling price is Rs. 30 per kg, loss on any unsatisfied demand is Rs. 8 per kg and unsold commodities at the end of the day have no saleable value.

Day	*Random no.*	*Supply Availability*	*Random no.*	*Demand*	*Buying cost Rs.*	*Selling cost Rs.*	*Loss for unsatisfied demand*	*Profit*
1	31	30	18	20	600	600	—	—
2	63	40	84	40	800	1200	—	400
3	15	20	79	40	400	600	160	40
4	07	10	32	30	200	300	160	–60
5	43	30	75	40	600	900	80	220
6	81	40	27	20	800	600	—	–200

During the simulated period of six days, the net profit of the retailer is

= (400 + 40 + 220) – (60 + 200)

= 660 – 260

= Rs. 400

PROBLEM 9.15

A single counter ticket booking centre employs one booking clerk. A passenger on arrival immediately goes to the booking counter for being served if the counter is free. If on the other hand, the counter is engaged, the passenger will have to wait. The passengers are served on first come first served basis. The time of arrival and the time of service varies from one minute to six minutes. The distribution of arrival and service time is as under:

Arrival/Service Time (Minutes)	*Arrival (Probability)*	*Service (Probability)*
1	0.05	0.10
2	0.20	0.20
3	0.35	0.40
4	0.25	0.20
5	0.10	0.10
6	0.05	—

Required:

(i) Simulate the arrival and service of 10 passengers starting from 9 A.M. by using the following random numbers in pairs respectively for arrival and service. Random numbers 60 09 16 12 08 18 36 65 38 25 07 11 08 7959 61 53 77 03 10.

(ii) Determine the total duration of

(1) Idle time of booking clerk and

(2) Waiting time of passengers.

(b) Random allocation tables are as under:

Time (Mts)	*Arrival (Prob.)*	*Arrivals Cum. Probability*	*Random No. allocated*	*Time (Mts)*	*Service. (Prob.)*	*Service Cum. (Prob.)*	*Random No. allocated*
1	0.05	0.05	00-04	1	0.10	0.10	00-09
2	0.20	0.25	05-24	2	0.20	0.30	10-29
3	0.35	0.60	25-59	3	0.40	0.70	30-69
4	0.25	0.85	60-84	4	0.20	0.90	70-89
5	0.10	0.95	85-94	5	0.10	1.00	90-99
6	0.05	1.00	95-99				

Simulation of ten trails:

R.No.	*Arrival Mts*	*Time*	*Start*	*R.No.*	*Time (Mts)*	*Finish*	*Waiting Time Clerk*	*Waiting Time Passanger*
60	4	9.04	9.04	09	1	9.05	4	
16	2	9.06	9.06	12	2	9.08	1	
08	2	9.08	9.08	18	2	9.10	—	
36	3	9.11	9.11	65	3	9.14	1	
38	3	9.14	9.14	25	2	9.16	1	
07	2	9.16	9.16	11	2	9.18	—	
08	2	9.18	9.18	79	4	9.22	—	
59	3	9.21	9.22	61	3	9.25	—	1
53	3	9.24	9.25	77	4	9.29		1
03	1	9.25	9.29	10	2	9.31	—	4
	Total						6	6

In half an hour trial, the clerk was idle for 6 minutes and the passengers had to wait for 6 minutes.

PROBLEM 9.16

A plant has a large number of similar machines. The machine breakdown or failure is random and independent.

The shift incharge of the plant collected the data about the various machines breakdown times, the repair time required on hourly basis, and the record for the port 100 observations. This is shown below:

Time between recorded machine breakdowns	*Probability*	*Repair time required (hours)*	*Probability*
0.5	0.05	1	0.28
1	0.06	2	0.52
1.5	0.16	3	0.20
2	0.33		
2.5	0.21		
3	0.19		

For each hour that one machine is down due to being or waiting to be, repaired, the plant loses Rs. 70 by way of cost production. A repairman is paid at Rs. 20 per hour.

(a) Simulate this maintence system for is breakdown.
(b) How many repairman should the plant hire for repair work?

Random number for breakdown			Random number for repair		
61	08	44	87	87	41
85	82	33	39	52	82
16	56	77	28	52	19
46	22	87	97	15	99
88	49	54	69	85	23

Solution

Time between break down (hour)	*Probability*	*Comulative Probability*	*Random numbers*
0.5	0.05	0.05	00–04
1	0.06	0.11	05–10
1.5	0.16	0.27	11–26
2	0.33	0.60	27–59
2.5	0.21	0.81	60–80
3	0.19	1.00	81–99

Repair time requried (hours)	*Probability*	*Comulative Probability*	*Random numbers*
1	0.28	0.28	00–27
2	0.52	0.80	28–79
3	0.20	1.00	80–99

S.No.	***RN for break-down***	***Time btw break-down***	***Time of break-down***	***Repair work begins at***	***Time***	***R.No. for repairs***	***Repair time required***	***Repair work end at***	***Waiting Time***
1	61	2.5	02:30	02:30	0	87	3	05:30	3
2	85	3	05:30	05:30	0	39	2	07:30	2
3	16	1.5	07:00	07:30	0:30	28	2	09:30	2:30
4	46	2	09:00	09:30	0:30	97	3	12:30	3:30
5	88	3	12:00	12:30	0:30	69	2	14:30	2:30
6	08	1	13:00	14:30	1:30	87	3	17:30	4:30
7	82	3	16:00	17:30	1:30	52	2	19:30	3:30

8	56	2	18:00	19:30	1:30	52	2	21:30	3:30
9	22	1.5	19:30	21:30	2:00	15	1	22:30	3:00
10	49	2	21:30	22:30	1:00	85	3	01:30	4:00
11	44	2	23:30	01:30	2:00	41	2	03:30	4:00
12	33	2	01:30	03:30	2:00	82	3	06:30	5:00
13	77	2.5	04:00	06:30	2:30	98	3	09:30	5:30
14	87	3	07:00	09:30	2:30	99	3	12:30	5:30
15	54	2	09:00	12:30	3:30	23	1	13:30	4:30
					21:30		35		56:30

Current maintain cost

= *** time cost and Repairman's wage

= (Repair time-1 waiting time) × 70 + (35 + 2: 30) × 20

= 56 : 30 × 70 + 37:30 × 20

= 3955 + 750 = 4,405

Maintenance cost with additional repairman

In that cost there would be no waiting time

∴ Repair time × 70 + (37:30 × 2) × 20

= 35 × 70 + 75 × 20

= 2450 + 1500 = 3,950

For clusion: As maintenance cost with additional repairman is less, so plant should keep additonal repairman.

PROBLEM 9.17

A small retailer has studied the weekly receipts and payments over the part 200 weeks and developed the following set of information:

Weekly Receipts (Rs.)	*Probability*	*Weekly payment (Rs.)*	*Probability*
3,000	0.20	4,000	0.30
5,000	0.30	6,000	0.40
7,000	0.40	8,000	0.20
12,000	0.10	10,000	0.10

Using the following sequences of random numbers, simulate the weekly pattern of receipts and payments for the 12 weeks of the next quarter, assuming further that the beginning bank balance is Rs. 8000. What is the estimated balance at the end of the 12 weekly period? What is the highest weekly balance clusing the quarter? What is the average weekly balance for the quarter?

Random Numbers

For Receipts	For Payments
03	61
91	96
38	30
55	32
17	03
46	88
32	48
43	28
69	88
72	18
24	71
22	99

Solution

Random number coding: (Weekly Receipts)

Weekly Receipts	Probability	Comulative probability	Random number
3,000	0.20	0.20	0–19
5,000	0.30	0.50	20–49
7,000	0.40	0.90	50–89
12,000	0.10	1.00	90–99

Random number coding: (Weekly Payments)

Weekly payments	Probability	Comulative probability	Random numbers
4,000	0.30	0.30	0–29
6,000	0.40	0.70	30–69
8,000	0.20	0.90	70–89
10,000	0.10	1.00	90–99

Statement showing the closing balance of cash at the end o every quarter

Quarter (A)	Opening. balance (B)	Random number for receipts (C)	Receipts (D)	Random number for payment (E)	Payment (F)	Closing balance (G = B + D – 5)
1	8,000	03	3,000	61	6,000	5,000
2	5,000	91	12,000	96	10,000	7,000
3	7,000	38	5,000	30	6,000	6,000
4	6,000	55	7,000	32	6,000	7,000
5	7,000	17	3,000	03	4,000	6,000
6	6,000	46	5,000	88	8,000	3,000
7	3,000	32	5,000	48	6,000	2,000
8	2,000	43	5,000	28	4,00	3,000
9	3,000	69	7,000	88	8,000	2,000
10	2,000	72	7,000	18	4,000	5,000
11	5,000	24	5,000	71	8,000	2,000
12	2,000	22	5,000	99	10,000	(3,000)
						45,000

Estimated balance at the end of the quarter = –3,000

Highest weekly balance during the quarter = 7,000

Average weekly balance = Rs. $\frac{45,000}{12}$ = Rs. 3,750

PROBLEM 9.18

ABC Cooperative Bank receives and disburses different amount of cash in each month. The bank has an opening cash Balance of Rs 15 crores in the first month. Pattern of receipts and disbursements from past data is as follows:

Monthly Cash receipts		*Monthly Cash disbursements (Rs crores)*	
Rs in Crores	*Probability*	*Rs in Crores*	*P Probability*
30	0.20	33	0.15
42	0.40	60	0.20
36	0.25	39	0.40
99	0.15	57	0.25

Simulate the cash position over a period of 12 months.

Required:

(i) Calculate probability that the ABC Cooperative Bank will fall short in payments.

(ii) Calculate average monthly shortfall.

(iii) If ABC bank can get an overdraft facility of Rs 45 crores from other Nationalized banks, what is the probability that they will fall short in monthly payments?

Use the following sequence (rowwise) of paired random numbers.

1778, 4316, 7435, 3123, 7244, 4692, 5158, 6808, 9358, 5478, 9654, 0977. ***(May, 2010)***

Solution

Monthly Cash receipts (Rs crores)				*Monthly Cash disbursements (Rs crores)*			
Cash	*Probability*	*Cumulative*	*R.N.*	*Cash*	*Probability*	*Cumulative*	*R.N.*
30	0.20	0.20	00-19	33	0.15	0.15	00-14
42	0.40	0.60	20-59	60	0.20	0.35	15-34
36	0.25	0.85	60-84	39	0.40	0.75	35-74
99	0.15	1.00	85-99	57	0.25	1.00	75-99

Months	Opening (Rs in Crores)	Receipts		Total	Payments		Closings (Rs in Crores)
		Random Number.	(Rs in Crores)		Random Number.	(Rs in Crores)	
1	15	17	30	45	78	57	−12
2	−12	43	42	30	16	60	−30
3	−30	74	36	06	25	39	−33
4	−33	31	42	09	23	60	−51
5	−51	72	36	−15	44	39	−54
6	−54	46	42	−12	92	57	−69
7	−69	51	42	−27	58	39	−66
8	−66	68	36	−30	08	33	−63
9	−63	93	99	36	58	39	−3
10	−3	54	42	39	78	57	−18
11	−18	96	99	81	54	39	42
12	42	09	30	72	77	57	15

(i) In 12 months, the bank falls short of cash in 10 months to meet payment.
Thus, probability of shortfall = 10/12 = 0.83

(ii) Total short fall of Rs 399 crores over 10 months
Average monthly shortfall during 10 months = Rs 39.9 crores

(iii) With an overdraft facility of Rs 45 crores is available, there will be a shortfall in 5 months (4,5,6,7,8).. Therefore, probability is = 5/12 = 0.42

PROBLEM 9.19

A car rental agency has collected the following data on the demand for five-seater vehicles over the past 50 days.

Daily Demand	4	5	6	7	8
No. of Days	4	10	16	14	6

The agency has only 6 cars currently.

(i) Use the following 5 random numbers to generate 5 days of demand fo the rental agency
Random Nos 15, 48, 71, 56, 90

(ii) What is the average number of cars rented per day for the 5 days ?

(iii) How many rentals will be lost over the 5 days? ***(May, 2011)***

Solution

Daily demand	*Days*	*Probability*	*Cumulative probability*	*Random No.*	*Day*	*Demand*	*Rented*	*Rental lost*
4	4	0.08	0.08	00-07	1	5	5	
5	10	0.20	0.28	08-27	2	6	6	
6	16	0.32	0.60	28-59	3	7	6	1
7	14	0.28	0.88	60-87	4	6	6	
8	6	0.12	1.00	88-99	5	8	6	2
	50	1.00					29	3

(ii) Average no. of cars rented = 29/5 = 5.8, (iii) Rental lost = 3

10 LEARNING CURVE THEORY

LEARNING OBJECTIVES

After studying this chapter, you should be able to understand:

- Learning Curve Theory
- Meaning of Learning Curve
- Meaning of Learning Curve Ratio
- Meaning of Learning Curve Equation
- Applications of Learning Curve

1.0 LEARNING CURVE THEORY

As the production quantity of a given item is doubled, the cost of the item decreases at a fixed rate. This phenomenon is the basic premise on which the theory of learning curve has been formulated. As the quantity produced doubles, the absolute amount of cost increase will be successively smaller but the rate of decrease will remain fixed. It occurs due to the following distinctive features of manufacturing environment:

(i) Better tooling methods are developed and used.

(ii) More productive equipments are designed and used to make the product.

(iii) Design bugs are detected and corrected.

(iv) Engineering changes decrease over time.

(v) Earlier teething problems are overcome.

(vi) Rejections and rework tend to diminish over time.

2.0 MEANING OF LEARNING CURVE

Learning curve is a geometrical progression, which reveals that there is steadily decreasing cost for the accomplishment of a given repetitive operation, as the identical operation is increasingly repeated. The amount of decrease will be less and less with each successive unit produced. The slope of the decision curve is expressed as a percentage. The other names given to learning curve are Experience curve, Improvement curve and Progress curve.

3.0 MEANING OF LEARNING CURVE RATIO

In the initial stage of a new product or a new process, the learning effect pattern is so regular that the rate of decline established at the outset can be used to predict labour cost well in advance. The effect of experience on cost is summarised in the learning ratio or improvement ratio:

$$\text{Learning curve ratio} = \frac{\text{Average labour cost of first N units}}{\text{Average labour cost of first 2N units}}$$

For example, if the average labour cost for the first 500 units is Rs. 25 and the average labour cost for the first 1,000 units is Rs. 20, the learning curve ratio is (Rs. 20/25) or 80%. Since the average cost per unit of 1,000 units is Rs. 20, the average cost per unit of first 2,000 units is likely to be 80% of Rs. 20 or Rs. 16.

4.0 MEANING OF LEARNING CURVE EQUATION

Mathematicians have been able to express relationship in equations. The basic equation

$$Y_x = KX^s$$

where, X is the cumulative number of units or lots produced

Y is the cumulative average unit cost of those units X or lots.

K is the average cost of the first unit or lots is the improvement exponent or the learning coefficient or the index of learning which is calculated as follows:

s = log of learning ratio/log 2

5.0 APPLICATIONS OF LEARNING CURVE

Some of the applications of learning curve are as follows:

1 Learning curve helps in analyzing cost-volume profit relationships during familiarisation phase of product or process to arrive at cost estimates. It helps in budgeting and profit planning.
2. It helps in pricing and consequent decision making – e.g. acceptance of an order, negotiations in establishing contract prices etc. with the advantage of the knowledge of decreasing unit cost.
3. It helps in setting standards in the learning phase.

ILLUSTRATION 1

The following information is provided by a factory manager who wants to use appropriate average learning rate on following activities:

(i) A set of very experienced people feed data into the computer for processing inventory records in the factory. The manager wishes to apply 80% learning rate on data entry and calculation of inventory.

(ii) A new type of machinery is to be installed in the factory. This is patented process and the output may take a year for full fledged production. The factory manager wants to use a learning rate on the workers at the new machine.

(iii) An operation uses contract labour. The contractor shifts people among various jobs once in two days. The labour force performs one task in 3 days. The manager wants to apply an average learning rate for these workers.

Required: Advise to the manager with reasons on the applicability of the learning curve theory on the above information.

Solution

(i) The learning curve does not apply to very experienced people for the same job, since time taken can never tend to become zero or reduce very considerably after a certain range of output. This is the limitation of the learning curve.
Data entry is a manual job so learning rate theory may be applied. Calculation of inventory is a computerized job. Learning rate applies only to manual labour.

(ii) Learning rate should not be applied to a new process which the firm has never tried before.

(iii) The workers are shifted even before completion of one unit of work. Hence learning rate will not apply.

ILLUSTRATION 2

XYZ Co. has observed that a 90% learning curve ratio applies to all labour related costs each time a new model enters production. It is anticipated that 320 units will be manufactured during 1999. Direct labour cost for the first lot of 10 units amounts to 1,000 hours at Rs. 8 per hour. Variable overhead cost is assigned to products at the rate of Rs. 2 per direct labour hour.

Required:

1. Find total labour and labour-related costs to manufacture 320 units of output.
2. Average cost of (a) the first 40 units produced (b) the first 80 units, (c) the first 100 units.
3. Incremental cost of (a) units 41-80 and (b) units 101-200.

Solution

Statement of Cost Projections on 90% Learning Curve

Cummulative Quantity	*Average time per unit*	*Cummulative time taken*	*Incremental Hours*
10	100	1,000	—
20	90	1,800	800
40	81	3,240	1,440
80	72.90	5,832	2,592
160	65.61	10,497.6	4,665.6
320	59.049	18,895.68	8,398.08

(i) **Total labour and labour related cost**

For first 320 units = 1,8895.68 x Rs. 10/hr = Rs. 1,88,956.80

(ii) (a) **Average cost of 40 units** $= \dfrac{3{,}240 \times 10 \text{ p.u.}}{40}$ = Rs. 810 per unit

(b) **Average cost of first 80 units** $= \dfrac{5{,}832 \times 10 \text{ p.u.}}{80}$ = 729 p.u

(iii) (a) **Incremental cost of units 41 – 80**

= (total time taken for 80 units – total time taken for 40 units) × 10

= (5,832 – 3,240) × 10 = Rs. 25,920

Now, the basic learning curve formula must be used to derive the average cost of the first 100 units and the incremental cost of units 101 – 200.

We have,

$$Y = ax^b$$

Here,

$$A = 1000$$
$$X = 10$$

and

$$b = \frac{\text{logarithm of learning ratio}}{\text{logarithm of 2}}$$

$$= \frac{\log 90\%}{\log 2} = \frac{\log \frac{9}{10}}{\log 2} = \frac{\log 9 - \log 10}{\log 2}$$

$$= \frac{0.9542 - 1}{0.3010} = -0.15216$$

Now,

$$A = 1000$$
$$Y = ax^b$$

Taking log on both sides

$$\log Y = \log ax^b$$
$$\log Y = \log 1000 + b \log 10$$
$$\log Y = 3 \times l + (-0.15216) \times 1$$
$$= \text{Antilog } 2.84784$$
$$= (7031 + 1\ 3) = 7044$$

Hence, Average Time for first 100 units = 70.4 hours

Therefore, Average cost per unit of first 100 units = 70.4 × 10 = Rs. 70.4 P.U.

(i.e. first 10 lots)

Due to 90% learning curve

Average Time taken for 200 units = 70.44 × 90% = 63.396 hrs/unit

Therefore, total time taken = 63.396 × 200 hrs = 12,679.20 hours

Therefore, total cost = 12,679.20 × 10 = Rs. 1,26,792

Therefore, incremental cost = Rs. 1,26,792 – Rs. 70,400 = Rs. 56,392

ILLUSTRATION 3

Bharat Tulsian Ltd has observed that learning curve applies to all labour related cost, each time a new unit enter into production. It is anticipated that 400 units will be manufactured during the current year. Direct labour hours for the first lot of 5 units is 80 hours. Material cost is Rs. 10 per unit and labour cost per hour is Rs. 2. Variable cost of manufacturing is Re. 1 per direct labour hour.

Calculate the cost of producing 400 units in each of the following alternative cases:

Case (a) *Learning Curve Rate is 90% and it applies when cumulative production volume becomes double.*

Case (b) *Learning Curve Rate is 90% and it applies when cumulative production volume becomes 1.5 times.*

Case (c) *Learning Curve Rate is 80% and it applies when cumulative production volume becomes double.*

Case (d) *Learning Curve Rate is 80% and it applies when cumulative production volume becomes 2.5 times.*

Solution

Labour hours required for the first unit $= \dfrac{80 \text{ hours}}{5} = 16$ hours.

Comulative average labour hour of 400 units.

$$Y_x = Kx^s$$
$$K = 16 \text{ hours}$$
$$X = 400$$
$$S = \frac{\log(0.90)}{\log(2)}$$
$$\log(0.9) = \log\left(\frac{9}{10}\right) = \log 9 - \log 10$$
$$= 0.9542 - 1.0000 = -0.0458$$
$$S = \frac{-0.0458}{0.3010} = -0.1522$$
$$Y_x = 16(400)^{-0.1522}$$

Taking log of both sides

$$\log Y_x = \log(16)(400)^{-0.1522}$$
$$= \log 16 - 0.1522 \log 400$$
$$= 1.2041 - 0.1522(\log 10 \times 4)$$
$$= 1.2041 - 0.1522 (\log 100 + \log 4)$$
$$= 1.2041 - 0.1522 (2 + 0.6021)$$
$$= 1.2041 - 0.1522 (2.6021)$$
$$= 1.2041 - 0.3960 = 0.8081$$
$$\log Y_x = 0.8081$$
$$Yx = \text{Antilog } (0.8081)$$
$$Yx = 6.428 \text{ hours}$$

Total hours = 6.428 × 400 = 2571.20 hours.

Statement showing the Cost of producing 400 units

Particluars	*Rs.*
Direct Material (Rs. 10 × 400)	4,000.00
Direct labour (2571.20 × Rs. 2)	5,142.40
Variable cost (2,571.20 × Re. 1)	2,571.20
	11,713.60

Case (b) Comulative Average Labour Hours for 400 units

$$Y_x = Kx^s$$
$$K = 16 \text{ hours}$$
$$X = 400$$
$$S = \frac{\log(0.90)}{\log(1.5)}$$
$$S = \frac{-0.0458}{0.1761} = -0.2601$$
$$Y_x = 16(400) - 0.2601$$

Taking log of both sides

$$= \log 16 - 0.2601 \log 400$$
$$= 1.2041 - 0.2601 (2.6021)$$
$$= 1.2041 - 0.6768 = 0.5273$$
$$\log Y_x = 0.5273$$
$$Y_x = \text{Antilog } (0.5273)$$
$$Y_x = 3.367$$

Total hours = 3.367 × 400 = 1,346.80 hours

Statement showing the cost of producing 400 units.

Particluars	*Rs.*
Direct Material (Rs. 400 × Rs 10)	4,000.00
Direct labour (1,346.80 × Rs. 2)	2,693.60
Variable Cast (1,346.80 × Re. 1)	1,346.80
	8,040.40

Case (c) Cummulative Average Labour Hour of 400 units

$$Y_x = Kx^s$$
$$K = 16 \text{ hours}$$
$$X = 400$$
$$S = \frac{\log(0.80)}{\log(2)}$$
$$= \log(0.80) = \log\left(\frac{8}{10}\right) = \log 8 - \log 10$$
$$= 0.9031 - 1.0000 = -0.0969$$
$$S = \frac{-0.0969}{\log(2)} = \frac{-0.0969}{0.3010} = -0.3219$$
$$Y_x = 16(400)^{-0.3219}$$

Taking log of both sides

$$\log Y_x = \log 16 - 0.3219(\log 400)$$
$$= 1.2041 - 0.3219\ (2.6021)$$
$$= 1.2041 - 0.8376$$
$$\log Y_x = 0.3665$$
$$Y_x = 2.325$$
$$\text{Total hours} = 2.325 \times 400 = 930 \text{ hours}$$

Statement showing the Cost of producing 400 units.

Particluars	*Rs.*
Direct Matarial (400 × Rs 10)	4,000
Direct Labour (930 × Rs 2)	1,860
Variable Lost (930 × Re 1)	930
	6,790

Case (d) Cumulative average labour hours of 400 units

$$Y_x = Kx^s$$
$$K = 16 \text{ hours}$$
$$X = 400$$
$$S = \frac{\log(0.80)}{\log(2.5)}$$
$$= \frac{-0.0969}{0.3979} = -0.2435$$
$$Y_x = 16(400)^{-0.2435}$$

Taking log of both sides

$$\log Y_x = \log 16 - 0.2435 \log (400)$$
$$= 1.2041 - 0.2435\ (2.6021)$$
$$= 1.2041 - 0.6336$$
$$\log Y_x = 0.5705$$
$$Y_x = \text{Antilog}\ (0.5705) \Rightarrow Y_x = 3.72 \text{ hours}$$
$$\text{Total hours} = 3.72 \text{ hours} \times 400 = 1488 \text{ hours}$$

Statement showing the Cost of Producing 400 units

Particluars	*Rs.*
Direct Material (400 × Rs 10)	4,000
Direct Labour (1,488 × Rs. 2)	2,976
Variable Cost (1,488 × Re. 1)	1,488
	8,464

ILLUSTRATION 4

Tushar Tulsian Ltd. invent a new product '*Kx*'. It is to be processed in 3 departments, i.e., Department A, B and respectively. The cost of producing first 100 units are given below:

Particluars	*Rs.*
Direct Material (100 × Rs. 8)	800
Direct Labour:	
Department A (100 × 2 hour × 5)	1,000
Department B (100 × 3 hour × 10)	3,000
Department C (100 × 2 hour × 10)	2,000
Variable Costs:	
Department A (200 hour × 2)	400
Department B (300 hour × 3)	900
Department C (200 hour × 4)	800
Total	8,100

These units are sold in market and obtained good response. Units are to be produced in a batch of 100 units. The company receives the further order for 200 units. What minimum price should the company quote considering the following:

(1) Department A is highly automated and learning curve effect does not take place there.
(2) Department B requires highly skilled labour so learning curve effect will take place there at a rate of 80%.
(3) Department C requires semi-skilled labour so learning curve effect will take place there at a rate of 90%.
(4) Company desires to earn a profit of 20% on quotation price.

Solution

Labour Hours at Department B

Average cumulative hours for producing 300 units in lot of 100.

$$Y_x = Kx^s$$

$$K = 300 \text{ hour}$$

$$X = 3$$

$$S = \frac{\log(0.80)}{\log(2)} = \frac{-0.0969}{0.3010} = -0.3219$$

$$Y_x = 300 \times 3^{-0.3219}$$

$$\log Yx = \log 300 - 0.3219 \log 3$$

$$= 2.4771 - 0.3219\ (0.4771)$$

$$= 2.4771 - 0.1536$$

$$= 2.3235$$

$$Yx = \text{Antilog}\ (2.3235) = 210.62 \text{ hours}$$

$$\text{Total Hours} = 210.62 \text{ hours} \times 3 = 631.86 \text{ hours}$$

$$\text{Incremented hours for 200 units} = 631.86 \text{ hours} - 300 \text{ hours}$$

$$= 331.86 \text{ hours}$$

Labours Hours of Department C

Average cumulative hours for producing 300 units in lot of 100 units.

$$Yx = Kxs$$

$$K = 200$$

$$X = 3$$

$$S = \frac{\log(0.90)}{\log 2} = \frac{-0.0458}{0.3010} = -0.1522$$

$$Y_x = 200 \times 3^{-0.1522}$$

$$\log Y_x = \log(200) - 0.1522 \log 3$$

$$= 2.3010 - 0.1522\ (0.4771)$$

$$= 2.3010 - 0.0726$$

$$= 2.2284$$

$$Y_x = \text{Antilog}\ (2.2284)$$

$$Y_x = 169.20$$

$$\text{Total Hours} = 169.20 \times 3 = 507.60$$

$$\text{Incremented Hours} = 507.60 \text{ hours} - 200 \text{ hours} = 307.60 \text{ hours}$$

Statement showing the Minimum Price to be quoted for the order

Particulars		*Rs.*
Direct Material (200 × Rs. 8)		1,600.00
Direct Labour:		
Department A (200 × 2 hours × Rs. 5)	2,000.00	
Department B (331.86 hours × Rs. 10)	3,318.60	
Department C (307.60 hours × Rs. 10)	3,076.00	8,394.60
Variable Cost:		
Department A (400 hours × Rs. 2)	800.00	
Department B (331.86 hours × Rs. 3)	995.58	
Department C (307.60 hour × Rs. 4)	1,230.40	3,025.98
Total cost		13,020.58
Add: Profit margin @ 25% on cost		3,255.145
Minimum Quotation Price		16,275.725

ILLUSTRATION 5

Calculate the expected average unit cost of making,

(a) 4 machines; (b) 8 machines

Using the data below:

Data:

Direct labour needed to make first machine 1,000 hours

Learning curve = 90%

Direct labour cost Rs. 15 per hour

Direct materials cost Rs. 1,50,000 per machine.

Fixed cost for either size orders Rs. 60,000.

Solution

Statement of Learning Curve

Cummulative Quantity	*Average time per unit*	*Cummulative time taken*	*Incremental Hours*
1	1,000	1,000	—
	900	1,900	900
4	810	3,240	1,340
8	729	5,832	2,592

Statement showing Expected Average Cost per unit

Particulars	*First 4 Machines (Rs.)*	*First 8 Machines (Rs.)*
Material	6,00,000	12,00,000
Labour	48,600	87,480
Fixed Cost	60,000	60,000
Total Cost	7,08,600	13,47,480
Average Cost per unit	177150	1,68,435

ILLUSTRATION 6

XYZ & Co. has given the following data:

80% Average – Time Curve

Cumulative Units (X)	*Average Hours*	*Total Hours*	*Marginal*
1	100	100	100
	80	**160**	60
	?	?	?
4	64	56	?

Required: Fill in the blanks.

Solution:

Know

$$Y = ax^b$$

Where Y = average time per unit

a = total time for the first unit

x = the cumulative no. of units manufactured

b = the learning curve

Now,

The learning coefficient, b, is determined as follows

$$b = \frac{\log 80\%}{\log 2} = \frac{\log 8/10}{\log 2} = \frac{\log 8 - \log 10}{\log 2}$$

$$= \frac{0.9031 - 1}{0.3010} = \frac{-0.0969}{0.3010}$$

$$= -0.3219 = -0.322$$

Now, Calculation of average time (Y) when x = 3, be

$$Y = ax^b$$

$$Y = 100 \times (3)^{-0.322}$$

Taking log on both sides

$$\log Y = \log 100 + (-0.322) \log 3$$
$$\log Y = 2 + (-0.322) \times (0.4771)$$
$$\log Y = 2 - 1536$$

Therefore,

$$Y = \text{anti} \log (1.8464) = (7015 + 6) = 70.21$$

Therefore $Y = 70.21$

80% Average Time Curve

Cummulative Units	*Average Time*	*Total Time*	*Marginal Time*
1	100	100	100(100 – 0)
	80	160	60(160 – 100)
	70.2	210.6(3 × 70.2)	50.6(210.6 – 160)
4	64	256(64 × 4)	45.4(256 – 210.6)

ILLUSTRATION 7

A customer has asked your company to prepare a bid on supplying 800 units of a new product. Production will be in batches of 100 units. You estimate that costs for the first batch of 100 units will average Rs. 100 a unit. You also expect that a 90% learning curve will apply to the cumulative labour cost on this contract.

Required:

(a) Prepare an estimate of the labour costs of fulfilling this contract.
(b) Estimate the incremental labour cost of extending the production run to produce an additional 800 units.
(c) Estimate the incremental labour cost of extending the production run from 800 units to 900 units.

Solution

(a) Statement Showing labour cost at 800 units

Cummulative units	*Average Cost per unit*	*Total Cost*	*Incremental Cost*
100	100	10,000	—
200	90	18,000	8,000
400	81	32,400	14,400
800	72.90	58,320	25,920

(b) Calculation of incremental labour cost to produce additional 800 units

Average cost for the first 1600 units = 72.90 × 90% = Rs. 65.61
Therefore, total cost = 65.61 × 1,600 = Rs. 1,04,976
Therefore, incremental cost = Total Cost of 1,600 units – Total Cost of 800 units
= (1,04,976 – 58,320) = Rs. 46,656

(c) Calculation of incremental Labour Cost of Production exceeding from 800 units to 900 units

We know

$$Y = ax^b$$

Where

$$a = 10{,}000$$
$$x = 9$$

$$b = \frac{\log 9/10}{\log 2} = \frac{\log 9 - \log 10}{\log 2}$$

$$= \frac{0.9542 - 1}{0.3010} = \frac{0.0458}{0.3010}$$

$$= -0.15216$$

Therefore $Y = 10000\ X(9)^{-0.15216}$

Taking log on both sides

$$\log Y = \log 10{,}000(9)^{-0.15216}$$

$$\log Y = \log 10{,}000 + \log 9^{-0.15216}$$

$$\log Y = 4 + (-0.15216) \times (0.9542)$$

$$\log Y = 4 - 0.14519$$

Therefore, $Y = \text{Antilog } 3.8548$

$= 7145 + 13 = 71.58$

Hence, Average Cost per unit = Rs. 71.58

Therefore, Cost of 900 units = 900 × Rs. 71.58

= Rs. 64,422

Therefore, required incremental cost from 800 units to 900 units

Total Cost of 900 units – Total Cost of 800 units

= Rs. 64,422 – Rs. 58,320 = Rs. 6,102

ILLUSTRATION 8

Comforts Ltd. makes household appliances. It is now examining a three-year old contract to make electrical bread toasters for sale through a departmental store. During the entire contract period, it will receive for its toaster a fixed price of Rs. 40 per piece for whatever quantity it can produce in the 3 years. Skilled labour is the constraint and this cannot be increased above that currently available in the Company for making the toaster.

Capital investment required Rs. 50,000 payable down cash with nil scrap value.

Additional Overheads	Rs. 25,000 per annum
Material	Rs. 30 per toaster
Labour (Skilled)	Rs. 5 per hour.

The production manager envisages a learning curve effect for labour in the form of $y = \text{at } x^{-0.3}$ where y = average labour hours per unit, a = labour hours per first unit and x = cumulative production. He estimates that the first toaster will take 10 hours to produce and the fixed amount of skilled labour available will enable 5,000 toaster to be produced in the first year. Assume all cash infows to arise at year end and the cost of capital is 15%. What is your advice?

Solution

Statement of Net Present Value

Year	*1st year*	*2nd year*	*3rd year*
Revenue	5,000 × 40 = 2,00,000	8,460 × 40 = 3,38,400	10,550 × 40 = 4,22,000
***Less:* Cost**			
Material	1,50,000	2,53,800	3,16,500
Labour	19,425 = 3,885 × 5	19,425 = 3,885 × 5	19,425 = 3,885 × 5
Fixed overhead	25,000	25,000	25,000

Year	1st year	2nd year	3rd year
Cash Inflow	5,575	40,175	61,075
Present value factor	0.869	0.756	0.657
Present value of cash inflow	4,845	30,372	40,127

Present Value of Cash Inflow = 4845 + 30,372 + 40,127
= 75,344

Less: Present Value of Cash Outflow = 50,000

Net Present Value (N.P.V) = 25,344

Comment: Project should be accepted sinθ N.P.V is positive.

Working Notes

(i) Calculation of total labour hours available in first year

Statement of Learning Curve (just for under standing)

Quantity	Average time per unit	Total hours	Incremental Hours
1	10	10	—
	8	16	6
4	6.4	25.6	
5	—	—	
—	—	—	
—	—	—	
—	—	—	
5,000	—	3,885 (see below)	

Labour hour available in first year

$$Y = ax^b$$

Multiply both sides by X

$$xy = ax^b \times X$$
$$xy = ax^{b+1}$$

Taking log on both sides

$$Y = ax^b$$
$$\log xy = \log ax^{-0.3+1}$$
$$\log xy = \log 10(5000)^{0.7}$$
$$\log xy = \log 10 + 0.7 \log 5000$$
$$\log xy = 1 + 0.7 \times 3.699$$
$$\log xy = 3.5893$$
$$xy = \text{Antilog } 3.5893$$
$$= 3882 + 3 = 3885$$
$$xy = 3885$$

Therefore, the available labour hours in the first year are 3885 which are sufficient to produce 5000 toasters only in the first year.

(ii) The Number of Toaster to be produce in second year from 3885 labour hours

Labour hours available in first year = 3885 hours

Labour hours available in second year = 3885 hours

Total hours available up to 2nd year = 7770 hours

Which are to be utilized to produce the number of toaster up to second year with the application of equation method.

$$X \times Y = ax^b \times X$$
$$= ax^{b+1}$$
$$7770 = 10(x)^{0.7}$$

Taking log on both sides

$$\log 7770 = \log 10(x)^{0.7}$$
$$\log 7.77 \times 10^3 = \log 10 + \log x^{0.7}$$
$$3 + \log 7.77 = 1 + 0.7 \times \log x$$
$$3 + 0.8904 = 1 + 0.7 \times \log x$$
$$3.8904 - 1 = 0.7 \times \log x$$
$$\log x = \frac{2.8904}{0.7}$$
$$\log x = 4.1291$$
$$x = \text{Anti log } 4.1291$$
$$x = 1346 \times 10$$
$$x = 13460$$

Hence, total number of toasters produced upto

Second year	= 13,460
Less: first year	= 5,000
No. of toasters produced in 2nd year	= 8,460

(iii) Calculation of number of toasters to be produced up to third year.

Labour hours available in third year = 3885

Total labour hours available up to third year = 3 × 3885 hours = 11655 hours

Now,

$$XY = ax^{b+1}$$

i.e.,

$$11655 = 10(x)^{0.7}$$
$$\log 11655 = \log 10 + \log x^{0.7}$$

Therefore

$$X = 24010$$

Hence, the total number of toasters produced

up to 3rd year = 24010

up to 2nd year = 13460

No. of toasters to be produced in 3rd year = 10550

ILLUSTRATION 9

An electronics firm has developed a new type of fire alarm system. A first unit assembled has a material cost of Rs. 18.000 and took 400 hours of direct labour to assemble. Labour rate is Rs. 25 per hour. This type of assembly is known to experience a learning curve effect of 80% (index of learning = 0.3219). Demonstration of this unit to potential customers resulted in an order for 20 units during the next quarter. The firm wishes to popularize this system and will therefore pass on the benefit of cost savings due to learning effect to the customers while setting the sale price.

(i) Determine the price to be set for the first lot of 20 units to be sold. The initial unit will not be sold as this is required for demonstration. The firm follows a practice of imputing a fixed overhead at 125% of direct labour cost and will set the selling price to earn a 20% gross margin on sale price.

(ii) Assume that a further order for a lot of 60 units was received on a contract basis from a single customer. The price was set on the basis of the contracted total. However, after delivery of 30 units against the contract, the contract was cancelled. Determine the deferred learning cost that may have to be written-off consequent to the cancellation of contract for balance not supplied.

Solution

Given data: X = 1, Y = 400 hours : Material cost Rs. 18,000;

Labour rate = Rs. 25 per hour. P = 80% (b = 0.3219)

First order lot 20 units. Since the first unit is not for sale to supply the first lot of 20, a total of 21 units would have been assembled. For the next contract of 60 units a total of 1 + 20 + 60 = 81 units would have to be assembled. For contract terminated halfway the total units assembled to date would 51 units.

Particulars	*X = 1*	*X = 21*	*X = 51*	*X = 81*
Y average labour hours	400	150.12	112.821	97.212
Total labour hours	400	3,153	5,754	7,874
Incremental total hours	400	2,753	2,601 (over 21)	4,721 (over 21)
Average labour incremental	137.65	86.7	76.68	

Pricing for the first sale lot of 20 units:		(Rs. per unit)
Material cost		18,000.00
Direct labour	(137.65 × 25)	3,441.25
Overheads	(@ 125% labour)	4,301.56
Total cost		25,742.81
Add: Profit 20% on sales or 25% on cost		6,435.70
Selling price		32,178.51

Price quoted for the contract lot of 60 units and for a 30 units:

Particulars	*Full lot 60*	*Half lot 30*
Material	18,000	18,000
Direct labour	1,967	2,168
Overheads	2,459	2,710
Totai cost	22,426	22,878
Add: Profit margin	5,606	5,719
Selling price	28,032	28,597

On the expectation of a full contract of 60 units the price quoted would have been Rs. 28,032.50 per unit. If it is expected that only 30 units will be supplied, then the price to be quoted is Rs. 28,597.50 per unit.

		(Rs.)
Actual cost of 30 units	(30 × 22,878)	6, 86,340
Less: Cost recovered based on full contract	(30 × 22,426)	6,72,780
Under recovered cast to be written off		13,560

SOLVED PROBLEMS

PROBLEM 10.1

Engine Ltd. manufactures engine mounting for wide bodied airlines. They have been asked to bid on a prospective contract for 90 engine mounting for the Jet aircraft. They have just completed an initial run of 30 of these mounting at the following costs:

		Rs.
Direct materials		20,000
Direct Labour	(6,000 hours @ Rs. 4)	24,000
Tooling cost	(re-usable)	3,000
Variable Overheads	(Re. 0.50 per Labour hour)	3,000
Fixed	(Re. 0.50 per labour hour)	6,000
	Total	56,000

An 80% learning curve is thought to be pertinent in this case. The marketing director believes that the quotation is unlikely to be accepted if it exceeds Rs. 1,10,000 and as the company is short of work, he believe the contract to be vital.

Required: Comment whether is it worth accepting at 1,10,000 State your assumptions clearly.

Solution

Statement of Learning Curve (80%)

Cummulative produce	*Average time per unit*	*Total time*	*Incremental hours*
30	200(*i.e.*, 6,000/30)	6,000	—
60	160(*i.e.*, 80% of 200)	9,600(*i.e.*, 160 × 60)	3,600
120	128(*i.e.*, 80% of 160)	15,360(*i.e.*, 120 × 128)	5,760

Incremental time for next 90 units = total time for first 120 units total time for first 30 units

= 15,360 – 6,000 = 9,360 hours

Statement of Revenue Cost

Cost to be incurred:

Material (20,000/30 × 90) = 60,000

Labour (9,360 × 4) = 37,440

Variable overhead (9,360 × 0.5) = 4,680

Tooling cost = NIL

Fixed overhead = NIL

Revenue Cost = 1,02,120

As relevant cost is less than quoted price. Hence, its better to accept the offer i.e. as the relevant cost Rs. 1,02,120 is less than quoted price Rs. 1,10,000. Hence it better to accept the offer.

PROBLEM 10.2

Company has accepted an order for making 15 items of a specialized machine at a price of Rs. 4 lacs each. The delivery is to be completed within 4 months. The company works 23 days a monthly and the normal direct wages per day amounts to Rs. 10,000. However in case of need, the company can work overtime up to 8 days during the said period at double the normal rate of wages. Overheads amount to Rs. 12,000 per normal working day but no overheads are charged on overtime working days. The material cost is Rs. 2,40,000 per machine. The company has estimated that it will take 10 working days to manufacture the first machine. The company is expected to experience a learning effect of 90% (b = 0.152). The contract stipulates a penalty of Rs. 40,000 per machine delivered beyond the schedule of 4 months.

Required: Calculate the costs and advise the company whether it is preferable to work only during normal working days and pay penalty for any delayed delivery of the machines or to work overtime to avoid paying penalty.

Solution

Statement of Comparative Cost (14th and 15th)

Overtime Premium		*Penalty*	
Overtime premium (8 × 10,000)	80,000	Extra cost (40,000 × 2)	80,000
Overhead cost	Nil	Overhead (12,000 × 8)	96,000
Total	80,000	Total	1,76,000

Hence, its better to introduce overtime working days

Working Notes:

Normal wages rate = 10,000 per day
Working days = 4 × 23 days = 92 days
Basic wages = 10,000 per day
Overtime premium = 10,000 per day
Overtime payment = 20,000 per day

Statement of Learning Curve

Cummulative Produce	*Average time per unit*	*Total time*
1	10	10
2	9	18
4	8.1	32.40
8	7.29	58.32
13	6.772	88.03
14	6.694	93.716
15	6.625	99.375
16	6.561	104.976

For first 15 machines:

$$Y = a(x)^b$$
$$\text{Log } Y = \log 10(15)^{-0.152}$$
$$\text{Log } Y = 1 + \log(15)^{-0.152}$$
$$\text{Log } Y = 1 - 0.152 \log 15$$
$$\text{Log } Y = 1 - 0.152 \log 15$$

By solving above equation, we get $Y = 6.625$

For first 14 machines

$$Y = ax^b$$
$$\text{Log } Y = \log 10\,(14)^{-0.152}$$
$$\text{Log } Y = 1 + \log(14)^{-0.152}$$
$$\text{Log } Y = 1 - 0.152 \times \log 14$$

By solving above equation, we get $Y = 6.694$

For first 13 machines

$$Y = ax^b$$
$$Y = 10(13)^{-0.152}$$

$$\text{Log } Y = \log 10 + \log (13)^{-0.152}$$
$$\text{Log } Y = 1 - 0.152 \times \log 13$$

By solving above equation, we get $Y = 6.772$

Hence, from above it is cleared that 14th and 15th machine cannot be completed within scheduled time.

PROBLEM 10.3

A company has 10 direct workers, who work for 25 days a month of 8 hours per day .The estimated down time is 25% of the total available time. The company received an order for a new product. The first unit of the new product requires 40 direct labour hours to manufacture the product. The company expects 80% (index is – 0.322) learning curve for this type of work. The company uses standard adsorption costing the cost data are as under:

Direct materials	Rs. 60 per unit
Direct labour	Rs. 6 per direct labour hour
Variable Overheads	Rs. 1 per direct labour hour
Fixed overheads	Rs. 7,500 per month

Required:

1. Calculate the cost per unit of the first order of 30 units.
2. If the company receives a repeat order for 20 units, what prices will be quoted to yield a profit of 25% on selling price?

Solution

(i) Calculation of Cost per unit of first 30 units

	Rs.
Material	60
Labour (13.38 × 6)	80.28
Variable Overheads	13.38
Fixed Overheads (13.38 × 5)	66.90
Required Cost	220.56

(ii) Calculation of Quoted Price of next 20 units

	Rs.
Material (60 × 20)	1,200
Wages (166.1 × 6)	996.6
Variable OH (166.1 × 1)	166.1
Fixed overheads (166.1 × 5)	830.5
Cost	3,193.20
Profit (l/3 of cost)	1,064.40
Selling price	4,257.60

Working Notes:

(*i*) *Calculation of Recovery Rate*

= Fixed Overhead/Budgeted Hours

= Rs. 7,500/[(2000 – 500 (Down Time)] = Rs. 5 per hour

(*ii*) Statement of Learning Curve

Cummulative Produce	*Average Time per unit*	*Total Time*	*Incremental Time*
1	40	40	
4			
8			

Cummulative Produce	*Average Time per unit*	*Total Time*	*Incremental Time*
16			
30	13.38	401.40	
—			
50	11.35	567.50	166.1

For first 30 units $Y = ax^b = 40(30)^{-0.322}$

Taking log on both sides

$$\text{Log } Y = \log 40(30)^{-0.322}$$
$$\text{Log } Y = \log 40 + \log (30)^{-0.322}$$
$$\text{Log } Y = 1.6021 - 0.322 \times \log 30$$
$$\text{Log } Y = 1.1264$$
$$Y = \text{anti log } 1.1264$$
$$Y = 13.38$$

For first 50 units $Y = ax^b = 40 \times (50)^{-0.322}$

Taking log on both sides

$$\text{Log } Y = \log 40 - 0.322 \log 50$$
$$\text{Log } Y = \text{Anti log } 1.055$$
$$Y = 11.35$$

PROBLEM 10.4

An electronic firm which has developed a new type of fire-alarm system has been asked to quote for a prospective contract.

Required: Prepare separate price quotations for each of the following.

Order	*Number of Fire-alarm systems*
First	100
Second	60
Third	40

The firm estimates the following cost per unit for the first order:

Direct materials Rs. 500

Direct Labour

Deptt. A (Highly automatic) 20 hours at Rs. 10 per hour.

Deptt. B (skilled labour) 40 hours at Rs. 15 per hour.

Variable Overheads 20% of direct labour

Fixed overheads absorbed:

Deptt.A Rs. 8 per hour

Deptt B Rs. 5 per hour

Determine a price per unit for each of the three orders, assuming the firm uses a mark-up of 25% on total costs and allows for an 80% learning curve. Extract from 80% Learning Curve table:-

X	1.0	1.3	1.4	1.5	1.6	1.7	1.8	1.9	2.0
Y(%)	100.0	91.7	89.5	87.6	86.1	84.4	83.0	81.5	80.0

X represents the cumulative total volume produced to date expressed as a multiple of the initial order. Y is the learning curve factor, for a given X value, expressed as a percentage of the cost of the initial order.

Solution

Statement showing Price per unit for each of three order

Particulars	*1st 100 units (Rs.)*	*2nd 60 units (Rs.)*	*3rd 40 units (Rs.)*
Direct material	50,000	30,000	20,000
Direct Labour			
Highly automatic Dept – A	20,000	12,000	8,000
Skilled Dept – B	60,000	22,656	13,344
Variable OH	16,000	6,931.20	4,268.80
Fixed OH			
Dept – A	16,000	9,600	6,400
Dept – B	20,000	7,552	4,448
Total Cost	1,82,000	88,739.20	56,460.8
Add: Profit Margin	45,500	22,184.80	14,115.20
Selling Price	2,27,500	1,10,924	70,576
Selling Price per unit	2,275	1,848.73	1,764.40

Working Note:

Statement of Learning Curve

Cummulative Unit	*Average Time per unit*	*Total Time*	*Incremental Time*
100 (=1)	40(100%)	4,000	—
130 (=1.3)	—	—	—
160 (=1.6)	34.44(86.1%)	5,510.40	1,510.4
200 (=2)	32(80%)	6,400	889.6

PROBLEM 10.5

(a) Your company has been approached by a customer to supply four units of a new product made to the customer's individual specification. The company experiences a 90% learning rate. The estimated labour time for the first unit of this product is 150 hours and the company's direct labour cost Rs. 5 per hour. (a) Estimate the labour cost for this order, (b) After receiving the first order, if the customer places a repeat order, what will be the labour cost for the second order, (c) If the customer had ordered all eight units at the same time, calculate the labour cost per unit for the combined order.

Solution:

(a) Calculation of Labour Cost

Units Produced (1)	*Cum. Production* (2)	*Avg. Time per unit (hrs.)* (3)	*Total Labour Time* (4) = (2) × (3)
1	1	150.0	150.0
1	2	135.0 (90% of 150)	270.0
2	4	121.5 (90% of 135)	486.0

Estimated Labour Cost for the order = 486 × Rs. 5 = Rs. 2,430

Labour Cost per unit = Rs. 607.50

(b) The first order relates to four units. The repeat order will be for another four units.

Thus, average labour hours for 8 units will be:

Average time per unit = 90% of 121.5 = 109.35 hrs.

Average time for 8 units = 109.35 × 8 = 874.80

Less: time spent on this order 486.00

388.80

Total labour cost for second order = 388.8 × Rs. 5 = 1 ,944 or Rs. 486 per unit, i.e., 1,944 ÷ 4

(c) Labour Cost of Combined Order

Units Produced (1)	*Cum. Production (2)*	*Avg. Time per unit (hrs) (3)*	*Total Labour Time (4) = (2) × (3)*
1	1	150.0	150.0
1	2	135.0	270.0
2	4	121.5	486.0
4	8	109.35	874.8

Estimated labour cost for the order = 874.8 x Rs. 5 = Rs. 4,374

Estimated labour cost per unit (4,374 ÷ 8) = Rs. 546.75

PROBLEM 10.6

You have been asked about the application of the learning curve as a management accounting technique. You are required to: illustrate the use of learning curves for calculating the expected average unit cost of making: (i) 4 machines; and (ii) 8 machines.

Using the data given below.

Data:

Direct labour needed to make the first machine 1,000 hours	
Learning curve	80%
Direct labour cost	Rs. 3 per hour
Direct materials cost	Rs. 1,800 per machine
Fixed cost for either size order	Rs. 8,000

Solution

(i) *Calculation of average time to be taken for different given levels.*

(a) Equation Approach, i.e., $y = (a)(x)^{-b}$

Learning coefficient for 80%

$$b = \frac{\log\text{(learning coefficient)}}{2} = \frac{\log(0.80)}{\log 2} = -0.3219$$

For 4 units $y = (1,000)$

$$\log y = 3.0000 - 0.3219(0.6021)$$
$$= 3.0000 - 0.1938$$
$$= 2.8062$$

y = Antilong 2.8062 = 640 hours per unit of cumulative production at this level.

For 8 units, $y = (1000)(8)^{-0.3219}$

= 512 hours per unit of cumulative production at this level.

(b) Doubling Approach: 80% learning curve, when the first unit required 1,000 hours.

Incremental qty. (units)	*Total number of units (units)*	*Average time to produce all units to date (Hrs.)*	*Computations*
1	1	1,000	(1,000 × 1)
1	2	800	(1,000 × 0.80)
2	4	640	(800 × 0.80)
4	8	512	(64 × 0.80))

(ii) Average unit cost for making:

(a) (*i*) 4 machines:

	Rs.
Direct material	1,800
Direct labour (640 hrs x Rs. 3)	1,920
Fixed cost (Rs. 8,000 ÷ 4)	2,000
	5,720

(b) (*ii*) 8 machines:

Direct material	1,800
Direct labour (512 hrs. x Rs. 3)	1,536
Fixed cost (Rs. 8,000 ÷ 8)	1,000
	4,336

PROBLEM 10.7

H Ltd. has produced its first 10 units of product B. The customer is enquiring about the cost of the further 30 units of Product B. The total cost of the original 10 units was:

	Rs
Materials	3,000
Variable labour costs (500 hours at Rs. 10 per hour)	5,000
Variable overheads*	1,000
Other overheads**	1,000
Machine tool costs***	2,000
Total cost	12,000

*Directly affected by variable labour costs.

** Estimated at 20% of variable labour costs.

***All machine tools can still be used although all costs recovered on first order.

Use an 80% learning curve to estimate the total costs for a new batch of 30 units to Product B.

Solution

Machine cost is ignored, since it is already absorbed by the first batch.

Table showing the labour cost projection considering 80% learning effect

Incremental Qty. (Units)	*Cumulative Qty. (units)*	*Average Labour hours for the batch of 10 units (hours)*	*Cumulative Labour Cost (Rs.)*	*Calculation of Labour (Rs.)*
10	10	500	Rs. 5,000	500 hrs. × 1 batch × Rs. 10
10	20	500 × 0.80	8,000	400 hrs. x 2 batches × Rs. 10
20	40	500 × 0.80 × 0.80	12,800	320 hrs. x 4 batches × Rs. 10

For 30 units:

Labour cost = Rs. 12,800 – Rs. 5,000 = Rs. 7,800

Variable overheads = 20% of Rs. 7,800 = Rs. 1,560

Other overheads = 20% of Rs. 7,800 = Rs. 1,560

Total estimated cost for additional 30 units:

Material	Rs.	9,000
Labour		7,800
Variable overheads		1,560
Other overheads		1,560
		19,920

PROBLEM 10.8

You have been asked to give a quote for the production of 50 units of a new product. Estimates for the assembly of the first unit are:

Direct materials	Rs. 100
Direct Labour	Rs. 50
Variable overhead	Rs. 30

Notes:

1. Labour costs are Rs. 5 an hour.
2. Variable overhead is based on labour hours (activity based) at a rate of Rs. 3 per labour hour.
3. The company quotes prices on a 20 per cent mark-up on the estimated costs to cover fixed overheads and profits.
4. The company operates an 80 per cent learning curve.
   (i) The company wishes to estimate the marginal cost of making the 50 units and hence calculate the quoted price per unit.
   (ii) What will be the impact, if the company decides to ignore the learning curve effect? Present the comparative data showing the price per unit.

Solution

(i) Calculation of average time to be taken for different given levels:

Equation approach, i.e. $y = ax^{-b}$

The company operates at 80% learning curve.

So, Learning coefficient for 80%

$$b = \frac{\log(0.80)}{\log 2}$$

For 50 units,

$$y = ax^{b}$$
$$= (10)(50)^{-0.3219}$$
$$\log y = 1.000 - 0.3219(1.6990)$$
$$= 1.0000 - 0.5469$$
$$= 0.4531$$
$$y = \text{Antilog } 0.4531 = 2.839 \text{ or } 2.84 \text{ hrs.}$$

So, Total time for 50 units = 50 x 2.84 hrs = 142 hrs

Hence, the estimated marginal cost of 50 units.

Direct materials (50 × 100)	Rs.	5,000
Direct labour (142 hrs × Rs. 5)		710
Variable overhead (142 × Rs. 3)		426
Total		6,136

Hence marginal cost of 50 units = Rs. 6,136

Therefore, price to be quoted for 50 units = 6,136 x 1.20 = Rs. 7,363.20

So, Price quoted per item = Rs. 7,363.20 ÷ 50 = Rs. 147.26

Barsands should, therefore, quote a price of Rs. 147.26 per item for the batch of 50 items.

(ii) If the company did not appreciate that learning curve effect was present, then the estimated priced based on the first unit cost would be:

	Price based on 1st unit costs	*Priced based on learning curve*
Direct material	Rs. 100.00	Rs. 100.00
Direct labour 10 × 5; (2.84 × 5)	50.00	14.20
Variable overhead (10 × 3); (2.84 × 3)	30.00	8.52
Total	180.00	122.72
Add: 20% Mark-up	36.00	24.54
Price	216.00	147.26

Hence ignoring the learning curve effect would lead the substantial overpricing to the competitors advantage.

PROBLEM 10.9

A company with two production departments has set the following standards for the forthcoming year:

Particulars	*Department*	
	S	*W*
Direct labour hours available per period	6,000	4,000
Standard wage rate per hour	Rs. 6	Rs. 5
Expected learning curve	80%	70%
Standard variable overheads per hour	Rs. 9	Rs. 5
Standard fixed overhead per hour	Rs.12	Rs. 8
Direct labour hours required for first 100 units	18	9

The direct materials are introduced in Department S. The company is able to negotiate the following prices for purchase of direct materials during the year.

Level of output	*Price of direct materials per (unit of output)*
100	Rs. 72.00
200	Rs. 64.80
800	Rs. 54.00

Overtime, if required, is paid at time and a half. The overhead rates as given above does not include overtime premium. It is the policy of the company to add profit margin as under in quoting the prices:

Department	*Percentage on total labour & overhead cost*
S.	25%
W.	15%
Sub-contracted work	5% on sub-contract price

The company has received a special order. Special tooling costs of the order amount to Rs. 1,200. If this order is for 200 units or less, it will be executed in the period which has a workload of 3840 direct labour hours in Department S and 2100 direct labour hours in Department W. For the work which is done in Department W, a subcontract price of Rs. 50 per unit is quoted by an associate company.

Required:

(i) If the company decides to get the work executed entirely within the company, what price, on cost plus basis, should be quoted for the order, if it consists of: (*i*) 100 units (*ii*) 200 units.

(ii) Assuming that the initial order placed by the customer is for 200 units, what lowest price should be quoted for a repeat order of 600 units? Assume that this order will be executed when there are no capacity constraints.

(iii) State the output level at which the company should close down Department W to get the work executed through sub-contractors.

Solution

Statement of Learning Curve

(Department – S) 80%			*(Department – W) 70%*		
Cummulative Produce	*Average Time per unit*	*Total Time*	*Cummulative produce*	*Average time per unit*	*Total Time*
100	18	1,800	100	9	900
200	14.40	2,880	200	6.3	1,260
400	11.52	4,608	400	4.41	1,764
800	9.216	7,372.8	800	3.087	2,469.6

Statement of Hours avalability

Particulars	*Department – S*	*Department – W*
Hours available	6,000	4,000
Less: regular working	(3,840)	(2,100)
Balance	2,160	1,900
(*i*) *less:* first 100 units	1,800	900
Balance	360	1,000
(*ii*) *less:* first 200 units	2,880	1,260
Balance surplus (Defcit)	(720)	640

Statement of Cost and Price per unit (Absorption)

First 100 units		*First 200 units*	
"S" Dept	Rs. Per unit	"S" Dept	Rs. per unit
Material	72	Material	64.80
Wages (18 × 6)	108	Wages (14.40 × 6)	86.40
Variable-OH (18 × 9)	162	Variable-OH (14.4 × 9)	129.6
Fixed-OH (18 × 12)	216	Fixed-OH (14.4 × 12)	172.80
		Overtime premium (2160/200)	10.80
"W" Dept		*"W" Dept*	
Labour cost (9 × 5)	45	Material	
Variable-OH (9 × 5)	45	Wage (6.3 × 5)	31.5
Fixed-OH (9 × 8)	72	Variable-OH (6.3 × 5)	31.5

		Fixed-OH (6.3 × 8)	50.4
		Overtime	NIL
Tooling Cost (1200/100)	12	Tooling Cost (1200/200)	6
Total	732	Total Cost	583.8
(+) Profit Margin		(+) Profit	
"S" Dept – 486 × 25% = 121.5		"S" Dept – 399.6 × 25% = 99.90	
"W" Dept – 162 × 15% = 24.3	145.8	"W" Dept – 113.4 × 15% = 17.01	116.91
Price	877.80	Price	700.71

PROBLEM 10.10

A company has designed a Prototype Electronic Starter for which the following information are available:

Direct Labour hours	260 hours
Direct material cost	Rs. 30,000
Direct labour rate	Rs. 20 per hour
Variable overhead	130% of direct labour
Fixed overhead	70% of direct labour

Based on the demonstration of the prototype, the company has received order for 50 units during first six months and another 75 units during the following six months thereafter.

A learning curve effect of 80% is applicable. It is expected that in view of large volume, a 5% discount on material cost will be available in first six months and a 10% discount thereafter. The rates of overhead will remain unchanged and the same percentages would apply.

The company sets the selling price with a 40% mark upon cost. Determine the selling price per unit for the first 50 units and the next 75 units.

(The index of learning rate of learning curve effect of 80% is 0.3219)

Solution

Incremental Labour Cost/unit

Hours *X*	*Y(x)*	*L(x)*	*M(x)*	*Incremental Cost/unit* *(Rs.)*
1	260	260	260	5200
51	73,334	3,740	69.9	1392
126	54,811	6,906	42.21	844

Selling Price Computation

Particulars	*1st lot of 50* *(Rs.)*	*2nd lot of 75* *(Rs.)*
Direct material	28,500 (30,000 – 1,500)	27,000 (30,000 – 3,000)
Direct Labour (as per statement)	1,392	844
Variable overhead	1,810	1,097
Fixed overhead	974	591
Total cost	32,676	29,532
Mark up 40%	13,070	11,813
	45,746	41,345

PROBLEM 10.11

A company has 10 direct worker, who work for 25 days a month of 8 hours per day. The estimated down time is 25% of the total available time. The company received an order for a new product. The first unit of the new product requires 40 direct labour hous to manufacture the product. The company expects 80% (index is - 0.322) learning curve for this type of work. The company uses standard absorption costing and the cost data are as under:

Direct labour hour	Rs. 60 per unit
Direct material cost	Rs. 6 per direct labour hour
Variable overhead	Re. 1 per direct labour hour
Fixed overhead	Rs. 7,500 per month

Required:

(i) Calculte the cost per unit of the first order of 30 unils.

(ii) It the company receives a repeat order for 20 units, what price will be quoted to yield a profit of 25% on selling price?

Solution

(i) Computation of Cost per unit of the first order of 30 units

Particulars		*Rs*
Direct Material Cost	(30 units × Rs. 60)	1,800.00
Direct Labour Cost	(401.4 hours × Rs. 6)	2,408.40
Variable Overheads	(401.4 hours × Rs. 1)	401.40
Fixed Overheads	(401.4 hours × Rs. 5)	2,007.00
Total Cost of 30 units		6,616.80
Cost per unit	(Rs. 6,616.80/30 units)	220.56

(ii) Cost per unit, when a repeat order for 20 units is also placed.

Particulars		*Rs*
Direct Material Cost	(20 units × Rs. 60)	1,200.00
Direct Labour	(567.5 hours – 401.40 hours) × Rs. 6	996.60
Variable Overheads	(166.1 hours × Re. 1)	166.10
Fixed Overheads	(166.1 hours × Rs. 5)	830.50
Total Cost of 20 additional units		3,193.20
Cost per unit	(Rs. 3, 193.20/20 units)	159.66

Price to be quoted to yield a profit of 25% on selling price.

It Selling Price is Rs. 100 then profit is Rs. 25 and cost of Rs. 75.

Hence Selling Price unit = $\frac{100}{75} \times 159.66$ = Rs. 212.88.

Working Notes:

(*i*) *By the theory of learning curve*

$$Y_x = KX^s$$

Hence X is the cumulative number of units or lots produced. Y is the cumulative average unit time of those X units. K is the average time of the first unit or lot, s is the improvement exponent or the learning coefficient or the index of learning.

Taking log on both sides of relation (i) we have

$$\log Y = \log K + s \log X$$

(*ii*) Time required for 30 units order (when the time required for first unit is 40 hours)

$$\log 40 + (-0.322) \log 30 = 1.6021 + (-0.322)(1.4771) = 1.6021 - 0.4756$$
$$= 1.1264$$

Antilog of 1.1264 =13.38

Hence hours required for 30 unit =13.38

Total time required for 30 units = 30 units × 13.38 hours = 401.4

(*iii*) Time required for 50 units order (when the time required for first unit is 40 hours)

$$\log 40 + (-0.0322) \log 50 = 1.6021 + (-0.0322)\ 1.6990 = 1.055$$

Antilog of 1.055 = 11.35

Hence hours required per unit 11.35 hours

Total time required for 50 units = 11.35 hours × 50 units = 567.5 hours

(iv) Fixed overhead recovery rate per labour hour

Total labour hours	(10 men × 25 days × 8 hrs)	2,000
Less: 25% downtime	(in hrs.)	500
Total effective hours		1,500
Total fixed overheads per month (Rs.)		7,500
Fixed overhead recovery rate per labour hour (Rs.)	(Rs. 7,500/1500 hrs)	5

PROBLEM 10.12

SV Ltd. which has a fairly full order book is approached by a customer with the offer of a contract for a model that is a variant, in terms of dimensions and materials used, of one of its existing products.

Though the customer expects to pay a normal price for the model he wants SV Ltd. to take account of an 80% learning curve in its price calculation; this level has been shown to be reasonable in SV Ltd's industry for relevant work.

The Prospective contract is for a total 464 units made up of an initial order of 160 units, two subsequent orders of 80 unit each, and three subsequent orders of 48 units each. SV Ltd. estimates the following costs for the initial order.

Direct materials:

P- 8 mtr.	At Rs. 3.50 per mtr.
Q-12Kg.	At Rs. 1.00 per Kg.

Direct Wages:

Department	*Hours*	*Rs. per hour*
1	100	
2	320	
3	160	1.00

Variable overhead: 20% of direct wages.

Fixed overhead Department Recover	*Rate per hour (Rs.)*
1	2.00
2	1.00
3	2.00

The nature of the work in the three production departments is as follows:- Department 1 uses highly automatic machines. Although the operators on these machines need to be fairly skilled, their efficiency only affects the quality of the work but can have little impact on the quantity of his departments output which is largely machine controlled. Department 2 and 3 the skill of operators is a major determinant of the volume of output.

Required: Calculate the cost per unit for:

(i) the initial order of 160 units

(ii) the second, third and fourth orders, if given successively but without guarantee of further orders and

(iii) the whole contract of six orders if given from the start but on the same basis of production and delivery.

Note: An 80% learning curve on ordinary graph paper would show the following relationship between the X-axis (volume) Y-axis (Cumulative average price of elements subjects to the learning curve):

X represents the cumulative total volume produced to date expressed as a multiple of the initial order. Y is the learning curve factor, for a given X value, expressed as a percentage of the cost of the initial order.

X	Y%	X	Y%
1.0	100.0	2.1	78.9
1.1	960	2.2	77.8
1.2	93.3	2.3	76.8
1.3	91.7	2.4	76.0
1.4	89.5	2.5	74.9
1.5	87.6	2.6	74.0
1.6	86.1	2.7	73.2
1.7	84.4	2.8	72.3
1.8	83.0	2.9	71.5
1.9	81.5	3.0	70.7
2.0	80.0	3.1	70.0

X represents the cumulative total volume produced to date expressed as a multiple of the initial order. Y is the learning curve factor, for a given X value, expressed as a percentage of the cost of the initial order.

Solution

Statement of Learning Curve of "Dept-2" (80%)

Cummulative Product	*Average Time per unit*	*Total Time*	*Incremental Time*
160(=1)	2 (=100)	320	—
176(1.1)	1.92(96%)	337.9_	17.92
240(1.5)	1.752(87.6%)	420.48	100.48
320(2)	1.6(80%)	512	91.52
368(2.3)	1.536(76.8%)	565.25	53.25
416(2.6)	1.48(74%)	615.68	50.43
464(2.9)	1.43(71.5%)	663.52	47.84

Statement of Learning Curve of "Dept-3" (80%)

Cummulative Product	*Average Time per unit*	*Total Time*	*Incremental Time*
160 (=1)	1(100%)	160	—
240 (=1.5)	0.876(87.6%)	210.24	50.24
320 (=2)	0.8(80%)	256	45.76
368 (=2.3)	0.768(76.8%)	282.624	26.62
416 (=2.6)	0.74(74%)	307.84	25.22
464 (=2.9)	0.715(71.5%)	331.76	23.92

(a) Calculation Cost of Initial Order of 160 units

		Rs.
Material:		
P – 8 × 3.50	= 28	
Q – 12 × 1.00	= 12	40
Wages:		
Dept-I – 100 × 1.25	= 125	
Dept-II – 320 × 1.50	= 480	
Dept-III – 160 × 1.00	= 160	765
Variable overheads		= 153
Fixed Overheads:		
Dept-I – 2 × 100	= 200	
Dept-I1 – 1 × 320	= 320	
Dept-III – 0.80 × 160	= 128	648
Total Cost	=	1606

(b) Statement showing Second, Third and Fourth Order Cost

Particulars	*2nd 80 units (Rs.)*	*3rd 80 units (Rs.)*	*4th 48 units (Rs.)*
Material	20	20	12
Direct Wages:			
Dept-I	62.5	62.50	37.50
Dept-II	150.72	137.28	79.875
Dept-III	50.24	45.67	26.62
Variable OH:	52.69	49.11	28.80
Fixed OH			
Dept-I	100	100	60
Dept-II	100.48	91.52	53.25
Dept-III	40.192	36.60	21.30
Total Cost	**576.82**	**542.68**	**319.35**

(c) Statement showing cost of whole contract (464 units)

	Rs.	Rs.
Direct material	=	116
Direct wages		
Dept-I – (290 × 1.25)	= 362.50	
Dept-II – (663.52 × 1.50)	= 995.28	
Dept-III – (331.76 × 1)	= 331.76	1,689.54

Variable Overheads	=		337.91
Fixed Overheads			
Dept-I – (2 × 290)	= 580		
Dept-II – (1 × 663.52)	= 663.52		
Dept-III – (0.80 × 331.76)	= 265.41		1,508.93
Total Cost	=		3,652.34

PROBLEM 10.13

SV Ltd., which has a fairy full order book is approached by a customer with the offer of a contract for a model that is a variant, in terms of dimensions and materials used, of one of its existing products. Through the customer expects to pay a normal price for the model, he wants SV Ltd. to take account of an 80% learning curve in its price calculation; this level has been shown to be reasonable in SV Ltd's industry for relevant work. The Prospective contract is for a total 464 units made up of an initial order of 160 units, two subsequent orders of 80 units each, and three subsequent orders of 48 units each. SV Ltd. estimates the following costs for the initial order:

Direct materials:

P-8 mtr. at Rs. 3.50 per mtr.
Q-12kg. at × Re 1.00 per kg.

Direct wages:

Department	*Hours*	*Rs. per hour*
1	4	1.25
2	50	1.50
3	15	1.00

Variable overhead: 20% of direct wages

Fixed overhead Department	*Rate per hour (Rs.)*
1	2.00
2	1.00
3	0.80

The nature of the work in the three production departments is as follows:

Department 1 uses highly automatic machines. Although the operators on these machines need to be fairly skilled. Their efficiency only affects the quality of the work but can have little impact on the quantity of his department's output which is largely machine-controlled. Department 2 is partially mechanized, whilst Department 3 is an assembly department.

In both departments 2 and 3 the skill of operators is a major determinant of the volume of output.

The terms of the contract price allow for:

Direct materials cost *plus* 2.5% profit margin
Conversion cost *plus* 12.5% profit margin

You are required to calculate the price per unit for

(a) the initial order of 160 units;

(b) the second, third and fourth orders, if given successively but without guarantee of further orders, and

(c) the whole contract of six orders it given from the start but on the same basis of production and delivery.

Note: An 80% learning curve on ordinary graph paper would show the following relationship between the X-axis (volume) and Y-axis (cumulative average price of elements subjects to the learning curve):

x	*y%*	*x*	*y%*
1.0	100.0	2.1	78.9
1.1	96.0	2.2	77.8
1.2	93.3	2.3	76.8
1.3	91.7	2.4	76.0
1.4	89.5	2.5	74.9
1.5	87.6	2.6	74.0
1.6	86.1	2.7	73.2
1.7	84.4	2.8	72.3
1.8	83.0	2.9	71.5
1.9	81.5	3.0	70.7
2.0	80.0	3.1	70.0

Solution:

(a) Initial Order *(Rs.)*

Deptt. 2			
Labour Costs	(50 hrs @ 1.50)	75	
Variable Overhead	(20%)	15	
Fixed Overhead	(50 × Re. 1)	50	140
Dept. 3			
Labour Costs	(15hrs@ Re. 1)	15	
Variable Overhead	(20%)	3	
Fixed Overhead	(15 × 0.80)	12	30
Total cost affected by l.c.			170
i.e., subject to reduction on(subsequent orders.)			
Other Labour Costs			
Dept.1	(4 hrs. @ Rs. 1.25)	5	
Variable Overheads	20%	1	
Fixed Overheads	(4 × Rs. 2)	8	14
Total Conversion Cost			184
Materials	P(8 × 3.5)	28	
	Q(12 x Re. 1)	12	40
Total Cost			224
Profit	(2.5% of Rs. 40)	1	
	(12.5%of Rs. 184)	23	24
			248

Selling price per unit for initial order = 248/160 = 1.55

Note: Department 1 is highly automatic as such not subject to LC effect.

(b) Second order of 80 units

Total output = 240 units (i.e., 160 + 80).

Thus the output due to second order increased by 50%.

160= 1.0= 100%

240 = 1.5* = 87.6% (overall average time)

*240/160 = 1.5 (1.5 = 87.6% as per given table)

Cumulative reducible cost*			223.38
Less: Charged to first order			170.00
Reducible cost for this order			53.38
Wages/Overhead of Deptt. 1	(50% of Rs. 14)		7.00
Total Conversion Cost			60.38
Materials	(50% of Rs. 40)		20.00
Total Cost			80.38
Profit	(2.5% of Rs. 20)	0.50	
	(12.5% of Rs 60.38)	7.55	8.05
			88.43

*(1.5 × Rs. 170) = Rs.255 (Rs. 255 × 87.6%)

Selling price for second order of 80 units = Rs. 88.43 / 80 units = Rs. 1.11 per unit.

Third order of 80 units

Total cumulative output 320 units (i.e., 2 times of the first order of 160 unit.)

Therefore L.C. as per given table will be 80% (overall average time).

Cumulative reducible cost*			272.00
Less: Charged to 1st and 2nd orders			223.38
Reducible cost of this order			48.62
Wages/Overhead of Dept. I	(50% of Rs. 14)		7.00
Total Conversion Cost			55.62
Materials	(50% of Rs. 40)		20.00
Total Cost			75.62
Profit	(2.5% of Rs. 20)	0.50	
	(12.5% of Rs. 55.62)	6.95	7.45
Selling Price of this order			83.07

*(2.0 × Rs. 170) = Rs. 340

(80% of 340) = Rs.272

Selling Price per unit= Rs. 83.07/80 units = Rs. 1.04

Fourth order of 48 units

Total cumulative output = 360 units (i. e., 2.3 times of first order of 160 units) = 76.8% (overall average time)

(Rs.)

Cumulative reducible cost*			300.29
Less: Charged to previous three orders			272.00
Reducible cost of this order			28.29
Wages/overhead of Dept.	(18/160) × Rs. 14		4.20
Total conversion cost			32.49
Materials	(48/160) × Rs. 40		12.00
Total cost			44.49
Profit	(2.5% Rs. 12)	0.30	
	(12.5% of Rs. 32.)	4.06	4.36
Selling price for fourth order of 48 units			48.85

*(Rs. 170 × 2.3)	= Rs. 391
(76.8% of Rs. 391)	= Rs. 300.29
Selling price per unit	= Rs. 48.85/48 units = Rs. 1.02

(c) Total Contract

Orders	*Total units*
1 × 160	160
2 × 80	160
3 × 48	144
	464

464 units or 2.9 times of initial order of 160 units

Cumulative Average Time = 71.5% of initial order time.

(Rs.)

Reducible costs*			352.50
Labour/Overhead Deptt.1	(2.9 x 14)		40.60
Total conversion cost			393.10
Materials	(2.9 × Rs. 40)		116.00
Total maximum cost			509.10
Profit	(2,5% of Rs. 116)	2.90	
	(12.5% of Rs. 393.10)	49.14	52.04
Total selling price of 464 units			561.14

*(2.9 × Rs. 170) = Rs. 493

(71.5% of Rs. 493) = Rs. 352.50

THEORETICAL QUESTIONS

1. Discuss the applications of the learning curve.
2. What are the distinctive features of learning curve theory in manufacturing environment?
3. Explain the Learning Curve Ratio.

APPENDIX IMPORTANT THEORETICAL QUESTIONS

1.0 LINEAR PROGRAMMING–FORMULATION

Q. 1.1 What is Linear Programming?

Ans. Linear programming is a powerful quantitative technique (or operational research technique) designs to solve allocation problem. The term **'Linear Programming'** consists of the two words **'Linear'** and **'Programming'**.

The word **'Linear'** is used to describe the relationship between decision variables which are directly proportional. *For example*, if doubling (or tripling) the production of a product will exactly double (or triple) the profit and required resources, then it is linear relationship.

The word **'Programming'** means planning of activities in a manner that achieves some 'optimal' result with available resources. A programme is 'optimal' if it maximises or minimises some measure or criterion of effectiveness such as profit, contribution (i.e. sales-variable cost), sales, cost.

Thus, 'Linear Programming' indicates the planning of decision variables which are directly proportional, to achieve the 'optimal' result considering the limitations within which the problem is to be solved.

Q. 1.2 Explain the terms—Decision Variables, Objective Function, Constraints, Non-Negativity Restriction, Divisibility with reference to LPP.

Ans.

Decision Variables	The decision variables refer to the economic or physical quantities which are competing with one another for sharing the given limited resources. The relationship among these variables must be linear under linear programming. The numerical values of decision variables indicate the solution of the linear programming problem
Objective Function	The objective function of a linear programming problem is a linear function of the decision variable expressing the objective of the decision maker. *For example*, maximisation of profit or contribution, minimisation of cost/time.

Constraints	The constraints indicate limitations on the resources which are to be allocated among various decision variables. These resources may be production capacity, manpower, time, space or machinery. These must be capable of being expressed as linear equation (i.e. =) *or* inequalities (i.e. ≥ or ≤ type) in terms of decision variables. Thus, constraints of a linear programming problem are linear equalities *or* inequalities arising out of practical limitations.
Non-Negativity Restriction	Non-negativity restriction indicates that all decision variables must take on values equal to or greater than zero.
Divisibility	Divisibility means that the numerical values of the decision variables are continuous and not limited to integers. In other words, fractional values of the decision variables must be permissible in obtaining optimal solution.

Q.1.3 List any four applications of LPP.

Ans. 1. Transportation Decisions
2. Assignment Decisions
3. Product Mix Decisions
4. Portfolio Mix Decisions
5. Capital Mix Decisions
6. Advertising Mix Decisions
7. Bending Decisions
8. Agriculture Decisions

2.0 LINEAR PROGRAMMING– GRAPHICAL METHOD

Q. 2.1 Explain the terms— Closed Half Plane, Feasible Solution, Feasible Region, Convex Set, Convex Polygon, Vertexes, Redundant Constraint with reference to LPP.

Ans.

Closed Half Plane	A linear inequality in two variables is known as a half plane. The corresponding equality or the line is known as the boundary of the half plane. The half plane along with its boundary is called a closed half plane. Thus, a closed half plane is a linear inequality in two variables which include the value of the variable for which equality is attained.
Feasible Solution	Any non-negative solution which satisfies all the constraints is known as a feasible solution of the problem.
Feasible Region	The collection of all feasible solutions is known as a feasible region.
Convex Set	A set (or region) is convex if only if for any two points on the set, the line segment joining those points lies entirely in the set. Thus, the collection of feasible solutions in a linear programming problem form a convex set. In other words, the feasible region of a linear programming problem is a convex set.
Convex Polygon	A convex polygon is a convex set formed by the intersection of a finite number of closed half planes.

Extreme Points or Vertexes or Corner Points	The extreme points of a convex polygon are the points of intersection of the lines bounding the feasible region. The value of the decision variables which maximise or minimise the objective function is located on one of the extreme points of the convex polygon. If the maximum or minimum value of a linear function defined over a convex polygon exists, then it must be on one of the extreme points.
Redundant Constraint	Redundant constraint is a constraint which does not affect the feasible region.

Q.2.2 Explain the terms— Multiple Solution, Unbounded Solution, Infeasible Problem with reference to LPP.

Ans.

Multiple Solution	Multiple Solutions of a linear programming problem are solutions each of which maximize or minimize the objective function. Under graphical method, the existence of multiple solution is indicated by a situation under which the objective function line coincides with one of the half planes generated by a constraint. In other words, where both the objective function line and one of constraint lines have the same slope.
Unbounded Solution	An Unbounded Solution of a linear programming problem is a solution whose objective function is infinite. A linear programming problem is said to have unbounded solution if its solution can be made infinitely large without violating any of the constraints in the problem. Since there is no real applied problem which has infinite returns, hence an unbounded solution always represents a problem that has been incorrectly formulated. *For example*, in a maximization problem at least one of the constraints must be an 'equality' *or* 'less than or equal to' (≤) type. If all of the constraints are 'greater than or equal to' (≥) type, then there will be no upper limit on the feasible region. Similarly for minimization problem, at least one of constraints must be an 'equality' or 'a greater than or equal to' type (≥) if a solution is to be bounded. Under graphical method, the feasible solution region extends indefinitely.
Infeasible Problem	A linear programming problem is said to be infeasible if there is no solution that satisfies all the constraints. It represents a state of inconsistency in the set of constraints.

3.0 LINEAR PROGRAMMING–SIMPLEX METHOD

Q.3.1 Explain the terms— Multiple Solution, Unbounded Solution, Infeasible Problem, Degeneracy with reference to LPP.

Ans.

Multiple Solution	Multiple Solutions of a linear programming problem are solutions each of which maximize or minimize the objective function under Simplex Method. Under Simplex Method, the existence of multiple optimal solutions is indicated by a situation under which a non-basic variable in the final simplex table showing optimal solution to a problem, has a net zero contribution. In other words, if at least one of the non-basic variable in the $(C_j - Z_j)$ row of the final simplex table has a zero value, it indicates that there is more than one optimal solution.
Unbounded Solution	An unbounded solution of a linear programming problem is a situation where objective function is infinite. A linear programming problem is said to have unbounded solution if its solution can be made infinitely large without violating any of its constraints in the problem. Since there is no real applied problem which has infinite return, hence an unbounded solution always represents a problem that has been incorrectly formulated. Under the Simplex Method, an unbounded solution is indicated when there are **no positive values** of Replacement Ratio i.e. Replacement Ratio Values are *either* infinite *or* negative. In this case there is no outgoing variable.
Infeasible Problem	A linear programming problem is said to be infeasible if there is no solution that satisfies all the constraints. It represents a state of inconsistency in the set of constraints. Under the Simplex Method, the problem is said to have no feasible solution if at least one of the artificial variable remains in the final simplex table as basic variable with non-zero quantity.
Degeneracy	Degeneracy in a linear programming problem is said to occur when a basic feasible solution contains a smaller number of non-zero variables than the number of independent constraints when values of some basic variables are zero and the Replacement ratio is same. In otherwords, under Simplex Method, degeneracy occurs, where there is a tie for the minimum positive replacement ratio for selecting outgoing variable. In this case, the choice for selecting outgoing variable may be made arbitrarily.

4.0 ASSIGNMENT PROBLEMS

Q.4.1 What is Assignment Problem?

Ans.

Meaning	Assignment Problem is a special type of linear programming problem where the objective is to minimise the cost or time of completing a number of jobs by a number of persons.

	The assignment problem in the general form can be stated as follows : *"Given n facilities, n jobs and the effectiveness of each facility for each job, the problem is to assign each facility to one and only one job in such a way that the measure of effectiveness is optimised (Maximised or Minimised)."*
Example	A manager has four persons (i.e. facilities) available for four separate jobs (i.e. jobs) and the cost of assigning (i.e. effectiveness) each job to each person is given. His objective is to assign each person to one and only one job in such a way that the total cost of assignment is minimised.

Q.4.2 What is Hungarian Method?

Ans. Although an assignment problem can be formulated as a linear programming problem, it is solved by a special method known as Hungarian Method because of its special structure. If the time of completion or the costs corresponding to every assignment is written down in a matrix form, it is referred to as a Cost matrix. The Hungarian Method is based on the principle that if a constant is added to every element of a row and/or a column of cost matrix, the optimum solution of the resulting assignment problem is the same as the original problem and vice versa. The original cost matrix can be reduced to another cost matrix by adding constants to the elements of rows and columns where the total cost or the total completion time of an assignment is zero. Since the optimum solution remains unchanged after this reduction, this assignment is also the optimum solution of the original problem. If the objective is to maximise the effectiveness through Assignment, Hungarian Method can be applied to a revised cost matrix obtained from the original matrix.

Q.4.3 Explain the terms— Balanced Problem, Unbalanced Problem, Dummy Job/Facility, An Infeasible Assignment with reference to Assignment .

Balanced Problem	Balanced Assignment Problem is an assignment problem where the number of facilities is **equal to** the number of jobs.
Unbalanced Problem	Unbalanced As assignment problem is an assignment problem where the number of facilities is **not equal to** the number of jobs. To make unbalanced assignment problem, a balanced one, a **dummy** facility(s) or a dummy job(s) (as the case may be) **is introduced** with zero cost or time.
Dummy Job/Facility	A dummy job or facility is an imaginary job/facility with zero cost or time introduced to make an unbalanced assignment problem balanced.
An Infeasible Assignment	An Infeasible Assignment occurs in the cell (i, j) of the assignment cost matrix if *ith* person is unable to perform *jth* job. It is sometimes possible that a particular person is incapable of doing certain work or a specific job cannot be performed on a particular machine. The solution of the assignment problem should take into account these restrictions so that the infeasible assignments can be avoided. This can be achieved by assigning a very high cost to the cells where assignments are prohibited.

Q.4.4 In an assignment problem to assign jobs to men to minimize the time taken, suppose that one man does not know how to do a particular job, how will you eliminate this allocation from the solution? [Nov. 2009]

Ans. In an assignment minimization problem, if one task cannot be assigned to one person, introduce a prohibitively large cost for that allocation, *say M*, where *M* has a high the value. Then, while doing the row minimum and column minimum operations, automatically this allocation will get eliminated.

5.0 TRANSPORTATION PROBLEMS

Q.5.1 What is Transportation Problem?

Ans.

Meaning	1. The transportation problem is a special type of linear programming problem where the objective is to minimise the cost of distributing a product from a number of sources or origins to a number of destinations. The origin of a transportation problem is the location from which shipments are despatched. The destination of a transportation problem is the location to which shipments are transported. The unit transportation cost is the cost of transporting one unit of the consignment from an origin to a destination. 2. The transportation problem indicates the amount of consignment to be transported from various origins to different destinations so that the total transportation cost is minimised without violating the availability constraints and the requirement constraints. The decision variables x_{ij} of a transportation problem indicate the amount to be transported from the *ith* origin to the *jth* destination. 3. A transportation problem can be formulated as a linear programming problem using decision variables with two subscripts.
Example	A manager has four Factories (i.e. origins) and four Warehouses (i.e. destinations). The quantities of goods available in each factory, the requirements of goods in each warehouse and the costs of transportation of a product from each factory to each warehouse are given. His objective is to ascertain the quantity to be transported from various factories to different warehouses in such a way that the total transportation cost is minimised.

Q.5.2 Explain the terms— Balanced Problem, Unbalanced Problem, Dummy Origin/Destination, with reference to Transportation.

Ans.

Balanced Problem	Balanced Transportation Problem is a transportation problem where the total availability at the origins is **equal to** the total requirements at the destinations. For example, in case the total production of 4 factories is 1000 units and total requirements of 4 warehouses is also 1000 units, the transportation problem is said to be a balanced one.

Unbalanced Problem	Unbalanced transportation problem is a transportation problem where the total availability at the origins is **not equal** to the total requirements at the destinations. *For example*, in case the total production of 4 factories is 1000 units and total requirements of 4 warehouses is 900 units or 1,100 units, the transportation problem is said to be an unbalanced one. To make an unbalanced transportation problem, a balanced one, a **dummy** origin(s) or a dummy destination (s) (as the case may be) is **introduced** with zero transportation cost per unit.
Dummy Origin/ Destination	A dummy origin or destination is an imaginary origin or destination with zero cost introduced to make an unbalanced transportation problem balanced one. If the total supply is more than the total demand an additional column is introduced in the Table which represents the surplus supply with zero transportation cost. Likewise, if the total demand is more than the total supply, an additional row is introduced in the Table which represents unsatisfied demand with zero transportation cost.

Q.5.3 What is Initial (or Basic) Feasible Solution? Enumerate the methods of obtainting Initial Feasible Solution.

Ans.

Meaning	In general, any basic feasible solution of a transportation problem with m origins (such as factories) and *n* destinations (such as warehouses) should have '$m + n - 1$' non zero basic variables. A transport problem is said to be a degenerate transport problem if it has a basic feasible solution with number of non zero basic variables less than $m + n - 1$. **According to Mustafit,** "*A degenerate basic feasible solution in a transportation problem exists if and only if some partial sum of availabilities (row) is equal to a partial sum of requirements (column)*".
Methods	Initial Feasible Solution can be obtained by any of the following three methods: 1. Least Cost Method (*or* LCM) 2. North-West Corner Method (*or* NWCM) 3. Vogel's Approximation Method (*or* VAM)

Q.5.4. Enumerate the practical steps involved in the Least Cost Method.

Ans.

Step 1	Make maximum possible Allocation to the Least Cost Cell depending upon the demand/supply for the Column/Row containing that Cell. In case of Tie in the Least Cost Cells, make allocation to the Cell by which maximum demand or capacity is exhausted.
Step 2	Make allocation to the Second Lowest Cost Cell depending upon the remaining demand/supply for the Row/Column containing that Cell.
Step 3	Repeat the above Steps till all Rim Requirements are exhausted, i.e., entire demand and supply is exhausted.

Q.5.5. Will the initial solution for a minimization problem obtained by Vogel's Approximation Method and the Least Cost Method be the same? Why? [May 2011]

Ans. The initial solution need not be the same under both methods. Vogel's Approximation Method uses the difference between the minimum and the next minimum costs for each row and column.

This is the penalty or opportunity cost of not utilising the next best alterative. The highest penalty is given the 1st preference. This need not be the lowest cost.

For example if a row has minimum cost as 4, and the next minimum as 3, penalty is 1; whereas if another row has minimum 5 and next minimum 7, penalty is 2, and this row is given preference. But least cost given preference to the lowest cost cell, irrespective of the next cost.

Vogel's Approximation Method will be result in a more optimal solution than least cost.

They will be the same only when the maximum penalty and the minimum cost coincide.

Q.5.6 How do you know whether an alternative solution exists for a transportation problem? [Nov. 2009]

Ans. The $\Delta\, i_j$ matrix = $\Delta\, i_j = C_{ij} - (u_i + v_j)$

Where C_{ij} is the cost matrix and $(u_i + v_j)$ is the evaluation matrix for allocated cell.

The $\Delta\, i_j$ matrix has one or more 'Zero' elements, indicating that, if that cell is brought into the solution, the optional cost will not change though the allocation changes.

Thus, a 'Zero' element in the Δi_j matrix reveals the possibility of an alternative solution.

Q.5.7 What do you mean by Degeneracy in transportation problem? How this can be solved?

Ans. In a transportation problem, if the no of occupied cells is less than $m + n - 1$, such a solution, in transportation problem, is called as degeneracy. Degeneracy can occur in two ways:

(i) The initial basic solution can turn out to be a degenerate solution. *Or*

(ii) an improved solution can turn out to be a degenerate solution

This can be solved by introducing an infinitesimally small allocation e (epsilon) to least cost empty cell so that the total number of allocated cells is equal to $m + n - 1$ independent cells.

6.0 CRITICAL PATH METHOD (CPM) — DRAWING NETWORK

Q.6.1 What is CPM? State its usefulness.

Ans.

Meaning	Critical path is a chain of activities that begin with the starting event and ends with ending event of a particular project. It is that path that runs through a network with the maximum length of time or it indicates the maximum possible time required for completion of a project. Critical path indicates the minimum time that will be required to complete a project. It is determined after identifying critical events. Critical path goes through critical events.
Usefulness	CPM plays an important role in project planning and control. 1. Network indicates the specific activities required to complete a project.

	2. Network indicates the **interdependence and sequence** of specific activities.
	3. It indicates the **start and finish time** of each activity of the project.
	4. It indicates the **critical path**.
	5. It indicates the **duration** of critical path.
	6. It indicates those activities for which extra effort would not be beneficial in order to shorten the project duration.
	7. It indicates those activities for which extra effort would be beneficial in order to shorten the project duration.
	8. It enables the project manager to **deploy resources** from non-critical activities to critical activities without delaying the overall project duration.
	9. It enables the project manager to **assign responsibilities** for each specific activity.
	10. It enables the project manager to **allocate resources** for each specific activity
	11. It can be used as a **controlling device** to monitor activities of the project by comparing the actual progress against planned progress.
	12. It can be used to determine **possible alternative solutions.**
	13. It can be used to determine various **cost variances** for initiating corrective action by comparing the actual costs against budgeted costs of the project.
	14. It enables the project manager to determine a **revised plan and schedule** of the project by recomputing the project's critical path and the slack of non-critical activities using the actual duration of activities already finished and the revised estimated duration of activities not yet finished.

Q.6.2 State the Assumptions of CPM/PERT.

Ans. 1. A project can be sub-divided into a set of predicable, independent activities.

2. The precedence relationships of project activities can be completely represented by a non-cyclical network graph in which each activity connects directly into its immediate successors.
3. Activity times may be estimated *either* as single point estimates or as three point estimates (i.e. optimistic, pessimistic or most likely) and are independent of each other.
4. Activity duration is assumed to follow the beta distribution, the standard deviation of the distribution is assumed to be 1/6th of its range.

$$\text{Mean } (t_e) \text{ is assumed to be } = \frac{t_0 + 4t_m + t_p}{6}.$$

Variances in the length of a project is assumed to be = Sum of Variances of activities on the critical path.

5. The duration of an activity is linearly related to the cost of resources applied to the activity.

Q.6.3 State the Limitations of the assumption of PERT and CPM.

Ans.
1. Beta distribution may not always be applicable.
2. The formulae for expected duration and standard deviation are simplification. In certain cases, errors due to these have been found up to 33%.
3. The above errors may get compounded or may cancel each other.
4. Activities are assumed to be indepedent. But the limitations on the resources may not justify the assumption.
5. It may not always be possible to sort out completely identifiable activities and to state where they begin and where they end.
6. If there exist alternatives in outcome, they need to be incorporated by way of a decision tree analysis.
7. Time estimates have a subjective element and to this extent, techniques could be weak. Contractors can mainpulate and underestimate time in cost plus contract bids. In incentive contracts, overestimation is likely.
8. Cost-time tradeoffs/Cost Curve Slopes are subjective and even experts may be widely off the mark even after honest deliberations.

Q. 6.4 Explain the term Activity (or Task or Job) with reference to CPM.

Ans. An activity or task or job is any portion of a project which consumes time or resources and has a definable beginning and ending. *For example*, "laying of foundation of a building is an activity which requires the use of resources. In network an activity is **represented by an arrow** which may be straight or bent but not broken. An activity must commence from some event. It may be noted that no activity can start untill all previous activities in the same chain are completed.

Predecessor Activities	The activities which immediately come before another activity without any intervening activities are predecessor activities.
Successor Activities	The activities which follow another activity without any intervening activities are called successor activities to that activity.

Q.6.5 Explain the terms—Event (or Node or Connector), Tail Event, Head Event, Merged Event and Burst Event.

Ans.

Events	The starting and finishing point of an activity or a group of activities are called events. In a network, an event is generally represented by a numbered circle [e.g. (1), (2)].
Tail Event	The starting point of an activity is called a tail event because it is connected to the tail of an activity. In a network, tail event is represented by symbol "*i*".
Head Event	The finishing (*or terminal*) point of an activity is called a head event because it is connected to the head of an activity. In a network, head event is represented by symbol "*j*". ***Note:*** Head events should always have a number higher than that of the tail events.

Merged Event	Merge event is an event which represents the joint completion of more than one activity.
Burst Event	Burst event is an event which represents the joint starting of more than one activity.

Q.6.6 Explain the term NetWork (or Arrow Diagram).

Ans. A network is a graphical representation of inter-relationship of the various activities of a project. While drawing network, the following rules must be kept in mind.

1. An activity cannot occur untill all activities leading to it are complete.
2. No activity can start untill its tail event is reached.

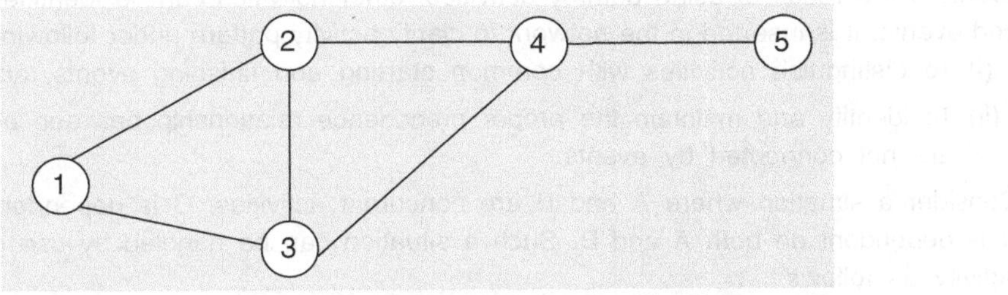

Activity	*Head Event*	*Tail Event*
1 - 2	2 (Burst Event)	1 (Burst Event)
1 - 3	3 (Merge Event)	1 (Burst Event)
2 - 3	3 (Merge Event)	2 (Burst Event)
2 - 4	4 (Merge Event)	2 (Burst Event)
3 - 4	4 (Merge Event)	3 (Burst Event)
4 - 5	5 (Merge Event)	4 (Burst Event)

The aforesaid graphical representation showing the inter-relationships of the various activities of a project is called '**Network**'.

Q.6.7 State the steps involved in Working Methodology of Critical Path Analysis. [Nov 2010]

Ans. The working methodology of Critical Path Analysis (CPA) which includes both CPM and PERT, consists of following five steps:

1. Analyse and breakdown the project in terms of specific activities and/or events.
2. Determine the interdependence and sequence of specific activities and prepare a network.
3. Assign estimate of time, cost or both to all the activities of the network.
4. Identify the longest or critical path through the network.
5. Monitor, evaluate and control the progress of the project by replanning, rescheduling and reassignment of resources.

Q.6.8 State the Conventions followed in drawing A Network.

Ans. The conventions followed in drawing a network are as follows:

1. Draw the arrow directing from left to right, that is, time and progress of the project flows from left to right.

2. As far as possible avoid drawing arrows that cross each other. Where ever crossing of arrows is unavoidable, bridging may be done.
3. An activity is always bounded by two events, called the start event and the end event. No event should hang loosely on the network.
4. Each node should be numbered without ambiguity. The numbers are assigned to events in such a way that the number assigned to the ending event of an activity is greater than the number assigned to the beginning event of that activity.

Q.6.9 Explain Dummy Activity/Arrow with reference to Network. **[June 2009]**

Ans. Dummy activity is a hypothetical activity which does not consume any time or resources for completion. Dummy arrow represents an activity with zero duration. It is represented by **dotted line**. It is used when two or more activities have same initial and terminal events. As a result of using dummy activities, other activities can be identified by unique end events. It is inserted in the network to clarify activity pattern under following situations:

(i) To distinguish activities with common starting and finishing events, and

(ii) To identify and maintain the proper precedence relationship between activities that are not connected by events.

Consider a situation where A and B are concurent activities, C is dependent on A and D is dependent on both A and B. Such a situation can be handled by use of a dummy activity as follows:

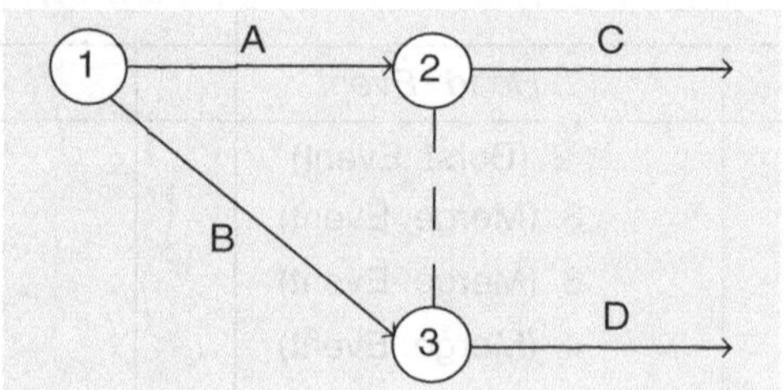

Avoiding duplication of desgination – In the figure below, two activities A and B are being designated as 1 - 3 in the network given on left hand side. This anamoly has been set right in the network given on right hand side by employing a dummy.

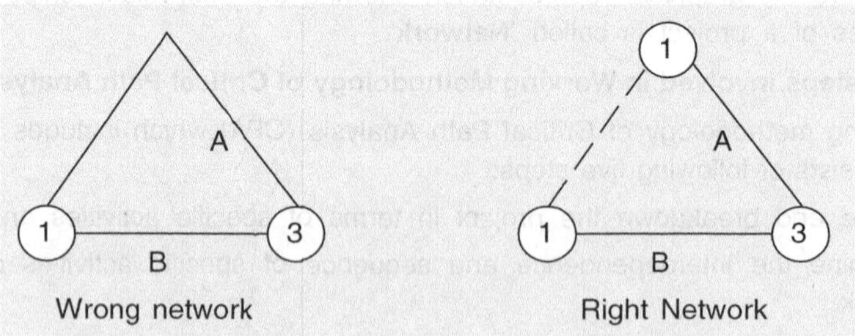

Q.6.10 Can a critical path change during the course of a period?

Ans. The critical path of a project will not remain static throughout its life, it can change during the course of project completion. Unforeseen circumstances sometimes may cause estimated duration of one or more activities to change. Due to variation in time duration of the project activities, if some activities take more or less time than their expected time, this may render some of the non-critical activities as critical and vice versa. Hence a non-critical path may become a critical path or alternatively a critical path may become non-critical. For this reason, the project leader is required to closely monitor the project's activities by comparing the planned progress to the actual progress. Such monitoring will enable him to quickly recognise and react to unpredictable events that may significantly alter the estimated duration of some activities. Using the actual duration of activities already finished and the revised estimated duration of activities not yet finished, the project leader can determine a revised plan and schedule of the project by recomputing the project's critical path, the slack of non-critical activities and then rescheduling the starting and finishing times of every activity not yet finished.

7.0 PERT

Q.7.1 State the meaning and process of PERT.

Ans.

Meaning	1. PERT stands for Programme Evaluation and Review Technique. 2. PERT is event oriented. 3. PERT is a probabilistic model i.e. it takes into account uncertainties involved in the estimation of time of a job or an activity. 4. PERT uses three estimates of the activity time - Optimistic, Pessimistic and Most Likely. 5. PERT is primarily concerned with project time.
Objective	The objective of PERT is to schedule and co-ordinate the various project activities so that the project can be completed on scheduled time.
Suitability	PERT is generally used for those projects which are not of repetitive in nature (e.g. Research and Development Projects) and where time required to complete various activities are not known in advance.
Process	The process of PERT analysis includes: **Step 1.** Identification of the activities of the project. **Step 2.** Estimation of activity time. **Step 3.** Defining inter-dependence relationships between the activities. **Step 4.** Drawing the net work. **Step 5.** Using the network to obtain the scheduling data.

Q.7.2 Distinguish between CPM and PERT.

Ans. CPM and PERT differ in the various respects:

Basis of Distinction	***CPM***	***PERT***
1. Orientation	CPM is **activity oriented** i.e. CPM network is built on the basis of activities.	PERT is **event oriented.**
2. Nature of Model	CPM is a **deterministic model** i.e. it does not take into account the uncertainties involved in the estimation of time for execution of a job or an activity.	PERT is a **probabilistic model** i.e., It takes into account uncertainties involved in the estimation of time of a job or an activity. It uses three estimates of the activity time –optimistic, pessimistic and most likely. Thus, the expected duration of each activity is probabilitistic and expected duration indicates that there is 50% probability of getting the job done within that time.
3. Emphasis	CPM places dual emphasis **on time and cost** and evaluates the trade off between project cost and project time. It enables the project manager to manipulate project duration within certain limits by deploying additional resources so that project duration can be shortened at an optimum cost.	PERT is primarily concerned with **project time**. It enables the and co-ordinate various activities so that the project can be completed on scheduled time.
4. Use	CPM is generally used for those projects which are **repetitive** in nature (e.g. construction projects) and where one has **prior experience** of handling similar projects.	PERT is generally used for those projects which are **not repetitive** in nature (e.g. Research and Development Projects) and where **time** required to complete various activities are **not known** in advance.

Q.7.3 Explain the Usefulness of PERT.

Ans.

1. Facilitates Planing	PERT facilitates planning. Planning involves the formulation of objectives and goals that are subsequently translated into specific plans and projects. The planning phase of the project is initiated by PERT because it requires the establishment of project objectives and specifications, and then, it provides a realistic and disciplined basis for determinining how to attain these objectives, considering pertinent time and resource constraints. Planners are required to specify not only all the activities necessary to complete a project but also their technological dependencies. PERT calculations then lay out clearly the implications of these inter-dependencies and aid the planners in finding problems that might be over looked in large complex problems. PERT provides a realistic way of carrying out more long range and detailed planning of projects including their co-ordination at all the levels of management.

	In developing a detailed and comprehensive project network, users often make significant improvements over their original ideas, they do a better job of early co-ordination with supplier, engineers, managers contractors and all other groups associated with the project.
2. Facilitates Controlling	PERT facilitates controlling. The function of control is to institute a mechanism that trigger a warning signal if actual performance is deviating (in terms of time, cost or some other measures of effectiveness) from the plan. PERT is unique in its emphasis on the control phase of project management because it uses statistical analysis along with probability calculations concerning the project completion by a certain period. As a result, it is easier under PERT to revise the plan each time changes are introduced in the network. With the information from PERT, the manager is in a better position to know where troubles may occur, supervision may be needed and where resources may be shifted to keep the project on schedule. It also helps in controlling the project by checking off progress against the schedule and by assigning the schedule manpower and equipments. It enables the managers to analyse the effects of delays and to revise the network in case any changes are required.
3. Facilitates the Application of MBE Principle	PERT **facilitates the application of the principle of management by exception** by identifying the most critical elements in the plan, focusing management attention on the 10 to 20 per cent of the project activities that are most constraining on the schedule. It continually defines new schedules and illustrates the effects of technical and procedural changes on the overall schedule. Thus, the manager can control the project in a better way.
4. Acts as Project Management Technique	Programme Evaluation is a **project management technique**. The project to be planned is broken into inter-dependent activities and a network of arrows is constructed to depict these dependency relationships, each activity being represented by one arrow. PERT, however is particularly suited to innovational projects (viz. oil exploration or introducing a new product) for the activities of which it is not possible to estimate the timings precisely.
5. Provides Feedback Information	PERT provides valuable feedback information about the status of the project. The management is provided with a convenient yardstick against which progress of various activities especially those which are critical may be measured. This information is extremely important for control. For example, any delay beyond the schedule completion time of an activity will be brought to management's attention. The cause of the delay can be investigated and remedial action taken. This increases the likelihood of completing the project. However, the success of the technique depends on the management's response to the feedback information provided. If this information is merely field and no remedial action is taken, the purpose of the technique

is defeated. It is important to recognise that there is no self-correcting mechanism built into the model that will cause automatic remedial action. Such action has to be initiated by the persons using the technique. Another problem that may destroy the success of PERT model is the tendency of many activity managers to delay in the reporting of the current status of progress. This causes delays in the updating of time schedule and the management begins to operate with outdated information which could be disastrous. To resolve this problem, it is crucial for the project manager to inform all activity managers about the relative importance of their activity's impact on the total project and where they 'fit in' in the overall project's success.

In short, there is nothing wrong with the PERT network technique. If the feedback information provided by it is properly utilised by the management, it will act only as wall decorates in a business enterprise. However, if proper remedial action is initiated for various information provided by it, PERT can prove to be a dynamic tool for planning, controlling and scheduling a project.

Q.7.4 How can uncertainty be incorporated in PERT Model?

Ans. Uncertainty can be incorporated in PERT network by assuming that the activity time has a **beta distribution**. This enables us to calculate the expected activity time and its standard deviation. For this purpose we have the following three different estimates for the completion time of an activity.

Optimistic Time (T_0)	Optimistic time for an activity is the **minimum time** required to complete an activity if everything goes all right. i.e. under ideal conditions.
Normal Time (or Most Likely Time) (T_m)	Normal time, is the **most probable time** which an activity will take. This is the time which lies between the optimistic time and the pessimistic time.
Pessimistic Time	Pessimistic time, is the **best guess-estimate** of the maximum time that would be required to complete an activity if bad luck were encountered at every turn. The estimate does not take into account such natural catastrophes as flood etc.
Expected Time	Expected time is the **average time** that an activity will take if it was to be repeated on large number of times and is based on the assumption that the activity time follows beta distribution. It is given by the relation. $$t_e = \frac{t_0 + 4t_m + t_p}{6}$$ *where t_o, t_m, t_p are the Optimistic, Most likely (or Normal) and Pessimistic Times.*

Activity Variance	Activity Variance is the square of 1/6th of the difference between the pessimistic and optimistic guess-estimates, i.e. $\sigma^2 = \left(\frac{t_p - t_0}{6}\right)^2$
Project Variance	Project Variance is the variance of the critical path duration which, in turn, is the sum of variances of the activities on it. From central limit therein it follows that critical path duration is normally distributed. As such variance can be put to use for finding the probability of completing the project by a given date. The physical interpretation of this term is that if the project were to be repeated on myriads of occasions its duration follows a normal distribution with the variance explained above. The formula presumes beta disribution of activity time. Thus, Project Variance = Sum of Variances of Critical Activities.

8.0 CRASHING, RESOURCE ALLOCATION AND SMOOTHING

Q.8.1 Explain the term Crashing.

Ans. Crashing is employed when we want to shorten the project completion time by spending extra resources i.e., ultimately money. In real life, it is always possible to employ more resources or 'book a lightening call'. Consider, for example, the activity of laying bricks which requires a gang of a mason assisted by a few labourers. By increasing the number of labourers the activity duration can be shortened or crashed. But there is a limit to this. Too many labourers per mason would not reduce the duration any more since they are liable to jam up. Concerned specialists would have to estimate the crashing limit for each activity as also extra money for crashing each activity. Once these estimates are available, an analysis can be made to determine the time cost trade off curve i.e., what (cost) it takes to crash the project to a given duration.

Since the additional resource associated with crashing activity times usually result in added costs, the management would want to identify the least cost activities to crash and the amount of duration by which activities may be crashed to meet the desired project completion date.

In order to determine just where and how much to crash activity times, management would need information about Normal Cost, Normal Time, Crash Time, Crash Cost, Activity Cost Slope.

Q.8.2 Explain the terms—Normal Cost, Normal Time, Crash Time, Crash Cost.

Ans.

Normal Cost (N_c)	Normal Cost is the **lowest possible direct cost** required to complete an activity.
Normal Time (N_t)	Normal Time is the **minimum time** required to complete an activity at normal cost.

Crash Time (C_t)	Crash Time is the **minimum possible time** in which an activity can be completed using additional resources.
Crash Cost (C_c)	Crash Cost is the direct cost that is anticipated in completing an activity within the crash time.

Q.8.3 Explain the Activity Cost Slope with the help of diagram.

Ans.

Meaning	Activity Cost Slope is the rate of increase in the cost of activity per unit with a decrease in time. A necessary measure for the cost analysis is the calculation of the cost slope for each activity. The cost slope indicates the additional cost incurred per unit of time saved in reducing the duration of an activity.
Diagram	It can be understood more clearly by considering the following diagram: 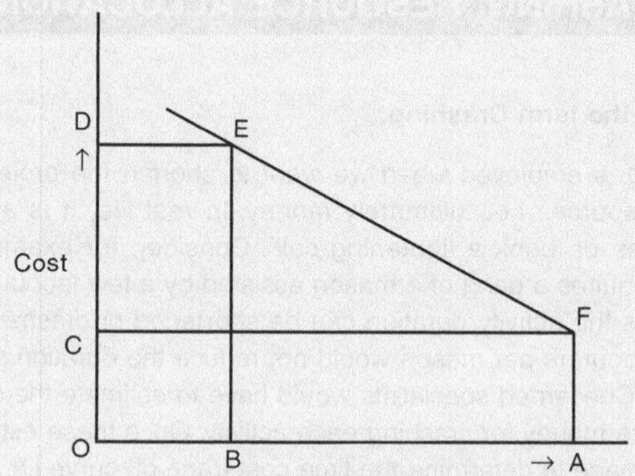 *Duration time for the Job* Let OA represent the normal time duration for completing a job and OC the normal cost involved to complete the job. Assume that the management wishes to reduce the time of completing the job to OB from normal time OA. Therefore, under such a situation the cost of the project increases and it goes upto say OD (Crash Cost). This only amounts to saying that by reducing the time period by AB the cost has increased by the amount CD. The rate of increase in the cost of activity per unit with a decrease in time is known as activity cost slope and is described as below: $\text{Activity Cost Slope} = \frac{CD}{AB} = \frac{OD - OC}{OA - OB}$ $= \frac{\text{Crash Cost} - \text{Normal Cost}}{\text{Normal Time} - \text{Crash Time}}$

Process of Crashing	Since the project duration is determined by the length of the critical path, it can be shortened by reducing the time of critical activities. As the objective of the management is to reduce the project duration at the lowest possible cost, the **critical activity with the lowest cost slope is selected for crashing**. The amount of time by which an individual activity can be reduced is limited by its crash time. However, during such a crashing other factors must be taken into account. For example, the next longest route may also become critical. There will be then two critical paths and any further reduction in project time must occur on both the paths for overall project time to be reduced. The process is continued in this manner and the sum of direct and indirect costs i.e. the total costs for each completion time are tabulated. The **optimum schedule corresponds to minimum total cost**.

Q.8.4 What is Resource Smoothing?

Ans.

Meaning	Resource smoothing is a useful technique to estimate the total resource requirements for various project activities. In this technique, the time-scaled diagram of various activities and their floats (if any) along with resource requirements are used. Time scaled diagram is a network diagram in which all critical activities are arranged as a straight line with non-critical events above or below it, on a horizontal time scale. Flotas are represented by dotted horizontal lines and dummics are represented by dotted vertical lines.
Process	Under Resource Smoothing technique — 1. The periods of maximum demand for resources are identified, and 2. Non-critical activities having floats are rescheduled or shifted so that a uniform demand on resources is achieved.

Q. 8.5 What is Resource Levelling?

Ans.

Meaning	Resource levelling is a process which is performed when the availability of the resources are less than their requirement.
Two types of Problems in Resource Levelling	Two types of problems are normally involved in resource levelling: 1. Levelling resource demands with constraint on the total project duration time. 2. Minimization of the project duration time with a constraint on the total availability of certain key resources. The first problem arises when one is able to procure sufficient resources to carry out the project being scheduled and is concerned with the utilization of these resources at a relatively constant rate during the life of the project. The second problem arises in such a case when the existing pool of resources can not be increased and the goal is to schedule the activities in such a way so as to minimise the total project duration subject to the

	present availability of resources. In this situation the total floats for the non-critical activities is utilised. By shifting a non critical activity between its ES and LF limits, one may be able to lower the maximum resource requirements. In essence this would mean a more steady work force.

Q.8.6 What is Time Cost Trade off?

Ans. By manipulating (*adding or reducing*) the resource in a project, we can have a range of possible solutions and obtain a number of project durations and the corresponding minimum cost. Concern should be to see whether this extra commitment of resources is worth spending and whether this extra expenditure is commensurate with the cost economics of the project. We have therefore, to find out an optimum time cost solution to the project. Hence "Time Cost Trade Off" is meant to determine the following three aspects:

1. Determination of that project duration for which the cost is least;
2. Determination of the least cost for reduction in project duration to a specified or stipulated date; and
3. Determination of the Time-Cost-Risk relationship of the Network Technique.

9.0 SIMULATION

Q.9.1 What is Simulation Technique?

Ans. Simulation is a quantitative technique developed for evaluating alternative courses of action by building a model of new system under the conditions of uncertainty and then conducting a series of repeated trial and error experiments to predict the behaviour of the system over a period of time before running the risk, of experimenting on the real system with a view to avoid the cost of real-world experimentation.

According to T.H. Taylor: *"Simulation is a numerical technique for conducting experiments on a digital computer, which involves certain types of mathematical and logical relationships necessary to describe the behaviour and structure of a complex real word system over extended period of time."*

Q.9.2 What are the Steps involved in carrying out simultation process?

Ans. Although simulations vary in complexity from situation to situation, in general one would have to go through the following steps:

Step 1	Define the Problem or System you inteneded to simulate.
Step 2	Formulate the Model you intend to use.
Step 3	Test the Model; compare its behaviour with the behaviour of the actual problem.
Step 4	Identify and Collect the Data needed to Test the Model.
Step 5	Run the Simulation
Step 6	Analyze the resuls of the simulation and, if desired, change the solution you are evaluating.
Step 7	Rerun the Simulation to test the new solution.
Step 8	Validate the Simulation; This involves increasing the chances of the inferences you may draw about the real situation from running the simulation to become valid.

Q.9.3 List any four Applications of Simulation.

Ans. Simulation can be used:

1. for learning about the operating characteristics of a New Airplane by simulating flight conditions in a wind tunnel,
2. for learning about the models of Production Processes
3. for learning about the Economic Systems,
4. for learning about the mathematical models of such real-life systems as Inventory Control, Production Scheduling, Network Analysis and so on.
5. for planning Military Strategy,
6. for Traffic Control,
7. for planning Management Games and Role Playing,
8. for Medical Diagnosis, Hospital Emergency Facilities,
9. for Gambling and Analysis,
10. for determining Optimal Location for Plants and Warehouses,
11. for evaluation of Industrial and Commercial Policies.

Q.9.4 List the Advantages of Simulation.

Ans. The four advantages for using simulation for solving management problems are given below :

1. ***Simulation techniques allow experimentation with a model of the system rather than the actual operating system*** – Sometimes experimenting with the actual system itself could prove to be too costly and, in many cases too disruptive. *For example*, if you are comparing two ways of providing food service in a hospital, the confusion that would result from operating two different systems long enough to get valid observations might be too great. Similarly, the operatioin of a large computer centre under a number of different operating alternatives might be too expensive to be feasible.
2. ***The non technical manager can comprehend simulation more easily than a complex mathematical model*** – Simulation does not require simplifications and assumptions to the extent required in analytical solutions. A simulation model is easier to explain to management personnel since it is a description of the behaviour of some system or process.
3. ***Sometimes there is not sufficient time to allow the actual system to operate extensively*** – *For example*, if we were studying long term trends in world population, we simply could not wait for the required number of years to see results. Simulation allows the manager to incorporate time into an analysis. In a computer simulation of business operation the manager can compress the result of several years or periods into a few minutes of running time.
4. ***The use of simulation enables a manager to provide insights into certain managerial problems*** where analytical solution of a model is not possible or where the actual environment is difficult to observe. *For example*, simulation is widely used is space-flights or the charting of satellite. Simulation allows a user to analyse these large complex problems for which analytical results are not available. For example, in an inventory problem if the distribution for demand and lead time for an item follow a standard distribution, such as the position distribution, then a mathematical or analytical solution can be found. However, when mathematically convenient distributions are not applicable to the problem, an analytical analysis of the problem may be impossible. A simulation model is a useful solution procedure for such problems.

Q.9.5 List the Disadvantages of taking a Simulation Approach.

Ans. Disadvantages of taking a simulation approach to solve a management problem are indicated below:

1. Simulation is not precise. It is not an optimization process and does not yield an answer but merely provides a set of the system's responses to different operating conditions. In many cases this lack of precision is difficult to measure.
2. A good simulation model may be very expensive. Often it takes years to develop a usuable corporate planning model.
3. Not all situations can be evaluated using simulation. Only situations involving uncertainty are candidates, and without a random component, all simulated experiments would produce the same answer.
4. Simulation generates a way of evaluating solutions but does not generate the solution techniques. Manager must still generate the solution approaches they want to test.

Q.9.6 What is HERTZ Simulation Model? List the Steps in this model.

Ans.

Meaning	Prof. David B. Hertz while evaluating the risky investments has proposed the use of a simulation model to obtain the expected return for an investment proposal. *To explain, let us take the following case:* A medium-sized industrial chemical producer is considering a $10 million extension to its processing plant. The estimated service life of the facility is 10 years the engineers expect to be able to utilise 2,50,000 tonnes of processed material worth $510 per tonne at an average processing cost of $435 per tonne. Is this investment a good bet? In fact, we wish to find out what is the return that the company may expect? What are the risk? In evaluating such an investment proposal, the following nine factors are considered (i) Market size (ii) Selling price (iii) Market growth rate (iv) Market share (in physical sales volume) (v) Investment required (vi) Residual value of investment (vii) Operating cost (viii) Fixed costs, and (ix) Useful life of facilities. To carry out the analysis, Prof. Hertz proposed the following steps:
Step 1	*Estimate the range of values for each of the factors like range of selling price, sales growth rates and so on and within that range, the likelihood of occurrence of each value i.e., develop the probability distribution of uncertain factors in the system.*
Step 2	*The next step in the proposed approach is to select at random (from the distribution of values for each factor) one particular value and associate each one of them with the respective probability distribution to determine the expected value for each factor in the model. Then combine the values of all the factors and compute the rate of return (or present value) from that combination.*

Step 3	*Do this over and over again to define and evaluate the odds of the occurrence of each possible rate of return. Since they are literally millions of possible combinations of values, we need to test the likelihood that various specific returns on the investment will occur. The result will be a listing of the rates of return we might achieve, ranging from a loss (if the factors go against us) to whatever maximum gain is possible with the estimates that have been made.*

Q.9.7 What are the Steps involved in carrying out Monte Carlo Simultation Model? [Nov. 2010]

Ans.

Meaning	The Monte Carlo method is the earliest method of simulation. It employs random numbers and is used to solve problems that depend upon probability, where physical experimentation is impractable and the creation of a mathematical formula impossible. It is a method of simulation by the sampling technique. That is, first of all, the probability distribution of the variable under consideration is determined; then a set of random numbers is used to generate a set of values that have the same distributional characteristics as the actual experience it is designed to simulate. The steps involved in carrying out Monte Carlo Simulation are:
Step 1	*Select the measure of effectiveness of the problem, that is, what element is used to measure success in improving the system modelled. This is the element one wants to maximise or minimise. For example, this might be idle time of a service facility, or inventory shortages per period.*
Step 2	*Identify the variables which influence the measure of effectiveness significantly. For example, the number of service facilities in operation or the number of units in inventory and so on.*
Step 3	*Determine the proper cumulative probability distribution of each variable selected under Step (2) plot these, with the probability on the vertical axis and the values of variables on horizontal axis.*
Step 4	*Get a set of random numbers.*
Step 5	*Consider each random number as a decimal value of the cumulative probability distribution. With the decimal, enter the cumulative distribution plot from the vartical axis. Project this point horizontally, until it intersects cumulative probability distribution curve. Then project the point of intersection down into the vertical axis.*
Step 6	*Record the value generated in Step (5) into the formula derived from the chosen measure of effectiveness. Solve and record the value. This value is the measure of effectiveness for that simulated value.*
Step 7	*Repeat Steps (5) and (6) until sample is large enough for the satisfaction of the decision maker.*

Q.9.8 What is meant by Pseudo-Random Numbers and Mid-square Method? Also state the limitations of Mid-square Method .

Ans.

Pseudo-Random Numbers	The Methods commonly used to generate random numbers are not random processes. Random numbers are called psuedo-random numbers when they are generated by some deterministic process but they qualify the predetermined statistical test for randomness. The sequence of numbers generated by such process is completely determined by the input data (or the first random number) used for the method.
Mid-square Method	This is one of the commonly used methods to generate sequences of Pseudo-random numbers. The method works as follows : Select a four-digit integer or seed to initialise the generator. The first random number is obtained from the seed in the following manner: The seed is squared, the resulting number is supposed to contain 8 digits (if less digits are there, leading zeros are inserted). From this number, the middle four digits are extracted as the required random number. This number is subsequently used as the new seed. Pseudo-random numbers are generated in this manner, each time using the previous random number as the new seed. To explain the process, consider the first seed as 1723. By squaring 1723, we get the number 02968729. From this number four middle digits 9687 are extracted which is the first random number. To get the next random number, we square 9687 which is 93837969. The next random number is 8379. This process is repeated until the required number of random numbers are obtained.
Limitations	1. The method has a tendency to degenerate rapidly. A random number may reproduce itself. **Example I** $x_3 = 7600$, $x_4 = 7600$, $x_5 = 7600$. **Eexample II** $x_4 = 2500$, $x_5 = 2500$, $x_6 = 2500$. 2. If the number zero is ever generated, all subsequent numbers generated will also have a zero value unless steps are provided to handle this case. 3. A loop may generate i.e. the same sequence of random numbers can repeat, **Example I** $x_1 = 1600$, $x_2 = 5600$, $x_3 = 3600$, $x_4 = 9600$, $x_5 = 1600$, **Example II** $x_1 = 6100$, $x_2 = 2100$, $x_3 = 4100$, $x_4 = 8100$, $x_5 = 6100$, $x_6 = 2100$, $x_7 = 4100$. 4. This method is slow since many multiplications and divisions are required to access the middle digits in a fixed word binary computer.

10.0 LEARNING CURVE THEORY

Q.10.1 List the Limitations of Learning Curve Theory.

Ans. 1. All activities of a firm are not subject to learning effect. (Activities that have not been performed in the present operational mode, those performed by new or unfamiliar employees are subjected to learning effect, while those performed by familiar or experienced workmen will not be subjected to learning effect)

2. It is correct that learning effect does take place and average time taken is likely to reduce. But in practice it is highly unlikely that there will be a regular consistent rate of decrease. Therefore any cost prediction based on conventional learning curves should be viewed with caution.

3. Considerable difficulty arises in obtaining valid data that will form basis for computation of learning effect.

4. Even slight change in circumstances quickly renders the learning curve obsolete. While the regularity of conventional learning curves can be questioned, it would be wrong to ignore learning effect altogether in predicting costs for decision purposes.

11.0 MISCELLENEOUS QUESTIONS

Q.11.1 State the limitations of the LPP technique.

Ans. 1. It assumes the linear relationship among variables whether it is objective function or the constraint. But in real world this may not be a situation.

2. In some problems only integer value can be assigned to decision variables. Like in case of indivisible project in capital budgeting. However linear programming cannot solve these types of problems.

3. The linear programming problems are more deterministic rather than stochastic. But in real life this may not be a case. Parameters assigned to variables whether in objective function or in constraint are assumed to be constant. However in real world they may change.

4. Linear programming consider only single objective but in real life there exists multiple objective.

Q.11.2 State the Basic Characteristics of a linear programming problem.

Ans. 1. There must be decision variables.

2. These decision variables should be linearly related.
3. Objective function must be well defined.
4. Presence of constraints.
5. Existence of several courses of action.
6. Non Negativity constraint.

Q.11.3 State the major assumptions of Linear Programming.

Ans.

1. Proportionality	This property requires the contribution of each decision variable in (a) Objective function, and (b) Constraint to be directly proportional to the value of the variable. *For example,* if decision variable X_1, X_2 then in objective function and constraint its contribution is directly proportional i.e. like $4X_1$ or $5X_1$ or RX_1. However if it is in form of X_1^2 or X_1^3 then it becomes non-linear and this property is not met. Similarly if contributions remain same for certain output level and thereafter it decreases due to quantity discount then this also becomes non-linear.
2. Additivity	This property requires the total contribution of all decision variables in objective function and in the constraints to be the direct sum of the individual contributions of each variable. *For example,* in objective function variables are given as $3X_1 + 5X_2$ or $RX_1 + DX_2$. However if the two products compete for market share in such a way that increase in sales of one adversely affects the other, then the additivity property is not satisfied and the model is no longer linear.
3. Certainty	All the objectives and constraints coefficients of the LP model are deterministic. This implies they are known constants. However in real life data are represented by probabilistic distribution. In such a case constant or LP coefficient can be taken as average value approximations of the probabilistic distribution. If standard deviation is small then LP model is acceptable. However, if deviations are large then stochastic LP algorithms or sensitivity analysis is applied to the optimum solution.
4. Divisibility	This assumption implies that in final solution variable may also take fractional value.

Q.11.4 What observations in the iterative process of the simplex solution of a linear programming indicate its degeneracy?

Ans. Degeneracy appears when value of any basic variable is zero during iterative process or in final solution. This happens, when there is tie between two minimum ratios that has to be replaced during iterative process. When tie happens then at least one basic variable will be zero in the next iteration and the new solution is said to be degenerate. However if this solution is optimal solution then final solution shall also be degenerate. But if this solution is not an optimal solution then degeneracy shall not appear in final solution provided degeneracy does not appear again during iterative process.

Q.11.5 How does the simplex algorithm indicate that:

(a) There is an alternate optimal solution.

(b) The problem has unbounded optimal solution.

(c) The problem has no feasible solution.

(d) A given solution is optimal

(e) A solution is degenerate.

Ans.

Alternate Optimal Solution	When "j row shows zero for any non – basic variable in an optimal solution.
Unbounded Optimal Solution	(i) **In case of Maximization Problem**: When "j row shows **positive value for any non – basic variable** but replacement ratio for all basic variables are *either* negative *or* infinity. (ii) **In case of Minimization Problem**: When "j row shows **negative value for any non – basic variable** but replacement ratio for all basic variables are *either* negative *or* infinity.
No Feasible Solution	When any artificial variable becomes basic variable in optimal solution with positive values.
Optimal Solution	(i) **In case of Maximization Problem**: When "j row shows **negative value for all non – basic variables** and no basic variable is an artificial variable then solution obtained is an optimal solution. (ii) **In case of Minimization Problem**: When "j row shows **positive value for all non – basic variables** and no basic variable is an artificial variable then solution obtained is an optimal solution.
Solution is Degenerate	When value of any basic variable in a solution is zero.

Q.11.6 "Quantitative analysis provides a systematic approach to decision making". Explain the statement with suitable example.

Ans. Meaning : Quantitative analysis is the application of scientific methods, techniques and tools to problems involving the operation of systems so as to provide those in control of operations with optimum solutions to the problems. Thus, it may be regarded as the scientific method employed for problem solving and decision making by the management.

Features of Quantitative Analysis

Decision Making	Quantitative analysis is mainly concerned with managerial decision making. It attempt to locate best solution to the given problem.
Scientific Approach	It uses scientific methods for obtaining the optimal solution.
Inter-disciplinary	It is inter-disciplinary in nature. Managerial problems have economic, physical, psychological, biological, sociological and engineering aspect. This requires an expertise in the various disciplines such as mathematics, statistics, engineering, economics, management, computer science etc.
Computer	Nowadays computers have become an integrated part of data processing and analysis. Computer is capable of handling many complex data and information very easily and without any loss of time. Iterative process which can take many human days can be processed with the help of a computer in the fraction of second.

Examples of Quantitative Analysis

Linear Programming	It is designed for models with linear objectives and constraint functions.
Integer Programming	In this type of problem, decision variables assume only integer values.
Dynamic Programming	In this model the original model can be decomposed into more manageable problems.
Non-Linear Programming	Where the constraints functions are non-linear (i.e. having a degree of more than one).

Q.11.7 What is the Model? What are the advantages of analyzing and experimenting with models as opposed to real object or situation ?

Ans.

Meaning	Models are abstraction of real world. They are designed to optimize a specific objective criterion subject to a set of constraints; the quality of resulting solution depends on the completeness of the model representing the real system. The majority of applications usually involve varying degree of approximations. First step is to abstract the assumed real world from the real situation by concentrating on the dominant variable that control the behavior of the real systems. In essence, simplification from the real world to the assumed real world is achieved by lumping several real world variables into a single assumed real world variable.
Advantages	1. If model is complete then solution obtained through model will be an optimal one and that cannot be obtained with experimenting with real world. 2. Experiment with real world shall involve lot of time and cost. But once model is developed then solution can be obtained within no time. 3. Experimentation with real world shall involve lot of uncertainty and risk. But this shall not be the case with models.